Complete Guide to

HOME
APPLIANCE
REPAIR

A Popular Science Book

Complete Guide to

HOME APPLIANCE REPAIR

by Evan Powell

with Robert P. Stevenson

POPULAR SCIENCE BOOKS

HARPER & ROW
New York, Evanston, San Francisco, London

First Edition, 1974

Four Printings

Second Edition, 1984

Manufactured in the United States of America

TO

Arnold Powell, my father, from whom I learned many things, the most important being the value of a job well done.

Robert P. Stevenson, my editor, who encouraged me to write this book and spent countless hours helping me to realize that goal.

Contents

How You'll Profit from This Book

By Robert P. Stevenson
Former Home & Shop Editor
Popular Science Magazine

The history of Evan Powell's book on home appliances began some years ago when a letter from him reached me in the New York City editorial offices of *Popular Science* magazine. Powell was then working full time in the field of appliance repairs. Would the magazine be interested in a series of articles, Powell asked, to help readers repair their own appliances? Would we, indeed!

Eventually, I also learned that Powell was teaching appliance repairs in an evening adult education course. He had found, he said, that none of the available appliance-repair books was adequate as a textbook for his class. So he proposed to write one, basing his chapters on the articles he hoped to produce for *Popular Science*.

As a long-time editor of do-it-yourself articles, I was aware of the strong reader demand for reliable—and understandable—information about appliance repairs. I agreed fully with Evan Powell's assessment of the books then on the market. Most were quick compilations of materials taken from technical manuals that manufacturers distribute to their servicemen. The information was reliable. But the instructions weren't understandable to home-owners.

Powell's background seemed exactly right for producing a series of articles and, eventually, a book. Besides teaching the evening class, he was working full time as director of a regional service center for an appliance distributor. He had helped pay his own way through college by spare-time work in appliance repairs. Moreover, he had one characteristic that I have always considered essential to any job of technical writing. He was enthusiastic about his subject matter. In his original letter, he wrote: ''I have stayed in this business because I feel that it offers a great challenge as well as great potential, and, primarily, because I love it.'' Combine that enthusiasm with his background information and experience, and how could his proposed articles (and book) be anything but helpful to those thousands of people who wanted—and were able to follow—the kind of guidance he could provide?

To develop a trial article, I visited Powell at his home. William W. Morris, long-time *Popular Science* photographer, went along to take the show-how illustrations that are such an important part of any successful do-it-yourself article. As Powell posed successive stages of repairing various small appliances in front of the cameras, I questioned him about points in his article that I felt might puzzle readers. When the article was complete, the editors of *Popular Science* introduced it with this preface:

"Readers have been asking for this article for years. We've held back until now for what we consider a good reason—the lack of an authority in whom we could have full confidence, a man qualified to tell you what you can do and what's better left to others. In Evan Powell, we believe we have that authority. We fully endorse his proposal that homeowners, especially young ones, can profit—both in convenience and actual cash saving—by learning how to service their own home appliances."

Readers responded enthusiastically to the article, and Powell went on to write a succession of others. With each one, he gained steadily in clarity of presentation, and gradually became his own expert photographer. During this time, I discovered that Evan Powell has infinite patience. This, I'm sure, has been of great help to him in writing the book into which the articles have now been expanded; for in that task I have been his Devil's Advocate, constantly

prodding him into amplifying or rephrasing material so as to benefit the greatest possible number of readers.

At the onset of our teamwork, Evan and I agreed to produce a manual for homeowners, rather than the classroom textbook toward which he originally had aimed. We reasoned that if our main objective were successful, the book then might naturally find classroom use in adult education programs throughout the United States. Now that the book is complete, I can confidently recommend it for use either in the home or classroom.

One of the book's chapters—the one on automatic ice makers—has already been endorsed by the appliance industry. Its information and illustrations first appeared as an article in *Popular Science* under the title "How Ice Makers Work . . . what to do if they don't." The article brought a 1972 Alma Award to Evan Powell and *Popular Science* for "outstanding communication of information to consumers about home appliances." The awards are given annually by the Association of Home Appliance Manufacturers. The manufacturers have continued their approval of Powell's work by making a 1973 award for his magazine writings in the field of appliance repair. Late in 1973 Powell joined the editorial staff of *Popular Science* as its Southeast Editor.

Evan Powell's qualifications for writing this urgently needed book have been steadily growing. Over the years he has taken part in several nationwide seminars on appliance design. He has originated many of the commercial servicing procedures and techniques currently in use. He has a top reputation in the field of product investigation, an activity that requires him to suggest remedies for design defects or operating problems discovered in appliances already in use. He has developed his own program for training appliance technicians; and national representatives of several appliance servicing divisions have adopted some aspects of his program.

Powell's two-step training concept has been closely followed in this book. You first learn how an appliance works. You then learn how to diagnose a problem and make repairs. The concept works.

I was interested in hearing Powell's opinion of a crash training program that attempts to teach beginning technicians how to make repairs "by the numbers." The beginner is shown how to replace a refrigerator compressor, for instance, by following a routine procedure. According to this theory, the man does not need to understand the workings of the equipment. He just follows outlined steps. Advocates claim this numbers training gets instant production and income from a novice.

"The training is successful only in a few isolated cases," Powell told me. "For one thing, there are no routine jobs in appliance servicing. Even expert technicians often run into unexpected problems after they have started a job, no matter how well it has been diagnosed. Secondly, the caliber of the work is usually poor, and the man gets little personal satisfaction from the job.

"On the other hand, our two-phase training concept puts the man on familiar ground with the first appliance he approaches. From then on, every job

becomes a training ground where he improves his knowledge and capabilities. He takes pride in his work. He becomes master of the situation."

In producing this book Powell and I have had the enthusiastic cooperation of many appliance manufacturers, as well as their trade associations. As a service technician involved with the operating problems of a wide range of brands, Powell has often been able to summarize these problems in terms of their common denominators. He can visualize the pitfalls into which amateurs might tumble. He can caution them away from the thoughtless, tear-apart approach to appliance repairs that in the past has so often resulted in what repairmen know as "basket cases"—parts strewn over the floor by a homeowner unable to get them back together again.

This unhappy result has occurred so frequently that a few manufacturers urged that this book *not* be produced. They argued that it would only lead to more basket cases, that some homeowners are constitutionally incapable of mastering the techniques of the simplest sort of repair operation. People of this sort do exist, and do-it-yourself books that contain phrases like "it's easy" and "anybody can do it" are constantly conning these people into making fools of themselves.

Let the following now be understood:

Making a repair to a home appliance takes brains. You *must* apply your mental powers. You can't get by with mere wishful thinking. It is not enough to read instructions. Rather, you must understand those instructions, contained in words, diagrams, and photographs. Human beings vary widely in this type of capability. Some are naturally inclined toward mechanical operations and problems. For these, repairing an appliance is a comparatively simple exercise. We say that they have an "aptitude" for such work. Other people do not. If you know, deep in your heart, that you are one of the latter, then you are going to have to really work to understand and follow the instructions found in this book. You are going to have to work *mentally*—the type of work that, for many of us, is the most difficult. Evan Powell and I both realize the truth of this, and we have tried, in every way we could, to ease the job for you.

I am confident that this book contains somewhere around 99 percent of all the facts that might ever be needed to solve *any* appliance problem. But keep in mind, always, that these facts will not do you a bit of good unless you are willing to try to understand them—and how to apply them. You *must* be willing to extend yourself mentally. Before you can successfully repair an appliance, you must understand—completely and fully—what you are doing.

In the chapters that follow, Evan Powell is your guide. The words and expertise are his. Read his words carefully. Heed his advice—well! Understand what you are doing before you act—and you ought to be able to solve just about any appliance-repair problem that you encounter. The best of luck!

ROBERT P. STEVENSON

Complete Guide to

HOME
APPLIANCE
REPAIR

1
Wait! Don't Call a Repairman—Yet

Chances are good that you will get your money's worth out of this book even though you never put a wrench to a single appliance. This will be true even if you are a woman—or perhaps it's better to say *especially* if you are a woman. For nine times out of ten, it's the woman of the household who first encounters the problem when trouble comes to an appliance.

What I want to tell you, first of all, is how to act and what to do in the first few minutes after you find out that something has gone wrong with the washer, the refrigerator, the air conditioner, or other household machine on which your family's well-being partly depends. My first bit of advice is a don't. Don't rush to the telephone and call the dealer from whom you bought the ailing machine. Wait! You really are smarter than you think you are, and there's a very good possibility you can do something constructive about your problem without calling a repairman.

Among my acquaintances are a number of appliance-service technicians, and almost all are honest, dedicated people. They know what they are talking about. My advice about not immediately calling a technician comes directly from the repairmen themselves. Any good technician would much rather that you wait until you are confident your problem is serious—and beyond your abilities—before giving him that call.

It is estimated nationally that fully 30 percent of all service calls are unnecessary, that the cause of the problem was something so simple, so nontechnical that the homeowner could have handled it himself. Some estimates of these calls range as high as 40 percent. The reasons for the calls generally fall under what the servicing industry classifies as "customer instruction." They involve factors outside the appliance itself. They include such things as improper use of the appliance, blown fuses, improper purchasing—the appliance lacks the ability or capacity to do the job desired—and, more often than you think, disconnected electrical plugs.

On such a service call, everybody loses.

1

Often there's a resentment transferred toward the appliance manufacturer. The servicing agency, even though it charges for the call, can seldom charge enough to cover actual expenses. You lose because the service charge you must pay could have been avoided, and often there's an inconvenient wait before the appliance is back in operation. Remember, I'm not speaking of the rare occasion; these causes account for one out of every three of the thousands of appliance service calls made in this country every day. Just being aware of this fact is a good starting point for you. Happily, if yours is the average family, you can immediately eliminate at least 25 percent of the service calls to your home.

Even under the very best conditions, the need for an appliance service call is not a welcome experience. It's usually unexpected and unbudgeted, and always seems to come at the most inappropriate time. Besides the cost of service, you face a certain amount of "down time"—the period when you can't use the ap-

pliance. It's a situation well worth avoiding if you can.

Here's what you can do to try to avoid a repair call:

1. Check the appliance plug. And don't just *look* at the plug. Take hold of it, and make sure its prongs are all the way into the outlet.

2. What about the fuse or circuit breaker that protects the circuit on which the appliance operates? Is the fuse blown or the breaker tripped? Make sure. Press the breaker knob toward the *reset,* then the *on* position. Unless you are absolutely confident that the fuse is good, substitute a new one of the proper amperage. Remember that a 230-volt appliance such as a dryer has two fuses. One blown fuse may knock out only part of the appliance, such as the heating element, but the motor may still run. Don't let it fool you.

3. Is your power off? Or is your neighbor-

You may save a repair bill by this simple test when an appliance fails to operate. Plug a desk lamp into the wall outlet that serves the appliance. If the lamp lights, you know that the circuit and its fuse (or circuit breaker) are both okay. In putting back the appliance plug, be sure it's all the way into the receptacle.

hood perhaps undergoing a power brown-out? If so, your appliances obviously won't work or at least they won't work right. In a severe brown-out, it's best to turn off or unplug automatic motor-operated appliances because of the possibility of a low-voltage motor burnout.

4. If the ailing appliance has a self-contained light, is the light working? If not, suspect a burned-out bulb—or that you still haven't made a complete checkout of the first three possibilities above.

5. Check to make sure that all of the appliance controls are properly set and that all buttons are all the way in.

6. If your ailing appliance is a refrigerator, is it perhaps in its defrost cycle? Technicians *have* been called because of this.

7. If there's a water leak, will something as simple as tightening a hose or hose clamp stop it?

8. If a washer fails to fill with water, be sure someone has not turned off the valves in the pipes leading to the machine.

9. Remember that in the damp-dry cycle, a washer basket may not spin unless the lid is closed.

10. What particular symptom do you notice about your appliance? Do you find this symptom in the instruction book that came with your appliance? Or do you find the symptom in the checklist accompanying the chapter later in this book that applies to the type of appliance that's giving you the trouble? Do the possible causes of the symptom offer you a clue about what to do?

11. Have you taken care of your appliance as recommended in your instruction book and later in this book? Is it possible that just a good cleaning is all that's needed? Grease in a gas jet? Dust on a refrigerator's coils? Lint in a dryer?

Don't give up until you have gone through all of these checkout points. Your next move then may be to call that technician unless you want to attempt the needed repair yourself. If you call the technician, be prepared to describe to him what you have learned and done. Also have at hand the serial and model numbers. He'll undoubtedly ask you for them.

If your appliance is still in warranty, attempt no repairs yourself or you will lose your benefits. Manufacturers are very touchy about this. The slightest change from the original condition can be called tampering, legal grounds for invalidating the warranty. Don't take a chance. Get in touch with the dealer from whom you bought the appliance. Ask him what to do about repairs.

Later in this book you can learn how to undertake the solution of the really difficult appliance problems—the ones that make up some 75 percent of a technician's work load. You will learn, too, when it's better for you not to attempt a repair. But for the present, learn that lesson about all of those unnecessary calls. Remember that by putting back just a single pulled-out electrical plug you might save at least twice the cost of this book.

2
The Use and Care of Your Appliances

You already have learned, in our opening chapter, that you can reduce your appliance repair bill by as much as one-fourth simply by making sure you don't call a technician without reason. Now I want to tell you another important money-saving fact of appliance life: If you use and take care of your appliances so as to reduce the *need* for repairs you'll save another goodly amount, as well as get increased satisfaction from the appliances themselves. No one, to my knowledge, has arrived at any reliable figures for this type of saving, but proper use and regular preventative maintenance, combined, surely have a high monetary value in the life of an appliance.

The instruction book that comes with an appliance is valuable. Read it. Study it. If there is something you fail to understand fully about the operation of the appliance, go back to the dealer and ask him to explain. For the most part you will find him willing and able to help. But if you do not learn everything you want from him, do not hesitate to write to the manufacturer. Address the service manager, or use the address that usually is supplied for sending in the appliance warranty card. Whirlpool and General Electric have a WATS line to help customers with any problem—even with repair advice.

Before you buy a new appliance, plan ahead and do some homework to be sure it's the best one for you. Consider life-cycle costs, consisting of three factors—initial cost, operating costs, and maintenance costs. Many appliances now have energy-consumption labels; look at the graph that illustrates the spread between high and low models of that appliance. If the spread is small, don't base your decision on this. If it's large, however, consider that during the appliance's lifetime the cost of operating the high-energy-consuming model can amount to hundreds of dollars more than the energy-efficient model.

Not long ago, we purchased the largest appliance that would fit the available space. But larger appliances generally consume more energy, so it's a good practice to size them realistically for your needs. Like many modern families, your next refrigerator may be *smaller* than your present one. Check the available space to be sure that it will fit. Be sure to allow sufficient room for servicing and proper ventilation. The specifications can be obtained from the dealer who carries the equipment that you are considering. If it is a particularly large appliance, check to be sure that doorways are large enough to allow it to be installed. Freezers and refrigerators are sometimes returned for this reason.

When you're shopping, give consideration to both the present and the projected requirements of your family, for an appliance is a durable purchase. Perhaps you determine that your needs require only the basic washing cycles on an automatic washer. On the other hand, perhaps they require most of the specialized choices available on top-of-the-line models.

Look also for signs of quality construction and for ease of cleaning. A wise salesman will be able to demonstrate these aspects of his product to you. And don't forget the all-important questions: how long does the warranty last? What does it include and what are its limitations? Does it include both parts and labor in its coverage? Does the dealer offer authorized service during the warranty period? If not, who should be contacted for service?

It's not a bad idea to ask for an owner's manual and instruction book before leaving the sales floor after purchasing a new appliance. Usually the dealer will be able to provide this for you. This gives you an opportunity to familiarize yourself with it before delivery.

Make learning all you can about the operation of the new appliance a family affair. As often as not in these days of working wives, the task of doing the family wash may often fall to the husband. But that is not the only reason we husbands should know all we can about the machines that too many of us still tend to banish to the woman's domain. The more we know about the use of the machines, the greater success we'll have in making repairs when they become necessary.

After both husband and wife understand fully the use of the new appliance, store the instruction book and other materials that usually come with it (wiring diagram, parts list, warranty, bill of sale, etc.) in a place where both of you will have ready access to them if needed. Unless the papers include the model and serial numbers, find these on the appliance and note them on the cover of the instruction book. Keep a file like this for every appliance, large and small, that you own. Some homeowners protect important papers like these in a loose-leaf folder. Suit yourself about the method of storage. But do it. If you become deeply involved in appliance repair, as outlined in later chapters, this file will include a lot of information that you are going to need (for example, the wiring diagrams).

When you replace one appliance with a newer model, don't take it for granted that the new one operates exactly like the old one. Manufacturers are constantly making improvements in appliances—and you may fail to get the advantage of the improvement unless you learn all you can about the new features.

Each time you get a new appliance, don't relax until you make sure that it has been installed properly, legally, and safely. Otherwise, you may not get full satisfaction from it. Men employed by reliable dealers will try to make a proper installation, but don't take it for

It's never too soon to learn about using and maintaining home appliances correctly. Owner's manuals contain a great deal of safety-related information that should be reviewed regularly; most manufacturers also provide updated information and tips upon request.

vidual circuits, usually protected by 20 ampere fuses or circuit breakers.

PREVENTATIVE MAINTENANCE

Auto mechanics will always advise that it's easier and less expensive to tighten a wheel nut than to repair the wreckage that may occur if the nut comes off. That's preventative maintenance. Through preventative maintenance of home appliances, you can avoid the inconveniences that accompany a breakdown. You also can often save money by taking corrective steps before a tiny trouble becomes a big one.

The simple act of application of oil or other lubricant to adjoining surfaces that function together is preventative maintenance. So is vacuuming or brushing away the lint and dust that accumulates within appliance enclosures. The wise homeowner will have a regular schedule for lubricating (but not overlubricating) and cleaning all household machines. Twice a year should be about right. When you have once checked over a particular appliance, a record of where to apply oil will speed future lube jobs. Some machines or parts, of course, are sealed and have lifetime lubrication.

Professional preventative maintenance is almost always a wise investment. Having your room air conditioner checked, cleaned, and oiled may prevent a motor bearing burnout on the hottest day of summer. Tightening a loose belt on a washer or dryer may save the same belt from replacement a few months in the future. During off seasons and periods of light work loads appliance service organizations sometimes advertise reduced rates for preventative maintenance work. Such offers are usually worthwhile. Watch for them.

granted. While the appliance is being installed, ask to see any installation instructions that come with it. If you can't be at home while the job is being done, request that the installation instructions be left behind for you. Follow them through and check out the installation as fully as you can. In any electrical appliance, make sure it has been safely grounded as required by local codes. This is the time to wonder, too, if the addition of the new appliance is overloading your household wiring. Most major appliances should have their own indi-

Consider the service contracts that several companies now offer. With one of those, you can budget your expense for service on the appliance. You have no dread of the major expense lurking behind the next twist of a timer. These contracts often go beyond the coverage of the original warranty, including such fringe benefits as preventative maintenance calls, replacement of lamps and fuses, etc. Whether or not they're worthwhile for you depends greatly on the amount of usage that you give your appliances. But consider a service contract or agreement carefully if you believe your usage is above normal. Ask a dealer whether such a service is available in your area. Prices of each contract vary with the age of the appliance. It's doubtful whether a contract is worthwhile as the appliance approaches replacement age.

In later chapters devoted to repair of specific appliances, you will find tips about what to do to keep the appliance in good operating condition: preventative maintenance. You will also find a listing of good habits of use and care for the particular appliance. These compilations summarize information developed by the Major Appliance Consumer Action Panel (MACAP), based on its exposure to a variety of appliance problems, plus related tips I have gleaned from my experiences in the home appliance industry. And you'll find pointers to help you use (or modify) your equipment to use less energy.

Certain use and care tips apply to all appliances. Among them are the following:

- Always unplug the appliance before cleaning or inspecting it.
- Provide a grounded (polarized) outlet for every appliance that needs one.

- Never use an appliance when your hands are wet or when you are standing in a damp location.
- At the slightest indication of a tingle or electrical shock, unplug the appliance and *don't use it again* until it is thoroughly tested.
- Use the appliance *exactly* as the manufacturer directs.
- Use the appliance for its intended purpose only. Do not make any unusual demands for which it was not designed.
- Use with the appliance only those products recommended by the manufacturer—that is, detergents, utensils, cleaning solutions, etc.
- Treat exterior and interior finishes with care. Metal finishes can scratch, porcelain enamel can develop hairline cracks or chips, and there are limitations to the impact plastics, and other materials, can absorb. Pay careful attention to advice provided in the user's manual.
- Exercise care in cleaning the appliance. Water can cause electrical short circuits.
- Grasp the plug, not the cord, when disconnecting an appliance from the outlet. Be on the lookout for worn cords and loose plugs.
- Do not operate an appliance that is partly disassembled.
- Don't attempt to defeat safety devices such as lid and door switches.
- Keep children away from any appliance that is in operation, including range door surfaces during self-cleaning operations. All appliances use an energy source for operation that presents a potential hazard for any person not instructed in proper use and care.
- An extension cord is not recommended. If one must be used temporarily, be sure that

it is at least as large as the appliance cord and keep it as short as possible.

- Gas appliances that use an external electrical supply should be grounded and wired in the same manner as electrical appliances.
- Make provisions for combustion air and venting for gas appliances, as specified in the owner's manual and instructions.
- Shut off the gas supply before moving a gas appliance. Relight the pilot when back in place.

You'll obtain best results if you use the material in this book as a three-part program of home-appliance maintenance and servicing. The first step begins with the proper installation and usage of the equipment. The second is to exercise proper preventative maintenance procedures as contained in the chapters devoted to each appliance. If you don't do this yourself, you're still ahead of the game even if you pay to have it done. The third step is to know how your appliance operates and what to do if it doesn't. This pays big dividends to you, often resulting in considerable savings in time and expense, plus a big bonus—the fun and satisfaction derived from a job well done.

But let us point out once again that this activity is not a one-sided affair—for either the lady or the man of the house. Proper use and maintenance ought always to be a joint consideration and habit for both of you.

For example, the person who *uses* the dryer ought to be the one who cleans out the lint, making the machine ready for the next user. Enough said?

3
How the Manufacturers Can Help You

Appliance manufacturers have spent a great deal of money setting up and operating service programs and repair centers. Each manufacturer has a strong interest in seeing that his appliance gives you satisfaction. His interest is largely self-interest, of course, for he wants your repeat business. But don't discount this. Manufacturer-inspired service programs offer you nothing but good.

In addition to trying to service what they sell, manufacturers generally are concerned with producing a product that will be safe and trouble-free. Quality control programs benefit the manufacturers themselves, for a safe and trouble-free product lessens the chances of liability suits and the costs of after-sale servicing. As a customer, you obviously reap many benefits, too, many of them unrecognized.

When you buy an appliance, don't fail to look for and demand the labels that are evidences of the manufacturer's concern for safety and quality—the Underwriters' Laboratories (UL) seal, the Association of Home Appliance Manufacturers (AHAM)

seal on major appliances, and the American Gas Association seal on gas appliances. After remarking to me that the majority of manufacturers of consumer products urgently want quality and safety, the representative of one manufacturer told me: "We strive for this, and we are constantly improving our technique to do so. UL has tightened down on many requirements and we have gone well beyond this in many cases. We are testing almost 100 percent for current leakage in production, have improved sealing techniques, and have reduced the possibility of shock hazard, plus providing better operation."

You may find it difficult to believe just how far some manufacturers have progressed in their efforts toward quality control. For instance, tolerances are often checked closely. The instruments used by one manufacturer to inspect refrigerator compressors are so critical that they will measure the expansion of metal caused by the "heat" from the beam of a flashlight held two feet away. New materials have been adopted to practically eliminate former

9

trouble spots. An example of this is the new polypropylene pumps now used on many automatic washers. These are virtually unaffected by water and chemical action.

How does this sort of thing benefit you? Let's consider the purchase of a new refrigerator today as compared to the average purchase in the 1940s.

Your new model might contain approximately 16 cubic feet of usable storage space as compared to some 8 cubic feet previously. It would probably also have such features as frostless refrigeration, meaning that you never have to defrost it during normal operation; shelving arrangements that adjust to suit varying needs; improved finish materials that won't rust and colors that won't fade; high-efficiency components and insulation for lower operating costs; and very likely an automatic icemaker. You would get all this at a price just slightly higher than you might have paid for a refrigerator in 1948. Yet the appliance industry has faced the same problems of inflation, rising wages, and material costs that confronted other American heavy industries. Compare this to other major products and you'll probably agree that it has taken no small effort on the part of the appliance industry to accomplish such savings. The example I've given is typical; the same findings would apply to practically any home appliance.

Do today's appliances require less service than post-war models? No, they require more. The same components that make them so much more useful and desirable to today's homeowners also add to their complexity. Simply speaking, there's a lot more to go wrong. This naturally causes an increase in the frequency of service. But if we compare the number of components in today's machines to those in older machines and rank service on a basis consistent with the same percentage, we find evidence of product improvement. Indeed, today's equipment requires significantly *less* service than appliances of 10–15 years ago.

Plastics have had a lot to do with this. Used in the right places, they're hard to beat. The polypropylene previously mentioned as being used in many automatic washer pumps is a plastic compound that resists the effects of water and chemical solutions such as chlorine bleach and detergent. In older machines, these chemicals caused aluminum alloy components to become pitted and "eaten away" after several years. Plastic tubs are being used in automatic washers, again largely to resist corrosion. Modern materials and new processes of applying porcelain give us a finish that will last much longer than previous coatings under the adverse effects found in dishwasher tubs over periods of many, many cycles.

Sometimes new materials result in savings to the manufacturer. If so, it's a bonus. Often as not, they cost more, especially during the initial process while they are being phased into the manufacturing operation.

The records show that manufacturers are only too willing to put ideas, practices, and materials into usage that will improve their product and allow them to remain competitive in the marketplace.

I have seen many examples of this during my career in several areas of the appliance field. Much of my work has dealt with transmitting ideas about products directly to the manufacturers and in helping consumers obtain better service and more usefulness from their home appliances. In a very real sense, I have always worked for the consumer.

Appliance engineers always listen to what's being said about their products. If it's positive, this is their reward for a job well done. If not, they want to know so they can develop a better component. I've had the experience of having novice technicians point out something that those of us who have been involved for years had not noticed. When the information was passed along, the manufacturer put it into use in the product. The new technician was amazed that a giant company listened to his ideas. There's a lot to be said for an industry where such things can happen.

I've never seen any real evidence of so-called "planned obsolescence" in the industry—in the sense of such practices as building component parts to wear out fast so as to increase parts sales. Such a tactic would be self-defeating. Manufacturers are much more interested in emblazoning their brand name upon the mind of the consumer so he will return for another appliance purchase.

As part of this consumer-pleasing program, many manufacturers are now building their appliances so as to make service easier. Here are some examples:

Besides offering a quality repair service, Maytag eases service of its washers by making it unnecessary to pull them from the wall; tops are hinged and front panels are removable. Whirlpool and Sears, too, have long featured hinged "snap-up" tops on automatic washers. Frigidaire's "design for service" policy resulted in a line of laundry equipment featuring lift-off consoles, tops, and front panels that practically eliminate moving the machines for servicing. In addition, a special electronic analyzer could be plugged into the wiring harness to quickly pinpoint evasive electrical faults. General Electric has a program called R-E-D (rapid electrical diagnosis) in use in some G.E. and Hotpoint appliances. This utilizes a special multi-circuit connector in the wiring harness. A special adapter and meter

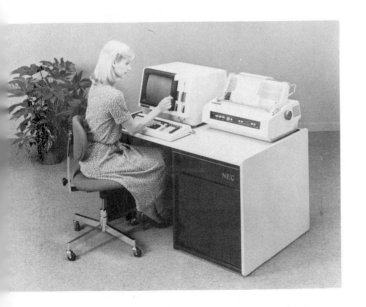

Service information is kept on file in computer in large organizations, on cards in smaller ones. Information on file should have records of customers' appliances and history of service. To speed process, be prepared to give travel directions, model and serial numbers, and purchase dates.

plugged into this connector allows fast, accurate diagnosis of electrical problems. And GE has experimented with service clinics, and has recently introduced "Quick-Fix" manuals and parts for those interested in doing their own repairs.

This activity on the part of the manufacturers adds up to one important fact that you should keep in mind—they really want to give you good service. For the most part, they are proud of their products, and they (some of them, at least) are not too sure that the rest of us ought to be tinkering with sophisticated machinery that we probably know very little about. Okay. I can do nothing but applaud the efforts of the manufacturers. But there comes a time when our own self-help seems to be needed and justified. Information to help you do this is what I am offering you in the later chapters of this book.

But attempt no repairs yourself during the period of warranty! The warranty you get with your new appliance is a valuable piece of property. Don't destroy it by undertaking a repair while it still is in force. We already have said this once before in our book—and we'll probably say it again a time or two. Check no further than to see that power (and water, if required) are reaching the machine, and consult your owner's manual to be sure that you are using it correctly. So long as your warranty is in force, let your dealer advise you about repairs. Call him and find out how to go about it. Or look in the telephone book yellow pages for the address of a firm that provides factory-authorized repairs. Look first under the brand name of your appliance.

Manufacturers offer service in two ways. First, many of them have skilled service technicians available to come to your home, espe-

cially for the larger appliances. Second, they have regional service centers where you can deliver the ailing appliance, especially if it's small and easily transported. Sunbeam, General Electric, and West Bend are among the companies that have invested heavily in such regional centers. In some cases, you can send a small appliance to a repair center by mail or other delivery service. Both types of service—in your home for a major appliance and at a repair center for a small appliance—are available, of course, whether your equipment is still in warranty or out of it, and let's be sure everyone understands the advantages of this. Many homeowners would be best advised to stick to services offered by the manufacturer. Perhaps you belong in this group. The services pro-

If the technician feels that he may need parts not on his truck, he will look them up on a parts drawing before he leaves for the day.

Parts requested by technician are removed from bins and checked out to him before he makes your call. If you have given him a good description of the symptoms of your problem, chances are good that he will have the right ones with him. A large back-up supply of repair parts is essential to an efficient service operation.

Service manager has a final chat with technician before he begins his day's work. During the day, technician will be in touch with the service office to report on his schedule and to take emergency calls.

NET REFRIGERATED VOLUME
AND NET SHELF AREA

AHAM
CERTIFIED

ASSOCIATION OF HOME
APPLIANCE MANUFACTURERS'
Refrigerator-Freezer Standard HRF 1

Look for this seal when you buy. You'll find it on many new appliances. It certifies that the manufacturers trade association has verified the ratings involved.

vided are usually expert and guaranteed. Consider well before undertaking the do-it-yourself repair procedures I will outline later. Be sure that you understand the operation of the equipment and can visualize each step in the job before you begin. If you can't do this, better call in a professional.

Most major manufacturers now have factory service centers in the largest cities, and all are constantly trying to outdo the others in improving speed and quality of service. Well remembered are the lessons learned during the "discount days" of the late 1950s when some dealers openly advertised "Cash and Carry—Low Prices, No Service." We all know the sad outcome of this policy.

Among companies that didn't pursue this course was Sears, Roebuck and Company. Sears now has a group of Technical Training Centers which offer a year-round curriculum of one and two week courses in appliance repair, geared for experienced as well as newer technicians. In addition, in Sears service centers repair parts are stocked and ordered by computers, and planes shuttle daily between centralized parts depots and factories, keeping the supply rolling. The Sears servicing organization is claimed to be the largest of its kind in existence.

Frigidaire was a pioneer in the training concept in the 1950s and when they were a division of General Motors, had permanent schools strategically located across the country. Here, thousands of their technicians were instructed each year in proper repair procedures. In addition, Frigidaire conducted an "Accredited Technician" program through its dealers as a means of recognizing and certifying individual technicians who met high standards in workmanship, experience, training,

attitude, and customer relations. The award was an annual one and a technician had to requalify each year. He was rated not only by his employer, but by the customers served. A verified customer complaint on the technician's record for the year meant automatic disqualification. Customers rated the technician on such points as courtesy, correction of the service problem, and respect for property.

General Electric has an excellent training program available for their dealers and service departments, and field representatives conduct regular training programs in their areas. G.E. has more than two hundred repair centers scattered throughout the country.

Whirlpool's Educational Center in Benton Harbor, Michigan, is a model training facility, and training aids furnished to their dealers and vocational schools are tops. They've installed a special telephone service through which they invite you to telephone—from anywhere in the U.S.—when you have trouble with a Whirlpool appliance. Calls are free. Call 800 253-1301. (In Michigan, call 800 632-2243.) The "Cool-Line" will even give you information to help you with your own repairs. Whirlpool also offers a home-study course related to appliance repair at reasonable cost, and it is available to anyone.

In this chapter, it was possible to provide credit to just a few of the consumer-oriented manufacturers for the good work they are doing. There are others. If we have failed to include the maker of your particular appliance, be assured that the omission is not intentional. The maker of your brand probably is doing more for you than you think he is. If you doubt it, write and ask about the problem you have. If your concern involves a small appliance, and you feel that you've exhausted every means of resolving the problem, write to the president of the company. Almost without exception that letter will get you the results you want.

The Association of Home Appliance Manufacturers (AHAM) is the national trade association of the appliance industry. The association conducts industry-wide programs in the statistical, technical, and safety areas, including safety inspection, certification, and governmental relations; advertising; consumer affairs; and public affairs. Practically anyone with the appliance industry would agree that the activities of this association are largely responsible for the success which the industry has achieved in many areas. No aspect is ignored, and even though the membership is composed of competitors, the trade organization provides a cement which welds them together on basic issues.

In addition to providing guidelines for manufacturing and production of home appliances, the association also takes a long-term outlook toward their products and the relationship of these products to the consumer. They've taken effective action in the fields of consumer education, both presale and postsale, and in service activities, developing recruiting and curriculum materials for the training of appliance technicians.

While much of AHAM's work goes on behind the scenes, practically everyone who has purchased a home appliance in recent years has been exposed to the AHAM certification program. The certification seal may be applied only to specific models which have been tested and verified as to the accuracy of the ratings involved. This may include such specifics as the water removal capacity of dehumidifiers, load size of automatic washers, cooling and

heating capacity of room air conditioners, and the net refrigerated volume and net shelf area of refrigerators and freezers. The AHAM seals provide a standard with which to compare various models of a particular brand and to compare brands to one another. Such third party certification provides technical verification of facts which simply can't be found by examining the product on the dealer's floor. The certification program is open to all manufacturers, both members and nonmembers of AHAM, and to firms that market private brand models. Participation is voluntary and AHAM is the sponsor and the certifying authority of the program.

Some of AHAM's certification effort is now being superseded by the government's energy efficiency labeling program for certain appliances. This information can tell you at a glance how a particular appliance compares in energy efficiency with other available models, and also exactly what it could cost to operate it.

While every successful appliance manufacturer was always aware that he must meet the needs of the consumer in order to sell his product and stay in business, still the most intense effort was placed upon getting the product into the marketplace. Sometimes there was a breakdown in direct communication between the manufacturer and the appliance owner.

Today there's another powerful authority on the scene in the appliance industry which has a very successful record in the area of representing consumer interest. This is the Major Appliance Consumer's Action Panel (MACAP), formed in 1970 to bridge the communication gap. MACAP consists of a group of consumer-oriented professionals who meet regularly to analyze consumer complaints and then recommend appropriate action to resolve them. The following major appliances fall within the scope of the panel: dehumidifiers, dishwashers, dryers, electronic ranges, freezers, garbage disposers, gas incinerators, humidifiers, microwave ovens, ranges, refrigerators, room air conditioners, trash compactors, washers, and water heaters. Although MACAP is sponsored by three industry trade associations, the Association of Home Appliance Manufacturers, the Gas Appliance Manufacturers Association, and the National Retail Merchants Association, it operates as an independent, voluntary, non-profit organization of consumer representatives. This provides a unique opportunity for a direct channel of communication among consumers, dealers, service agencies, and the appliance manufacturer. Through MACAP's complaint handling procedure, the consumer can receive fair and equitable handling of what otherwise might be an unresolved appliance problem. The panel also makes recommendations to appliance manufacturers for better complaint handling procedure, improved customer service, and appliance design.

Here's what MACAP recommends if a problem develops: Double check the electric plug, fuses, operating controls, and consult your instruction manual to make sure you don't waste money on an unnecessary service call. When you require service, call your dealer, the service agency he recommends, or an organization franchised by the manufacturer to repair your brand. If you cannot resolve the problem locally, write or call the manufacturer giving all details. If you are not satisfied with the action taken by the manufacturer, write or call MACAP collect, 20 North Wacker Drive, Chicago, Illinois 60606, Telephone 312 236-3165.

This is what's going on in the thinking of the appliance manufacturing industry today. While their record is good, there's lots more to be done. But the makers are listening to your ideas as an appliance owner about the things you want in future appliances. There's a lot of work going on now in the areas of making appliances more energy-efficient; making owner's manuals easier to read and understand, telling appliance owners why their machines operate as they do in addition to the basic information of how to use them and care for them; providing better, faster appliance service and supplies of parts; and testing hundreds of new materials each year to help keep prices in line and provide you with better, more reliable products. Where there are shortcomings, there's an honest effort going on to alleviate them. And for all the accomplishments, it's time we gave credit where credit is due.

That competing firms working both cooperatively and independently are capable of such accomplishments speaks well for the appliance industry. Guenther Baumgart, the president of the Association of Home Appliance Manufacturers, speaking to a University of California graduate school symposium sums this philosophy up well: "The companies we work with are competitors. They vie with one another to capture sales. In most situations consumers benefit from these efforts as one company seeks to develop a better product or to offer it at a lower price or to create an innovative approach. Vigorous competition is basically good, socially desirable, and should be encouraged."

4
Why Learn About Appliance Repairs?

The question that heads this chapter might have a variety of answers, but I want to discuss just two of them. You may answer that you are aiming toward maintaining the many appliances in your own household. That's reason enough for most people. Or you may say that you intend to become a professional appliance technician. That, too, is an excellent reason. Both objectives hold great potential rewards. This book can give you a sound start toward either or both of these laudable goals.

Let's consider first the maintenance of your own appliances. Whatever percentage of your life expectancy still lies ahead of you, you and other members of your family are going to be depending for a long time on household appliances, your present ones and new ones, for a lot of the satisfaction that you expect from life. These appliances are very important to you. Taken as a whole, your appliances probably rank as an investment only behind your house and your car or cars. A young homeowner will benefit for many years from the information he can learn from this book. I would recommend,

however, that he use the book just as the beginning—that he go on and get further training and practice from a correspondence course in appliance repairs or by taking an adult education course in the subject. If no course of this type is available in your vicinity, see if a few of your neighbors may not like to join you in asking that an adult course be offered at your local high school or vocational training center.

As you gain in proficiency, however you get it, friends and neighbors who know about your growing knack with appliances will tend to call on you for help. First thing you know, you just might have a profitable moonlighting activity.

And this advice by no means applies only to men; there's no reason that you girls can't be perfectly qualified to master the technology of your home equipment. In fact, you have an immediate advantage; as I noted in a previous chapter, the chances are very high that you will be the one to encounter the problem first when an appliance begins to act up. Why wait for the man of the household to arrive home before attempting a repair? You might very well get the problem out of the way before then. If this book stimulates your interest, and you then find that an adult education course is offered locally, by all means take it—even if you have to go alone. Let your husband do the babysitting.

I'd like to tell you now about a course in major appliance repair that I developed and taught at the Technical Education Center in Greenville, South Carolina. This was an invaluable experience for me. I learned a lot from the students. The course gave me a unique opportunity to test some theories that I had developed from my career in the appliance industry. It also enabled me to observe how information about home appliances was put to use by the students.

Many of my students had little or no experience with home appliances. Others had attempted some limited work on their own equipment. Still others were engaged in appliance repair as a part-time business and some were professionals who were interested in increasing their knowledge or picking up a few pointers that might be of help to them. The scope of the material was arranged so that all might receive maximum benefit from the time that they spent in class.

At the beginning of each year, I asked the students to fill out a brief questionnaire. This included two questions which were extremely important to me. These were (1) what previous experience do you have, if any, in the appliance field or in any electrically or mechanically-oriented field, and (2) what are your reasons for taking this course, including any long range plans or goals that this course may help you realize?

I still have those papers. Their purpose at the time was simply to allow me to get to know each student on a personal basis and to help me plan material so that each might obtain maximum benefit. Since I then had some knowledge of each individual's experience, I could answer any questions that he might have on a level directly related to his experience or to phrase material in a way that he could understand it. Over the years, these papers have served a gratifying purpose. Through occasional meetings and telephone calls from my ex-students, I have been able to "keep tabs" on several hundred of them. Many were able to realize their ambitions. Many whose primary goal was to repair the appliances in their own homes call from time to time to tell me of a particularly challenging job that they've conquered. They're proud of it—and so am I. Some, particularly a few who were retired, began part-time businesses of their own. A number of younger students who were employed in other fields but enjoyed this type of work and felt that they were interested in making a career of it, have done just that. One example is that of a student, now a close personal friend, who answered my "Why?" with this statement: "For enjoyment. I like to do things around the house." That simply. Before long he transferred his enjoyment to a small part-time business. Some time later he left a job which he had held for many years, even though he wasn't overly happy with the work, to enter the appliance servicing field. Today he is regarded as one of the top technicians of the largest servicing unit in the area.

My purpose in this reminiscing is not to extoll the merits of the course. It is to say simply this: the wonderful world of home appliances is a fascinating and challenging field, one in which you can very easily and unexpectedly become absorbed. The information which is conveyed here is intended to help you repair your own home appliances and hopefully to stimulate your interest in them. But it can also be a starting point for much more.

Should you become an appliance technician? If you feel that you are interested in a career in appliance servicing, my advice to you is this: get some experience by using the information in this book to work on your own appliances, or disassemble and diagnose an old appliance no longer in use. When you have done enough of this, you may have found that you gain a great sense of accomplishment from putting an ailing appliance back into service. After diagnosing the fault and making the repairs, you are rewarded with the sight and sound of the equipment whirring back to life. This personal satisfaction is a rare commodity in many jobs these days. But you'll discover other things, too. It can be hard work because appliances are heavy and they usually must be moved for servicing. The work can be greasy and dusty; for example, when you're lying on your back changing the pump on an automatic washer. But you'll probably agree with expert technicians that the enjoyment of seeing the end result of your labor exceeds the discomfort. It's a creative process that can provide some of the best therapy you'll ever find.

Another thing that makes appliance servicing so interesting is the fact that it's a continual learning process. This book is only a beginning—you'll need more refined training in the technical field as well as in the fields of human relations and business. Appliance servicing involves handling people as well as equipment, and it's hard to say which is the more important to a successful technician. There are also reports to be made out, important reports which record the type of work done, the amount of income received for parts and labor, and product reports that are invaluable to the manufacturer in developing quality control programs.

Your training can begin where you are. If you are a high school student, take all the shop courses you can in math and physics. Take some shop courses which emphasize craftmanship. Other training is available at both public and private technical schools and through several very good home study courses such as the one offered by Whirlpool. In any case, you'll find no shortage of training available. For the most current detailed information about training programs in appliance service, you can write to the National Association of Trade and Technical Schools and the National Home Study Council, 1601 18th Street, N. W., Washington, D. C. 20009; and the Association of Home Appliance Manufacturers, 20 North Wacker Drive, Chicago, Illinois 60606.

After your basic training, you'll find a large market for your talents. There are over a billion home appliances in use today with more than one hundred fifty million new units being produced annually. The sales of major appliances for more than ten years have generally grown at a rate of almost ten per cent each year. A chief engineer of one of the nation's largest manufacturers of dishwashers, for instance, recently told me that his company was producing more than 6,000 units per day. This means that as more and more new homes become filled with an ever-growing variety of home appliances, many more service technicians will be needed to provide the necessary installation and maintenance services. There's already a great shortage of qualified personnel, and opportunities are practically unlimited.

Salary levels are good and increasing. Many manufacturers offer desirable fringe benefits as well as opportunities to advance to such areas as quality control, management, and instruction.

At some point, you may find that you are more interested in one type of appliance than another. You may even feel inclined towards certain brands of appliances. When you do, it's time for some on-the-job training. Chances are you'll be able to apply to the servicing agency of your choice in your community and get a part-time job in their shop or as a service technician's apprentice during busy seasons. Here you can learn more about the business aspects of appliance servicing as well as become involved in the service techniques of the particular organization. From this point you'll be available to enter the field on a full-time basis with the same agency or you'll be gaining valuable experience for starting your own business. In either case, if you satisfy yourself beforehand that this is the field for you, and if you develop your training and potential along these guidelines, you're on solid footing for a successful career.

When you begin this career, you'll find that your training begins all over again. Each manufacturer has his own training programs and procedures that he recommends and provides. Many of these are conducted at regional centers or even at the factory itself, and in larger units may be conducted on a local basis. In the beginning your training will be oriented toward the basics: electrical diagnosis, proper use of special tools and equipment, etc. Even years later, when you reach the advanced technician stage, there's regular training available. New products are introduced each year and

new servicing techniques are developed. It takes concentration to stay abreast of all of them. The appliance manufacturers have done an outstanding job in making training available to their employees and their dealers.

The capable technician of today is a respected, well-paid professional who is highly skilled and takes pride in his work. As such, he contributes much to our modern technological society. I like to think that the stigma cast by early postwar "jacklegs" has been largely erased by the conscientious and courteous technicians who form the vast majority of those in the field today.

But the potential of saving time and money, and the satisfaction to be gained from making a repair on your own appliance, are reasons enough for every homeowner to learn more about the equipment in his home. Whatever your reason for reading this book, you'll gain most from it if you'll take pride in every aspect of the work that you do.

I was impressed recently as I watched a technician that I know to be very competent repairing a television set. Even though he was unaware that anyone was watching, he had placed a protective cloth on the cabinet to protect the finish from tool scratches. When he was done, he took a bottle of cleaner from his tool kit and wiped the face of the picture tube, and then he produced a small brush which he used to dust lint away from the crevices around knobs and switches.

Obviously, this was a habit, and one that denoted pride in his work and consideration for the equipment. It's a habit that you would do well to cultivate. There's no better time than when you are first learning to work with appliances.

5
The Tools You Need to Repair Appliances

Before you can work on appliance problems, you must have on hand certain tools and test instruments. Surprisingly enough, two of the finest test instruments already are available to you—your own eyes and ears. Even before you read further in this book it would pay you to begin developing skill in using them. The practice in using eyes and ears that I'm going to suggest has given expert technicians what may seem like a sixth sense when you first encounter it. You can gain the same skill.

Whatever your goal in learning about appliance repair, you can begin by becoming better acquainted on an individual basis with each of the appliances in your home, using just your eyes and ears.

Whenever you have a chance, during the evening or on a weekend, take a few minutes off and spend them with one of your appliances. Three to five minutes is enough. Walk up to the family washing machine while there is a load of wash in it. Listen. Note the sounds it makes during each part of its cycle. Use your eyes to see whatever there is to see. Correlate

sight and sound and then dig out the instruction booklet that came with the machine and read all the facts you can find about the operations you are hearing and seeing. Get acquainted with the dishwasher in the same way.

Next month when the water won't pump out of the automatic washer, you won't have to be an expert to make an accurate preliminary diagnosis. Even if you don't attempt to make the repair yourself, being able to give knowledgeable information over the telephone to the servicing agency can often save you time and money, for the technician will probably be able to bring along the part needed to repair the washer.

Remember, look and listen for *symptoms* of the appliance problem. Take nothing for granted. What is the appliance doing or not doing that differs from its normal operation? From previous acquaintance with the appliance, you should soon have some idea where the problem exists. But look closely.

Here's a step-by-step example:

If a refrigerator is on the fritz, check to see

whether the lights are working. If they are, this means the fuses are good and power is being supplied to the refrigerator through the plug. Keep in mind what I've told you before —that technicians are sometimes called unnecessarily when a refrigerator is simply in a defrost cycle. Are the blower fans operating in normal fashion? Do you hear the compressor running? What about the condenser fan that circulates air around the compressor? Is the condenser clear? If nothing seems to be working, including the lights, perhaps a fuse is blown. No. The fuses check okay. Maybe the appliance is unplugged. No, couldn't be. It was working fine, last night. Did someone vacuum behind the refrigerator this morning? Hmmm. The plug. That's why you should never take anything for granted—especially if you want to avoid one of those unnecessary service calls we discussed earlier in the book. And from this simplified reasoning process you should be able to see that your familiarity with the appliance directly affects the speed and accuracy of your diagnosis.

You should understand by this time that you'll always be using your eyes and ears to supplement the hand tools and at least one important test instrument—a volt-ohm meter —that you ought to have on hand if you are really serious about making your own appliance repairs. Chances are that you may have to buy some of the tools that I'm about to list. But these tools are an excellent lifetime investment for any householder, just like insurance. Even in these days of developing inflation, its unlikely that you'll need to spend any large sum for the lot.

Your work in repairing appliances divides itself into mechanical and electrical phases. The tools you need divide somewhat the same way, although some can be used in both mechanical and electrical fields.

These basic tools will allow you to service small appliances, many major appliances. You probably already own many of them. The tools: (1) ¼"-inch drive socket set with pull bar and ratchet handle; (2) 10" utility pliers or arc joint pliers; (3) Phillips screwdriver set, including sizes 0 and 1; (4) setscrew wrench set; (5) small soldering gun; (6) pocket screwdriver, ⅛" blade and 4" screwdriver, ³/₁₆" blade; (7) 6" screwdriver, ¼" blade; (8) 5" ignition pliers; (9) 6" long-nose pliers with side cutters and insulated handles; (10) hose clamp pliers.

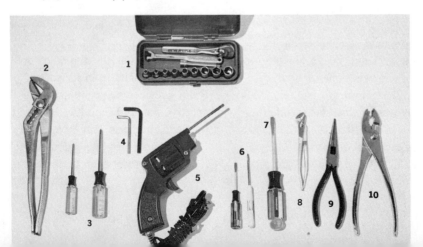

MECHANICAL TOOLS

From the mechanical standpoint, you'll need a pair of slip-joint pliers, Phillips screwdrivers size 0 and 1, setscrew wrenches, small pocket screwdrivers (I'd choose one with a ⅛-inch blade and one with a 3/16-inch blade), a pair of ignition pliers, 6-inch long-nosed pliers with side cutters and insulated handles, hose clamp pliers, and a ¼-inch six-point socket set with an extension and a ratchet handle.

As you progress toward larger appliances, you may find that you want to add to your tools. Additions that I would suggest are pictured as a supplementary set in an accompanying photograph. These include a set of ⅜-inch, six-point sockets with ratchet handle and extension, a set of open-end wrenches (I personally like combination wrenches which are open end on one end and box end on the other) ranging up to ¾ inch in size, a terminal tool

for electrical terminals, a propane torch, nutdrivers, and you may want to increase the range of screwdriver sizes in your collection. Of course, the list could go on and on—but once your skill has outgrown the basic tools, you'll know which additions suit your needs best.

With such an array of tools at your disposal, there's hardly any appliance problem you won't be able to handle. With one exception, you should have no problem finding any of them in hardware departments and automotive stores. The possible exception—hose clamp pliers. Try an automotive parts house, and you're almost certain to find several types on hand. They come in two basic types. Some have swiveling ends, and others are rigid like a set of standard pliers with notches to hold the clamps cut into them. I own and use both. Often one will fit a certain situation better than others. The straight, rigid type tends to hold

Supplementary tools allow full repair capabilities when combined with basic tools. These are tools you will want to add to your collection as you progress in appliance repair work. Tools as shown below are: **(1)** ⅜″ socket set, including pull bar and ratchet handle; **(2)** set of nut drivers, 3/16″ to ½″; **(3)** additional sizes of screwdrivers; **(4)** electrical terminal tool and spare terminals; **(5)** set of open-end or combination (shown) wrenches, ¼″ to ¾″.

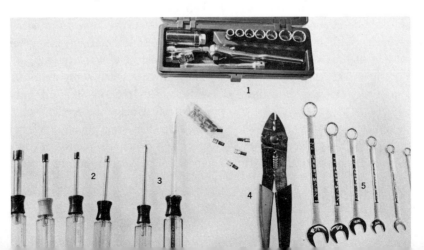

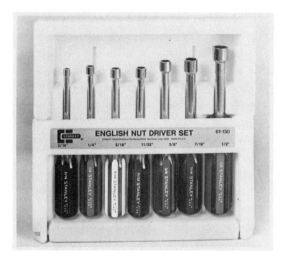

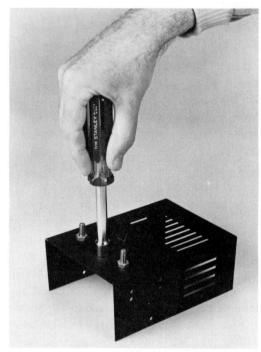

Nutdrivers are like screwdrivers with socket permanently mounted on end, but with one unique advantage—the hollow shaft accepts a protruding bolt and still allows you to reach the nut to loosen or tighten it. Sizes in Stanley set shown range from ³⁄₁₆ to ½ inch, ideal for appliance repairs.

the hose clamp in position a little more firmly. The swiveling type reaches easily into tight places that can be awkward with the rigid tool. I recommend that you look at both types. You may prefer one over the other.

When purchasing hand tools, look for quality. You may spend a little more, but as we mentioned before this is a long-term investment. You'll be using them for much more than appliance repair. With proper care, a good tool can last a lifetime. In fact, some hand tools now on the market carry a lifetime warranty. This may be worth paying a little more to obtain.

Hand tools should be cared for both in and out of use. Store them in a dry place. If they become rusty, clean and wipe them down with an oily cloth, leaving a light film of oil on the metal parts. Store them neatly in a toolbox or on a wall of your shop area. All of the tools mentioned, both basic and supplementary tools, can be placed in a medium-size tool box and kept in an unused corner of a closet.

You can also care for your tools by using them correctly. If you use a screwdriver with a ⅛-inch blade in a large screw with a ¼-inch slot, you're almost certainly asking for trouble. Use the correct tool for the job, and hold it firmly in place when applying force. Move it with a steady motion—this prevents slipping which can damage the tool. If you're joining wires together, use a pigtail or Western Union splice as shown in the photos. If you're attaching an electrical terminal to a wire, use the

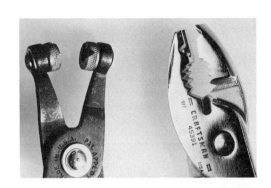

Which style is for you? This photo shows the difference between two basic types of hose-clamp pliers. Swiveling heads on style at left are more easily used in cramped spots, but rigid grip of style at right can be an advantage in some instances.

terminal tool to clinch the connection, then solder if necessary. Be sure to use the proper size terminal for the wire. Most electricians and technicians will give such a bond a firm tug to be sure that it is firmly connected before applying solder. Many such terminals of this type require no solder at all.

SOLDERING TOOLS AND TECHNIQUES

Before you begin to make a solder connection, get the gun ready for the job. If the tip is corroded or dirty, heat the gun just to the point that the solder begins to melt. Now scrape it gently with a knife or sandpaper until the copper shows through. Then touch solder to the tip of the gun, leaving a thin coat. This is called "tinning," and it goes a long way toward insuring a good job.

Solder must be used in conjunction with a flux, a material which cleans the parts to be joined and protects them from oxidation until the solder has flowed into the joint. In the past it was necessary to use a paste, applying it to the joint after cleaning and before heating. Now, however, the job is much easier; many soldering materials have the flux contained in

a hollow core of the solder itself, making it a one application operation. But there are two types of solder available, and you have to be sure to use the right one for the job. Acid-core solder (and acid paste fluxes) are used on some heavy-duty plumbing jobs where the joints can't be perfectly cleaned. Rosin-core solder and flux is made for use on electrical connections. *Never use an acid-core solder for any sort of electrical work.* The connection will soon corrode to the point that it will break or burn off.

Solder comes in various lengths and diameters. Be sure to select a supply marked for electrical work; this signifies that the tin-lead alloy proportions and the flux are specifically designed for the purpose, and that it has been tested in this type of application. I prefer the smaller diameter sizes, either $1/16$-inch or $1/32$-inch. You might not find these at the hardware counter, but they're available from any radio-TV parts supplier. The advantage of the small diameter solder is that the work doesn't have to be as hot for the solder to flow. Large diameter solder can act as a heat sink, absorbing heat from the work and requiring more heat to make the solder flow.

To make a good solder joint, first clean the

Here's how to get a good mechanical connection and a smooth job after taping. This is called the "Western Union" splice; conductors are wrapped around each other before soldering, not twisted together. Trim ends of wire and smooth down before soldering to prevent sharp edge which might cut tape.

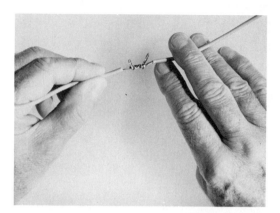

This one is the "pigtail" splice, and it's nothing more than twisting the wires tightly and cutting them before soldering. When soldering stranded wires such as those in photos, you will find that the solder will flow between each conductor when properly applied to the heated wire. This is "capillary action," and illustrates the tendency of the solder to flow toward the source of heat (the tip of the soldering gun).

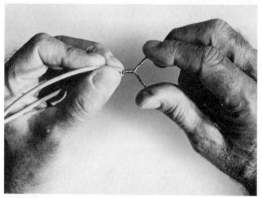

Taping is as important as the splice itself, and it takes practice to develop proficiency. When taping pigtail splice, start with wrap around tip of soldered conductors, then between the base of the splice before you begin to wrap the connection. This assures "double coverage" of vulnerable points.

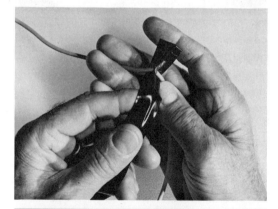

The wrap is important for a neat, secure job. Most amateurs go wrong by failing to stretch the tape while making the wraps. This results in the loosely wound "globs" of tape sometimes found. To avoid this, pull the tape tightly as you wind it, stretching it as you go. It will conform to the shape of the joint and provide a tight, neat seal.

parts to be joined thoroughly. A small piece of sand cloth or light abrasive material is good for this. Steel wool is often used but has an oil film which protects it from rusting. Under some conditions, the film left on the joint could prevent good bonding of the alloy. For the same reason, avoid touching a previously cleaned joint with your hands. Pull the trigger to energize the gun, and touch the tip to the largest piece of the work. Apply solder to the joint, and allow the heat from the work, not the gun itself, to melt the solder. While practicing this, you will probably notice that the solder tends to flow toward the heat source, or the hottest portion of the work. You can often use this to your advantage, even making solder flow uphill if the situation warrants. Hold the gun so that the broadest section of the tip is in contact with the work; the actual physical position of the gun may vary depending upon the shape of the work. This allows maximum thermal connection between the gun and the work.

Allow the solder to flow completely into the joint, but don't try to "build up" the connec-

tion—this leads to sloppy, insecure connections which aren't as strong as those which use much less solder. Use only enough to fill the gap or opening in the work. Hold the work perfectly still for a few seconds after the job is completed. You'll soon develop a "sixth sense" that tells you when the work is cool. The solder takes on a shiny, hard appearance at this point. If it has moved, however, it is suddenly filled with tiny fissures and cracks, presenting a cold, dull appearance. This is in fact called a "cold" joint, signifying that the joint was not hot enough to allow the solder to flow freely or the work was moved before the solder solidified. In either case, it should be redone. Under normal conditions, you'll be able to watch the solder harden into a smooth silvery mass.

VOLT-OHM METER

The last tool that I'm going to discuss, but probably the most important of all to proper

A strong mechanical connection is the first requirement for a perfect soldering job. Here a terminal is crimped to the wire after both wire and terminal ends have been cleaned. Terminal tool used with proper terminal may eliminate need for soldering such a connection and speed the work.

The second important rule of soldering is: Always apply soldering-gun heat to the object being soldered, as you see here, never to the solder itself. Heat from the work then melts the solder when correct temperature is reached, assuring good flow into all crevices of the connection.

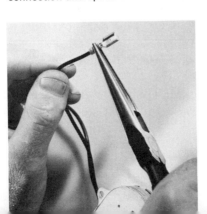

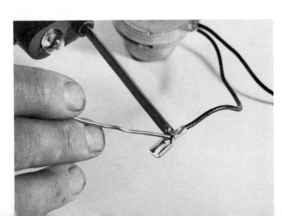

appliance diagnosis and care, is the volt-ohm meter (VOM). There are many people, including some appliance servicemen, who would take issue with me on this. They contend that all that is necessary is a test light, and possibly a battery-powered light or buzzer to test continuity. And they can prove their point by using these to pinpoint most problems in an appliance. I've tried it both ways, and have come to this conclusion: if you're already accustomed to using a test light, and if you prefer it, fine —go ahead and use it. But if this is something new to you, and you want to learn to service and diagnose appliances in the quickest, easiest, and most accurate fashion, you're far better off to invest in one of the good but inexpensive volt-ohm meters now on the market. The most inexpensive VOM is far superior to any test light I've seen. Sometimes it's not enough to know that voltage or continuity exists. You need to know how much—*exactly* how much, is present. Considering the cost of materials to build a good test light and buzzer rig, there would be little if any savings realized.

The VOM has become as essential to home maintenance as a portable drill. Those of us who work in electrical and automotive fields take this test meter so for granted that we're surprised to find the average homeowner is unfamiliar with it and most likely thinks he'd have to be an electronics buff to use one. Not true. The VOM is a simple measuring tool that should be standard equipment in every home.

What's ailing that toaster you tucked away months ago? Is that dead brake light getting 12 volts—or is there an almost invisible break in the lamp filament? When the vacuum cleaner gives out, is there something wrong with the motor or just a break in the line cord? When-

ever an electrical malfunction occurs, you need a VOM to pinpoint the cause.

A volt-ohm meter does two jobs: It measures the voltage across an electrical circuit, and it measures resistance within a circuit. (Actually, most VOMs have a third function —indicating current flow on a milliammeter— but you'll rarely need this for electrical-appliance repair.)

Everything around us is made up of electricity. All atoms consist of positively charged protons in a nucleus with negatively charged electrons orbiting outside. Electrons in the outermost orbits are less attracted to the nucleus, and by "bumping" these "free electrons" from atom to atom, we cause electron flow. This chain reaction is like pushing a marble into one end of a tube already filled with marbles, expelling another from the opposite end.

The atomic structure of any substance determines whether it will permit easy electron flow or not. Materials with large numbers of free electrons (aluminum, copper) are "conductors." Those with only a few (plastic, glass) are "insulators."

Voltage is the pressure, or force, which bumps electrons through a conductor. Your VOM measures this pressure in units of volts.

Current is the volume, or flow rate, of electrons, measured in amperes.

Resistance is the restriction of electron flow. Insulators have high resistance, conductors have low. Lowering the resistance in a circuit permits greater current flow for a given voltage. Your VOM measures resistance in units of ohms.

Most people find electrical flow puzzling because they can't see it. But if you visualize these factors in terms of their counterparts in a water system it all becomes clear.

Once you understand what the terms mean, you can apply them by using Ohm's law, the basic law of electrical calculations. With it, you can find the voltage, resistance, or current in a circuit if you know any two of the three values. Ohm's law simply states that $E = I \times R$, where E is the symbol used for voltage, I for current, and R for resistance. From this, you can also see that $I = \dfrac{E}{R}$ and $R = \dfrac{E}{I}$. If you have trouble remembering this, simply draw (or picture in your imagination) the pie-shaped sections shown in the illustration. By covering the value that you want to know, you can find the correct formula for obtaining it.

There's another calculation that you should know, also. This is the power formula $p = EI$, which states simply that power (which is expressed in watts) is the voltage times the current.

You won't have to make use of these formulas to repair an appliance, but in some cases they're helpful. Perhaps their greatest impor-tance is to show you that all of the values of an electrical circuit, voltage, power, resistance and current, are interrelated and interacting. If you change one of them, you change the others as well. As you will see later on, this is important—especially, in these days of energy scarcity, for an understanding of the ways in which reduced voltages affect appliances and for determining the energy consumption of an appliance or component.

You make two types of tests with a VOM, a test for resistance and a test for voltage.

Resistance tests are made to check a part that has been removed from a circuit, to check for a ground, or to check equipment with the power supply disconnected.

This is how to make a resistance test:
1. Plug test leads into meter jacks.
2. Set function switch on $R \times 1$.
3. Zero meter.
4. Disconnect equipment from power, remove one lead from test part.
5. Touch test probes to terminals of part, read resistance in ohms. If needle movement is slight, switch to higher scale.

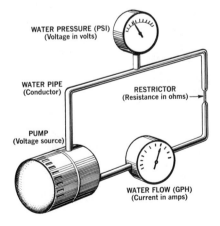

WATER PRESSURE (PSI)
(Voltage in volts)

WATER PIPE
(Conductor)

RESTRICTOR
(Resistance in ohms) →

PUMP
(Voltage source)

WATER FLOW (GPH)
(Current in amps)

If one visualizes electrical flow in terms of a water system it is more easily understood. Here the parts of a typical water system are shown with their counterparts in an electrical circuit. These are the terms used in calculating with Ohm's law.

An easy way to remember the functions of Ohm's law is to cover the unknown factor with one hand; the "pie" will tell you how to find it.

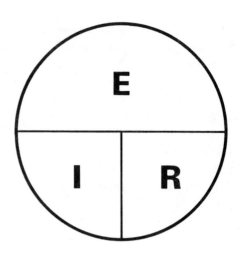

DC voltage: Function switch is set to find amount of voltage at direct current (DC) sources, such as battery. Set range switch to position that includes the voltage you would expect.

Resistance (ohms): Small battery in VOM sends current through unit you're testing; meter shows opposition current meets, in ohms. Voltage is kept from circuit to avoid meter damage.

AC voltage: Set switch here to find amount of voltage at alternating current (AC) sources, such as wall outlet. Select the test range as before.

Calibrated scales correspond to various settings of range switch. Voltage readings increase, left to right, while resistance readings decrease similarly.

Zero ohms: Adjust with probes touching until pointer is at zero on ohms scale. Insures precise amount of current flow through resistance tested.

Input jacks: Put red probe in positive jack and black probe in common (COMM. or NEG.) one. In DC tests, "polarity" of these probes is critical.

Range switch puts various values of resistance into the circuit. Select highest scale if you don't know what voltage level to expect in tested appliance.

Continuity tester can often be helpful and fast in pinning down a problem area—but back up its diagnosis with a resistance reading on your VOM. It's often necessary to know just how much resistance is in the circuit.

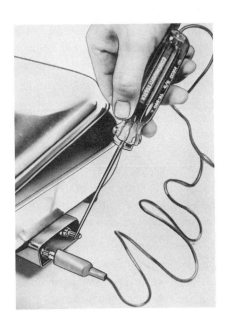

While a VOM is usually employed to measure single components rather than the entire appliance, the test shown here can tell you a lot about the condition of the equipment. A high resistance reading might point to corroded contacts in the bimetal control switch. Also, turning the switch to *off* should break the circuit.

The first step in using the VOM for measuring resistance is to select a scale (in appliance work, it will usually be the lowest numerical ohms scale), clip the two leads together, and move the *ohms adjust* or *zero adjust* knob until the pointer rests on 0. This is necessary to insure accuracy each time the scale is changed with range switch knob. Resistance reading is made of electric iron with switch and thermostat turned to *on* position. On *R × 1* position, reading is taken directly from scale (about 15 ohms in photo). Other resistance scales require that the reading be multiplied by 10, 100, 1,000, or 10,000 to obtain correct resistance in ohms.

How to interpret reading. No needle movement on any scale indicates part is open. A reading between terminals and body or case of part indicates a short to ground. Replace part in either case.

You should know why and how to make a voltage test, but, as I will explain later in this chapter, you may never need to use it to diagnose a line-voltage appliance or component. But when there is no other alternative, here's how you should make a voltage test to check a part that's hooked into an operating circuit:

1. Plug test leads into meter jacks.
2. Set function switch to lowest voltage range above reading you expect. Use AC range for line voltage, DC range for batteries.
3. Unplug appliance or turn circuit off.
4. Locate suspected part. Clip test probe to terminals (which terminal is critical in DC tests only).
5. Turn circuit on.
6. Note reading on meter—unplug appliance again before removing test probes from terminals.

How to interpret reading. Proper voltage across the terminals of a non-operating "load" component pinpoints trouble within the part itself. No voltage indicates trouble is not in the tested part but elsewhere in the circuit.

There are two types of voltage measurements, and you must set your VOM switch and place the two test probes accordingly. One type is the voltage present at ordinary household outlets: alternating current (AC). Current means electrons are flowing in the circuit. When you throw a switch to light a lamp or run a motor in a common 60-Hz (60-cycle) circuit, the electrons flow first in one direction,

and then reverse and move in the opposite direction, 120 times each second, completing 60 cycles. When you measure AC voltage, therefore, it doesn't make any difference which probe you put where; current is moving both ways in both probes.

But direct-current (DC) voltages—such as you get from batteries—require care in probe placement. You'll note that a VOM's jacks are labeled POS. or + for *positive;* NEG. or − or COMM. for *negative.* The last is an abbreviation for common, and in DC circuits it's a "shared" point for all negative leads. In most cars, for example, the negative battery terminal is "grounded" to the car chassis. The common point for all negative connections in the car's electrical circuit is, then, the metal chassis.

Electron flow in a DC circuit is always from the negative terminal (which has an excess of electrons) to the positive terminal. The positive terminal attracts electrons, creating a one-way flow.

Always attach the red lead to the positive terminal of the VOM and the black to the negative. Failure to get the positive (red) probe on the positive terminal of a DC circuit will cause the meter needle to "peg" against a stop on the left, instead of sweeping to the right. If the voltage is high, this can damage the meter.

The VOM has a small built-in battery that feeds a current through whatever you touch the probes to, once you set the meter for resistance tests. Since the amount of this current is known (you "told" the meter this value when you zeroed the meter), the meter can be calibrated to register how much opposition it encounters in the circuit you're measuring.

When you place the probes at opposite ends of a piece of copper wire, the current from the

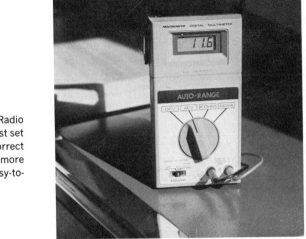

Range-seeking digital volt-ohm meter from Radio Shack is ultimate in ease of operation—you just set the function you want and it selects the correct range automatically. Digital instruments are more expensive but offer great accuracy and easy-to-read display.

Snap-around ammeters are useful to measure amount of current appliance uses, now have resistance and voltage readouts as well. Ammeter's jaws snap around one line of circuit; meter senses induction surrounding conductor without direct connection into circuit.

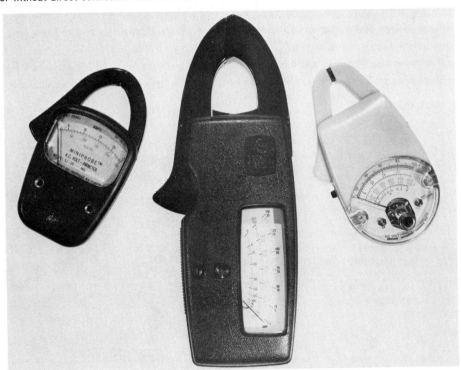

VOM battery will encounter little resistance. But when you place them at the ends of the graphite from a mechanical pencil, the current meets a higher resistance. You see these results as low and high readings on the VOM scale. (A short circuit offers zero resistance—unlimited current flow.)

For troubleshooting your car's wiring, nothing beats a VOM. It will diagnose circuit problems, pinpointing which circuits are live, dead, open, or shorted. It lets you check bulbs (switch to low-ohm scale, zero meter, and touch one probe to bulb's base, other to its contact; if filament is burned out, scale will show infinite resistance). It lets you test fuses (set and zero meter as for bulbs, then touch probes to ends of removed fuse; if fuse is good, needle shows zero resistance).

You can also find resistance under load in the starting-motor circuit, test the car clock and the panel gauges, and make various tuning checks in the ignition system.

Once you grasp these basics, you can buy a VOM with confidence that you'll be able to use it with ease. And just consider: You'll pay for the meter with what you save the first time you don't have to call in a service technician because you're able to track down and repair the trouble yourself.

How much will a VOM cost? There are some pocket-size meters selling for under $10, but these lack some features you'll probably find useful. However, if you'll be using the meter only on rare occasions, a $10 model might suffice.

Better meters are in the $10–$25 range. You can buy them from Radio Shack and stores and catalogs, at electrical supply dealers, at many radio-TV parts suppliers, and at appliance parts suppliers. Practically all of the meters seen in the photographs in this book are in this price bracket.

Of course, you can spend much more. Several manufacturers (RCA, Simpson, Triplett, etc.) offer a range from $45 up; a few models run over $250.

But you've no need for an expensive VOM. There is little practical difference in accuracy,

To read DC volts, select the appropriate scale, insert probes in the proper jacks (– for the black probe, + for the red). Always use the red probe on the positive end of the circuit or battery when testing for DC voltage, black on the negative side. If needle jumps backwards violently when you touch the leads to the battery, reverse the probes immediately. Battery pack in the radio in photo registers slightly less than 3 volts.

In this DC voltage test on an automobile, battery terminals indicated 11 volts when engine was cranked, but other end of cables showed only 6 volts. Cleaning corroded terminals restored power.

for our purposes, between meters above $10. Features to look for include a large, legible scale and rugged construction. But keep in mind that even the most expensive instruments won't take much abuse. A rotary switch for selecting the function of the meter is more convenient than plug-in jacks and generally more durable than the pushbuttons used on some models.

Once you've made your choice, learning to use your meter is standard for all makes.

Remember that all the elements in an electrical circuit—the components and the wiring that connects them—must be continuous for the circuit to function. Current won't flow properly across a gap. The circuit may be interrupted intentionally (by opening a switch) or due to a failure (blown fuse, broken wire).

When a part of a circuit doesn't work, chances are that voltage isn't reaching that part (as when a motor's fuse is blown) or the part itself doesn't have continuity (as when a motor winding wire is broken). With a VOM you can quickly test for the presence of voltage at the terminals of a component and/or the resistance within the component to pin down the problem.

The secret of electrical diagnosis is: simplify. Complex circuits are composed of many simple ones. Concentrate your efforts on the part of the circuit that could produce the symptoms you've detected.

Never forget that you're working with voltages that can be dangerous when servicing home appliances. For this reason, which will be emphasized later, I strongly recommend that you make every test using the resistance test procedures rather than testing for the presence of voltage. Usually, there is a choice between the two, and resistance measurements are just as indicative and often quicker. They are always the best choice from the standpoint of personal safety.

But in those situations where voltage tests are necessary, I repeat the following procedure: first of all, unplug the appliance or dis-

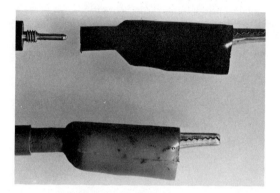

Dual-purpose test leads for VOM like these allow fast changeover from probes to clips. Always use insulated clips for making voltage tests, and be sure to turn off power.

To check receptacle with a VOM, main switch at entrance panel was pulled and VOM leads inserted into receptacle. Then power was restored and reading taken.

connect the circuit. Then, using insulated alligator clips on the test probes (some meters now are using test leads with threaded posts for the purpose of attaching insulated clips), clip the two leads to the terminals under test. Plug the appliance in and note the reading on the meter scale; then disconnect the appliance and remove the leads.

Using this procedure, it's not necessary for you to be in direct contact with the appliance or the meter when voltage is present. In the chapters to follow, testing procedures will be outlined which make use of the resistance checks rather than voltage tests in practically every case. But where voltage tests are the only alternative, be sure to follow the procedure outlined above.

When I use the term "continuity" in this

book, I am referring to resistance tests which simply indicate that the electrical circuitry through the component is complete. A solenoid may have a resistance of 400 ohms, while a switch or conductor may (and should) have a resistance of 0 ohms. However, they both have "continuity," since they are capable of allowing current to flow, even though they may have different resistance values and may be measured on different scales on the VOM.

If a component does not have continuity, it is "open." There will be no deflection of the needle of the VOM on any of the resistance scales. This means, of course, that no current can flow through that component while the "open" condition exists.

Don't treat your VOM roughly. Keep the face and jacks clean; oil and dirt can insulate and give you false readings. Always check the position of the rotary switch before using the meter; and when the meter isn't in use, place this switch in highest DC voltage position. If a carrying case is listed as an accessory for the meter you select, it probably would be a worthwhile investment. It will protect the meter from jolts while in use, and will keep dust out when the meter is stored.

Each chapter in this book is designed to "build" upon the preceding ones so that you develop practice and skill as you progress from simpler appliances to more complex ones. The information you get from the book and the practice in working with the appliances relate to the more complex jobs ahead. In the chapter about the basic parts of appliances, you will find a series of exercises which will utilize

open, visible switches and heating elements to help you see what your meter is telling you about these components. Keep in mind, as you progress, that it's telling you the same thing about the switch in a washer timer, even though you may not be able to see it with your eyes. This ability to let you visualize what is happening electrically to components that you can't see is the forte of the VOM.

From this point on, practice with your hand tools, soldering equipment, and VOM as you learn. Remember, nine times out of ten a neat job is a good job. It not only looks good, but it lasts well. Take pride in each detail of every repair job that you do on a home appliance. This is the professional way—and it's the way that will provide you with the maximum satisfaction for the effort you've expended.

6
How to Develop Good and Safe Work Habits

Good work habits go hand in hand with safe work habits. Together they provide that touch of craftsmanship that sets an outstanding job apart from a mediocre one.

The end result of a repair job may be the same, of course, whether or not you observe good work habits. The washer is running again, you can put clothes in it, and they'll come out ready for the line or dryer. But if the front of the cabinet is scratched up from being placed directly on a concrete floor, the fact that it runs again is little consolation to your customer (even if that customer happens to be yourself). The earlier you begin practicing good work habits, the earlier you become aware of the little touches that make up good work habits, and the more you'll gain from repairing home appliances.

Good work habits are not hard to visualize if you will picture the things that you look for yourself when a technician comes into your home. They all usually boil down to respect for property and equipment. For instance, if a refrigerator rests on a tiled kitchen floor, espe-

cially one of the cushioned type, don't try to pull or even roll it out without first placing something down for it to move on and to distribute the weight to prevent floor damage (small strips of Masonite are good for this purpose). Then there's the good habit of placing a dropcloth on the top of a washer to protect it before putting a tool there. Placing a quilt on the floor before turning a washer on its side or front and moving the appliance correctly by the cabinet and not by the console or exposed knobs (which can be damaged) are other examples of good work habits. Greasy fingerprints are unavoidable in most appliance repair jobs, but the careful technician will wipe them away when he's through. Some technicians carry a small container of wax for buffing up the surface of the appliance after finishing a repair. This takes only a few minutes, and it leaves a mighty good impression.

A list of the little traits representing good work habits could go on and on, and you'd still be likely to find new ones to put into use with every job. But the habits themselves are not so

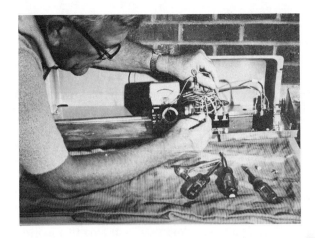

A good habit to develop early in your appliance repair experience: Protect finished surfaces by placing a cloth on them. Here, the cloth was placed on top of the dryer before the console was removed. It then provided protection for the tools and the console.

Place a quilt or other padded surface on the floor before turning an appliance over for servicing. Note that homeowner is moving appliance by keeping his back straight and using his legs to lift or otherwise move the weight of equipment. Dryer is relatively light. Heavier appliances may require two people to prevent strain.

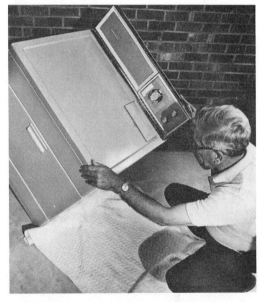

important as the attitude behind them. It's well worth developing.

You must also develop *safe* work habits. In this, you can be both student and teacher; student because I can't overemphasize the importance of learning to practice safe working procedures in every aspect of the work you do

in repairing appliances; teacher because I hope that you'll teach all members of your family the safety aspects of using household equipment.

Appliance manufacturers are always working for new ways to make their products safer. Testing laboratories, design departments, home economic departments all work toward this common goal. Independent testing laboratories such as Underwriters' Laboratories and the American Gas Association laboratories are commissioned to double-check the manufacturer's efforts. AHAM maintains an engineering standards and safety board that is directly responsible for developing industry guidelines regarding safety.

The user and technician must be as safety conscious as the manufacturer. There are two potential danger sources. One is mechanical: moving parts, sharp edges, etc., and for our purposes will also include such things as damaged gas lines. The other danger source is the electrical supply.

The safe use of home appliances begins even before your purchase is made. First, make your selection from a reputable dealer in your community who is likely to have good servicing and installation personnel. Since he knows that your satisfaction with your purchase may be determined in large part by proper installation, you're much more likely to have the job competently done.

Second, buy equipment built by a reputable manufacturer. With major appliances, you won't likely run into a problem here. But with small portable appliances the possibility is somewhat greater of purchasing a poorly designed or sloppily built appliance. If you're in doubt, look for the seal (UL) of the Underwriters' Laboratories on the appliance itself, the AHAM seal, or in the case of a gas appliance the seal of the American Gas Association. This means that the appliance has been tested and that the equipment, cords, and plugs are reasonably safe for the use for which the appliance and parts are designed. Don't be fooled, however, by a UL sticker affixed to the cord. This is intended only for the cord and plug, not for the appliance. The seal should be located in both places. Remember, too, that the seal of approval by such national standards organizations means that the equipment is reasonably safe as purchased new.

Finally, take time to read all the information through regarding your appliance before putting it into use after making sure it has been installed properly.

Look for sharp edges and projections on the appliance at the time it's delivered. Normally,

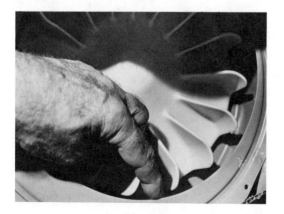

Beware of sharp edges when disassembling appliances or working behind access panels. Stamped metal surfaces are sometimes razor sharp. This is a view of blower in a dryer, after cover and duct have been removed.

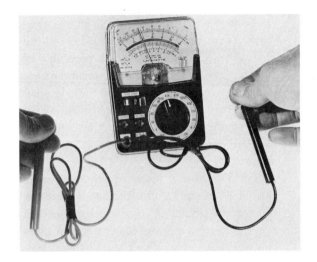

Wet hands permit considerable current to flow through your body—as shown in this simple test with a VOM. For how to make it, see the text.

these can be trimmed off or filed with no problem, but it's best to call them to the installer's attention.

ELECTRICAL SAFETY

My father, one of the most conscientious electrical engineers I've ever known, gave me good advice about this many years ago—advice that I've never forgotten. In his work it was often necessary for him to deal with equipment carrying thousands of volts and amperes. One day while watching him test a substation I asked if he wasn't ever afraid of electricity. "I've never been afraid of it," was his reply, "but I always respect it." This philosophy overcomes the complacency that sometimes develops about the dangers of electricity.

Perhaps you subscribe to the school of thought that voltages and currents found in homes, being relatively low, are safer than those found on industrial equipment or on high tension lines. You couldn't be more mistaken. A great number of fatalities are caused by our standard 115-volt, 60-cycle supply. Carelessness and a lack of respect are one big reason. Another: With higher voltages a violent muscular reaction may knock you away from the power supply.

You've probably experienced an electrical shock. Almost everyone has. And you've probably wondered why you felt only a tingle in situations where others were seriously injured. This results from a number of variables that you can't afford to take a chance on.

When the skin is dry, the body offers a considerable amount of resistance to current flow. When your body is exposed to moisture or when you have been perspiring (and particularly if there is an open cut on the hand) it's much more capable of carrying fairly large amounts of electrical current. You can test this for yourself if your VOM has a scale marked *R × 10,000* or even *R × 1000*. Simply set the meter to read this range of resistance and grasp each meter lead tightly. Note the resistance on the meter scale. Next, moisten the fingers and grasp the leads again, and you'll see what a tremendous difference occurs. This is also why electrical equipment with current leakage may cause only a slight tingle; after you go outside, do heavy work, and return to it, the same equipment could give you a very serious or fatal electrical shock.

How much current flow is dangerous? It depends to some extent upon the individual person and also his general health conditions. But on a 115-volt power supply, 5/10,000ths to 2/1000ths of an ampere produce a noticeable shock. A small amount of current indeed, considering that the average household circuit is capable of conducting at least 15 amperes. Somewhere between 5/1000ths and 25/1000ths of an ampere a strong shock occurs, and often the victim is unable to control his muscles to release himself. At 50 to 200 milliamperes (50/1000ths to 200/1000ths of an ampere), ventricular fibrillation can occur. This is a twitching of the heart muscle that prevents its normal rhythmic pumping action. At 100 milliamperes or more the electrical current can interrupt the breathing process. That's a very small amount of current flow. That's only 1/150 of the amount of current that the circuit in your home is capable of carrying—less than it takes to light a flashlight bulb.

Be sure all of your appliances are grounded. Electrical current always takes the path of least resistance. If an appliance is grounded to a cold water line or through a polarized, three-wire plug to *an electrical system that is properly grounded,* any current leakage will flow through the grounding conductor rather than through your body. Combine this with a safe-

ty-designed appliance in which all electrical terminals and conductors are shielded and you have practically eliminated the possibility of an electrical shock while using the appliance. Most power tools are grounded through a polarized cord. The use of double insulation does not require grounding since it allows the tool to "fail safe" in the event of an insulation breakdown.

For a number of years the national electric code has required a third wire to be used for equipment grounding in most home electrical circuits. Properly installed, this system gives protection by grounding the metal enclosure of any appliance with polarized plugs. If you have any doubt about the grounding system in your home, have an electrician check by using a "megger," an instrument designed to test the condition of a grounding electrode. You'll notice when you insert a polarized plug that the grounding prong is slightly longer than the others. Entering the receptable first, the longer prong grounds the equipment before electrical power is applied to the rest of the plug.

It's always a good idea to run an external ground wire from the cabinet of a major appliance to the cold water line. Attach it to any screw that will firmly tighten the wire against the frame. Scrape away any paint under the contact portion of the wire. A clamp for attaching the ground wire to the water line is available at any electrical supply house. Use at least an 18-gauge wire as the grounding conductor. In most parts of the United States, the frame of 230-volt, single-phase equipment is grounded directly to the neutral line of the power supply by an internal connection. Even in this case, there's never any harm done by providing an external ground as well.

Many new appliances come with an adapter

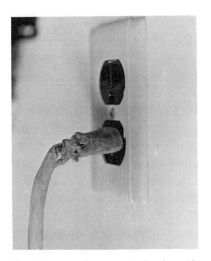

Double trouble—not only is this washer cord obviously in poor condition, but it's also an ungrounded type. Replacement with heavy-duty polarized cord will make this washer even safer than when it was new.

External ground wire is run from cabinet of washer to cold-water line. Grounding clamp like this is obtained from electrical supply house. It's not bad practice to ground a washer even though it has a polarized cord.

for the polarized plug in case a polarized receptacle isn't available. These are acceptable if the adapter is attached to the center screw of the receptacle cover and *if the receptacle box itself is properly grounded.* Chances are it may not be. Therefore I'd recommend strongly that an external ground wire be run from the receptacle cover plate screw to a cold water line. The best bet of all is to have a competent electrician install a grounded receptacle. If your home doesn't have them, chances are that it's time for a check of the wiring anyway.

Additional protection against line-to-ground shock hazards can be gained by using a ground fault circuit interrupter in place of the conventional circuit breaker. This affords protection for small appliances (which normally do not have the three-wire grounding plug and cord) and power tools. The GFCI opens the circuit in the event of overload, like an ordinary circuit breaker, and it also interrupts it almost instantaneously when there is a leakage of current to ground, as there would be if a person contacted a live wire or other part of the circuit. The National Electric Code now requires GFCI's on certain high-risk circuits such as those in bathrooms, garages, and outdoor receptacles. I also recommend this protection for the kitchen.

You can make a simple test light to check whether polarized receptacles are properly wired and grounded. Use at least a 100-watt lamp so you'll know that the grounding connector is well grounded and capable of carrying a fair amount of electrical current. All you need is the bulb, a socket (preferably of the pigtail type), and a polarized plug. In the plug, attach one wire from the socket to the grounding prong. Attach the other wire to the smaller of the two flat blades. If it doesn't light the receptacle is not wired correctly or grounded. If it does light brightly, you can be assured that proper grounding procedures were followed. If the bulb lights but is dim, it's an indication of a poor connection. Commercial testers are also available for this purpose.

In using electrical equipment in your home, every member of the household should be aware of these points.

- Locate and remedy any condition that produces an electrical shock; be sure the appliance is properly grounded before it's put back into use.
- Never use a piece of electrical equipment in a wet location or when you are wet, and never use it when touching another grounded object such as a water pipe or even the frame of the appliance itself.
- Always turn the equipment off before removing the plug from an outlet. Always grasp the plug and not the cord to remove it from the receptacle. If a cord disconnects from the appliance as well as from the receptacle, always plug the cord into the appliance before plugging it into the wall; conversely, also remove the plug from the wall outlet before disconnecting from the appliance.
- Never run a cord over hot pipes, radiators, or other hot objects and don't allow the cord or the appliance to become wet.

An awareness of the foregoing points while servicing home appliances offers you a good opportunity to improve the safety of the equipment. Take note of broken or frayed cords and replace them promptly. Check immediately any situation that might produce an electrical

shock. Check the grounding of all home equipment.

In the servicing procedures you should note that the recommended tests always advise use of resistance checks rather than voltage checks. This means that in all cases when the appliance is being tested and serviced, the cord is unplugged and it is disconnected from the electrical supply. In some cases, such as testing a receptacle, technicians sometimes insert test prods into the receptacle for testing, although it's easier, faster, and safer simply to plug a table lamp into it. If you use such procedures, remember the one-hand rule. *In using your VOM to test voltages, keep one hand in a pocket. Attach one clip to one of the terminals and touch the prod to the other terminal with the hand.*

Here's the reason for using this method. If a slip occurs, the current's path through the body can have a direct effect on the extent of injury. Current flowing from the hand to the elbow, for instance, will not likely be as serious as that flowing through both hands since it then must pass directly across the chest and heart. Keeping one hand "out of action" lessens the possibilities of this. However, I no longer recommend even this procedure. It's far safer to attach both leads with power removed from the circuit and keep hands off completely.

Capacitors are found in many motor-driven appliances. They act as "storehouses" for electricity, *and must be discharged before handling or testing them.* To avoid blowing an internal fuse used in many capacitors, discharge them with a 20,000-ohm, 2-watt wire-wound resistor. You can purchase one at any TV-radio parts supplier. Wrap the resistor with tape and handle it so you don't come in contact with the uninsulated leads. Touching the resistor across the capacitor terminals will bleed away any residual charge. After doing this, you can test it safely.

MECHANICAL SAFETY

In servicing mechanical equipment, you must often expose mechanical components to observe the operation before you begin testing. Use reasonable caution and you should have no problem. Keep hands and fingers away from moving belts and pulleys and from electrical connections. Do not wear loose clothing. Roll up your sleeves and take off your tie before removing the service panels. Avoid cuts from sharp edges of stamped metal, particularly on the interior portions of appliances. Be sure all panels are put back on the machine when servicing is completed. If you must leave an appliance inoperative for any length of time, whether it's to get a tool from the workshop or to purchase a repair part, be sure it's unplugged and that all water supply lines are turned off. Place a note on it to be sure that no one attempts to use it in the meantime. Lift with your legs and not with your back when it's necessary to move an appliance. Make a check of the wiring harness and connections a part of every servicing and maintenance job you do. Replace or repair any broken or damaged wiring and use your VOM to test the equipment for any leakage to ground before plugging it back in.

There's some danger in using any tool, even a hand tool. You would not, for instance, hold one hand behind a screw while you tighten it with a screwdriver. Keep a secure grip on all tools and use them so that if they were to slip your hands could not fly into any sharp or moving parts of the machinery. Use goggles or glasses when you're operating a grinder, an electric drill, or any equipment where dust or flying particles is produced. Keep your fingers and hands away from drill bits and any moving parts on tools. Use all the protective devices with which your tools are equipped. Keep your work area clean and position yourself so that you're balanced and not likely to slip. Keep all your concentration focused on the work that you're doing. Be sure that your tools and all equipment are in good shape, both electrically and mechanically. And don't attempt to clean, adjust, or oil any part of any appliance while it is running. Except for observations, it should always be unplugged and disconnected from the power supply when the access panel is removed.

7
Understanding the Parts of an Appliance

Although some home appliances are rather complex mechanisms as a whole, they are all composed of simple mechanical components and simple electrical circuits. Understand these components and circuits first and you have taken the first steps toward understanding what goes on inside an appliance. That's the big secret of all appliance repair. Understand how an appliance works—and you'll have a better chance of a successful repair.

Every brand of appliance differs in some respects, but there are enough similarities to allow us to discuss each type of appliance later in this book and start you on the happy road to a repair. Later chapters will explain what happens inside a typical appliance and then give you the simplest and best techniques and methods of servicing particular appliances. You will also learn about some areas where you should not attempt service unless you are a technician with specialized equipment at your disposal. It will be up to you to draw the line as to how far you want to go in servicing

appliances, depending on your own mechanical ability, tool accessibility, etc. It's all a pleasant chain of circumstances, however. You'll probably find that the more you do, the more you'll be able to do; and the more you can do, the more you can save.

But remember that all of this begins with the basics—an understanding of the mechanical parts and electrical circuits you find inside an average appliance.

One trade secret will be of great advantage in repairing appliances: it's the word *simplify*. Diagnosis is the key to solving any appliance problem. Simplification is the key to diagnosis. Simplification starts with the appliance as a whole. When you look at it, you should simplify by breaking it down mentally into its various assemblies. And when you look at the assemblies, you must simplify these and their problems by breaking them down into their simplest components. This is what this chapter is all about—the simplification of components, how they work, what they do.

THE CONDUCTOR

In home appliances, the conductor is usually a wire. In some cases, it may be a bus bar, a strip of metal which carries electrical current. It is a means of conducting the current from one point to another without loss of voltage. It is a means of getting the current from the power supply to the load, the part of the circuit which actually does the work. It is at the load that power is used, and it is the conductor which transports it there. Some examples of loads are motors, heating elements, lights and buzzers.

When you test with the volt-ohm meter, a conductor should read 0 resistance. Any break in the conductor will keep the appliance from functioning. Any change in the dimensions of a conductor, which could occur when you strip the insulation off and cut down into the wire itself, actually reduces the size of the conductor. The smaller the conductor, the less current it will carry, just as a quarter-inch water pipe with a force of 100 pounds per square inch will deliver less water than a 1-inch pipe when the same amount of force is applied. Therefore, it's necessary to use extreme care when you're attaching terminals, or handling a conductor in any way, to keep from breaking or cutting any part of the conductor.

Several types of insulation are used on the conductors in home appliances. Some conductors have no insulation at all—for instance, a terminal where it attaches to a timer or, in some instances, conductors within an enclosure such as a range console that carry current to a number of switches mounted very closely to each other. Yet even these are insulated from the cabinet and from surrounding terminals by air space. Other conductors are insulated with an asbestos-impregnated or heat-resistant thermoplastic insulation which serves to protect the conductor from heat. Most conductors in modern home appliances are insulated with a plastic covering that is highly resistant to cracking, breaking, deterioration from oil, and exposure to moisture. Also most conductors in appliances consist of a number of strands, or small wires, instead of a single large wire. This allows more flexibility.

Even with conductors (the simplest single component in a home appliance) pride in craftsmanship is necessary. Though a problem will seldom be directly attributable to a broken conductor, you'll constantly be working with conductors in replacing timbers, controls, etc. You will find it necessary to loosen connections and remake them, and sometimes to even change the connections. Wherever conductors are involved, handle them with care.

THE SWITCH

A switch provides a means of opening and closing a conductor to control the circuit. Switches come in all shapes and sizes, and range from simple, double-contact switches to highly complex switching devices such as a timer in an automatic washer. But here again, more complex switches are simply a matter of multiple arrangements of a single switch.

To understand what a switch does, suppose you have a battery, some conductors, and a light connected into a simple electrical circuit to make the light burn. With a wire cutter, you snip one of the conductors, and then strip the insulation from the two cut ends of the wire. You soon find that touching the two cut ends together closes the circuit and allows the lamp

A PRACTICE SESSION WITH THE VOM

In the accompanying photographs, the basic elements of an electrical circuit as used in home appliances are easily seen. The conductors, open-type knife switch, and the heating-element "load" can be tested just as their counterparts in the actual equipment would be.

After setting the meter to the $R \times 1$ scale and adjusting the zero ohms knob, disconnect power from the circuit and close the switch. You should get a reading of 0 ohms. Note that one lead from the component under test is removed; this is always good practice when making resistance tests, as it eliminates all possibility of "feedback" from other resistances in the circuit.

An enclosed switch would be tested in exactly the same manner. When a switch in its closed position is tested on the resistance scale, it should always indicate 0 ohms resistance — otherwise, you can consider the contacts pitted or damaged, and the switch should be replaced.

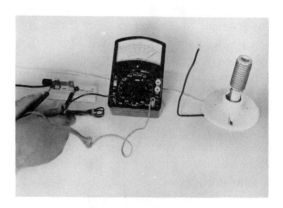

When the switch is opened, the needle indicates infinite resistance (no movement), indicating that no current could flow through the circuit should it be energized. An open switch should always check in this manner — any resistance noted on the meter means that the switch will pass some current when it should open the circuit. Typical causes of the problem are sticking or "welded" contacts, or damaged internal components in the switch itself.

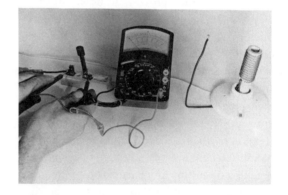

With the heating element acting as the load, the porcelain base socket is placed on its side and the resistance of the element is checked through the terminals on the base. Note that one lead is disconnected. Depending upon the wattage of a particular element, some resistance should be noted; it should test neither open nor completely to 0 ohms, but should have a slight resistance reading. If the element read 0 ohms, it would be "short-circuited," another term which we commonly use for 0 resistance in the load of a circuit. When this occurs for any reason, the fuse or circuit breaker will immediately trip in a properly protected circuit.

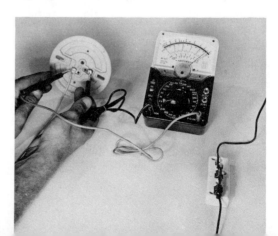

to burn, and that taking them apart opens the circuit, and the light goes out. We can put a switch in the circuit at this point, and have the switch perform the same function of turning the light on and off. This is all any switch does, regardless of the means used to initiate the switch in action—it opens and closes the circuit. It's a very important operation.

Here's a place where your familiarity with the VOM can pay off quickly. Cartridge-type fuses are often used in conjunction with large current-carrying capacity appliances such as clothes dryers and air-conditioning units, as well as for ranges and main lighting circuits in many homes. But when they blow (or one of them blows), they give no outward indication of their condition. Your VOM will tell you. Since the fuse is part of the conductors of the circuit, it should indicate 0 resistance just as the conductor should. If it is open or indicates partial resistance, it should be replaced. When testing and changing fuses, be sure that all contacts are tight and free of corrosion. When testing a fuse in a "live-front" switch box, where wiring and switches are open, use extreme caution. Pull the switch and keep clear of all interior components of the switch box. When working around an electrical panel, stand on a dry board or other insulating material to isolate you from the ground.

Switches are highly specialized, and in many cases, are designed on purpose for the duties to which they are applied. Miniature microswitches require very small space, yet perform their switching functions at exactly the right time to get the job done. Where heavy loads are involved, large heavy-duty switches control the load with a minimum of arcing due to the fast snap-action of the switch contacts and the material from which the contacts are made. This is one of many good reasons for always using the manufacturer's specified component as a replacement.

Except in the case of the leaf switch, there's usually some sort of mechanism attached to the contacts themselves. This may be in the form of a toggle, such as that within a light switch in a home. A toggle, usually spring-loaded, provides a convenient means of initiating the switching action quickly, thus reducing arcing. In some cases, a device called a sole-noid is attached to provide the mechanical action initiated electrically from a remote location. In any case, the switch still performs the same function as touching the two wires together—it completes the circuit to the load.

In home appliances, the contacts of the switch (the two surfaces that meet to complete the circuit) are critical. If they don't meet perfectly, there's some resistance to the electrical flow. Resistance means heat, and heat will soon destroy the switch contacts. If the switch contacts are badly pitted or burned, the switch should be replaced. In cases of mild pitting, they can often be cleaned, but *only* if you catch them in time to prevent severe pitting of the contacts. The best method of cleaning pitted switch contacts is first of all to use a point file, the type used for automotive points (which again are a type of simple switch). Then, the contacts should be cleaned or burnished with a hardwood stick. The striking surface from a

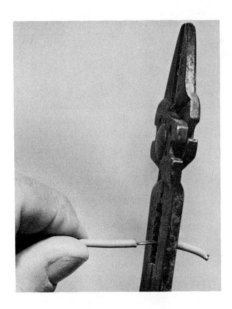

Wire stripping is made easy with a stripper such as the one found on many terminal tools. To use it, just select the proper wire gauge and insert the wire, squeeze the handle of the stripper to make the cut, and pull the wire through leaving the unwanted insulation. This doesn't damage or nick the wire, a problem which causes high-resistance connections in some instances. If you use a knife to strip insulation, practice until you can remove the insulation without the blade of the knife actually touching the copper.

book of paper matches will polish the contacts in many cases. Often this may be only an emergency repair, but it will put the equipment back in operation until you can obtain a replacement part.

Switch contacts are mounted to some sort of movable arm on one side and often to a stationary surface on the other, providing a means of connecting and disconnecting the two contacts. In most cases, the arms also serve as conductors, carrying the current to the point of contact. As you observe the condition of the various switches in an old appliance you may be working on, make a mental note of the appearance of the switches and the reading you obtain through the switches with your volt-ohm meter. A switch should always indicate 0 resistance with its contacts closed, just as a conductor should. Any resistance here causes heat. You'll find that in mildly pitted contacts you'll seldom notice resistance, while in those that are badly pitted, you may well notice quite a bit of resistance. Many contacts will not be visible; they'll be within a plastic housing or within a component itself. Your VOM, however, lets you "see" their condition by the resistance reading it provides. If there is some resistance, chances are that the contacts are pitted and the switch should be replaced. If there is no resistance, the contacts should be in good shape. This can save a lot of time in disassembling a timer, or other enclosed type of switch. Just rely on your volt-ohm meter to "look" inside the component and tell you something of its condition.

THE SOLENOID AND RELAY

The solenoid is a coil of wire arranged to concentrate the magnetic flux from current flowing through the conductors in the coil. This magnetism can move a linkage or otherwise do mechanical work. Any conductor with current flowing through it has a magnetic field or line of flux surrounding it. If you coil that conductor many, many times, you concentrate this magnetic force in one small area, and thus

The tiny microswitch is tested in the same manner as a large, exposed knife switch—it's just not possible to see what's going on with your eyes. This one is used on an automatic ice maker.

form an electromagnet. Add a movable bar, and it's a solenoid.

Technically, a solenoid is a device for changing electrical energy into mechanical energy, and that's just what this electromagnetic coil does. It provides the means of causing motion to occur in some component. By arranging the size of a conductor and the size of the coil you build, you can form any number of devices from the simple electromagnetic coil. It may be designed to lift the plunger in an inlet valve of an icemaker of a refrigerator, or shift the gears in a washer transmission. The solenoid has many applications in home appliances, and in many components you'll see that it is one of the basic elements which causes a component to function.

In checking a solenoid, the volt-ohm meter must always indicate continuity (a continuous electrical circuit) because there has to be a path for the current to flow through this coil. Unlike the switch and conductor, the solenoid will be classified as a load device since it actually does work and since power is consumed at that point.

These three basic elements, the switch, the conductor, and the solenoid, can be combined with each other or with various other mechanisms to form compound devices. As an example of this, take a switch and attach a solenoid to the movable contact so that when the solenoid is energized, the contact is closed, and when it's deenergized, a spring pulls the contact open. This is the basis of a simple relay, or contactor, as it is sometimes called. From this description you see that this component has two elements which must be tested—the coil section and the contact (switch) section of the relay.

Relays have many applications in the home.

Relays with coils operated by a low current are often used to control a high-current, high-voltage load. An example of this is the circuitry controlling your central air conditioner, where the thermostat acts as a switch, completing a 24-volt circuit to a relay coil at the control panel of the system. When the heavy contacts are closed by the small current flowing through the coil, they complete a 230-volt circuit which starts the compressor and cools the house. Another application is in a high current load such as in a clothes dryer, where a relay is often used to control the heating element. The coil of the relay is energized by the timer contacts or by a centrifugal switch in the motor. Since the high current flowing through the circuit to the heating element can cause arcing of the contacts, this load is taken up by the relay rather than by the lighter contacts found within the timer or motor.

Relays are used in most electronic or "solid state" appliances. Electronic "switches" such as diodes and transistors control relays with minute currents. The relays in turn do the heavy-duty work such as controlling motors, heaters, etc.

THE HEATING ELEMENT

In home appliances, heating elements are usually formed from a wire made of an alloy of nickel and chromium called nichrome wire. It has good heating characteristics and it's durable. Elements may be classified as open elements if the coil of nichrome wire is suspended in the air by a porcelain insulator, or classified as enclosed type elements when the wire is enclosed within a metal sheath with an insulating compound filling the void. In the enclosed

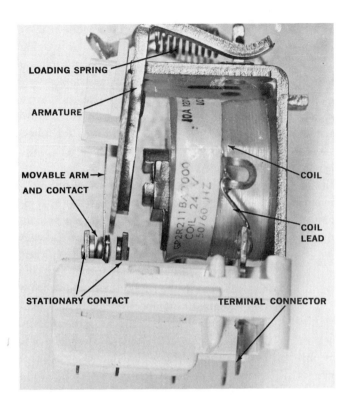

LOADING SPRING

ARMATURE

MOVABLE ARM →
AND CONTACT

COIL

COIL
LEAD

STATIONARY CONTACT

TERMINAL CONNECTOR

This photograph illustrates the major components of a relay. Two separate electrical tests are involved in testing the relay. First, the coil is tested for continuity. The coil on a miniature relay such as this one is composed of thousands of turns of wire no larger in diameter than a human hair. One of the electrical leads from the coil can be seen attached to the right front terminal in the photo. With the test meter set on $R \times 1000$ (the small wire has fairly high resistance) and probes touched to the two coil leads, this section of the relay can be tested. The contact section is tested like a switch. This relay is closed to one side while open to the other. When it moves to the opposite position as the coil is energized and pulls the armature in by electromagnetic force (you can do this manually for testing purposes), the side which is now closed will be open and vice-versa. This is called a single-pole, double-throw switching arrangement (SPDT).

Contact points on this relay are being cleaned with ignition file. Then they will be burnished for temporary repair. While this relay is constructed like that previously illustrated, it is much larger in physical size. Large relays like this, used for starting large motors like air-conditioner compressors, are often called contactors.

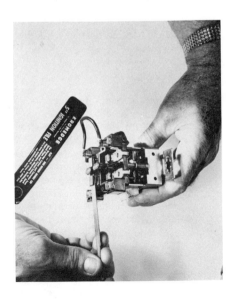

element the entire sheath may glow red in some applications such as the surface unit on an electric stove, but the nichrome coil itself is not visible. The size, the shape, and the resistance of these elements varies, depending upon the applications and the temperature range in which it operates. The volt-ohm meter should always indicate continuity, and there should *never* be a ground caused by the element touching either the enclosing sheath or, in the case of an open type element, a metal housing of any sort. Various styles and applications of these heating elements will be discussed with the appliance on which they are used.

THE THERMOSTAT

This is a switch which is either opened or closed by temperature change. The most common thermostat found in home appliances is the type known as a bimetal thermostat, so-called because of the way in which the mechanical action to open and close switch contacts is derived. In a bimetal thermostat, two dissimilar metals are bonded together. As they

are heated or cooled, the differences in their rate of expansion cause a bending or warping action of the piece of metal. This mechanical action is used to operate switch contacts.

Bimetal thermostats are found in a large variety of shapes and sizes and temperature ranges. A few common applications are found in controlling heat in electric irons, automatic toasters, electric water heaters, clothes dryers, and motor protecting devices. In testing a thermostat, it is imperative to know the temperature at which the switch should actuate and also know whether you should read that the switch is closed or open when you put your VOM on it. Specifications are found in service manuals, but in the case of fixed temperature thermostats, the temperature point will usually be stamped on the body of the thermostat. For instance, L 150 found on the body of a bimetal thermostat would indicate that this thermostat opens at 150 degrees.

Another class of thermostat is usually adjustable, the kind found on stoves and refrigerators. These are capillary tube or hydraulic 'stats. Switch contacts are connected by linkage to a flexible metal bellows which has a

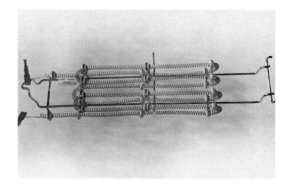

Open-coil heating element from a clothes dryer is a good illustration of this type of element construction. The coil is supported by porcelain insulators and held in the proper position by the wire frame. When replacing nichrome wire on open elements, be sure that no sags or looseness are left in the coils. If stock wire must be stretched for replacement, measure old coil and stretch new one to size.

Sheathed element is cut to reveal inner construction. Outer metallic sheath prolongs element life by protecting the coil from the effects of moisture and air. Manganese powder fills the void between sheath and nichrome element, pulled from center as indicated.

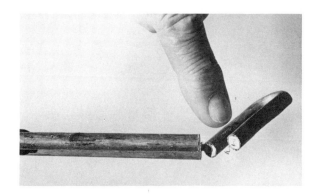

This hydraulic thermostat shows the sensing bulb, capillary tube, and bellows assembly (indicated by pencil point). The linkage from bellows is attached to contacts to provide switching action.

Cutaway view of water heater thermostat reveals bimetal construction. These switches are not serviceable — if any section of the thermostat fails, it must be replaced.

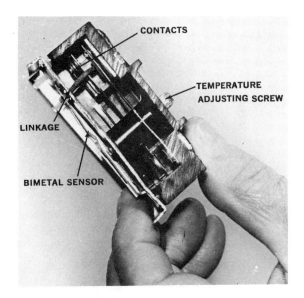

CONTACTS

TEMPERATURE
ADJUSTING SCREW

LINKAGE

BIMETAL SENSOR

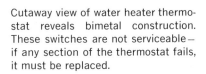

HOW A BIMETAL THERMOSTAT WORKS

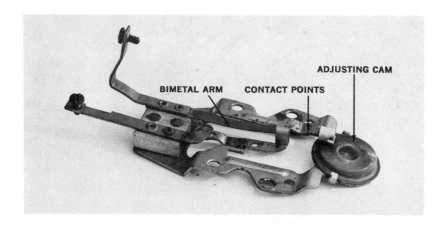

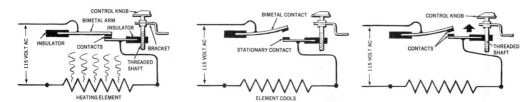

Bimetal thermostatic control in photo, removed from an electric iron, illustrates the principle shown in the series of three drawings. In the drawing at left, current flows through closed contacts of the bimetal switch and through heating element, which supplies heat to both appliance and to the switch itself. In center drawing, heat has caused bimetal arm to warp upwards, breaking electrical circuit. Appliance now cools until bimetal arm again makes contact. Cycle repeats and temperature of the iron stabilizes at a point that is dependent on the time of cycling. Drawing at right shows how heat range can be adjusted by varying position of second contact. By raising it on the threaded shaft, more heat is needed to lift bimetal contact. Shorter cool-down period is effected, resulting in higher overall temperature of the iron.

small tube called a capillary tube connected to it. The length of the tube is determined by the application for which it is to be used. This tube is usually filled with a substance such as freon gas of the type used in refrigerators. The tube is crimped and sealed at one end, the other end opening into the sealed bellows. When a por-

tion of the tube is exposed to heat, the refrigerant inside will expand, causing the bellows at the other end to move and to open or close the switch depending upon the design and application of the thermostat. As the tube is cooled the refrigerant contracts, causing the bellows to contract, and again this reverse movement initiates switch action. The rate of expansion and contraction may be adjustable by a spring load upon the bellows or switch linkage. For instance, when you set your oven thermostat to 300 degrees, what you're actually doing is setting up a precalculated spring load against the bellows of your oven's thermostat. As the oven heats, the pressure within the bellows builds up to a point where it finally overcomes the spring load, which should occur at approximately 300 degrees. This movement opens the contacts, and the heating element within the oven is turned off. Again, as the oven cools below 300 degrees, the bellows contracts and the switch is closed, completing the

circuit to the heating element. It continues to cycle in this manner until the thermostat is turned off or set to a different temperature. Thermostats such as these are durable and extremely accurate.

THE TIMER

On most major appliances, whenever a malfunction occurs, the timer is usually the first thing thought to be at fault. In fact, however, it's one of the least likely culprits. Proceed very cautiously when checking out the timer, and remember that here, probably more so

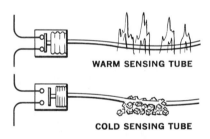

WARM SENSING TUBE

COLD SENSING TUBE

Here's how a basic capillary tube thermostat works. The tube and charge of gas, which is designed to work at a particular temperature range depending upon application, is attached to a set of switch contacts. This one is designed for use in a refrigerator. When the temperature becomes warmer, the bellows expands and closes the contacts, starting the compressor. When the temperature becomes colder, the bellows contracts and opens the contacts.

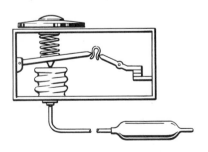

A thermostat as simple as the one above has two shortcomings: It doesn't allow for any means of control, and the contacts don't snap open quickly enough to eliminate arcing. The thermostat at left has a counterforce to the bellows action, in the form of a spring, which is adjusted by the setting of the dial knob. The toggle spring now imparts a snap action to the contacts. This is basically how the majority of these thermostats operate on modern refrigerators. *Courtesy Whirlpool Corp.*

than with any other component, it is important to simplify its inner elements. These will consist of four parts:

1. A set of switches numbering from one to twenty. Each one is just a plain switch, with stationary and movable contacts.
2. Cams which rotate and upon which the movable switch contacts rest. The lobes and indentations of the various cams cause the switches within the timer to be opened and closed.
3. A drive train or escapement, a mechanical gear train which turns the cam in a jerking motion approximately once each minute. Each segment of this movement, called an increment, causes the switch contacts to open and close quickly, thereby reducing electrical arcing.
4. And finally a small synchronous motor which turns the drive train.

Failure of any of these components may require replacement of the timer. The motor should always indicate continuity and not be grounded. Motors are usually easy to check and they may in most cases be detached from the timer body. Cams are seldom defective, unless they should break, an unlikely occurrence. The drive train may be checked visually. As for the switch contacts, even though there may be twenty contacts within the timer,

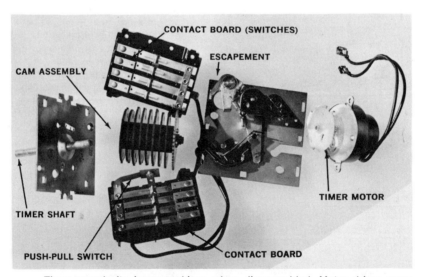

Timer reveals its inner workings when disassembled. Motor drives cams through escapement, which imparts sharp, "jerky" motion to motor's smooth output. This causes contacts to open quickly, prolonging their life and preventing arcing. The *on-off* contacts indicated are the ones which are energized by the *push-pull* timer shaft movement to turn the washer off and on. Learning to identify a faulty switch saves many wasted minutes rushing down dead-end streets in appliance repair.

And this is where that diagnosis be-gins — by observing the position of all switches and controls, and especially the timer, when the machine quit working as it should. Then, by piecing together the facts, you should be able to pinpoint the problem in one specific area. No need to test all seventeen contact surfaces in the timer in the previous photo; only one or two are likely to be suspect.

you've only got one symptom or one problem, and by looking at the wiring diagram you can eliminate all but one or possibly two sets of these contacts. A point to point check with the VOM should then indicate whether they are at fault.

I can't overemphasize the importance of simplifying within your own mind every step you take as you proceed in diagnosing a fault within an electrical appliance. As each compo-nent is discussed in the section dealing with the particular appliance, think how one chain of components (switches, conductors, etc.) in the machine can affect the other. In most cases you'll be able to eliminate 90 percent of the machine elements before you even begin to make your tests, simply by observing what the equipment is doing and listening for signs of unusual operation. And as we mentioned be-fore, as you become more familiar with the world of home appliances, you'll find that the best test instruments available are still your eyes and your ears.

The wiring diagram of an appliance is like a road map—it tells you where to go to find the electrical problem which you are tracing. Many different types of diagrams have been used by appliance manufacturers, making any one explanation of the checkout procedure im-possible. But here are some general tips which will allow you to make use of the ones on your appliances.

Again, the key word is simplify. If you are going on a trip and consult the road map, you don't try to take in all of the lines tracing roadways within an entire state. You find your destination and disregard all routes except the one which will lead you to that point. When you look at the wiring schematic it is easy to become confused by the maze of electrical cir-cuits pictured; yet you should only be inter-ested in a very small portion of that web. Just as you would use a road map, you should first locate your destination (the part which is not operating) and plot your course from one side of the power line, through the part which is inoperative, to the other side of the power line. In this manner you have plotted a complete electrical circuit, since you have passed from one side of the line to the other; and you will find that this "routing" procedure takes you

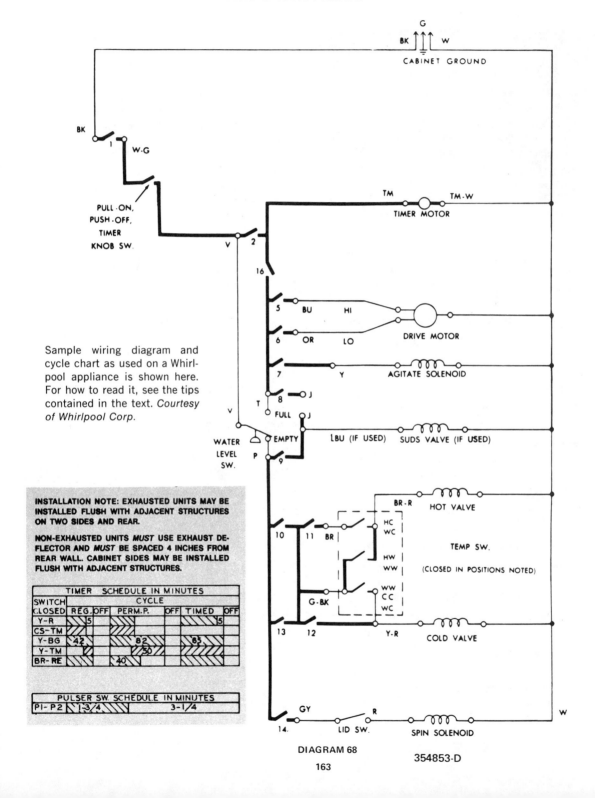

Sample wiring diagram and cycle chart as used on a Whirlpool appliance is shown here. For how to read it, see the tips contained in the text. *Courtesy of Whirlpool Corp.*

INSTALLATION NOTE: EXHAUSTED UNITS MAY BE INSTALLED FLUSH WITH ADJACENT STRUCTURES ON TWO SIDES AND REAR.

NON-EXHAUSTED UNITS *MUST* USE EXHAUST DE-FLECTOR AND *MUST* BE SPACED 4 INCHES FROM REAR WALL. CABINET SIDES MAY BE INSTALLED FLUSH WITH ADJACENT STRUCTURES.

TIMER SCHEDULE IN MINUTES					
SWITCH	CYCLE				
CLOSED	REG.	OFF	PERM.P.	OFF	TIMED	OFF
Y-R		5				5
CS-TM						
Y-BG	42		82		83	
Y-TM				50		
BR-RE			40			

PULSER SW. SCHEDULE IN MINUTES	
PI-P2	1-3/4 3-1/4

DIAGRAM 68

354853-D

163

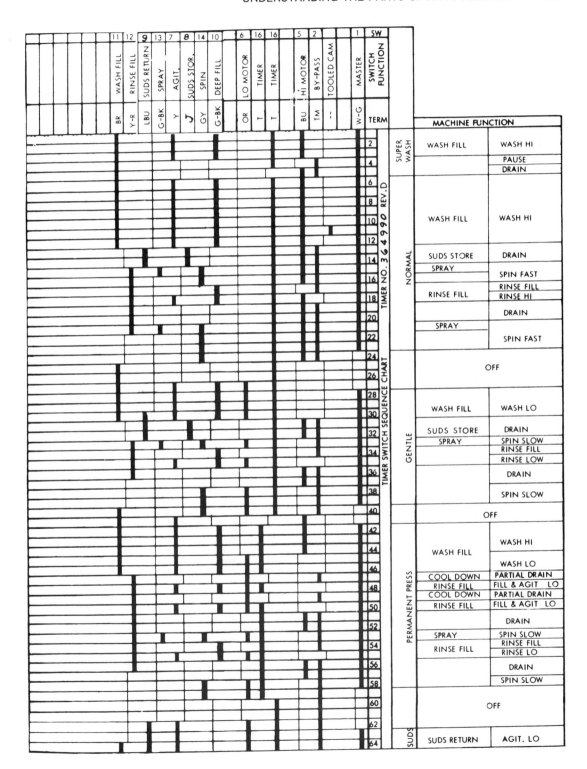

through every switch and connection which could cause the problem component to be inoperative. Now, by taking your meter and checking only those components involved in your route, you should be able to pinpoint the faulty one.

There are two assets on your side that ease this procedure. The first of these is your own powers of deduction—where the Sherlock Holmes in you comes out. When you first became aware of the problem with the appliance, your first observation will give you many clues to the solution of the case. You will learn to make a mental note of every one of these, and then pursue them further to eliminate various components which may not be at fault. As an example of this procedure, you find that the motor is not running on your automatic washer. You note the position of the timer dial when it stopped, and the setting of other controls. When you find the motor on the wiring diagram, you see that it also has two speeds other than the high speed used on the normal cycle. Turning the machine on and placing the timer in another cycle allows you to see that the motor does operate on the medium and low speeds. Now, returning to the diagram and tracing the circuit through the conductor marked "high" to the motor, you see that this is controlled by a switch on the console of the washer and by a contact within the timer. Since the diagram shows you which timer contact is involved, this is the only timer test you

have to make. You find that the contacts of both timer and console switch check OK, the motor runs on other speeds so the centrifugal switch on the motor is OK. What's left? The conductor. Checking from motor terminal to plug you find no continuity. Narrowing your search, you find no continuity between the motor and the timer on the high-speed motor wire. But there is a terminal block where the wiring harness passes through the top into the cabinet, and here is where you find your problem. A loose connection, easily repaired, hardly the budget-blasting blow that you had expected—a total cost of $0.00 if you repaired it yourself. And you just saved more than enough to pay for your new volt-ohm meter.

Another aid to your detection of the problem is a cycle chart, now provided alongside the wiring diagram by many manufacturers. With a cycle chart, you simply look at the increment showing on the timer when the trouble occurred, and the chart will show you all of the circuits in use at that time. Equally helpful are switch charts which show you which contacts are open and closed, and particular positions of the switch. All switches, timers, and wires are marked with a code to correlate these to the diagram. And remember, practice makes perfect. Try to perfect your skill in using the VOM and tracing diagrams on an old appliance in the house, and don't forget to exercise those powers of deduction.

8
Finding Troubles Before They Happen

There's no need to wait for problems to arise before putting your VOM to work. Use it to make a record of the appliances in your home. Then, when one acts up, you can compare the new and old readings and often pinpoint the problem area quickly. This is also a great way to develop proficiency with the VOM.

Mechanical problems in home appliances often announce themselves with squeals and clanks. Electrical troubles do not. But with a record of the electrical characteristics of your appliance during periods of "good health," you have fine help in solving a problem. In fact, you may even be able to locate a weakened part *before* it fails.

I had this experience in preparing data for this chapter. The heating element of my dryer failed to give the expected reading. The resistance was too high. Three days later the element failed completely. Years of use had taken their toll. The element had corroded, producing a "hot spot." Before it failed, I had another one on hand.

To develop the accompanying check-up chart, at least three brands of appliances were used in each category and the readings were averaged. But use my findings as "ball-park" figures only. You need to know the exact readings for your own appliances. So use the VOM to take and list them. A few manufacturers now save you the trouble of compiling a list, since they indicate the resistance of each component on the wiring diagram. Check this before you begin to chart the appliance.

If you can find time to do it, you then would do well to get out your chart at least once a year and check all your appliances. No method has yet been devised to eliminate appliance problems—but a checkup helps to find them at your convenience.

In the chart, the "Load" represents the part of the appliance that does the work. This part produces resistance in an electrical circuit. It is the primary point to check and record in your tests, for trouble and normal wear are most likely to occur there.

Consider any electrical appliance in your home; to recognize the load point, ask your-

GUIDE TO KEEPING ELECTRIC APPLIANCES
IN WORKING ORDER

Use this form and a VOM to record present readings for all your home appliances. When trouble occurs, check new readings against your record for a clue to the problem.

	Load	Test Point	Scale	Reading*	Your Appliance	
Clothes washer	inlet-valve solenoid	solenoid terminals	R X 100	400		
	timer motor	motor leads	R X 100	1,050		
	shift solenoid	solenoid terminals	R X 1	18		
	machine motor	motor terminals: high-speed low-speed	R X 1	0.81 0.75		
Clothes dryer	machine motor	motor terminals	R X 1	1.5		
	timer motor	motor leads	R X 100	1,100		
	element (double)	element terminals	R X 1	15, 22		
	element (single)	element terminals	R X 1	9.5		
Dishwasher	machine motor	motor leads: start winding run winding	R X 1	5.5 2.9		
	heating element	element terminals	R X 1	15.5		
	pump motor	motor leads (some use main motor for pump also)	R X 1	6.3		
	inlet valve	solenoid terminals	R X 100	280		
Stove	5" element, 2-wire	element terminals	R X 1	50		
	9" element, 2-wire	element terminals	R X 1	30		
	5" element, 3-wire	terminals: common to outer coil inner coil	R X 1	60 80		
	9" element, 3-wire	terminals: common to outer coil inner coil	R X 1	40 65		
Water heater	heating elements	element terminals: 1,000w element 2,000w element 4,500w element	R X 1	58 28 13		
Refrigerator	compressor (varies greatly among brands & sizes)	terminals: common to start to run	R X 1	11 1.9		
	defrost heater	heater leads	R X 1	18		
	mullion heater (between doors)	heater leads	R X 100	490		
	stile heater (surrounds cabinet)	heater leads	R X 100	525		
	drain-pan heater	heater leads	R X 100	21		
	evaporator fan	motor leads	R X 1	48		
	condenser fan	motor leads	R X 1	65		
Air conditioner (room)	compressor (varies greatly among sizes & brands)	terminals: (14,000 Btu comp.) common to start to run run to start	R X 1	5.5 1.0 6.5		
	fan motor (varies greatly among sizes & brands)	leads: common to high speed med. speed low speed	R X 1	38 47 58		
Coffee maker	heating element	plug terminals	R X 1	33		
Frying pan	heating element	plug terminals	R X 1	12		
Iron	heating element	plug terminals	R X 1	11.5		
Waffle iron	heating element	plug terminals	R X 1	11		
Toaster	heating element	plug terminals	R X 1	11.5		

GUIDE TO KEEPING ELECTRIC APPLIANCES
IN WORKING ORDER

	Load	Test Point	Scale	Reading*	Your Appliance	
Blender	motor	plug terminals: high medium low	R X 1	 24 30 40		
Can opener	motor	plug terminals	R X 1	7.5		
Mixer (hand; 3-speed)	motor	plug terminals: high medium low	R X 1	 40 51 60		
Mixer (table; inf. speed)	motor	plug terminals	R X 1	20		
Vacuum cleaner	motor	plug terminals: high low	R X 1	 2.5 3.5		
Other						
Other						
Other						
Other						
Other						
Other						

*These figures represent the average of readings obtained from three appliances of different makes. Your normal reading may be more or less than the figure given.

Every time you buy a new appliance, use your VOM to make a record of its normal electrical characteristics, add this to the records you have previously made of all other appliances, and you will have good help when trouble comes to one of them.

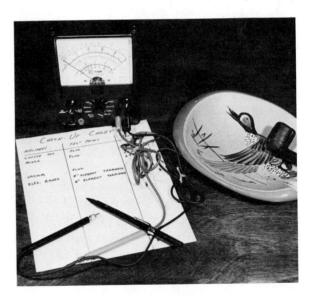

self, "What actually does the work in this appliance?" In a waffle iron, it is the heating element; in your vacuum cleaner, it is the motor; in your automatic washer, it is the machine motor, the water inlet valve solenoids, the timer motor, etc.

In many small appliances with only one load, such as an iron or toaster, you may obtain readings for the chart by simply unplugging the appliance, turning all switches and controls to *on* position, and reading across the terminals of the plug. Accuracy is of extreme importance. Zero your meter carefully, touch only the insulated portion of the probe, and select a range that gives you a reading as close to midscale as possible.

Complex appliances with more than one load require isolation of the individual components before readings are made. Unplug the appliance and remove one wire from the component under test before recording your result.

Closed switches and conductors should always indicate 0 resistance on your meter. They're relatively easy to pinpoint in the event of failure. Any reading higher than 0 resistance in a switch indicates bad contacts or loose connections. The job of these components is simply to get the electricity to the load where it can be put to work.

There is no need to list voltage readings in the chart, because these are known (either 115 or 230 volts on all home-appliance loads) and there is no need to make a voltage test even if the appliance fails to operate (see chapter 5).

Later, if the appliance becomes inoperable, check to see if voltage is reaching the receptacle by plugging in a table lamp. Perhaps a fuse is blown or a circuit breaker is tripped in the household circuit. If voltage is present, unplug the appliance, remove one lead from the load,

and take a resistance reading. If it compares favorably with the figure in your chart, all is well; if not, you ought to replace it. These two simple VOM tests can pinpoint any electrical problem quickly when used with your own chart.

You've probably noticed tags on your appliances that state the operating voltage and power consumption of the appliance. These nameplate ratings are required on most appliances by the Underwriters' Laboratories. You may compare your own readings to those of the manufacturer by applying Ohm's law. Since the meter tells you the resistance in the load, you can divide this into the voltage, which is known. This one simple calculation gives you the current in amperes flowing in an AC circuit. To convert amperes to watts, simply multiply by the voltage (example, 5 amperes in a 115-volt circuit is equivalent to 575 watts).

Don't be alarmed if your own readings vary somewhat from the nameplate rating. When in operation, the effects of heat and induction can alter the actual power consumption. This is another good reason for maintaining your own chart. You can see at a glance the exact readings that your meter should record.

This is the secret of spotting troubles before they hit. In your original check, you establish a standard for your appliances in normal operation. In subsequent checkups, evaluate carefully any reading that varies more than 10 percent from your standard.

If the resistance is higher, it could mean a loose or corroded connection or a burned and pitted contact point. Cleaning and tightening now could prevent inevitable failure. A lower reading could mean the normal deterioration of a heating element or a short between windings in a motor. Consider replacement. At this point, the life of a component would definitely be limited.

Include a tune-up while you are making the rounds with your VOM, and allow enough time to lubricate, check linkages, adjust belts, etc.

Check the resistance from each plug terminal to the equipment frame. On 115-volt non-polarized (two-terminal) plugs you should never read continuity to the frame. On polar-ized plugs (two flat terminals and one round "ground" terminal) no reading should be obtained from either flat terminal to the frame, but continuity should always be read from the ground terminal to the frame.

On 230-volt appliances, the middle terminal is the grounded neutral, and in most localities it is required to be attached to the frame. If it isn't in your case, consider running an external ground from the appliance to a cold-water line as a safety measure.

Total resistance of defrost heaters in frost-free refrigerators and freezers may be determined when refrigerator is cold by attaching meter leads to plug and turning defrost timer to the defrost cycle, usually around 2:00 on the clock indicator.

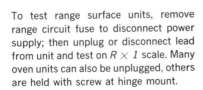

To test range surface units, remove range circuit fuse to disconnect power supply; then unplug or disconnect lead from unit and test on $R \times 1$ scale. Many oven units can also be unplugged, others are held with screw at hinge mount.

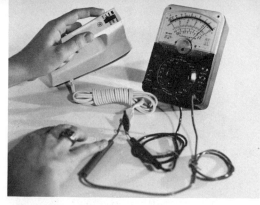

Many small appliances such as this mixer have tapped field windings to provide several motor speeds. List readings obtained with switch in each of the available positions.

Handle must be depressed and unopened can must be in place to energize switches on many electric can openers. Bottom of empty can "fools" switches for testing purposes.

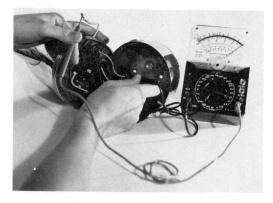

Resistance of portable appliances with removable cord is read at terminals. Check to ground also. A reading might indicate broken or sagging heating element.

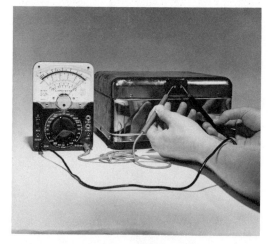

Resistance of electric-iron element is read across terminals of plug. Be sure that switch or thermostat knob is in *on* position before reading test meter.

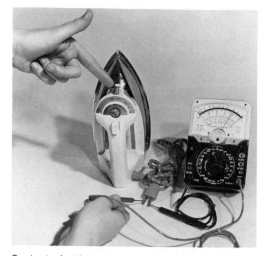

Contacts in thermostats or switches should always indicate 0 ohms resistance when closed. Don't list these components on chart, but remember that they should be tested as above if appliance malfunctions.

To test timer motors, find the two leads attached to motor and trace them to terminals on timer body. Remove one lead from terminal before testing. Appliance must be unplugged before panels or console is removed.

Compressor terminals on refrigerators and freezers are reached after unplugging leads or relay case from compressor housing. Terminals are marked *C* (common), *R* or *M* (running winding), and *S* (starting winding).

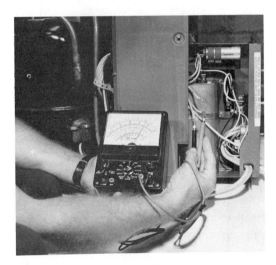

Dishwasher inlet valve solenoid terminals as well as heater and motor leads are accessible after removing front toe panel.

Many newer air conditioners have control panels which allow electrical components to be tested from one central point. Fan motor is tested after consulting wiring diagram for color-coding of respective windings.

9
Repairing Small Appliances with Heating Elements

Now the fun begins! I hope that you will find, as I have, that it really is fun to repair an appliance that's out of commission. There's a great reward in seeing an appliance working again as a result of your own handiwork.

Repair costs can approach the cost of a new small appliance. That's because assembly lines zip out small appliances so fast that no man could take one apart by hand, repair it, and reassemble it for anything that approximates the original cost of assembly. Manufacturers are all aware of this cost factor. It's the primary reason for the "immediate replacement" warranties now common for small appliances. Before you attempt a home repair, however, consider that you may void your warranty by making it. But out of the warranty period, it's often not economical to repair a small appliance unless you do it yourself.

Reputable manufacturers are all trying to overcome rising labor and materials costs to provide efficient and economical appliance repairs. Several small-appliance manufacturers (among them Sunbeam, West Bend, and General Electric) have numerous repair centers to which you can take or ship an ailing small appliance. However, it is often to your advantage to know how to repair it yourself. You can reduce both the time the appliance is out of commission and the cost of service.

Small appliances with resistance heaters are quite numerous in the average household. They are the simplest appliance to repair. What's more, they make a good starting point for learning to repair the more complex ones. The primary load of these appliances—the part that does the work—is a heating element, often referred to as a resistance heater, because resistance to electrical flow causes it to become hot. The heating element may be an open type, comprised of a coil of special wire suspended on ceramic insulators, or it may be the enclosed type, with the coiled wire inside a metal sheath. When enclosed, the coil is separated from the sheath by an insulating compound. In some irons and frying pans, this element may be part of the base casting.

Not just any wire can serve as a heating

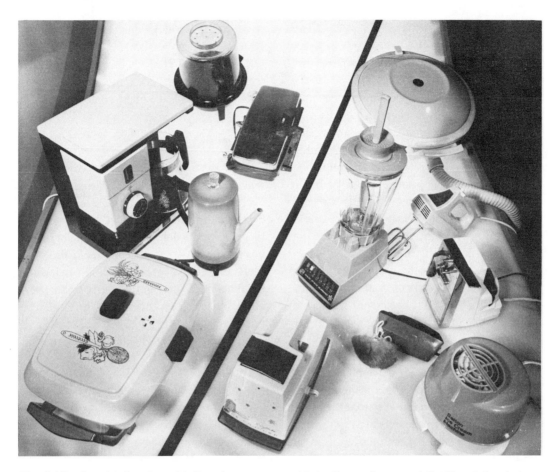

The dividing line—heating element is the primary component in heating appliances on left, although there's some overlap since some appliances use both motor and element.

element, for correct resistance and physical characteristics are necessary to provide an element that heats efficiently and has a reasonable life. An alloy of nickel and chromium is commonly used for this purpose. It is formed into nichrome wire.

The diameter and length of this wire determine its resistance. Since resistance also determines the wattage (remember Ohm's law and the power formula?), it is important that you match a replacement element to the wattage of the appliance on its nameplate. Nichrome wire for open heating elements is often sold from spools of 100 feet or more. After matching the diameter of the wire to that of your appliance, the parts distributor can cut it to length to suit the wattage. Such bulk wire is usually rated at a certain number of watts per inch.

When you replace an element, however, you will find that even though you have the correct wattage you still must stretch it to fit. There are two ways to do this. The easiest is to remove the old element, temporarily fasten any breaks together, and use the old as a pattern for the new. If a section of the old element is missing, use a tape measure to trace its path and determine the length. When you stretch the new element, be sure to fasten one end in a vise or other secure mount and stretch it from the extreme opposite end. Never try to stretch a section at a time. It is impossible to stretch each portion exactly the same. Unless stretching is even, the element will have "hot spots" and sags will shorten its life. When stretching a new element, wear safety goggles and don't stand directly in front of it. An element being stretched is like a mild spring and could cause injury if the gripped end suddenly slipped loose.

In some instances the heating element is energized when you plug in the appliance. Normally, however, you will find a thermostatic control and/or a switch in the circuit with the resistance element. In many cases, the switch is incorporated into the thermostat simply as an *off* position.

BASIC REPAIR PROCEDURE

Here, then, are the basic components with which you will deal in repairing small appliances with heating elements: (1) the conductor (plug, cord, and any connecting wiring); (2) the switch or bimetal thermostat; and (3) the heating element itself.

If you don't now have a broken heating-element appliance, get one from a neighbor for practice in making repairs. There is no better training ground for the work that lies ahead of

you in repairing major appliances. Basic components are usually visible in appliances that you work with in this chapter. This can be of tremendous value when the more complex ones (and less visible ones) come along.

Diagnosing the Problem

The first step in any repair procedure is correct diagnosis of the problem. Using those two deluxe test instruments, your eyes and ears, make a close examination and determine what the appliance is doing that it should not do (or what it is *not* doing that it should do). Are there any unusual sounds accompanying the malfunction? Where in the course of the operation is the problem occurring? These could be important clues.

Before attempting a diagnosis, find out what the primary user of the equipment has to say about the malfunctions. If you happen to be the lady of the house, you'll be able to answer your own questions. If you're the man of the house, you may have to rely on your wife's interpretation. Then plug the appliance in (unless the complaint is that it's shocking) and use it (or attempt to use it) in a normal manner, listening for any peculiar noises and keeping your eyes open. Somewhere along this path, you'll find some indication of the problem.

This indication can be important. By taking careful notice, you can eliminate many areas which might otherwise be time-consuming to investigate. For instance, if a toaster toasts the bread on one side but not on the other, you can eliminate the fuses, line cord, and thermostat. Failure of any of these would keep the toaster from operating at all. The only thing left would be a heating element or some of its connecting wiring. You can also apply this same thinking to larger appliances: if the light in the refrigerator burns but the unit doesn't cool, you needn't bother checking the fuse or supply cord. Concentrate your efforts on the cooling or air circulation system. Just remember that if there is a failure in the fuse, wiring, plug, cord—anything involved in supplying the power to the equipment—it won't work at all. Observe the symptoms; think them through. It'll save a lot of work.

The popcorn popper shown in accompanying photographs is an excellent starting point and a good example because of its simplicity. There are only two basic components to test: the heating element and the conductors, consisting of the plug(s), cord, and connecting wiring. Much is visible. You should be able to see a break in the element or a ground. But even though the fault may be visible, use your VOM to make tests. In the complex appliances ahead, you'll have to rely on it to "see" these electrical faults.

This is also the time to develop the habit of "thinking through" the problems you encounter and to ask yourself why the fault occurred. Then you're much more likely to remember a particular problem, even years from the time you first encounter it. If the element is broken, you immediately recognize that current can't flow. If the element has sagged and touches the metal housing or support, the resulting ground makes the appliance a shock hazard. But what caused the element to open or stretch? Was it due to age and usage, or was the element damaged or stretched by improper handling or overheating? The answers to such questions may prevent a repeat performance of many appliance ills.

Take a close look at the heating appliance that you've found for personal training. If you have determined the problem, the next question is what to do about it. Obviously the next step should be to test the appliance to pinpoint faulty components. Hopefully your preliminary diagnosis has eliminated some and pointed the finger at others.

Suppose the appliance doesn't heat at all. You've plugged a table lamp into the receptacle and it worked. So you know that the fuse, receptacle, and household wiring are all right. Now the knowledge that you have of the specific appliance comes into play. If you're scrutinizing a waffle iron, for example, you will notice that it has two heating elements, one each for the top and bottom griddles. It is highly unlikely that both would fail at the same time. The appliance cord and the thermostat-switch assembly are prime suspects, however. A failure in either of them could put the entire heating section out of commission.

Testing the Cord

Now the problem is how to get to various components—even the cord itself. On many new appliances, the screws and nuts which must be removed for disassembly are hidden. This is primarily a styling consideration by the manufacturer, but it does make your job of servicing the appliance more difficult. Look under trim and chrome nameplates and you'll most likely find them. Steam irons are notoriously hard to disassemble. Often there is a metal plate in the center of the lower portion of the handle which can be snapped off, providing access to the stud attaching the base to the handle assembly. But in many places it's necessary to pull the steam fill spout from the handle or pry adhesive-backed trim strips away to gain access. This will damage the trim beyond repair, so that portion must be re-placed.

A small appliance is usually also a portable appliance and many are moved about often in the course of normal use. This causes the cord to flex, and over a period of time results in a great deal of stress on the cord, plug, and terminals. If the stranded copper wires break, an open circuit results and the appliance is inoperative. This is probably the most common trouble in a small home appliance. It is also the easiest to repair.

Look at the point where the cord enters the appliance. There will be a cover in the vicinity that either snaps on or is held in place with a screw. Remove the cover, exposing the cord terminals. Look for corroded or broken terminals. Unplug the appliance and plug a table lamp into the same receptacle. If it doesn't light, the home circuit is at fault—the fuse is blown or the circuit breaker tripped (most likely), or the receptacle itself is defective (possible). If you do find voltage here, but the appliance doesn't operate, suspect the cord.

There is a trick to checking the cord. Remove the cord from the appliance by releasing the push-on or screw-type terminal connections. Inside the cord are two electrical conductors, each attached to one of the prongs on the plug, and each one must show continuity. With the VOM set to $R \times 1$, touch one test lead to one prong of the plug. Touch the other lead to both of the terminal ends in turn. Continuity should be indicated to one, and only one, of the terminal ends.

Now, take a small clip and clamp one test lead to the conductor showing continuity and the other test lead to the prong on the plug. Bend, twist, and pull the cord, especially in the area of the plug itself and at the strain relief where the cord entered the appliance. The meter must continue to indicate continuity; if the needle should fall during this test, it indicates an internal break in the conductor, and the cord must be replaced. Always be sure to test both conductors in the cord in this manner. An internal, erratic break such as this is invisible and is almost impossible to detect in any other way. If a cord is frayed or the terminals are burned or corroded, replace the cord with one of the same size and type. Heating appliances use special cords with heat-resistant insulation, and are widely available. Never replace this type with a common fixture cord. Before reassembly, always clean the electrical terminals until they are bright and shiny. And, as the final step, be sure that all connections are tight.

Testing the Bimetal Thermostat

The heart of a heating device is the bimetal thermostat. Metals expand at a certain rate when heated and contract at a certain rate when cooled. This rate of expansion and contraction varies with each metal, and is dependent on its molecular structure.

To understand the bimetal thermostat, imagine that you take two thin strips of unlike metals and fuse them together. Hold one end of the new double strip and heat it in the middle. Since one metal expands at a higher rate than the other, it will begin to push against the other. Because they are bonded together, however, this pushing action becomes a warping action, and a noticeable (and useful) mechanical action is obtained.

Insulate the fixed end of the strip and attach a wire to the strip itself. On the movable end put a silver contact. Take another strip (al-

CHECKING AN APPLIANCE CORD

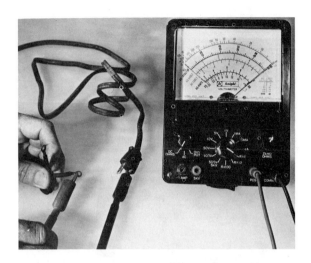

To check for internal breaks, fasten meter probes to each conductor and to one prong of plug in turn, as in photo left. Small alligator clips will hold cord in place. Continuity should be indicated from one side of line to one side of plug only. Now twist, pull and bend the cord all along its length (below). Should needle drop, it indicates break in conductor inside. Replace the cord. An alternate method is to clip the test leads to each prong of the plug, then twist the two conductors together at the opposite end. Twist and bend the cord, and note any drop in meter needle. This checks both conductors at the same time — it's the quickest method if the cord is entirely removed from appliance.

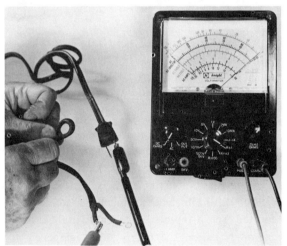

though not necessarily a bimetal strip) and make another contact on this to rest against the one on the bimetal. Then attach a wire to this strip and bring the wire to one terminal of a heating element. Also put a threaded shaft against the second contact base, so that you can move it up and down in relation to the bimetal contact strip.

You have now constructed an adjustable bimetal control very similar to that used in irons, heaters, toasters, waffle irons, etc. When you apply voltage to the circuit, electrical current

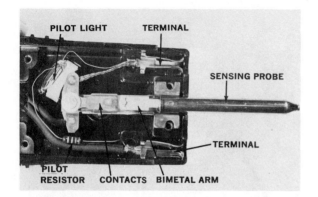

Top view of removable thermostatic control from electric fry pan shows typical location of components. Be sure to check wiring connections closely. This is view from underside — knob is still attached on opposite side.

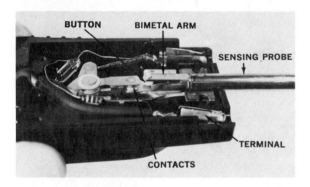

View from side of control indicates positioning of contacts and bimetal arm extending from probe. Contacts can be burnished with matchbook cover or very light sandpaper.

flows through the two contacts, energizing the heater. The bimetal, exposed to this heat, warps and separates the contacts. As the device cools, the bimetal again makes contact and the cycle is repeated. The length of the on and off cycles, and the corresponding temperature, is dependent upon the relation of the two contacts, which you can adjust with the threaded shaft. The more tension you apply to them at room temperature, the more heat you will need before the contacts will open.

Thermostats in modern small appliances rarely have to be adjusted. If the range has shifted greatly, it is usually wise to replace the control as a unit. Adjustments must be made

on special temperature testers, and if the control is not stable, an adjustment will usually be only a temporary repair. Inspect carefully all wiring connections at the control and also check the contact points. All terminals should be cleaned when found corroded. Should the threaded shaft become rusted, a drop of penetrating oil (or vinegar) followed by a drop of light lubricating oil will usually free it. Never allow oil to touch a contact point, and avoid touching the contact points with your fingers.

Many portable appliances with heating elements have a detachable heat control which plugs into the base of the appliance. Electric fry pans, skillets, and fondue pots are examples of small heating appliances which use this arrangement. In most instances, the element of these appliances is molded into the base casting.

The thermostat assembly of these appliances must be removed before the base is washed. The sensing element of the control is the long probe that is inserted into the appliance. Within the probe is a bimetallic rod that extends into the contact area, and is secured at the opposite end. At the end of this arm is a button which presses against contact arms, allowing the contacts to open and close. If the contacts are badly pitted, they can be cleaned with a point file. The control is calibrated with a screw in the bimetal contact section or, most

often, by adjusting the position of the knob on the shaft of the control. Look closely before attempting to remove this knob. In many appliances it is held in place with a setscrew, located in the side of the knob. In others, a nut or screw accessible after removing the decorative button or trim from the top center of the knob must first be removed.

To adjust the temperature range, put approximately one inch of water in the container, and adjust the knob to the point where the water just begins to maintain a constant boil. This should be near the 212-degree setting. If not, unplug the appliance and remove the knob from the shaft and position it correctly.

One of the most common requirements of

Plug-in thermostatic control of the type found on electric fry pans, griddles, electric fondue pots, etc. is easily tested (along with the cord and plug) by method shown here. With a jumper placed across the prongs of the plug and the meter set to the lowest resistance scale with the test leads pushed into position where the terminals on the pan would normally enter, turn the switch to the *on* position. The meter should indicate continuity. When the switch is turned to *off,* the needle should then drop back to show that the circuit is open. Heating the sensing element with switch *on* should also open the circuit. Control is similar to bimetal shown on facing page, but sensing portion is located in insertion tube so that temperatures within the pan are accurately detected.

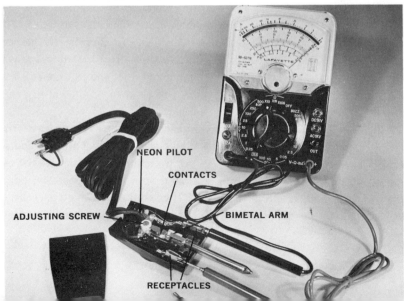

NEON PILOT

CONTACTS

ADJUSTING SCREW

BIMETAL ARM

RECEPTACLES

thermostatic controls after long usage is simply a good cleaning job. Vapors from greases, lint, and food particles can find their way into the seemingly unpassable openings in the control, and result in unsatisfactory and often erratic control operation. After carefully removing the control cover, use a soft brush and some television tuner contact cleaner (available from any radio-TV parts supplier) and spray the inside of the control thoroughly, wiping away the residue. Several applications of spray may be used if much grease is present. Don't use varsol or petroleum-base derivatives on electrical contacts. A thin, oily film can remain which acts as an insulator and can lead to early contact failure.

Sometimes it's necessary to tighten the electrical terminals on these controls. The first indication of this problem would be arcing or perhaps pitting of the male terminals on the appliance itself. Clean these terminals well; then open the control housing and check the condition of the terminals within the control. It may be necessary to bend the retaining tabs slightly to obtain a tight connection. Be sure that the plug is removed from the wall receptacle before testing a thermostatic control.

Testing the Heating Element

To test the heating element, remove one lead and check for continuity at the two terminals; also check from each of the terminals to ground (the frame of the appliance) with the VOM set to the highest resistance scale. If the element is open (no meter deflection noted), or if it is grounded (a meter reading is obtained when checking to ground), the element or casting must be replaced. It might appear that open-type elements, which are tested in the

same manner, could be repaired by simply twisting the parted wires together. Don't try it! The lowered resistance of the element, as well as the poor resulting connection, will cause it to burn out within a short period.

Enclosed elements, or those which are part of the base casting, are tested in much the same manner. The biggest difference lies in the fact that you can't see the element; you must rely on your meter to advise you of the existing conditions. The two terminal pins to which the thermostatic control attaches are the only visible portions of the heating element assembly. This is also the point where you test for open circuits and grounds within the heating element. Use the $R \times 1$ scale across each terminal to test for continuity; a low resistance reading should be noted. Use the highest resistance scale (such as $R \times 10,000$) to test for grounds. Attach one probe to each of the terminals in turn while pressing the other probe tightly against the base casting. No reading should be noted. Here, you must rely on your test readings to "see" inside the mass of metal and tell you what's going on within it.

If you noticed a reading during the ground test, indicating a leakage of electrical current to ground, it is possible that it is caused by moisture around the terminals. This is especially likely just after the pan has been washed. Thoroughly dry the terminal area and make another test. If the leakage still remains, the base of the pan or the entire pan should be replaced.

When replacing components in appliances, always get the model number and serial number from the nameplate as well as any part numbers on the component itself.

If you did not receive a parts list or diagram with your appliance, it may be a good idea to list the order in which you disassemble small linkages, perhaps even sketching their position to guide you when reassembling. Also, keep this in mind: Whether you're making repairs for a living or for your own convenience, be professional. Try to think ahead. Place the appliance on a soft cloth to avoid scratching the finish. Always unplug an appliance before disassembling, and never have "live" electrical connections exposed.

RULES FOR THE USE AND CARE OF PORTABLE APPLIANCES

- Always unplug a small appliance before cleaning.
- Clean regularly according to manufacturer's instructions. Pay particular attention to such things as crumb trays on toasters and motor filters on vacuum cleaners. Wipe spills and splashes off housings before they can get to electrical components.
- Use no more than one heating or two motor-driven appliances on a circuit at the same time.
- On appliances with detachable cords or thermostats, always plug cord into appliance before plugging into wall outlet. Also, remove plug from wall outlet before removing from appliance.

- Never immerse an appliance in water unless it is specifically designed for this purpose. Be sure to remove such items as detachable cords and thermostats before immersing.
- Don't force removable components into place.
- Keep all utensils (and hands) away from moving parts.
- Use distilled water in steam irons (rainwater or condensate water from a dehumidifier, after straining, can also be used).
- Keep sufficient space around heating appliances.
- Never operate an appliance when your hands are wet or when you are standing in a damp location.

ELECTRIC IRONS

The electric iron common in almost every home today is directly descended from the hand irons used in pioneer times. The electric iron, however, is a self-contained appliance with its own heat source and in many models a built-in steam system. The first electric models used a nichrome element wrapped around a mica support, but most built in recent years have the heating element enclosed in the base casting. These elements are nonrepairable, but should be tested for grounds and for continuity whenever a malfunction occurs.

The bimetal is located adjacent to the heating element, and controls the temperature of the base casting. In a steam iron, a reservoir for water sits above the element and thermostat. A needle valve controls the flow of water through ports in the hot base. When the water strikes the base on the way through the outlet port, it becomes steam and is forced into the clothing being ironed.

To disassemble the iron, be sure it is unplugged and then look closely for screws and retainers under trim plates. On many models, the fill spout must be pried away before the upper portion can be removed. Some irons have heat shields in the form of "layers" of covers above the heating element, and these have to be removed in order. To begin, remove the obvious screws first; lift away any components that can be moved and look further. One good bet is to remove the handle, for there are often retaining screws hiding under it.

The user should remember that it's important to keep the iron interior as clean as possible to prevent mineral buildup within the ports. The best way to do this is to be sure that clean water is always used. Distilled water and even rainwater is good. Special water filters, some contained within plastic squeeze bottles, are used to reduce impurities. If the steam action is reduced noticeably when the iron is in use, it's likely that the ports are becoming clogged. Often a pipe cleaner can remove the deposits without disassembling the iron, especially in the early stages of clogging.

Thermostats are often adjustable simply by changing the position of the knob on the thermostat shaft. Some have a calibration screw built onto the bimetal arm support. The contacts of the thermostat can be cleaned with an automotive point file if they are badly pitted.

When reassembling an iron, be sure to use new seals and gaskets around the tank. The old ones will probably be damaged in removal. High-temperature silicone sealant-adhesive may be specified for use in some irons, and it can also make a good temporary repair in an emergency. If the fill spout was removed, a new one will be needed.

Light 'N Easy steam iron from GE weighs only 2.5 pounds. Modern features include break-resistant cooler-to-the-touch shell, nonstick soleplate. Wide heel support adds stability and serves for cord storage.

To take an iron apart, look for hidden screws under the trim plates and knobs—a good rule for all small appliances. Steam iron is taken apart by snapping up the trim plates and removing nuts.

To test for continuity through contacts of bimetal switch, component must be isolated by removing wires. Reading shows contacts are okay.

Bimetal contacts may be cleaned with point file (available from auto-supply stores) if they are found to be pitted. Avoid bending bimetal arm or linkage. After points are filed, burnish them with hardwood stick or matchbook striking surface.

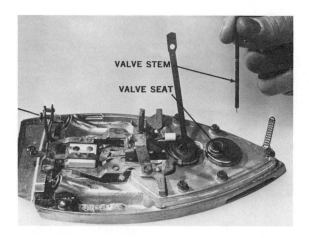

VALVE STEM

VALVE SEAT

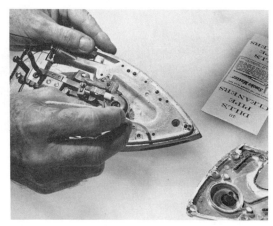

Two special jobs on steam irons are shown here. Valve meters water from tank of steam chamber. Take iron apart to clean the ports or valve if badly clogged (left). If ports are badly restricted, a pipe cleaner can be used to remove the mineral deposit, as at right. Also use a pipe cleaner to open spray outlet in irons that are so equipped. Use of distilled water will prevent such clogging. Second best choice is water from dehumidifiers, air conditioners, and rain water—but filter it through a cloth before adding it to your iron.

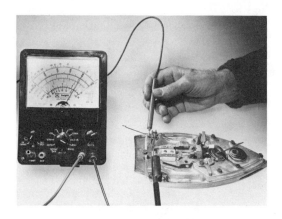

Heating element is checked from each of the two terminals. The reading that you get will not indicate 0 ohms resistance like a switch does, due to the resistance of the heating element—it will probably be around 12 ohms. If no reading is obtained, the element is open and must be replaced.

If continuity of heating element checks okay, check to ground from each of its terminals using highest resistance range. If you get a reading to ground, a shock hazard is indicated.

QUICK-CHECK CHART FOR

ELECTRIC IRON

Symptom	Possible Cause	Remedy
Will not heat	No voltage to receptacle	Check with table lamp—replace fuse or repair receptacle
	Defective cord or terminal connection	Test and inspect—replace only with heat-resistant cord
	Open thermostat	Inspect and replace if defective
	Open heating element	Test for continuity—replace if open or grounded
Overheats	Thermostat not operating	Test with meter and inspect visually—replace burned contacts
Steam will not exit from ports on sole plate, or rusty water spits out	Tank and/or ports clogged	Disassemble and inspect—replace tank and seal if badly clogged. Emptying iron after each use allows heat to evaporate remaining water and helps prevent clogging
	Valve inoperative or sticking	Inspect valve and linkage; clean or replace as necessary
Iron shocks user	Grounded element or wiring connection	Test with meter for ground *with iron unplugged;* replace element or isolate ground as required. Never operate appliance in this condition

COFFEE MAKERS

To service a coffee maker, unplug it and look for and remove any knobs which may extend from the adjustable thermostat. These are usually held in place with a setscrew or small screw recessed into knob. Then look for any screws on the bottom of the coffee maker.

Electric coffee makers can usually be disassembled by removing base and knobs. Sometimes screws holding feet on base also hold base to top. Pump in bottom of stem must be replaced as an assembly.

They may be the same ones which hold the feet in place. In some models a large hex nut is used in the bottom of the base.

Removing the bottom cover allows you to check the element(s) and the thermostat. If it is necessary to remove the element, this may be done in some models by loosening a retaining bolt and pulling the element from inside the tank. When replacing this type element, be sure to use a new gasket.

Thermostat contacts can be cleaned with automotive point file and burnished with a matchbook cover striking surface. These bimetal thermostats sometimes have an adjusting screw, but if it is the disc-type thermostat the temperature range is preset.

The pump chamber and tube is easily removable and should be flushed with clear water after each use.

Heating element is at left. Many newer elements have three leads. One part of the unit is the operating element, the other is for warming. Continuity should show from the middle (common) lead to both others.

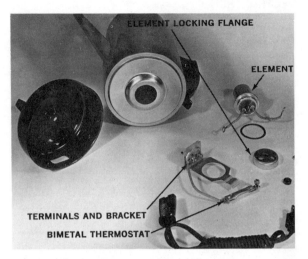

Stud attached heating element holds entire operating portion of this coffee maker together. Removing two nuts from this stud allows base and element to be removed. Element passes through bottom into tank bottom. Gasket should be replaced whenever element is removed.

In electrical assembly of this coffee maker, note that element is enclosed type and there will be no visible indication of failure. Bimetal switch is also encapsulated within metal enclosure.

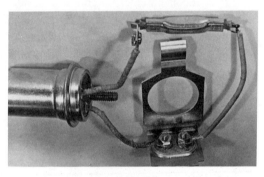

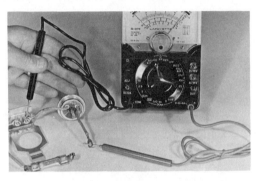

Use lowest resistance scale to test element of coffee maker. Note that one lead is disconnected, always a good practice when measuring resistance on a VOM.

GE's deluxe coffee maker features small gauge on handle to indicate amount of coffee remaining in tank, "Cool-Tip" extension to allow easy removal of hot basket, a small insert basket for use when only two or three cups are desired, and a signal light and adjustable thermostat.

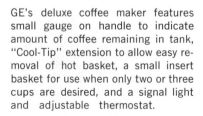

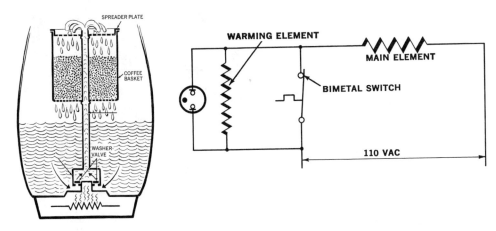

When bimetal contacts are closed, as shown in wiring diagram, current flows through main element. When contacts open, warming element and pilot lamp are energized. Warming element serves to maintain coffee temperature and prevent bimetal switch contacts from resetting, which would cause coffee to become too strong. In typical percolator pump assembly, seen in section drawing, tube has valve at bottom that seats on top of heater in percolator base. When tube is inserted into percolator, water rises to same level as in percolator. As element heats this water, pressure is exerted but water cannot pass back into tank because of valve, and is forced up tube where it flows across spreader plate at top and into basket filled with coffee, where it drains through and back into tank. At the same time, pressure loss from water evacuated from tube and chamber lifts valve from seat, allowing more water from tank to enter for heating, and the cycle repeats itself.

QUICK-CHECK CHART FOR
AUTOMATIC PERCOLATOR

Symptom	Possible Cause	Remedy
Will not heat	No voltage to receptacle Defective cord or terminal connection Open thermostat Open heating element	Check with table lamp Replace with heat-resistance cord Inspect and replace if defective—check linkage to control knob carefully Replace—also check connections to element
Coffee too strong (or too weak)	Thermostat linkage improperly set Thermostat defective	Remove pump assembly, fill with cold water—thermostat should open between 185°-195° as measured with thermometer Replace
Pilot lamp won't operate	Pilot lamp burned out Warming element open Thermostat not opening	Check for voltage to lamp with thermostat open; if voltage is present and lamp out, replace lamp Check for continuity—replace if open Check thermostat as above
Water heats but will not percolate	Pump not sealing Pump inoperative	If tube bent, realign or replace Clean. Washer should be free in pump. If it or seat is pitted, replace
Percolator leaks	Loose gasket, seal, or screw	Replace seals or tighten fasteners

Note: Coffee makers that lack thermostatic control may have fusible link to protect appliance.

GE's drip-filter coffee maker now has electronic timer on some models to get coffee brewing by the time you awake.

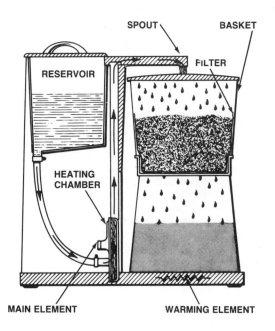

Drip-filter coffee maker differs from percolator in that water being heated is kept entirely separate from that which is already brewed. Water flows from reservoir into heating chamber which contains main element; temperature is closely controlled by a thermostat. As water heats, it is forced up the tube and out the spout where it falls across the coffee. Filter in coffee container controls the rate at which the water passes through. Coffee which drips through into serving container is undiluted and ready to drink. Warming element built into base keeps coffee at serving temperature.

QUICK-CHECK CHART FOR
DRIP FILTER COFFEE MAKERS

Symptom	Possible Cause	Remedy
Will not heat—water won't pump from reservoir.	No voltage to receptacle Defective cord or terminal connection Open thermostat Open heating element	Check with table lamp Replace with heat-resistant cord Inspect and replace if necessary Check with VOM and check connections
Water heats but will not pump into filter container.	Pump not sealing	Check visually and clean openings, replace if necessary.
Pilot lamp won't work	Lamp burned out	Check terminals, replace lamp if OK
Leaking	Overfilled Defective seal on reservoir or crossover	Don't fill above upper level indicator Examine and replace if necessary
Shocking	Grounded component	Discontinue use, check with VOM set to R X 1, replace component or repair wiring.

AUTOMATIC TOASTERS

Toasters can be tricky to disassemble. They are more complicated than you might expect. Before you disassemble one, try the test described in an accompanying photograph on page xx. If the problem is related to the degree of toasting, check to see if a calibration screw is provided to adjust the thermostat without disassembling. If so, it is often located under a removable crumb tray under the bottom of the toaster. Unplug it before attempting any adjustments.

But if disassembly is necessary, begin by removing any knobs and the operating lever handle. Then look underneath for any screws which serve to attach the shell to the bottom of the heater. Sometimes it's necessary to depress the sides of the shell to unlock it from the base. When the outer cover is removed, don't turn the toaster upside-down—the bread guard wires will fall out, and there are quite a few of them in the toaster.

Automatic toasters use small, ribbon-type heating elements, often wrapped around a support formed from mica. A sensitive thermostat determines the temperature in one of the racks where the bread is inserted. This opening is usually designated to use when only one slice

A General Electric two-slice toaster.

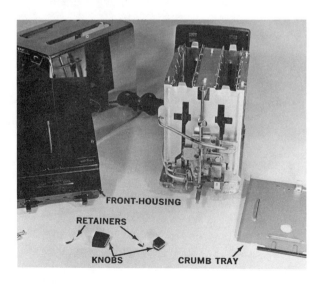

FRONT-HOUSING

RETAINERS

KNOBS

CRUMB TRAY

Disassembly of toaster requires looking under the trim and plates. Front and rear housings often retain wrap-around shell in place—removing the housings releases the shell as well. Note the spring retainers used to hold knobs in position.

of bread is being toasted. The rack rises and lowers in its linkages and latches in position when the handle is depressed by the user. The rack is released by some sort of timing mechanism, often a bimetallic arm which is designed to hold the bread rack in position until the proper temperature is reached, as shown in the accompanying photographs. In others a timing arrangement with a spring motor is used. Still another arrangement uses a small heater directly adjacent to or wrapped around a bimetal arm. The best bet here is to take a close look before proceeding to disassemble any part of the timing or release linkage.

When the rack is released, a shock absorber of some type cushions the release so the bread is not ejected from the toaster.

When replacing heating elements in a toaster, you should know that inner and outer elements are often different. Be sure to specify which one you need when obtaining a replacement. The elements are tested by using the $R \times 1$ scale. Be sure to remove one of the leads before making the test. Thermostat contacts are also tested on $R \times 1$ scale, and should indicate 0 ohms resistance with the contacts closed. Typical servicing operations are seen in the accompanying photographs.

To remove toaster cover, first take off the knobs (left). These usually are held in place by a setscrew or spring clip such as those shown in previous photo. Some covers can then be removed by simply depressing the sides of the toaster. In others, such as the one shown at right, you find the cover screws after dropping the crumb tray. For full work on the mechanism, you may need to remove the entire cover. But you can reach some of the control assembly at point shown. Bimetal switch acts as timer and energizes solenoid to work pop-up mechanism. Adjustment can be made to vary toasting.

 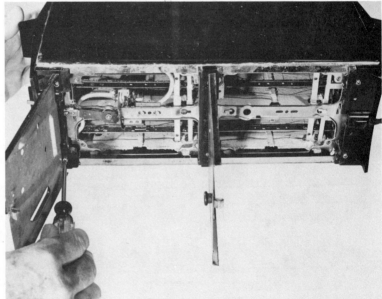

Solenoid movement in this toaster actuates trip lever (at pencil point) that releases pop-up mechanism. In some toasters, bimetal unit trips it mechanically. If there's trouble, look for broken springs or bent linkages (be sure that power is off).

Contact points that energize heating elements are linked to pop-up unit to turn heat off when toast is released. Clean points with point file, burnish with striking surface of match cover for better contact.

Close-up of solenoid shows how coil causes armature to pull inwards, releasing trigger which releases bread rack, allows toast to pop up.

PIVOT

TRIGGER

ARMATURE

COIL

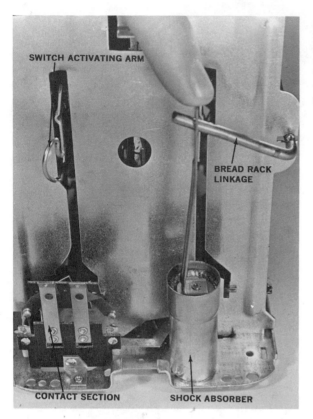

Linkage connected to spring-loaded bread rack is detained in upward movement by the damper at bottom right. This "shock absorber" prevents toast from being thrown out of toaster when rack springs up.

In testing heating element, note that one wire has been removed. Inner and outer elements often have different wattage ratings—be sure to specify which one you need when buying replacements. Use lowest resistance scale on VOM for this test.

Close-up of contact assembly. Points are below the end of retracted ball-point pen, shown to illustrate relative size. Hooked arm pushes contacts together when pop-up mechanism is depressed at start of toasting cycle.

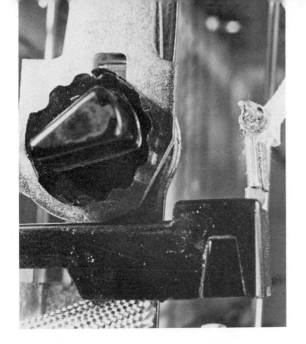

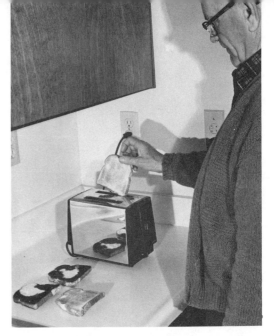

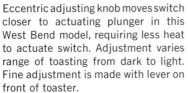

Eccentric adjusting knob moves switch closer to actuating plunger in this West Bend model, requiring less heat to actuate switch. Adjustment varies range of toasting from dark to light. Fine adjustment is made with lever on front of toaster.

Toast unevenly done sometimes? This may result from extra moisture in a certain part of the loaf—nothing to worry about. To find out, put test slices in each of four positions—top up, top down, top to front, top to rear. Uneven toasting is from moisture.

QUICK-CHECK CHART FOR
AUTOMATIC TOASTER

Symptom	Possible Cause	Remedy
Will not heat	No voltage to receptacle	Check with table lamp—replace fuse or repair receptacle
	Defective cord or terminal connection	Test and inspect—replace only with heat-resistant cord
	Open thermostat	Inspect and replace if necessary—check for binding linkage
	Heating element(s) open	Test and replace as necessary—often are replaced as pairs
Toast will not pop up	Binding slide lever or knob	Inspect and realign as necessary
	Broken latch spring	Replace as needed—do not stretch
	Latch mechanism binding	Inspect carefully and repair as needed; check by testing with several slices of bread
Toast will not stay down	Latch mechanism not functioning	Inspect and repair—should operate freely without oiling
Toast burns or does not brown enough	Thermostat inoperative—contacts welded or not closing properly	Inspect and replace as required
	Timing mechanism inoperative	Inspect with bread in toaster—adjustments are critical
Uneven toasting	Moisture content of bread	Test with several brands of bread
	One heating element inoperative	Test and replace as necessary

ELECTRIC FRY PANS, SKILLETS AND GRIDDLES

These appliances differ only in the shape of the base. They consist of two sections. The base, usually cast aluminum, contains the heating element. Since the element is molded into the base, only the terminal pins are accessible for checking; the element itself is nonrepairable. The testing procedure is described in the photos below. Unplug before beginning any test.

The second section, the heat control, is de-

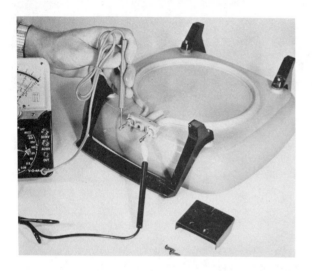

Element outline is visible within base casting of this West Bend fry pan. It is tested for continuity with meter set to lowest resistance scale, applying test probes to the terminal pins and testing for continuity.

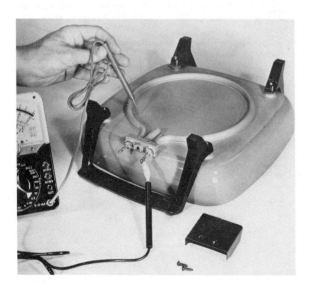

Base of cast appliances like this fry pan should be tested for grounds using highest resistance scale of VOM. If ground is detected, appliance should be discarded—but first check for moisture around terminals.

tachable from the base. The control should never be immersed in water. Most controls can be disassembled for testing by removing two small screws on the plastic housing of the control.

The temperature of the control is adjustable, and is calibrated on the knob. If the calibration is not accurate, you can usually set this by altering the position of the knob on the shaft. A screw or nut, often located under a piece of trim in the center of the knob, holds the knob to the shaft.

Be sure to check the condition of the terminals on both the heat control and the element. If they are corroded or rusted, clean and polish them with light sandpaper before considering the job complete.

If it is necessary to replace a cord on these appliances, be sure to use heat-resistant material of the same type and size as that originally used or recommended by the manufacturer.

Clean the control any time that it is necessary to disassemble it. If a ground develops in the sealed heating element, the appliance should be discarded—never attempt to use one in this condition. Be certain, however, that the ground isn't caused by the presence of moisture around the terminals. To avoid this possibility, be sure that the pan is thoroughly dry before using it.

Skillet differs from fry pan primarily in handling—rather than a long handle, it has two handles which also form the feet of the appliance. Many such appliances such as the GE model shown here now use a nonstick coating on the inside surface of the base. *Photo courtesy of GE.*

ELECTRIC FONDUE POTS

The electric fondue pot is a member of the same family of heating appliances as the electric fry pan, differing only in the shape of the base. The same comments apply.

The legs of the fondue pot are often part of the same component as the handles. It is especially important that they remain secure and undamaged, since the pot is often filled with hot oil and a spill could result in painful injury to the users.

Well-designed fondue pots such as this West Bend model have firm support from feet to prevent tipping. Be sure that feet are tight when inspecting the appliance.

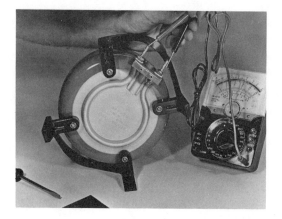

Heating element of fondue pot is molded into base and is nonreplaceable. Now you have to rely on your VOM to "see" the condition of the element and tell you if it is open or grounded. It's easily tested at terminals with VOM on lowest resistance scale. The shield surrounding the terminals was removed for this photo. Actual test could be made with shield in place.

QUICK-CHECK CHART FOR THERMOSTATIC HEATING APPLIANCES
ELECTRIC FRY PANS, FONDUE POTS, BROILERS, GRIDDLES

Symptom	Possible Cause	Remedy
Won't heat at all	No voltage to receptacle	Check with table lamp—replace fuse or repair circuit
	Defective cord or terminal	Test with VOM—replace only with heat-resistant cord
	Open heating element	Test with VOM—replace if defective
	Open thermostat	Test with VOM—repair contacts or replace thermostat as needed
Overheats	Thermostat inoperative	Test with VOM and inspect visually—replace if defective
Shocks user	Grounded element	Test with VOM—replace pan if element grounded
	Damp thermostatic control	Open control carefully and place in oven at 140°. **Do not immerse** control unit when washing pan

POPCORN POPPERS

The circuit is easily visible in the popcorn popper. The element is attached to the conductor at one end, and a bimetal thermostat is often used in series with the element to turn it off when the correct temperature is reached. One side of the bimetal is connected to the other line conductor. The current flows from the conductor through the bimetal to the element and to the other conductor. Be sure that the popper is unplugged before attempting to service it.

Everything is exposed in most poppers, but some models may have a cover or shield over the element and thermostat. In this case, you will have to remove the screws holding the cover in place (they are usually the same ones that hold the feet to the base of the popper). When the cover is removed, take a close look at terminals, element, and insulators or sup-ports which hold the element in place. Be sure that no break exists and that no electrical components are touching the base of the popper.

Although everything is visible (except the contacts of the bimetal thermostat), it is still wise to use the VOM to test the popper. You will have a better understanding of the way the meter reacts to defects in those appliances which are not so exposed, and you will also be able to verify what you see when looking at the element. Sometimes a ground or a break is not apparent.

Before reassembling a popper, be sure that terminals are clean and tight. If not, polish them with light sandpaper and retighten. When assembly is complete, check again for grounds before plugging the popper into the outlet.

The newest version of this favorite appliance

is the hot-air corn popper, which contains an electric motor and fan in addition to the heating element. The corn is deposited in a hopper with a wire-mesh bottom, with the fan located below. When the unit is turned on, the fan circulates hot air around the corn. When the corn is heated sufficiently, it pops and the air stream carries it out of a chute into an awaiting bowl. No oil is used in this type of popper, but a butter cup is provided on some models to melt butter from the heat generated during the popping.

QUICK-CHECK CHART FOR NONTHERMOSTATIC HEATING APPLIANCES

SOME MODELS OF TOASTER-OVENS, POPCORN POPPERS, RADIANT HEATERS

Symptom	Possible Cause	Remedy
Won't heat at all	Fuse blown on circuit Defective cord Burned or corroded terminal Open element	Check with table lamp Test with VOM, replace if defective— Use heat-resistant cord only Clean connection, replace terminal Test with VOM, replace if defective
Shocks user	Grounded element Defective wiring or connection Pinched wiring or connector	Test with VOM, replace element Test with VOM, repair as necessary Test with VOM, repair cord or connector and relocate to eliminate pinching

Hot-air corn popper has element located in base with motorized fan and swirling disc to circulate corn and push it up chute. No oil is required for cooking corn. Butter and salt are added after popping, if desired.

Self-buttering popcorn poppers are popular item. Element is covered in base, top forms handy container for popped corn when inverted.

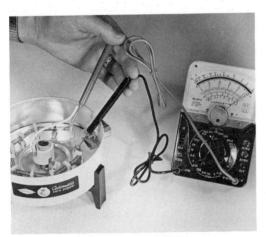

Popper is checked for ground when repairs to element are completed. VOM is set to highest resistance scale for this test. With one lead applied to the frame or housing of the appliance, the other test lead is touched to each terminal in turn. Any reading on VOM here indicates current leakage, a shock hazard.

Testing a popcorn popper. This West Bend model has a bimetallic thermostat, spring-loaded to fit tightly against bottom of corn hopper so that temperature is sensed directly. VOM is being used here to test thermostat for continuity. Element would be tested in same manner, only test leads would be applied to both ends of element. Many such poppers have only element and cord, no thermostat. Many electric heaters would be tested in exactly the same manner.

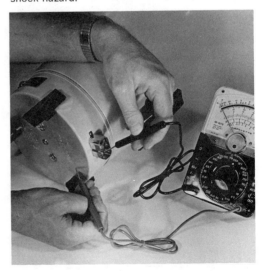

Hot plates are very much like an element from an electric range, with a switch or infinite heat control to turn the 115-volt element on and off. The infinite heat type of control has a bimetal arm and heater within the switch itself, to act as a timing device and cycle the element on and off, thus controlling heat input.

The element can be removed after the hot plate is unplugged by lifting and pulling it from its receptacle, or by removing the receptacle. The element receptacle is usually held with only one screw fastening it to the top stamping. With the element loose, it may be pulled forward to reach wiring and terminals.

If an element fails to function, check first to be sure that there are no loose wires. If terminals appear to be corroded, clean them with a small file or sandpaper and attach a new termi-nal to the wire (or, if screws rather than termi-nals are used to attach the wire to the element, apply solder to the end of the wire) and put the wire back into position. This wire leading from the switch to the element should not be spliced; if it is necessary to replace it, run it all the way to the switch.

The switch can usually be removed by pulling the knob off and removing the mounting screws beneath it. It is sometimes necessary to loosen and remove the top to gain access to the switches. The top is held in place with sheet-metal screws.

Check the element by testing for continuity on the $R \times 1$ scale, and check for grounds on the highest resistance scale. Check the switch by testing for continuity through the contacts. It should read 0 ohms resistance with the switch in the closed position.

QUICK-CHECK CHART FOR

HOT PLATES

Symptom	Possible Cause	Remedy
Won't heat at all	No voltage to receptacle	Check with table lamp—replace fuse or repair circuit
	Defective cord or connection	Test with VOM on R × 1. Use only heat-resistant cord for replacement
	Element open (single element type)	Test with VOM on R × 1. Replace if defective
	Open switch	Test with VOM on R × 1. Should indicate 0 ohms resistance across contacts. Replace if defective
Can't adjust heat level (infinite heat control type only)	Contacts welded in control	Replace control
Shocks user	Grounded element, switch, or wiring	Use VOM to isolate ground and repair as necessary

BROILER-OVENS, CONVECTION OVENS, ROTISSERIE BROILERS ————

These appliances differ from the cast appliances in that their heating elements are replaceable, and their thermostat, if they are so equipped, is not detachable. They range from the simple, inexpensive broiler with a single open element and cord (the only electrical components), to a deluxe broiler-oven with glass front, upper and lower enclosed elements, and adjustable temperature control. As with any appliance, unplug it before beginning your tests.

The simpler appliances are easily serviced with stock nichrome wire for the element (purchased by wattage and size) and standard cord

Toaster-Oven from GE has controls for adjusting browning of toast and for regulating temperature when used as oven. Variety of meals can be cooked in these handy devices.

Differences between cast appliances such as this griddle at right and the rotisserie-broiler at left are readily apparent. Griddle uses detachable control, broiler has no need for temperature control on this model. Both appliances are by West Bend.

to fit the terminals. Be sure that heat-resistant wire is used for the cord. If a protective guard is not installed beneath the element, you should use extreme caution to keep the metal pan away from the element. If it touches, there is the danger of a shock hazard and the likelihood that the element will be damaged.

The rotisserie broiler usually has no thermostat. It is an open pan or reflecting bowl with an enclosed element. The pan is often built to contain water during use. The appliance consists of a reflecting bowl with a rack and heating element. A motor-driven rotisserie unit sits atop this pan. For a detailed photo of one of these motor units, see Chapter 11. The heating element is specially formed to reflect the maximum amount of heat towards the food on top of the rack.

The element can be replaced by removing

Countertop convection ovens, like this one from Farberware, reduce cooking time for some foods by 30 to 50 percent compared to conventional ovens.

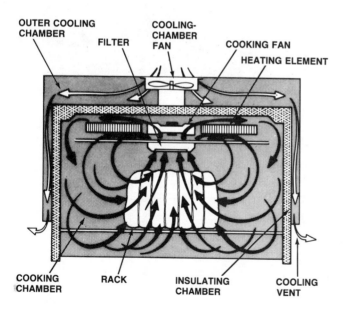

OUTER COOLING CHAMBER
FILTER
COOLING-CHAMBER FAN
COOKING FAN
HEATING ELEMENT

COOKING CHAMBER
RACK
INSULATING CHAMBER
COOLING VENT

Farberware's design uses three-chambers for insulation and energy savings. Internal fan continuously circulates heated air around food for more even heating; elements and circulating fan are behind divider in oven. Cooling fan pulls room air into area behind outer wall to keep outside of oven cool to the touch. Elements and controls are serviced like other tabletop ovens.

the retaining screws, which are clearly visible. Be certain that the terminals of the cord and the element are clean. If the element is grounded or open, it must be replaced. Don't attempt to substitute an element that is made for another application, even though the terminals may line up and the wattage is the same. Most elements used in this appliance are designed to concentrate the heat in certain locations, and the shape of the element is critical.

The more elaborate broiler-ovens have top and bottom elements. If only one element operates, be sure to check the wiring connections to the other. All wire within the unit must be of the heat-resistant type, and all connections must be tight and clean.

Convection ovens have the heating element contained in a cavity outside the oven, or have it shielded so that the food is not heated directly. Instead, a fan gently circulates heated air around the food. The convection oven is claimed to provide faster cooking and more consistent temperatures than an ordinary oven.

Thermostats may be the bimetal type or the sealed diaphragm type like those used on electric ranges. They are usually held in place by screws located under the knob, and are accessible by removing the control panel. The location of the sensing tube is important, and it should be supported by clips. If the clips become broken, others can usually be fabricated by bending a piece of tempered steel.

QUICK-CHECK CHART FOR
BROILER-OVENS

Symptom	Possible Cause	Remedy
Won't heat at all	Fuse blown in circuit Defective cord terminal	Check with table lamp. Test with VOM, replace if defective —use heat-resistant cord only
	Open thermostat	Test with VOM on R × 1 scale— clean contacts or replace.
	Open element	Test with VOM on R × 1 scale— replace
Overheats	Thermostat contacts welded or thermostat out of calibration	Test and adjust or clean contacts or replace as necessary
Shocks user	Grounded element, control, or wiring	Test with VOM using highest resistance scale. Check from plug with oven turned on to frame of appliance Isolate ground and repair as necessary

WAFFLE BAKERS

The waffle baker is a heating appliance using two elements, one in the top section and one in the lower section. They are usually the open type with coiled nichrome wire supported by porcelain insulating blocks. The elements are connected in parallel so that both are cycled off and on by the action of the thermostat, which is usually located in the lower section toward the center of the element or toward the front. The grids of the waffle iron are usually removable for cleaning. Some are reversible, with a sandwich grill on one side and the waffle grids on the other.

Unplug the waffle baker before removing any components. The grids on most newer waffle bakers are held in place with retainers or clips. Removing the grids gives good access to the element and the thermostat assembly.

On older models it may be necessary to remove several screws to remove the top and bottom cover. The screws for the top cover are often under the top handle and at the hinges.

The heating elements are tested by using the VOM on the $R \times 1$ position. They should each indicate continuity, and there should be no grounds when tested on the highest resistance scale. Be sure that there are no sags or bends; if you find them, eliminate them if possible. They will surely lead to later problems.

The wiring that connects the two elements can be a source of trouble also. It's usually contained within a metal sheath or coil to control its flexing as the waffle baker is opened and closed. This greatly prolongs the life of the wiring within the enclosure, but it can become brittle and break after long periods of use. Be

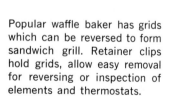

Popular waffle baker has grids which can be reversed to form sandwich grill. Retainer clips hold grids, allow easy removal for reversing or inspection of elements and thermostats.

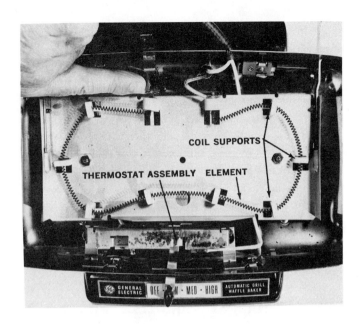

Open heating element on this waffle-baker-grill is supported by porcelain insulators. Terminal connection is indicated at rear of element. Sliding lever at front determines position of bimetal thermostat arm.

QUICK-CHECK CHART FOR THERMOSTATIC DUAL-ELEMENT HEATING APPLIANCES

WAFFLE IRONS, GRILLS

Symptom	Possible Cause	Remedy
Won't heat at all	No voltage to receptacle	Check with table lamp—replace fuse or repair circuit
	Defective cord or connection	Test with VOM—replace cord only with heat-resistant type
	Open thermostat	Test with VOM—repair or replace as necessary
Partial heat (waffles or sandwiches may brown on one side only)	One element open	Test with VOM—replace element if defective. Pilot is often glass "eye" which transmits light from element, may give clue to inoperative element
Overheats	Defective thermostat	Test with VOM and inspect visually—replace if defective
Shocks user	Grounded element	Test with VOM, replace element if grounded
	Grounded control or wiring	Test with VOM, repair fault or replace grounded component

sure to include this as part of your testing procedure. The symptom of this problem is that the upper element will not heat.

Thermostat contacts can be cleaned with an automotive point file, then burnished with paper or a matchbook cover.

You can usually judge if the thermostat range is correct by the condition of the waffles that it cooks. When correctly set, the temperature is in the vicinity of 410 degrees when the thermostat opens, signaling that the waffle is done. On adjustable models, the range is from around 400 degrees to 450 degrees. Adjustment can be made at the thermostat, which is the bimetal type and is located in the center of the element or near the front, in close proximity to the grid. If the waffle is overdone, adjust the calibration screw about a quarter turn toward the "cooler" direction; if not done enough, adjust it toward the "warmer" direction, as indicated near the screw. If the control is not marked, the direction that applies *less* tension to the bimetal arm is the cooler direction.

INSTANT HAIR SETTERS

Instant hair setters are made by using a cast or stamped base as a heat sink, with a heating element located directly below the base. The curlers, which also have a metal insert to retain heat, are placed over projections from the top of the base. As the base is heated, it heats the curlers. When they are removed, the heat is retained for some time because of the metal inserts within each curler.

Unplug the appliance before attempting to

The base of this hair setter is divided into two parts — the heat sink at top and the lower base, which serves as a stand and a cover for the element and thermostat. Top portion can be removed by first removing retaining screws.

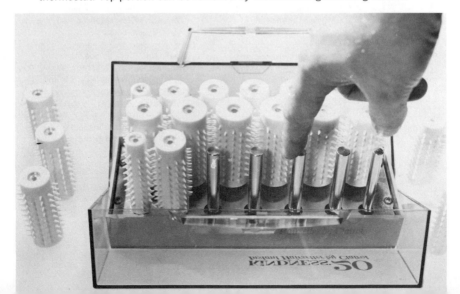

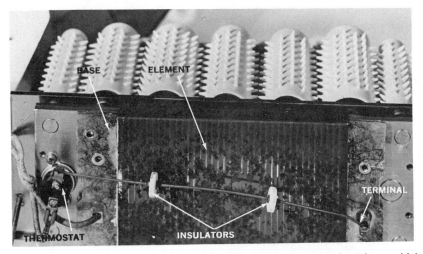

Electric hair setter uses mica-insulated ribbon element to heat base, which acts as a heat sink. Porcelain discs on wire passing across element to terminal at right insulate the bare conductor from adjacent surfaces.

service it. The top is usually removed by loosening small screws on the base that supports the hair curlers. The lower portion can then be separated from the upper. Be sure that all components and the cord-strain relief are in place when it is reassembled.

The element of the hair setter is often a thin ribbon of nichrome wrapped around an insulating support of mica, and attached below the base. A bimetal thermostat, usually a disc type, is also attached to the base and senses its temperature. Once the heat of the base has reached the correct level, the thermostat opens the circuit to the element and does not close

Heated curling brush works on same principle as hairsetters, but has the advantage of portability. GE's Style 'n Go II has two interchangeable barrels; bristles allow shaping without clamp marks.

again unless the temperature drops significantly. The thermostat is usually replaceable; the element often is not and is riveted to the base.

If the hairsetter doesn't work, check the element and the thermostat on the $R \times 1$ scale. The element should indicate continuity and a low resistance, and the thermostat should indicate 0 ohms resistance when it is cool. Be sure to look closely for loose or corroded terminals.

QUICK-CHECK CHART FOR

INSTANT HAIRSETTERS

Symptom	Possible Cause	Remedy
Won't heat at all	No voltage to receptacle	Check with table lamp—replace fuse, reset breaker, or repair circuit
	Defective cord or connection	Test with VOM—use specified cord for replacement
	Open thermostat	Test with VOM on $R \times 1$—repair or replace as necessary
	Open heating element	Test with VOM on $R \times 1$. Replacement is generally not possible, but look closely for corroded or loose connections
Overheats	Limit thermostat doesn't open	Remove bimetal thermostat and heat with match while VOM is connected across contacts and set to $R \times 1$ scale. If contacts don't open, the t'stat should be replaced
Shocks user	Grounded element or wiring	Test with VOM, repair as necessary to isolate ground

VAPORIZERS, BOTTLE WARMERS AND STEAM-TYPE HAIR SETTERS

These small appliances are considered in one group because each one uses the water it contains as the heating element. Two electrodes extend into the water reservoir, one connected to each side of the line. Since water offers some resistance, the electrical current passes through and, as in any resistance, forms heat. The electrodes are placed near each other, but of course they must not touch or you would have a short circuit.

The electrodes in a vaporizer are usually contained within a plastic housing, which has a small orifice drilled through it to admit a small amount of water. As the water within the housing is boiled away, more water is admitted to take its place. In the bottle warmer

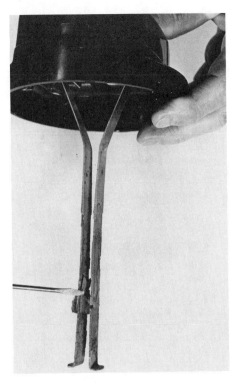

Electrodes from vaporizer can become caked with minerals as shown here. After scraping heavy deposits away, electrodes can be polished with light sandpaper. Be sure to maintain proper gap when replacing electrodes.

and hair setter, a measured amount of water is placed into the container. As the water is boiled away, the steam bathes the bottles or curlers and heats them. The designated amount of water is sufficient to raise the bottles to the correct temperature. Of course, with either appliance, when all of the water has been evaporated no current can flow and the unit is automatically off. Always unplug the appliance before removing the top, filling or testing it.

The electrode cover is usually removed by first loosening a screw or screws which attach it to the lid or base, depending on the appliance. These are simple appliances, and the methods of disassembling them are fairly obvious and should present no problem. If an insulating spacer is used between the electrodes, be sure that it is back in place before reassembling. Be sure also that any gaskets are in place when reassembling.

Sometimes it may be necessary to remove the electrode covers and clean the electrodes. Most of the mineral deposit which forms over a period of time, especially in hard water areas, can be scraped away. Then light sandpaper can be used to finish the cleaning job. If any medication is used in the vaporizer, the vaporizer and reservoir should be washed in hot soapy water after each use. Do not attempt to alter the spacing of the electrodes in any way.

Vaporizer steam is often a necessity in infant's room. Clean electrodes allow a vaporizer to operate efficiently.

VAPORIZERS AND BOTTLE WARMERS

Symptom	Possible Cause	Remedy
Won't heat at all	No voltage to receptacle	Check with table lamp — replace fuse, reset breaker, or repair circuit
	Defective cord or connection	Test with VOM — use only heat-resistant cord for replacement
	Electrodes coated with minerals or film	Inspect and clean as necessary. Be sure to observe proper gap
Partial heating only	Electrodes coated with minerals of film	Inspect and clean as necessary
	Orifice hole partially plugged	Open to original size
Blows fuses or trips circuit breaker.	Electrodes touching	Check electrode gap
	Defective cord or connection	Check with VOM, repair as necessary
"Spits" water out	Extremely high mineral content in water	Mix with distilled water or rain-water. (if water is completely free of minerals, however, it will not conduct and will fail to produce heat)

HEATING PADS

Heating pads are made of a material much like a blanket. They contain elements of different resistances, which means that they also have different wattage ratings. These elements can be switched in and out of use, or can both be used together to provide three separate heat ranges. Typically, a 40-watt and a 20-watt heater may be used. On the low setting, only the 20-watt heater is turned on by the switch. On the medium setting, the 40-watt heater is used. On the high setting, both heaters are used giving a total of 60 watts heat output.

I don't recommend that you attempt to open the heating pad itself to service the ele-ment or safety thermostat sewn into the material—but don't throw a heating pad away if only one element fails, for it still may be worthwhile to use with the remaining heat range. The switch and cord can often be repaired, however. The switch is fastened together with two screws, easily found on the side of the switch. After unplugging the pad, this switch can be disassembled and inspected. When opening it, note the position of the slide switch; this must be reinstalled in exactly the same manner.

The switch is usually on the line going to the heating pad. If contacts become corroded,

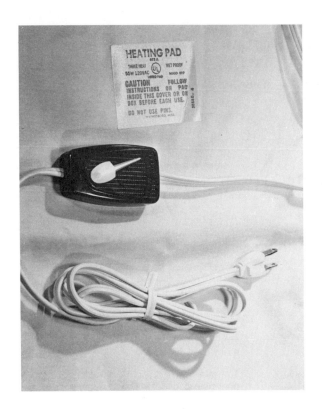

Heating pad shouldn't be opened for servicing, but switch and cord are usually at fault when problems arise.

Heating pad switch uses slide to energize contacts which vary heating capacity of dual elements. Terminal 1 is attached to one side of line. Terminal 2 is connected to low-wattage element, terminal 3 to high-wattage element. Clean corroded contacts.

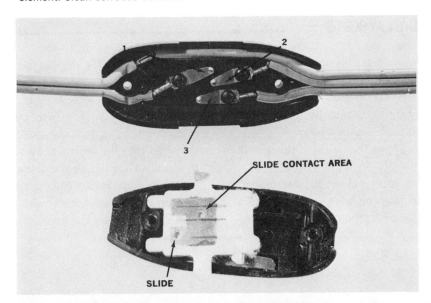

they can often be cleaned. If a conductor becomes loose, it can be tightened by cleaning and tightening its attachment screw or by soldering, if the conductor was held in place by a rivet.

Clean the switch by spraying with television tuner contact cleaner (available from radio-TV parts suppliers) and brushing away any remaining lint and dust.

QUICK-CHECK CHART FOR

HEATING PADS

Symptom	Possible Cause	Remedy
Won't heat at all	No voltage to receptacle	Check with table lamp — replace fuse, reset breaker, or repair circuit
	Defective cord or connection	Test with VOM. Use specified cord for replacement
	Open switch contacts	Try switch on other heat settings. Test with VOM on R × 1 scale. Clean by brushing and applying television tuner contact cleaner
	Open thermostat or elements in pad	Test with VOM on R × 100 scale. Will usually heat partially with one element out
Partial heating only	Open element in pad	Test with VOM in R × 100 position from connections in switch housing. Don't open pad to attempt repair
	Open contact in switch	Clean and repair as necessary
	Loose connection in switch	Tighten or solder as necessary

ELECTRIC BLANKETS

Electric blankets have flexible heating elements woven into the blanket material, and use several safety thermostats to prevent overheating. The control operates from room temperature, and increases or decreases blanket heat depending upon the setting of the control knob.

The control uses a bimetallic thermostat, usually in conjunction with a compensating heater. This heater is in series with the heating element, and when the element is energized by the control the compensator gives off a small amount of heat within the body of the control. The effect of this is to shorten the cycling times of the control and "smooth out" the on-off cycling so that the user is not aware of long *off* periods when the blanket is cool and long *on* periods when it may become too warm. It also operates in conjunction with room temperature—the cooler the room, the longer the

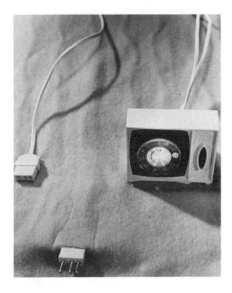

Electric blanket components are located in two places. Those components (element and safety thermostats) within the blanket are not serviceable, but the control unit can often be repaired when things go wrong. Check switch section first.

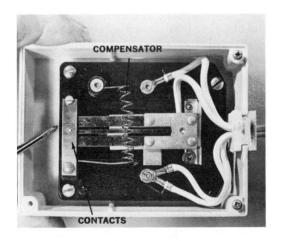

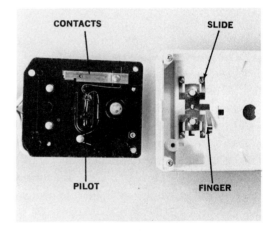

Bottom view of electric blanket control shows positioning of bimetal arm, contacts, and compensator resistor. *On-off* switch and pilot light are on opposite side, as seen at right. Switch arm is held tightly against contact beneath it unless it is raised by slide switch finger, which breaks the contact and turns blanket off.

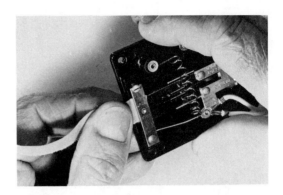

Blanket control contacts can be cleaned with strip of paper. Use care in handling—these contacts are delicate and their positioning is critical.

on periods at a given setting.

Blankets with dual controls operate in the same manner except that the elements are separated, one on each side of the bed, with a separate control for each.

To service the control, first unplug the control circuit from the wall receptacle. Then pull the control knob off, if it has one; if it has only a slide switch and the dial is recessed, it is not necessary to remove the switch knob. Then look at the back side or bottom of the control for any screws that may be present. Removing them should allow you to "split" the control and gain access to the works. Use the VOM to test the contacts and the compensator heater.

When servicing a control, check the switch section if the blanket won't heat at all. Remember that the compensator (which looks like a coil of nichrome wire) is in series with the blanket elements, and if it is open or has a bad connection the blanket won't heat. Use care when handling contacts. They are small, sensitive, and delicate. Clean them only with a

small scrap of paper, and never touch your fingers to any electrical contact—the resulting film of oil can insulate them and cause a quick failure.

The elements and/or internal thermostats are easily tested at the socket on the blanket. Use the $R \times 1$ scale, and test from the terminal farthest from the other pair (the common terminal) to each of the other two on dual control blankets. If they are open, I would not recommend that you attempt a repair. The thermostats are encapsulated in plastic, and the entire assembly is waterproof. But don't throw the blanket away if an element should open—it still makes a good blanket, even with its automatic warming features inoperative.

Some types of blankets had temperature sensors woven into the blanket with the elements. They usually can be identified by a four-conductor hookup to the blanket. If this circuit is open, it must be returned to the factory for repair.

RULES FOR THE USE AND CARE OF ELECTRIC BLANKETS

- Place the control in a position where it can sense an average temperature in the room. Since this control responds to room temperature, if it is in a drafty area or in the direct flow of warm air from a heat duct, the blanket temperature could be erratic. A bedside table is usually an ideal spot.
- Be sure that the blanket plug is on the outside of the blanket as it is placed on the bed. This prevents contact with any exposed electrical connections. The plug and receptacle should be fully mated.
- Follow the manufacturer's instructions for washing. *Never* dry clean an electric blanket.
- Don't sit or place any object on the blanket. This causes heat to be retained within the blanket and leads to erratic performance. Under extreme conditions, it could also damage the thermostats or wiring contained within the material.
- Don't use a blanket that is not in good working order or one that has frayed, broken or cut cords.

QUICK-CHECK CHART FOR

ELECTRIC BLANKETS

Symptom	Possible Cause	Remedy
Won't heat at all	No voltage to receptacle	Check with table lamp — replace fuse, reset breaker, or repair circuit as necessary
	Defective cord or connection	Test with VOM, repair as necessary
	Open compensator in control	Test with VOM on R × 1. Be sure to check connections carefully
	Open element or thermostat in blanket	Test with VOM set to R × 100 scale. Don't open blanket to attempt repair
Blanket overheats	Control out of calibration or sticking	Inspect condition of control contacts. Adjust if possible. Most controls have limited calibration
	Compensator heater jarred out of position	Move compensator closer to bimetal
	Spread or other weight placed on top of blanket	Remove object from blanket
Pilot light doesn't work	Defective connection or resistor in pilot line	Disassemble control and check connections. Check resistor on highest resistance scale — it's usually rated at 30 to 50 thousand ohms

10
Understanding and Troubleshooting Electric Motors

Almost everyone has placed iron filings on a piece of paper or glass, then held a magnet underneath and watched the filings align themselves with the lines of magnetic flux. Magnetic devices play important parts in the operation of home appliances. We have already mentioned the solenoid and the relay. But the most important magnetic device of all is the electric motor.

A simple motor is built by placing magnets on a stationary plate called the stator (usually referred to as the field) of the motor. If another magnet is placed in the center of the field magnets and suspended so that it is free to revolve, it will move to a point where unlike poles are adjacent. If the polarity is changed while the center magnet (the rotor or armature) is moving, its momentum will carry it past the stator pole, and it will continue to rotate as long as the polarity continues to alternate. There must also be a force to put it into motion (spin it) at the outset.

Most motors in home appliances accomplish this by making use of the alternating current power supply. Electromagnets are formed as the stator or field by windings of wire wrapped around pole pieces, which are laminations stamped from soft iron. When current passes through the windings, a magnetic field is formed much as it is in a solenoid. There are two or more of these fields in a motor (but there is always an even number).

The electromagnet is magnetized only when current flows through the coil, and its polarity is reversed when the current flow is reversed—120 times each second on our 60-cycle alternating current. This supplies the magnetic field necessary for the operation of the motor.

With the exception of the universal motor, motors found in home appliances use rotors which have no direct connection to the power supply. These rotors make use of the principle of induction as they cut the lines of force surrounding the field (stator) windings, which induces a current in the rotor. This current is exactly opposite to that in the stator.

The speed of the motor depends upon the number of poles in the field and the frequency

114

of the current on which it is being operated. Theoretically a two-pole motor operating on a 60-cycle-per-second (cps) power supply would adjust itself to a speed of 3600 revolutions per minute (rpm). The formula is:

$$speed = 120 \times \frac{frequency}{no.\ of\ poles}$$

However, because of "slip," which usually runs from 4 to 5 percent, the actual speed would be around 3450 rpm. If the motor had 4 poles in the stator windings, the synchronous speed would be 1800 rpm; the actual speed would be approximately 1725 rpm.

The simple motor described will operate with the alternating-power supply applied directly to the stator from the line and an opposite current being induced in the rotor *if* we first start the rotor spinning by giving it a twist. This brings us to a motor which is used in many home appliances called the split-phase motor.

SPLIT-PHASE MOTORS

To make a basic motor self-starting, something must be added to provide a twist to start the rotor spinning. This twisting force is called torque, and is usually referred to as "starting torque" in the sense that it is being used here. In the split-phase motor, it is obtained by adding another winding called the starting winding. The starting winding has a higher resistance than the running winding, is made of lighter wire with fewer turns, and usually is wound on top of the running winding in the stator slots. It obtains an electrical shift of approximately 20 to 30 degrees, which is sufficient to provide enough starting torque to start the rotor spinning.

Now the motor can start from standstill, but there is another problem. When the rotor reaches 75 to 80 percent of its theoretical top speed (synchronous speed), the running winding develops as much torque as the combined windings. Above this point, the starting winding actually becomes a hindrance. The torque of the motor is reduced and excessive current is drawn through the line. It can also damage the windings.

The problem is solved by using a centrifugal

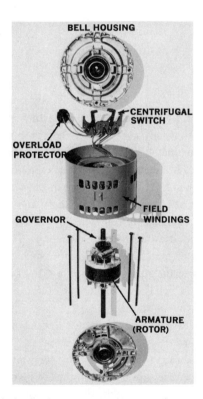

In typical split-phase motor, governor on the armature or rotor controls the centrifugal switch, which serves to break circuit to the starting windings when the motor approaches normal running speed. Many motor housings in newer appliances are sealed, but use an external centrifugal switch that may be replaced without disassembling the motor.

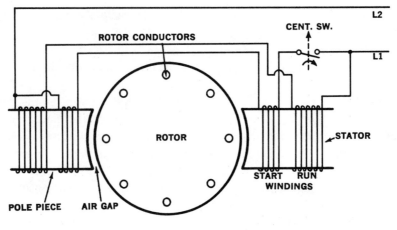

SPLIT-PHASE MOTOR

switch or relay to open the starting winding circuit when the speed of the rotor reaches approximately 80 percent of synchronous speed. If a centrifugal starting switch is used, the opening is controlled by a mechanical governor attached to the rotor shaft. If a relay is used, it is usually controlled by the amount of current draw of the motor windings. The relay must be matched to the motor, since it is set to open the start contacts at a rate of current draw which is a characteristic of that motor at a particular speed.

Solid-state semiconductor devices are now used as relays in some equipment, and are available as replacements for relays and starting switches in existing motors. When replacing a starting switch, the governor is eliminated since the solid-state device is current operated and needs no external mechanism to deactivate it. Such starting devices must always be matched to the type, size, and current rating of the motor to which they are attached.

Split-phase motors and most appliance motors use some sort of overcurrent and overheating protective device, usually referred to as the overload protector. This is a switch which opens the circuit to the motor windings if excessive loads are placed upon the motor, if it overheats, or if for any reason the temperature and/or current draw becomes excessive. Some of these overload protectors are attached to the motor housing, and others are embedded in the motor windings. In either case, they are designed to sense the temperature and the current draw of the motor.

Motors are called upon to turn in either clockwise or counterclockwise directions, depending on their applications. A split-phase motor can be reversed by changing the relationship of the start and running windings. Many single-speed motors can be reversed by simply removing the terminal cover and swapping the winding leads at terminals provided for this purpose.

HOW SPLIT-PHASE MOTORS ARE REVERSED

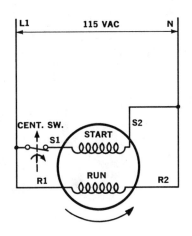 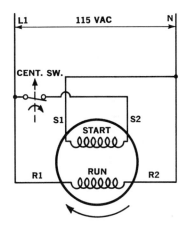

This diagram shows how split-phase (and some capacitor motors) are reversed by changing the relationships of the starting winding to the running winding. Sometimes this is done with a timer, as it is in many automatic washing machines, using the contacts to change the connections; at other times, it is done with a reversing switch; and often, it must be set to the correct rotation for the application of the motor by removing the cover plate and changing the connections on a terminal board.

In diagram at left, the starting winding lead marked *S1* is connected to the centrifugal switch, which in turn is connected to *L1*; starting winding lead *S2* is connected to the neutral line, designated *N*. The running winding leads *R1* and *R2* are connected to *L1* and *N* respectively.

In diagram at right, the leads from the starting winding have been reversed. *S1* is now connected to *N* and *S2* is now being fed from *L1*.

Note that *R1* and *R2* remain connected to the same line input in both instances. If these were also reversed, the motor rotation would not change because the relationship between the running and starting winding connections would not be changed.

CAPACITOR MOTORS

A major improvement on the split-phase motor is the capacitor-start motor. In this motor, a capacitor is placed in series with the starting winding. The effect of the capacitor is to cause the current in the starting winding to lead the running phase voltage, obtaining a greater displacement angle between the running and starting windings. The result is that the well-designed capacitor-start motor has twice the starting torque of a standard split-phase motor, yet line current at start is some two-thirds less.

Some larger refrigeration compressors (found primarily in air-conditioning units) use capacitor-start capacitor-run motors. This motor has the running capacitor permanently connected in series with the start winding and in parallel with the starting capacitor. At start-up, the capacitance of both are added to the circuit to obtain a high starting torque. When the motor reaches approximately 80 percent synchronous speed, the centrifugal switch

Capacitor-start motors are easily recognized by the presence of the starting capacitor, often secured directly to the motor housing. To check capacitor, it is only necessary to remove the screws securing the capacitor cover. If motor leads were disconnected at terminal board, you don't have to unsolder lead at capacitor. *Discharge capacitor per special instructions before handling.*

opens and the starting capacitor is dropped out of the circuit. The running capacitor remains in, giving the motor a higher running torque.

The capacitor serves as a "storehouse" for electricity; when it is applied correctly, it can give an extra punch to the circuit. This is the role that it plays when used with electric motors.

Permanent-split-capacitor motors are used in many larger air-conditioning systems. Both the running winding and the starting winding, with its starting capacitor connected in series with it, are permanently connected to the line at all times. The major difference is that no starting switch is used with this motor. The same capacitance is used during starting and running operations. The large capacitor causes a phase shift: when current is high during the starting operation, the starting winding acts as a conventional starting winding. As the motor

speed increases, the current decreases, and the starting winding begins to act like a running winding. Compared to the capacitor-start and the capacitor-start capacitor-run motors, the PSC motor has low starting torque and must be used in applications where little starting torque is required.

SHADED-POLE MOTORS

These are used on some small fans. They require both a stator and rotor, but the stator has a slot cut into its face. Within this slot is a coil of wire which must form a closed circuit or loop. It is not connected directly to the line. The main field windings are then wound around the remainder of the field pole piece. When these coils are energized, a magnetic field is set up between the pole pieces and the rotor. A portion of the magnetic field is also

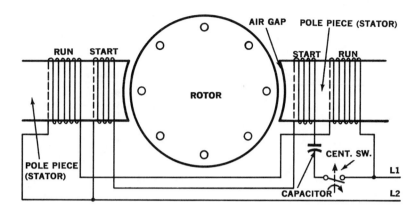

CAPACITOR-START MOTOR

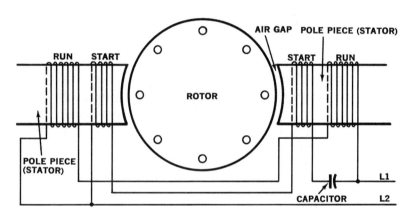

PSC MOTOR

cut by a portion of the shading coil. The lines of force which are cut by the shading coil are slightly out of phase with the remainder of the lines coming from the pole piece. This shift, slight as it is, is sufficient to start the small motor. Because of its low starting torque, the motor is limited to such applications as small fans. Speed is not constant and can vary over a wide range depending on the load and the applied voltage.

UNIVERSAL MOTORS

Used in many portable appliances, universal motors can be recognized easily by the presence of carbon brushes which attach the wound rotor to the line and the field coil.

The windings are arranged so that as the current alternates, the polarity changes from north to south and vice versa. By changing the polarity of the field action on the rotor, the

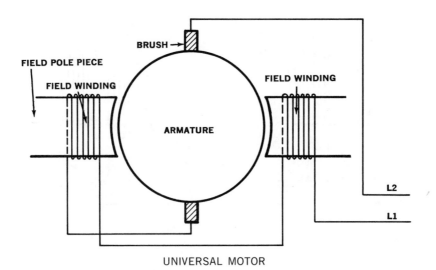

FIELD POLE PIECE
FIELD WINDING
BRUSH →
FIELD WINDING
ARMATURE
L2
L1

UNIVERSAL MOTOR

rotor begins to turn. It is called a universal motor because it is designed to operate equally well on either alternating current (AC) or direct current (DC).

To supply the current to the rotor (called an armature in the universal motor), a device called a commutator is used. The commutator reverses the connection to the conductors in the armature at the instant that the current in the conductors is reversing. Each end of the armature conductor loop is connected to one segment of the commutator, and each segment is insulated from the adjacent ones.

Carbon brushes (which are conductors) are held against the commutator by spring pressure. They are set so that current flows from one end of the conductor into the brush and out into the other end of the loop. This occurs regardless of the direction of current flow, and current flows in one direction only through the brushes.

The no-load speed of universal motors is high, usually around 3500 rpm. It can be made adjustable by using a variable resistor placed in series with one lead of the motor. This controls the amount of magnetic flux in the motor and the speed of rotation. The control used on sewing machines is a good example of this.

Another method of speed control is through the use of a governor connected into the circuit with the motor. This consists of opening and closing the circuit to the stator while the motor is in operation. Centrifugal force obtained from the motor armature rotation is used to open or close the governor contacts. In a sense, the motor controls itself. This method maintains constant voltage and higher torque than the variable resistor. The "solid state" controller acts in much the same manner, using a SCR to switch pulses of current on and off very rapidly to control motor speed. Varying the timing of these pulses alters the motor speed. This type of control is widely used on portable power tools.

The point at which the governor opens can be preset, usually by a knob or slide lever. Below the speed at which the opening point is set the contacts remain closed.

Tapped field windings are used on many small appliances to control the speed of a universal motor. With this system, the field coil is entered at several points and a lead is provided which goes to the switch. The number of speeds depends upon the number of taps. As a lesser number of coils are energized, the magnetic field becomes weaker and the speed (and the torque) is reduced. Only *one* of the taps should be energized at any given time. The switch is designed to break the circuit to one as it energizes another.

Still another method of controlling the speed of universal motors is called the brush-shift method. The physical position of the brushes is actually changed to cause the speed of the armature to vary as the brushes move to or away from the neutral position.

SYNCHRONOUS MOTORS

Small synchronous motors are used on some clock timers and on appliance control timers. These small motors have a rotor in which the poles are slotted to accept small bars of copper or brass. Unlike large synchronous motors, which must be externally started and excited by a DC power supply, these small motors start easily with alternating current. Because of their constant-speed characteristics, they are ideally suited for their application in home appliances.

FINDING THE PROBLEM

Once you have isolated the motor as the source of a problem in an appliance, you'll probably have to remove it to pin down the problem. The chances are good that you will be able to repair it yourself.

A visual inspection is the first step. Look closely at the terminal board where the leads

This synchronous timer motor can be observed in action through "window" in cover, shown removed in photo. With cover off, rotor can be rotated manually and cleaned or straightened if necessary. Use *R × 100* scale for checking tiny windings in motors like this.

enter the motor. Broken leads and loose terminals are often the source of motor failures—but hardly a cause for replacement. Check to see that the motor shaft is turning freely after belts or other devices that connect it to the drive mechanism are removed. If it doesn't, or if the previous tests fail to turn up a solution, the motor must be disassembled.

The motor housing consists of three basic parts: the body, which contains the field windings; the bell housings (there are two of these); and the rotor or armature. The bell housings are the end plates of the motor. In most motors, four long bolts hold this assembly together. Before the bolts are loosened, it's a good idea to mark the housing at each end bell to make sure that it can be realigned exactly as it came apart. You can do this with punch marks at the point where the end bell and housing meet, or you can simply make scratches on the housing that carry over to the end bell or even use a permanent felt-tip pen. Regardless of the method you choose, make two marks at one end and one at the other so you align the proper bell with the correct end of the housing.

Some appliances made within recent years use a "T-frame" motor which is sealed and inaccessible. The centrifugal switch is mounted on the outside of the housing, but all other components are inside and nonserviceable. Their record is a good one thus far, however, and in most cases small motors can be replaced about as inexpensively as they can be rewound.

After the through-bolts are removed and the housing marked, it's time to "split" the motor. Note carefully the number and placement of any spacer washers on the rotor shaft—they should be replaced in exactly the same order.

If it might be several days before the motor is reassembled, you might even go so far as to make a rough sketch of the parts as they are removed.

Bearings can be replaced in most motors which can be disassembled. Most larger towns have distributors who specialize in bearings; look in the yellow pages of your telephone directory under the heading "Bearings." If you install them yourself, be sure to press them in place carefully using a wooden block to protect the surfaces. If you take the motor to a motor shop for the job, the charge for bearings and the labor is usually quite reasonable.

The centrifugal switch is often mounted to the rear of the terminal board. A close inspection of the contacts will usually reveal any problem. Check the governor assembly on the rotor shaft to see that it is not binding and that the springs and flyweight linkages are not damaged.

The windings can be checked with the VOM, using the $R \times 1$ scale. If a starting winding is used, it is necessary to isolate it from the running winding. This can usually be done at the terminal board, but it is sometimes necessary to unsolder a connection. Before removing any leads, it is wise to tape both the lead and its terminal with adhesive tape and number or otherwise mark it. It is imperative that these leads be replaced on the correct terminal.

The leads should indicate continuity through each individual winding, but not to each other—if they do, they are shorted together. The resistance will be low, but should not be 0, using the $R \times 1$ scale. If the insulation on a winding has broken down (this is the condition often referred to as a "burned winding"), it will usually be visible as a darkened

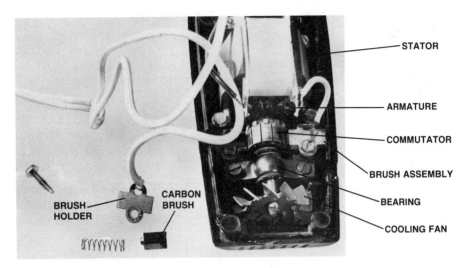

STATOR

ARMATURE

COMMUTATOR

BRUSH ASSEMBLY

BEARING

COOLING FAN

CARBON BRUSH

BRUSH HOLDER

Photo of motor in food mixer shows brush holder with brush removed. To clean commutator, use sandpaper only and burnish with hardwood block. Never use emery cloth.

area when compared to the other windings. It may also have an acrid odor.

A final test for the windings is to test for grounds from each lead of each winding to the motor housing, using the highest resistance scale on the VOM. No reading should be noted.

If there is a malfunction in the windings, the best bet is to replace the motor. It seldom is economical to have fractional horsepower motors rewound.

The motor capacitor is tested by turning the VOM to the *R × 100* scale and checking between the terminals of the capacitor *after discharging the capacitor with a 20,000-ohm resistor*. The needle of the meter should rise and then fall back toward infinity. Reversing the leads should repeat this sequence. If a resistor is attached across the terminals of a starting capacitor, it may still be tested in this manner by either making a resistance allowance in the reading or by disconnecting one side of the resistor. While this is not a sure-fire test (a

special capacitor tester can tell you the exact capacitance of the capacitor), I've seen only a very few problems that this test wouldn't pinpoint.

The physical difference between running capacitors and starting capacitors is usually quite obvious. The starting capacitors found in appliances are usually 3 to 5 inches long, 1 to 1½ inches in diameter, and have a dark Bakelite housing. Running capacitors are 6 to 18 inches long and 3 to 4 inches in diameter (they are usually rectangular or oval in shape) and have a metal housing. If the housing of a capacitor is distorted or leaking, it should be replaced.

If you have opened up a universal motor, you will also find the brushes and commutator inside the housing. Replace the brushes if they are ⅓ inch or less in length. Check the commutator carefully, and use care in handling it. Clean it with a soft, dry cloth before reinstalling it, and if it is scratched polish the surface with a hardwood stick. If the mica insulation

123

between the commutator segments is above the level of the copper segments, it can be undercut by using a broken hacksaw blade. This is a condition known as "high mica," and it can cause severe arcing between the brushes and commutator. Be sure that the brushes move freely in their holders when reassembling the motor.

If you encounter a problem with the small synchronous motor used in a timer, test the windings first (the only two leads into the motor). Use the $R \times 100$ scale on the meter. If they test okay, look closely for a cover which can be pried from the rear of the timer. Many of these motors have one. Remove the cover and examine the small rotor carefully for damage, dust, or lint which may be keeping it from operating. If the small shaft in the center of the rotor has become gummed, a very light oil (one drop only) on the shaft has kept many of them in operation for years.

RULES FOR THE USE AND CARE OF AN APPLIANCE MOTOR

• Keep motors free of dust and lint which can restrict the flow of air across their windings. Vacuum them at least once a year.

• Lubricate motor bearings (where caps or ports are provided) on a regular basis, usually once a year unless otherwise recommended by the manufacturer. Use recommended lubricant, or SAE 20 non-detergent oil if no special lubricant is specified.

• Don't overtighten belts. This can cause premature bearing failure. Be sure that belt and motor pulley are in alignment.

• Replace brushes when they no longer make good contact with the commutator in universal motors.

• Follow the manufacturer's instructions for loading and using appliances. Overloading places undue strain on the motor and drive assemblies and can lead to early failure.

QUICK-CHECK CHART FOR

SPLIT-PHASE MOTORS

Symptom	Possible Cause	Remedy
Won't run—no sound	Fuse blown or circuit breaker open	Check with VOM, replace or reset. Time-delay fuses are usually recommended on circuits with major appliance motors
	Overload protector open	Locate and check protector with VOM. Protector must be cool before reading can be obtained. Use R × 1 scale
	Open windings	Test with VOM, inspect visually. Unless *both* windings were open, motor would hum. Use R × 1 scale
	No power to motor	Check for broken leads and terminals on incoming line. FOLLOW SPECIAL INSTRUCTIONS FOR MAKING VOLTAGE TEST IF IT IS ABSOLUTELY NECESSARY
Won't run—makes humming sound. May also click on and off on overload protector.	Low voltage	Check by FOLLOWING SPECIAL INSTRUCTIONS FOR VOLTAGE TEST at receptacle. Voltage must be within ten per cent of nameplate rating. Check with appliance in operation
	Overloaded	Check to see that appliance mechanism is not jammed by turning manually or by removing belt from motor
	Bearings frozen	Turn motor manually. If bearings locked or broken, disassemble and replace
	Centrifugal switch open	Disassemble motor and check switch contacts with VOM set to R × 1 scale. File contacts if pitted using automotive point file
	Overheated	See symptom "Motor starts and immediately clicks off"
	Winding open	Test with VOM on R × 1 scale for open or grounded winding.
Motor starts and immediately clicks off or shuts off after a few seconds. May blow fuse.	Centrifugal switch sticking in closed position or governor not opening switch	Check operation of centrifugal switch and governor. Clean contacts with automotive file or replace switch if contacts are welded together. Use R × 1 scale on VOM to check contacts—should read 0 ohms resistance

SPLIT-PHASE MOTORS *(cont.)*

Symptom	Possible Cause	Remedy
	Motor overheated	Openings in motor housing restricted by lint and dust, blocking air flow. Vacuum clean Overloaded. Check appliance drive mechanism as described previously Bearings binding. Remove belt and rotate rotor by hand. Check for free movement. Be sure that bearings are lubricated Rotor dragging on stator. Check for worn bearings
	Windings shorted	Check with VOM on R × 1 scale as described in text. Look for cause: worn bearings, over-loading, defective starting switch, subjected to moisture or chemicals such as detergents. If windings are burned severely, an acrid smell and smoke may be noticed
Windings burned: symptoms vary, but are usually associated with smoke and/or odor. Fuse may blow	See "Windings Shorted" above	See above
Motor noisy	Worn or damaged bearings Not aligned with appliance drive mechanism Broken or damaged governor Loose laminations in field or part of rotor causing interference with stator. Dirt or foreign object in air gap.	Disassemble and check. Check for proper lubrication Check to be sure that motor pulley or sprocket is in alignment Disassemble and check. May usually be detected by turning rotor manually before disassembling Disassemble and check Disassemble and clean as necessary

QUICK-CHECK CHART FOR

CAPACITOR MOTORS

Symptom	Possible Cause	Remedy
Won't run—no sound	Fuse blown or circuit breaker open	Check with VOM, replace or reset. Time-delay fuses are usually recommended on circuits with major appliance motors
	Overload protector open	Locate and check protector with VOM. Protector must be cool before reading can be obtained. Use R × 1 scale
	Open windings	Test with VOM, inspect visually. Unless *both* windings were open, motor would hum. Use R × 1 scale
	No power to motor	Check for broken leads and terminals on incoming line. FOLLOW SPECIAL INSTRUCTION FOR MAKING VOLTAGE TEST IF IT IS ABSOLUTELY NECESSARY
Won't run—makes humming sound. May also click on and off on overload protector.	Low voltage	Check by FOLLOWING SPECIAL INSTRUCTIONS FOR VOLTAGE TEST at receptacle. Voltage must be within ten per cent of nameplate rating. Check with appliance in operation
	Overloaded	Check to see that appliance mechanism is not jammed by turning manually or by removing belt from motor.
	Bearings frozen	Turn motor manually. If bearings locked or broken, disassemble and replace
	Centrifugal switch open	Disassemble motor and check switch contacts with VOM set to R × 1 scale. File contacts if pitted using automotive point file
	Overheated	See symptom "Motor starts and immediately clicks off"
	Open start capacitor (capacitor start motors)	Check with VOM as described in text. Replace if open, shorted or grounded
	Open windings	Check with VOM on R × 1 scale. Replace motor if open
	Open running capacitor (PSC motors)	Check with VOM as described in text. Replace if shorted, grounded or open
Motor turns slowly, lacks power	Open running capacitor (PSC motors)	See previous remedy
Motor lacks starting torque	Shorted starting capacitor (capacitor start motors)	Check with VOM as described in text. Replace if open, shorted or grounded

QUICK-CHECK CHART FOR

CAPACITOR MOTORS *(cont.)*

Symptom	Possible Cause	Remedy
Motor starts and immediately clicks off or shuts off after a few seconds	Centrifugal switch sticking in closed position or governor not opening switch (capacitor start motors)	Check operation of centrifugal switch and governor. Clean contacts with automotive file or replace switch if contacts are welded together. Use R × 1 scale on VOM to check contacts—should read 0 ohms resistance
	Motor overheated	Openings in motor housing restricted by lint and dust, blocking air flow. Vacuum clean. Overloaded. Check appliance drive mechanism as described previously
Bearings binding. Remove belt and rotate rotor by hand. Check for free movement. Be sure that bearings are lubricated.
Rotor dragging on stator. Check for worn bearings
	Shorted running capacitor (PSC motors)	Check with VOM as described in text. Replace capacitor if grounded, shorted, or open
	Defective overload protector	Have current draw of motor tested; will require ammeter test, can be done at any motor shop. Replace protector if current draw is less than rating of protector
	Windings shorted	Check with VOM on R × 1 scale as described in text. Look for cause: worn bearings, overloading, defective starting switch, subjected to moisture or chemicals such as detergents. If windings are burned severely, an acrid smell and smoke may be noticed
Windings burned: symptoms vary, but are usually associated with smoke and/or odor. Fuse may blow	See "Windings Shorted" above	See above
Motor noisy	Worn or damaged bearings	Disassemble and check. Check for proper lubrication
	Not aligned with appliance drive mechanism	Check to be sure that motor pulley or sprocket is in alignment
	Broken or damaged governor	Disassemble and check. May usually be detected by turning rotor manually before disassembling
	Loose laminations in field or part of rotor causing interference with stator.	Disassemble and check
	Dirt or foreign object in air gap.	Disassemble and clean as necessary

QUICK-CHECK CHART FOR

UNIVERSAL MOTORS

Symptom	Possible Cause	Remedy
Won't run—no sound or attempt to turn	No power to receptacle	Check with table lamp. Check fuse or circuit breaker if doesn't light
	No power to motor	Check motor control or governor for continuity using R × 1 scale. Check all leads and terminals
	Brushes not making contact with commutator	Worn or sticking brushes. Replace if worn. If sticking, check condition of brush holder and spring tension
	Dirty commutator	Sand lightly with sand paper, *never with emery cloth* which is a conductor. Burnish with hard-wood stick
	Open windings	Test with VOM, inspect visually. If *either* winding is open in field motor will indicate open circuit. Use R × 1 scale
Won't run—makes humming sound or attempts to start	Drive mechanism jammed	Check and free problem in mechanism
	Brush making poor contact	See "not making contact" above
	Dirty commutator	See "dirty commutator" above
	Bearings frozen	Turn motor manually. If bearings are locked or broken, replace them. Take to motor shop for test
	Shorted rotor (armature)	on growler. Inspect visually. Replace if shorted.
Excessive arcing at brushes	High mica	Check armature for roughness. Undercut mica insulator between commutator segments with broken hacksaw blade
	Weak brush springs	Check condition of springs
	Distorted brush holder	Check condition of brush holder
	Worn brushes	Check and replace if badly worn
	Dirty commutator	See dirty commutator above
	Shorted armature	See "shorted armature" above
	Loose commutator bars	Replace armature
Burned windings	Overloading	Check condition of mechanism attached to motor
	Worn bearings	Replace as necessary
	Moisture	Replace windings—this condition may be caused by immersing in water to clean the appliance
	Solder or bar slinging off armature damaging fields	Replace both armature and fields if damage is severe

QUICK-CHECK CHART FOR

UNIVERSAL MOTORS *(cont.)*

Symptom	Possible Cause	Remedy
Excessive brush wear	Weak brush springs Dirty commutator High mica Overloading Governor not operating correctly	Check condition of springs See previous remedy See previous remedy Check condition of mechanism Check for binding rotor caused by dry or damaged bearings, foreign object in air gap, appliance mechanism binding. Also check for burned contacts or binding governor mechanism. Light oil applied to governor mechanism (not contacts) allowed to soak for several minutes and then wiped clear should free it
Motor noisy	Worn or damaged bearings Not aligned with appliance drive mechanism Broken or damaged governor Loose laminations or commutator bars causing interference with stator. Dirt or foreign object in air gap. Loose fan or armature	Disassemble and check. Check for proper lubrication Check to be sure that motor is in alignment with mechanism Disassemble and check. May usually be detected by turning rotor manually before disassembling Disassemble and check Disassemble and clean as necessary Repair if possible — this condition usually requires armature replacement

130

QUICK-CHECK CHART FOR
SHADED-POLE FAN MOTORS

Symptom	Possible Cause	Remedy
Won't run-no sound (hum may be hard to detect in small motors)	No power to motor	Check receptacle with table lamp. Check leads and motor control (if any) for continuity
	Open windings	Check with VOM set to R× 100 scale
Won't run-makes humming sound	Bearings frozen	Lubricate or replace as necessary (some of these motors are sealed and cannot be disassembled)
	Fan blade locked or binding	Check for free movement, clean and free as necessary
Motor noisy	Loose or damaged bearings	Lubricate or replace as necessary
	Fan blade making contact with part of cabinet or grill	Check and free as necessary
	Fan blade hub loose	Replace fan blade or secure hub
	Loose internal parts	If possible to disassemble, check and repair as necessary

QUICK-CHECK CHART FOR
SYNCHRONOUS TIMER MOTORS

Symptom	Possible Cause	Remedy
Won't run (Be sure that power is reaching motor- FOLLOW INSTRUC- TIONS FOR MAKING VOLTAGE TESTS AND DO SO ONLY IF ABSOLUTELY NECESSARY TO MAKE TEST)	Open windings	Check with VOM set to R × 100 scale. if open, replace motor
	Rotor binding on cover	Check cover for dents or nicks. Remove (if possible) and straighten cover or align rotor. Reinstall cover
	Jammed mechanism	Many of these motors are attached to built-in, non-serviceable gear trains. Check for evidence of binding or slipping in gear train. Replace motor assembly if defective
Noisy	Rotor tapping damaged cover	Check for dents or nicks in cover. Remove (if possible) and straighten cover or align rotor. Reinstall cover
	Defective gear train	See "jammed mechanism" above

11
Repairing Small Appliances with Motors

Motors of practically every type are found on small home appliances. Those with clocks and timers use a synchronous or shaded-pole motor. Many smaller and lower-power appliances use a shaded-pole motor, primarily for turning fans. Larger fans use capacitor-run, permanent split capacitor, and even split-phase motors. Many electric shavers are powered by a contact-point "motor" which is simply a vibrator.

But you'll find that the great majority of small appliances that you will be called on to service make use of the universal motor because of its high-speed and high-torque characteristics. The motor consists of a wound field (the stator, or nonmoving part) and a wound armature (the rotor, or revolving part), which are wired in series. To pass electrical current from the stationary field to the moving armature, carbon brushes rest against a circle of copper bars, the commutator, at one end of the armature.

After long use, these brushes may have to be replaced. Always check to see that a brush moves freely in its holder without binding. The field windings may be checked for continuity in the usual manner, and should be checked for grounds, also. If your tests do not indicate the problem, take the armature to a shop specializing in motor repair for testing.

Bearings should be cleaned and lubricated when removed. Burned windings, as well as many other motor defects, are usually visible on examination.

There are four motor-speed control methods: In one type, a variable resistor (rheostat) may be placed in the line ahead of the motor. This regulates the amount of current flow in the line and limits motor speed. A second method shifts the brushes mechanically, which also limits the speed of the rotor. Third, the windings may be tapped at certain points, varying the resistance (and thus the current flow) to control the speed.

In the fourth, a governor may be employed, which is arranged through a mechanical linkage to travel a certain distance within the speed range of the motor. At one end of the

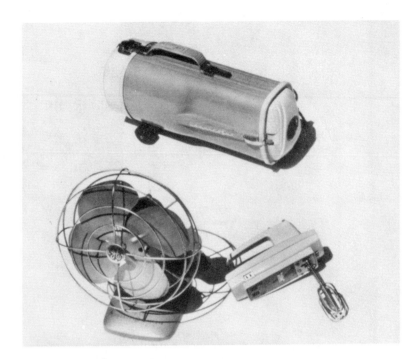

Typical motor-
driven appliances

linkage there is an adjustable control plate with contact points that control the motor circuit. When this plate is positioned toward the governor, the linkage will open the points at a certain speed; then, as the rotor slows, close them again. This happens so rapidly that it gives the effect of limiting the motor speed. The solid-state control is a variation of this, allowing a portion of the cycle of alternating current to pass. The length of the interruptions determines the operating speed.

In a motor-driven appliance, the motor and its speed-control device may be the only electrical components in the appliance. The appliance might be a combination of motor-drive and resistance heat. An example of this is a hair dryer. Both electrical sections of this appliance would be treated individually when testing or diagnosing the problem.

It is usually easy to pinpoint the appliance's problem as either mechanical or electrical without taking it apart, or at the most by taking off only the cover. Then attempt to operate it manually by turning the motor shaft or by turning the mechanism. If the mechanism is binding or slipping, you've found the source of the problem.

If you find that it is necessary to disassemble the mechanism, be sure and note the position of each part as you remove it. It's not a bad idea to make a rough sketch or drawing showing the location of each part, numbered by the order in which you disassemble it. Be particularly observant of the location of any spacers

REPAIR STEPS FOR ELECTRIC HAIR STYLER
ARE TYPICAL FOR A SMALL APPLIANCE

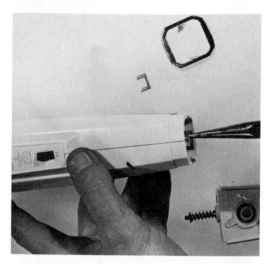

These photos made during the repair of an electric hair styler show some of the things to look for in repairing a small appliance. A grill at rear of housing was removed by first turning out two screws, an obvious procedure. Chrome trim at front of motor was then removed by prying two tabs from housing, then slipping trim off.

Removal of U-shaped retainers from front of plastic housing was next step. However, the housing still would not part. So it was necessary to look closer. The final elusive retainer was found as shown here—under the switch decal. The decal is adhesive-backed, but can be reused. In such appliances, styling features often hide screws and retainers. So you have to look closely.

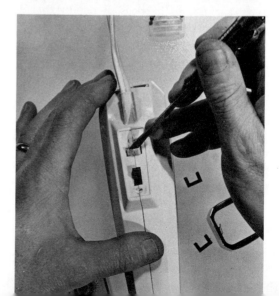

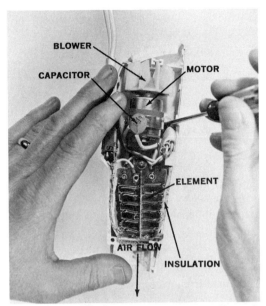

Here the problem is solved. The unit had been dropped on a countertop, causing the motor to slip in its retainer and jam against the housing. Loosening the retaining band and repositioning the small motor restored the operation. Be sure that all insulation and shields are in place before reassembling such a unit.

Inside view of rotisserie motor drive train illustrates how sufficient torque and slow movement is obtained from small shaded-pole motor. Coil of motor can be tested with VOM after removing one of soldered leads, but aside from lubrication of a noisy gear train there is little service you can perform since parts aren't readily available. It's worth a look however—the only problem may be a gear out of position or a loose rivet.

or shims which are taken out. These must go back in the same order.

If you discover a worn or chipped gear, don't stop your investigation until you determine whether this occurred during normal use or if it was caused by jamming elsewhere in the mechanism. If you don't uncover every defect, you may have to repeat the repair job.

If you replace a broken or chipped component in a mechanical-drive assembly, be sure to clean away all of the particles and pieces that are left. Varsol (available from most dry cleaners) used in a well-ventilated area is a good solvent to flush away oil and particles. A solution of liquid dishwashing detergent and water can also do a good job of cleaning, but keep it away from electrical components.

In many cases, bearings may be pressed into the frame of a small appliance. Sometimes they are actually cast into the frame and cannot be replaced. But if they are pressed in, they are usually available as a replacement part. Otherwise, it is necessary to buy the casting to which the bearing is attached, but it is still worthwhile if you are doing the job yourself.

If the bearing is a press fit, check the parts

list that came with the appliance or check with a servicing dealer to see if it is available. Do this *before* you attempt to remove it.

If the pressed-in bearing can be removed, it is done easily enough by boring a hole slightly larger than the outside diameter of the bearing in a block of wood. Then, locate a piece of pipe, tubing, or even a socket the same size as the bearing. Place the housing or casting on the block of wood with the bearing over the hole, then hold the pipe directly on top of the bearing and tap it out.

When replacing the bearing, you can use a small vise as a press after covering the jaws with a block of wood. Lubricate the outside of the bearing before pressing it into place, place the housing and bearing in alignment between the jaws, and turn the vise slowly and smoothly until the bearing is seated.

When reassembling an appliance, remember that cleanliness is important. Dirt and grit left in will make your repair job short-lived. Lubricate with clean lubricant of a type specified by the manufacturer. Some makers package their own lubricants for use in gearboxes of mixers, polishers, etc. If no specific lubrication instructions are provided, here are general guidelines that will serve the lubrication needs of many such appliances:

1. The motor bearings often have oil holes which are accessible from the outside of the housing. A few drops of SAE 20 nondetergent motor oil every twelve to sixteen hours of use should keep these bearings well lubricated.

2. Gearboxes should be cleaned and flushed thoroughly before refilling. Fill the gearbox approximately one-half full of a grease such as Gulf #3 or its equivalent.

When you've finished the job on a motor-driven appliance, take your VOM and check for grounds *before* trying it out, just as you should with any appliance. Turn the control switch on with the equipment unplugged. Then read from each prong on the plug to the housing with the meter set to the highest resistance scale. There should be no reading. Be sure to make this same test with the control switch on the appliance set to each of its positions.

Double-insulated equipment (found mostly in power tools) *must* be returned to the factory or to an authorized service center for repair. Special tests must be conducted on the tools before they can be released after a repair.

The foregoing information applies generally to all small motordriven appliances. We now are ready to consider repairs to specific small appliances that you may have in your home.

FOOD MIXERS

Home food mixers cover a wide range of chores—often with other attachments, such as a juicer and knife sharpener. This calls for substantial power and a means of varying speed.

A universal motor is used. A worm drive

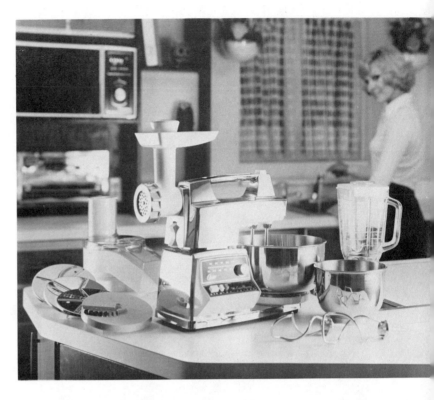

An Oster stand mixer with
bowls and accessories.

machined into the armature shaft drives two
gears. These usually incorporate the socket for
the beater shaft. If attachments are used (as
they often are on a tabletop mixer) another
shaft may extend from the gears to the top of
the unit. The second shaft serves for power
takeoff.

Small mixers which have a limited number
of speeds (usually three) most often use a
tapped-field method for speed control. Larger
mixers with infinite or large number of speeds
use governor control or the brush-shift
method of control. When a governor is used,
a capacitor is often connected across the contacts to reduce arcing. The governor can be the
source of some unusual problems, as you will
notice in the quick-check chart. Solid-state

controls are used on some newer blenders.
These work by passing only a portion of each
cycle of alternating current; the faster the
speed, the larger the portion of the cycle that
is fed to the motor. If the control should be
open or shorted so the mixer runs at a constant
speed or does not run at all, the entire control
unit should be replaced.

You service most mixers by "splitting" the
housing. Look for screws under the housing,
then separate the two halves. The motor, governor, and bearings should be visible. Sometimes the gear drive is open; in other models
it is enclosed within a housing. Clean away
crumbs, grease, and other matter by wiping
the surface with a clean cloth. A detergent
solution can be used on all but electrical parts

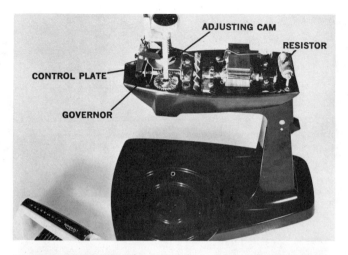

ADJUSTING CAM

RESISTOR

CONTROL PLATE

GOVERNOR

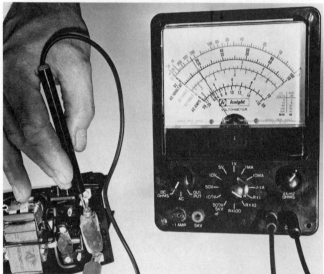

Centrifugal force exerted by a motor-mounted governor regulates speed in this mixer. Contact points on control plate shunt across resistor and apply full line voltage to windings. When governor motion opens contacts, voltage must pass through resistor, shown being tested for continuity (center). Thus motor slows, and rapid opening and closing of contacts on adjustable control plate regulate speed. Capacitor, connected across contacts to reduce arcing, is tested in same way for continuity, except that meter should rise quickly, then fall back. (Discharge capacitor first.) Switch in mixer is checked for continuity (bottom). Most three-speed mixers of this type have tapped field windings to vary motor speed. Observe proper wiring connections when replacing parts, such as switch. Some appliances may have plugs on outside of housing which retain brushes in holder.

Gears on this Westinghouse mixer are matched by dots. When replacing, set one dot opposite the two-dot marking on opposite gear. This insures proper timing of beaters.

and bearings. If the motor is disassembled, mark each component in the order in which it is removed. When reassembling, put one drop of SAE 20 motor oil on the inner surface of each bearing. Look for notches or retainers on the bearings.

Check the condition of governor contacts carefully. If pitted, they can often be restored to service by filing with an automotive point file and burnishing. If brush holders must be replaced, it will often be necessary to unsolder one lead and resolder it to the new holder. Be sure that the governor mechanism is not binding. A drop of oil on the pivot points, allowed to soak for a minute and then wiped away, will usually cure any problems.

QUICK-CHECK CHART FOR REPAIRING A FOOD MIXER

Symptom	Possible Cause	Remedy
Motor will not run	No voltage to receptacle	Check with table lamp
	Defective cord or terminal connection	Test and inspect—replace as necessary
	Governor contacts open	Replace if burned or bent. Some mixers use separate switch—replace if open
	Broken wiring connection	Repair as necessary
	Brush sticking or brush holder broken	Inspect and replace brush or holder—be sure new brush seats properly
	Armature binding	Inspect bearings—motor will hum if binding
	Open field windings	Test with meter and replace if open
Cannot adjust motor speed	Governor linkage sticking	Free linkage and springs
	Governor contacts not opening	Check for welded contacts—replace control plate
	Shorted capacitor	Test with meter—good capacitor should cause meter needle to sweep forward and fall back, repeat with leads reversed; no resistance indicates short
Mixer makes loud noise or knocks	Worn bearings	Lube dry bearings, replace scored ones
	Chipped tooth in gear train	Inspect and replace damaged gears
Beaters won't revolve—motor runs	Stripped gear or broken coupling	Inspect drive assembly and replace damaged components
Mixer shocks user	Grounded component or connection	Check with meter and isolate ground—do not use appliance until repaired

If you are replacing the beater gears, look for timing marks to set them in a position so the beaters will not hit. Some mixers use the same gears for right and left sides, but they will have two timing marks, usually marked 1 and

2. Don't align identical marks: set 1 opposite 2.

Beater blades can usually be straightened, but the shafts are hard to align so they won't hit. If the beater is badly bent, replace it.

ELECTRIC BLENDERS

Electric blenders consist of two distinct sections. The base contains a universal motor, speed control (usually by the tapped-field method in conjunction with a push-button switch), and a coupling device attached directly to the rotor of the motor. The coupling is often made of rubber and is sometimes threaded to the shaft with a left-hand thread. To loosen the coupling, remember to turn it in the direction of motor rotation. The coupling is designed so that the upper section, the container with the blade unit or cutter unit within it, can be removed by lifting it from the base.

Some motors are removed by loosening a large hex nut which extends through the top of

the base. Most, however, are accessible through the bottom. Look closely for any screws or nuts on the bottom of the base. They are often located inside the rubber feet.

The cutter unit is threaded to the bottom of the container, making it easy to remove for cleaning. If this unit is disassembled, be sure that all shaft seals and spacers are reassembled in order. If bearings or seals become worn, it's usually best to replace the cutter blades as a unit.

Be sure to reinstall the treated-fiber motor shield when the motor is serviced. This prevents dust and crumbs from entering the motor housing easily.

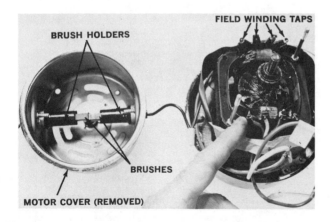

Blender uses tapped field windings to vary speed. Be sure that all shields are back in place before reassembling motor base. Brushes are accessible after base is removed.

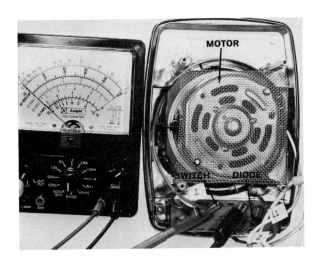

Multi-position switch is tested with VOM on *R × 1* scale. Mark leads with tape before removing when replacing switch. Contacts should measure 0 resistance. Diode should pass current in one direction only. If it gives high reading with leads in one direction and low when leads are reversed, it's okay.

QUICK-CHECK CHART FOR

BLENDERS

Symptom	Possible Cause	Remedy
Motor will not run	No voltage to receptacle	Check with table lamp, replace fuse or reset circuit breaker
(See 'Universal Motors in text, chapter 10)	Defective cord or terminal connection	Test and inspect with VOM on R × 1, replace cord if open or damaged
	Broken wiring connection	Inspect visually and repair as necessary
	Open switch	Test with VOM on R × 1 for continuity with switch in "on" position. Test with switch in each speed position of selector switch
	Brush sticking or brush holder binding	Inspect and repair or replace as necessary
	Open windings	Check with VOM R × 1 scale. Check each lead of tapped winding

Chart cont. on next page.

BLENDERS *(cont.)*

Symptom	Possible Cause	Remedy
	Overloaded — motor or blender blades locked or binding	Remove container (with blade assembly) and try motor. If it runs, problem lies in blades or bearing. *Be sure that blade unit is clean;* syrups and juices can "glue" it together. Soak in hot detergent water solution should cure problem. If seals are bad or bearings worn or locked, replace cutter unit
Motor runs, cutter won't turn	Loose or stripped coupling	Remove container and see if coupling turns when light force is applied manually. Some couplings are threaded to motor shaft with left hand threads. To loosen, hold shaft and turn coupling opposite direction of motor rotation
Lacks power	Brushes worn Brushes not making good contact with commutator or commutator dirty Cutter unit binding	Inspect and replace as necessary Inspect brush condition and holder. Clean commutator and burnish Clean and inspect, replace if worn
Arcing at commutator	Brushes worn or not making good contact	See "brushes not making contact" above
Excessive noise	Damaged motor or cutter unit loose	Visually inspect motor and cutters, repair as necessary
Leaks from container	Seal in cutter unit worn or damaged Damaged gasket	Remove cutter unit and inspect. Replace seals or unit if defective Check gasket on cutter unit, replace if torn or damaged

FOOD PROCESSORS

The food processor might be considered a giant, heavy-duty blender. It uses a heavier motor and often has only a single speed, with a push-and-hold "pulse" switch in addition to the constant-on switch. The blade is also much larger than the one in a blender, and various cutting discs and shredders can be used for slicing and cutting vegetables, cheeses, etc. A safety interlock switch is provided that will not let the motor be energized unless the top is in position.

Check the motor as you would any universal motor, paying particular attention to the condition of the carbon brushes. The switch should be tested with the VOM set on the $R \times 1$ scale. With one of the wires removed, the needle should sweep upscale when the switch is in the "on" position; on the "pulse" position, the needle on the meter should not move. The pulse switch should cause the meter to move upscale when it is depressed; the needle should remain at rest when the switch is in the normal position. The safety interlock switch should be open unless the container and top are installed on the base.

Never operate a processor if the interlock switch is not working, since the power of the motor and sharpness of the blades and attach-

Food processors are serviced like blenders; biggest difference is in size of cutting blades or discs and design of food compartment, which has provision for feeding food in while blades are spinning. Use care when handling cutting surfaces.

ments could be a safety hazard when proper protection is not present.

VACUUM CLEANERS

The heart of a vacuum cleaner is a high-speed universal motor coupled directly to a fan unit. Often two or more fans are "stacked" to increase efficiency.

In a canister vacuum, the fan unit is often inside a metal container that is clamped or staked shut. The entire motor-fan unit is then placed inside the vacuum housing, which is designed to pull air in through a plastic or

Vacuum hoses are often the culprits when poor suction is noted. Twist and flex hose with vacuum running to release any trapped object. Inner hose linings may also become detached, blocking air flow.

woven hose supported with a metal spiral. As the air enters the vacuum, it must pass

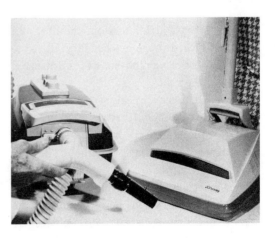

Filter protecting motor from dust and dirt should be replaced at least once a year. Don't let the vacuum bag become overfilled. Even the best filter cannot protect motor from severe dust conditions.

Fan and motor assembly of vacuum cleaners are often made as one unit. Replacement of entire assembly is necessary in case of failure of such a unit. Be sure all seals are in place when reassembling.

through a bag which filters out the dust and dirt, and then through a secondary filter, before it passes through the fans and is exhausted back into the room.

The bag may be a closely woven fabric or a disposable paper bag. In either case, it is designed with enough porosity to allow minimum restriction to air flow without allowing dust to pass through.

The principle of the upright vacuum is the same, but the housing is designed so that the motor unit is on a carriage at floor level. A

handle extends upwards at the rear. The bag is suspended from the handle or is placed within a plastic box that is mounted to the handle. The user guides the vacuum across the floor by pushing or pulling the handle.

The biggest difference between the two types is the presence of a revolving brush on the upright. The brush is placed directly in front of the suction nozzle inlet and is belted to the motor. The brushing action helps pull dirt from carpet fibers.

There are also "combination" vacuums on

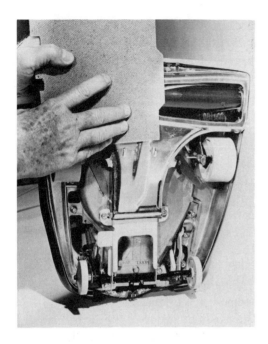

Belts on motor-driven brushes or upright vacuums may slip when worn. Check with vacuum running by applying load to brush, using hardboard. Avoid touching revolving brush.

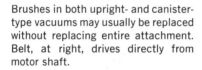

Brushes in both upright- and canister-type vacuums may usually be replaced without replacing entire attachment. Belt, at right, drives directly from motor shaft.

the market. These use a canister vacuum for suction while an accessory tool has a motor-driven revolving brush for use on carpets. These combinations would be serviced in much the same manner as individual units, except that two motors are used—one in the vacuum for the fan unit, the other in the revolving brush attachment for the brush only.

Central vacs are a giant-sized version of the canister, using a power unit located in the basement or other out-of-the-way place that pulls and exhausts through a series of tubes that pass under floors and between walls. Connecting the hose to one of the "suction outlets" in the living area turns on the vac and pulls through the hose. The advantages: more power, more capacity (some hold up to two bushels of collected dirt), and outdoor exhaust.

Switches on all units are usually accessible without disassembling the entire vacuum. Canister types often use foot switches; some of these require loosening a hex nut on the switch, then removing the switch from the inside. Slide switches are found on uprights and combination power units, and these can be removed by first removing one or two screws at the switch itself.

The motor-fan unit is usually held in place by screws or by retainers which are fastened to the housing with screws. Be sure to reinstall all seals which prevent air from bypassing the fan unit. The motor brushes can often be serviced without removing the unit.

It usually serves no purpose to try to remove the container which surrounds the fans. If a fan becomes damaged or loose, the unit (except in uprights where an open fan is used) must be replaced as a balanced assembly.

This points out the importance of protecting the vacuum motor by keeping the filter clean and replacing it regularly. If dirt enters the fan unit, it "sandblasts" the internal parts and can lead to early failure.

If the vacuum bag becomes overfilled, dirt and lint can build up and block the air passageways in the nozzle of uprights and in the hose of canister types. Be sure and remove all of this blockage if you detect an overfilled bag—otherwise, the dirt will build up within the passageways instead of in the bag. Pick up pins, large sticks, etc., before vacuuming—they can lodge in hoses and chutes and you will soon have a buildup there. If a hose becomes clogged, carefully run a length of garden hose or other flexible tube through it from the end that connects to the vac, forcing the blockage back out.

Be sure that any treated-fiber or cardboard shields are back in place around the motor and bearings as you put the vacuum back together. These prevent dust from reaching vital areas which can be easily damaged.

If lint builds up around the revolving brush —especially at either end of the brush—the lint should be removed. If belts become slick or cracked, they should be changed. Be sure to clean the motor pulley and brush pulley first to remove particles of old belt and any other foreign matter which could cause the new belt to slip and wear quickly.

QUICK-CHECK CHART FOR
REPAIRING VACUUM CLEANER

Symptom	Possible Cause	Remedy
Motor will not run	No voltage to receptacle	Check with table lamp
	Defective cord or terminal connection	Test and inspect—replace as necessary; check closely at plug and strain relief
	Broken switch	Check continuity—should get reading with switch on, none with it off
	Brush worn or sticking; brush holder broken	Replace as needed; be sure curved end of brush seats firmly on commutator
Motor noisy	Broken fan or foreign material in fan	Inspect and replace or clean
	Worn bearings	Lubricate or replace as necessary; in sealed motor-fan unit, replace entire unit
Lack of suction at cleaner	Bag full	Clean—also inspect filter
	Filter clogged	Should be replaced twice a year
	Broken fan	Inspect and replace as necessary
	Air leak at housing	Inspect seals—tighten or replace
Lack of suction at hose— okay at cleaner	Leak in hose or connection	Inspect, cement all fittings
	Lining in hose loose or separated	Replace hose
	Clogged hose	Put on blower end of vacuum—if still clogged, run flexible tube through
Rug attachment or upright vacuum not cleaning carpet	Worn or broken belt or brush	Inspect and replace as necessary
	Brush drive motor inoperative	Check motor and wiring connections
	Vacuum suction low	Check as in suction symptoms

COOLING FANS

Fans are in again as a low-energy method of finding cool comfort on hot days. GE's 16-inch oscillating fan has push-button controls, automatically turns 45 degrees to right and left.

Home cooling fans qualify as the simplest of all motor-driven appliances. In basic form a fan consists only of a motor and a blade attached directly to the motor shaft.

In smaller fans, the shaded-pole motor is the primary type used although universal motors have been used in some models. As fans become larger in size, split-phase and PSC motors are often used. All of these, with the exception of the universal motor, have low starting torque. Since the starting load is relatively low anyway, it's a good application.

Some fans use a reactor, a device like a transformer, to vary speed of the motor. It is "tapped" at several points to allow a different speed according to the portion of the winding selected. It can be checked for continuity with the VOM on the $R \times 100$ scale by reading

from the common lead (one end from the incoming line will usually be attached here) to the other leads going to the switch. If there is no continuity, the reactor is open and should be replaced. Others use a variable resistor to change the voltage into the motor.

Table fans often have a small gearbox to allow the fan to oscillate. This is linked from the motor head to the base. If gears become worn and have to be replaced, the assembly should be repacked with a light grease.

Larger fans such as window fans often use tapped windings to vary the speed of a PSC motor. They are serviced by removing the grill, then removing the motor assembly or the control cover. Since a running capacitor is used on these models, be sure to check it if the fan won't start or turns slowly. Discharge the

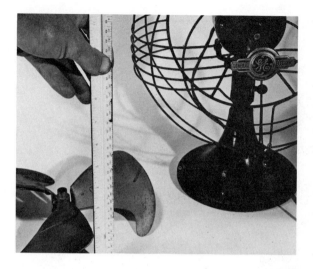

Fan blades should be handled carefully to avoid disturbing their pitch. Check pitch by removing blades and placing on flat surface. Measure height of blade tips. Measurement should be same on all blades.

Oscillation of fan head strains wiring connection to base. Check each conductor for continuity. Gearbox that causes fan to oscillate may become worn; replacing gears or assembly is only solution.

capacitor first with a 20,000-ohm 2-watt wound resistor (available from any radio-TV parts supplier). With the VOM on the $R \times 100$ scale, read from the two capacitor terminals. The meter needle should rise, then fall back to a lower reading. This should repeat itself when the leads are reversed. If not, or if a ground reading is obtained, replace the capacitor.

In even larger applications, such as attic fans, a split-phase motor with starting switch is sometimes used. This appliance adds three additional components; the starting switch, the belt, and the mandrel (shaft and bearing assembly) which turns the fan. Oil the motor and the mandrel yearly if oil caps or ports are provided, and vacuum lint accumulations away. Avoid overtightening the belt; ½- to

Shaded-pole fan motor is tested by placing test leads on motor leads. *R × 100* scale should be used for most of these small motors. Be sure that rotor is free and that bearings are clean.

QUICK-CHECK CHART FOR
REPAIRING AN ELECTRIC FAN

Symptom	Possible Cause	Remedy
Motor will not run	No voltage to receptacle	Check with table lamp
	Defective cord or terminal connection	Test and inspect—repair as necessary; check cord from base to fan head
	Reactor open	Test for continuity with meter
	Switch broken	Should have continuity with switch on, none with switch off
	Brushes worn (if used)	Inspect and replace as necessary—many small fans use no brushes
	Windings open	Check with VOM on R × 1. Replace if open
	Variable resistor open	Check with VOM on R × 100
Fan is noisy	Blade bent or damaged	Inspect and realign as necessary
	Motor bearings dry or worn	Lubricate or replace
Will not oscillate	Worm gear worn	Check gear mechanism—replace broken or badly worn gears
	Linkage broken or damaged	Inspect and realign, or replace
Fan turns only at low speed	Reactor defective or switch open	Check to see if 115 volts present with selector at high position; check between motor and base
	Motor bearings dry and binding	Lubricate
	Blade loose on motor shaft	Tighten
	Capacitor open (PSC motors)	Check with VOM, replace if open or grounded

¾-inch deflection with moderate pressure between the pulleys is fine.

Since large quantities of air move through fans, their motors are more subject to linting than most. Make lint cleaning regular maintenance. Oil regularly if oiling ports are provided. If a fan seems to be off-balance and vibrating, check it as soon as possible. If the condition is not corrected, the bearing life will be greatly reduced and the equipment will not be pleasant to use in the meantime.

Use caution when checking fans. Keep hands and fingers away from revolving blades, and be sure that grills are in place when the fans are in use.

Preventative maintenance is most important phase of home-appliance repair. Clean, well-lubricated fans run for years without failure. A few drops in each oil port is sufficient for a year's operation. Keep lint cleaned from openings in motor.

FLOOR POLISHERS

Floor polishers use a universal motor to drive a pair of revolving brushes to scrub and polish the surface of a floor. (Some commercial models use a capacitor-start motor to drive a single brush through a gear box.) A worm gear is machined into each end of the armature shaft on many such polishers intended for home use. Each worm turns a large drive gear, which also contains the socket for the brush spindle in its hub. The gearing reduces the speed of the motor to a slower, more powerful speed at the brush.

Most home polishers are furnished with several brushes and polishing pads. It is important that the correct brush is used for the job. If the polisher has more than one speed, it's also important that the correct speed be selected. Failure to do so can damage the motor by overloading it.

All of the component parts will be found in the head of the polisher except the switch, which is in the handle. The switch can usually be removed by removing two screws which hold it in position. The other components can be serviced by removing the bottom cover plate of the head.

Since a double-shaft armature is used in many units, the right and left drive gears are often not identical and not interchangeable. Many armature bearings have a slot to locate them. Look for it. Be sure that spacers and shims are properly positioned when reinstalling an armature, and check for binding before starting it.

With motor shielding removed, works of this floor polisher are easily accessible for servicing. Before base can be removed from housing, handle must first be removed. Look for retaining screws on handle socket and for large nut inside socket at base.

QUICK-CHECK CHART FOR

FLOOR POLISHERS

Symptom	Possible Cause	Remedy
Motor will not run (See Universal Motors in text, chapter 10)	No voltage to receptacle Defective cord or terminal connection Broken wiring connection Open switch Brush sticking or brush holder binding Open windings Overloaded—motor or gear train locked or binding	Check with table lamp, replace fuse or reset circuit breaker Test and inspect with VOM on R × 1, replace cord if open or damaged Inspect visually and repair as necessary Test with VOM on R × 1 for continuity with switch in "on" position Inspect and repair or replace as necessary Check with VOM on R × 1 scale Inspect by turning manually, locate and repair or replace damaged part
Motor runs, floor brush won't revolve	Broken or stripped gear or socket	Inspect visually, repair as necessary. Lubricate when reassembling gear train
Floor brush won't stay in socket	Worn or broken socket	Inspect for tight fit with floor brush spindle. If loose, replace socket. It is often combined with drive gear
Lacks power	Brushes worn Brushes not making good contact with commutator or commutator dirty Gearbox binding	Inspect and replace as necessary Inspect brush condition and holder. Clean commutator and burnish Inspect and repair or lubricate as necessary
Arcing at commutator	Brushes worn or not making good contact	See "brushes not making contact" above
Excessive noise	Damaged gear or motor	Visually inspect motor and drive train, repair as necessary

ELECTRIC HAIR DRYERS

Hair dryers are either hand-held or portable units, the latter usually equipped with a plastic hose and a hood. The motor and heating elements of portable dryers are located in a base which is placed on a table alongside the user. A variation of this type has a rigidly attached hood that protrudes from the base, much like the dryers found in beauty salons. Hand-held models consist of a housing, which contains the motor and elements, and a "snoot" to direct the warm air.

In most hair dryers, a shaded-pole motor drives the fan, although a few hand-held units use a universal motor. Several heat ranges are available, obtained by using a dual heating element, with one side typically double the wattage of the other. A four-position switch can give the following functions: cool, fan only with no heat; low, low-wattage element on; medium, high-wattage element on; and high, both elements on. On stationary dryers, this can be 400–500 watts; handheld dryers go up to 1400 watts, approaching the limit of a con-

ventional household circuit's capacity. The fan, of course, is working at all times when the heater is in operation.

If a fan fails to work due to a malfunction or blockage, the heaters must be controlled safely. This is accomplished by using a bimetal thermostat near the heating element. Any restriction of air flow, which allows the heaters to become abnormally hot, will open the bimetal and shut the heaters off until the unit has again cooled.

When servicing a hair dryer, clean all passageways thoroughly with a vacuum. Be sure to use heat-resistant wire whenever it is necessary to repair the wiring harness. If the bimetal thermostat replacement comes with a shield or bracket, use it when replacing the bimetal; this

GE's Do-It Dryer has six separate heat/air speed settings for fast blow-drying or soft styling. Powerful portable hair dryers like this use up to 1400 watts; be sure nothing else is plugged into same circuit when in use to prevent blowing fuse in electrical panel.

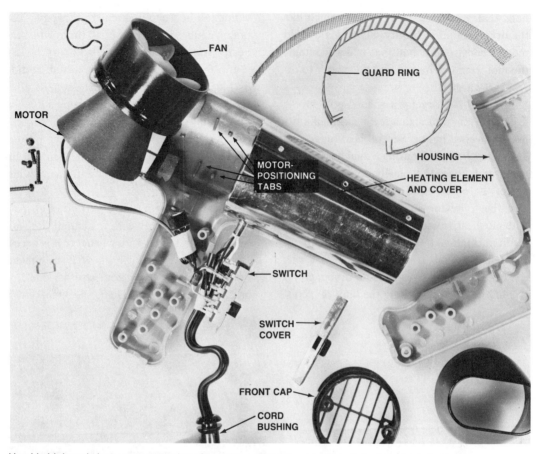

FAN

GUARD RING

MOTOR

MOTOR-
POSITIONING
TABS

HOUSING

HEATING ELEMENT
AND COVER

SWITCH

SWITCH
COVER

FRONT CAP

CORD
BUSHING

Hand-held dryer is just compact version of portable unit less hose and hood. Arrangement of components in this exploded view is typical. Some hair dryers of 1970s used asbestos as insulation for element. If you're unsure about yours and it is of this vintage, discontinue use and consult manufacturer for instructions.

locates it properly and assures proper operation.

Switches used in hair dryers often make use of self-locking terminals. The end of the conductor is pushed into place (although it should be tinned with solder first) and is held firmly by a spring that provides the electrical connection. To release one of these locks, look for a tab or opening directly behind the point where the wire enters the switch. Press a small screwdriver into the opening. With the spring lock held down, the wire can be withdrawn for testing the switch. *Caution:* Some hair dryers have been constructed using a shield of asbestos to insulate the heating element from the housing. This has been determined to present a hazard in the form of asbestos fibers which can be inhaled; dryers containing the material should not be used. It is hard to tell whether the insulator is asbestos or a substitute material from its appearance. If you suspect that your dryer may contain this material, and you find no markings that indicate that it does not contain asbestos, check with the manufacturer before using it.

QUICK-CHECK CHART FOR

ELECTRIC HAIR DRYERS

Symptom	Possible Cause	Remedy
Won't run at all	No voltage to receptacle	Check with table lamp, replace fuse or reset circuit breaker
	Defective cord or terminal connection	Test and inspect with VOM on R × 1, replace cord if open or damaged
Heats, motor won't run	Broken wire or terminals to motor	Inspect and repair as necessary. Check leads for continuity with VOM on R × 1
	Selector switch contacts to motor circuit open	Check contacts with VOM on R × 1 scale. Should indicate continuity
	Open motor windings	Check motor with VOM on R × 100 scale. If open, replace motor assembly
	Motor binding	Check for hairpins, etc
Motor runs but no heat	Safety thermostat open	Check with t'stat at room temperature. Should indicate 0 ohms resistance with VOM set to R × 1 scale
	Heating element open	Check for continuity with VOM on R × 1 scale. If open, replace element
	Broken leads or terminals to heating element	Inspect and repair or replace leads as necessary. Use only heat-resistant wire
Motor runs but no air flow	Fan slipping on motor shaft	Inspect for damage, tighten or replace fan
	Air passageways blocked	Inspect and clear as necessary
Noise	Fan out of balance or striking cabinet	Inspect and adjust fan positioning on motor shaft
Overheats	Restricted air flow Defective safety thermostat	Check and clear passageways Check with VOM on R × 1 while heating with match. Replace if does not open

PORTABLE ELECTRIC HEATERS

Since convection-type portable electric heaters have a blower to circulate heat within the room, I am classifying them as a motor-driven appliance. This blower is used in conjunction with a reflecting panel, usually chrome-plated sheet metal, to take advantage of radiation as well as convection. The blower circulates air behind the panel and out into the room through openings in the front grill. A shaded-pole motor turns the fan.

An adjustable thermostat is often used to control the heat range, turning the element assembly on when the room temperature drops below a designated point. These thermostats aren't marked with definite degrees, since the location of the heater will have a great deal of effect on the immediate temperature. Rather, they are intended to serve as reference points. When you find a setting that suits your

Hottest energy-saving appliance around is the electric quartz heater; it's used for spot heating after turning main heating system's thermostat down. Elements enclosed in quartz tube raise heat output to radiant levels; pleasant warmth can be felt almost immediately, even in cold room.

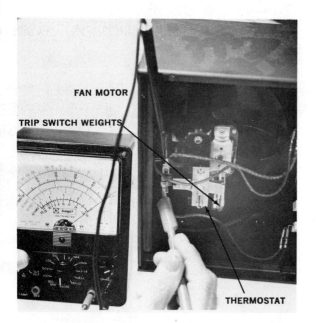

FAN MOTOR

TRIP SWITCH WEIGHTS

THERMOSTAT

Controls and fan are located at air intake end of most heaters. Keep lint and dust cleaned away from fan motor; check it at least twice a year if it sees heavy use. In this photo, meter is clipped to thermostat leads to read continuity. Since contacts of tip switch are part of the same circuit, it checks them at the same time.

desires and your installation, you can turn it to that point whenever you are using it.

Some heaters also have a switch to call various wattages into play. This can be quite useful if the heater is used in several different locations and if it is used on a circuit where the available current is limited. Two heating elements are often used in combination to provide the heat ranges. Typical ratings might provide stages of 1000, 1300, and 1600 watts.

Some heaters use a section of nichrome wire as voltage-dropping resistors to change the heat output. They are mounted near the main element, suspended on insulators, and appear like a short section of nichrome element wire.

Most units have a "tip switch," usually a weighted arm pivoted at the top which controls the action of a set of contacts. If the heater is tipped over, the contacts break and shut the heater off.

The heater should be checked and cleaned

each year. If dirt bakes onto the reflecting surface or blocks air passages, the efficiency of the heater will be greatly reduced. Oil the fan motor with non-detergent SAE 20 motor oil if openings are provided at the bearings.

Three types of elements are used. One of these is a nichrome coil, often wrapped around a ceramic block. In many heaters without a fan (radiant heaters) this has a base like a light bulb, and is simply screwed into the socket or an element enclosed in a quartz glass tube. Other heaters may use a nichrome ribbon strung out over porcelain insulators, and still others use elements enclosed in a metal sheath. When removing an element, be sure not to stretch the wire if it is in coil form. When the new element is in place, adjust it so that no sags or sharp bends are present.

Thermostats should be replaced as an assembly. In addition to cleaning the contacts, the calibration of most thermostats can easily

Reflective panel on electric heater helps reflect radiation into room area. Ribbon-type elements on this heater are suspended from porcelain blocks.

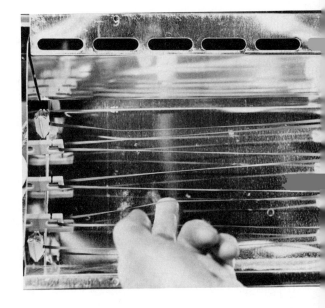

QUICK-CHECK CHART FOR
PORTABLE ELECTRIC HEATERS

Symptom	Possible Cause	Remedy
Won't run at all	No voltage to receptacle	Check with table lamp; replace fuse or reset circuit breaker
	Defective cord or terminal connection	Test and inspect with VOM on R × 1, replace cord if open or damaged
Heats, motor won't run	Broken wire or terminals to motor	Inspect and repair as necessary. Check leads for continuity with VOM on R × 1
	Selector switch contacts to motor circuit open	Check contacts with VOM on R × 1 scale. Should indicate continuity
	Open motor windings	Check motor with VOM on R × 100 scale. If open, replace motor assembly
	Motor binding	Check for accumulation of dust, etc. Clean and lube motor bearings
	Thermostat open (safety or oper.)	Check using R × 1 scale. Replace if defective
Fan runs but no heat	Broken leads or terminals	Inspect and repair or replace leads as necessary. Use only heat-resistant wire
	Voltage dropping resistors open	Check with VOM, replace if open
	Heating element open	Check for continuity with VOM on R × 1 scale. If open, replace element
	Broken leads or terminals to heating element	Inspect and repair or replace leads as necessary. Use only heat-resistant wire
Motor runs but no air flow	Fan slipping on motor shaft	Inspect for damage, tighten or replace fan
	Air passageways blocked	Inspect and clear as necessary
Noise	Fan out of balance or striking cabinet	Inspect and adjust fan positioning on motor shaft
Overheats	Restricted air flow	Check and clear passageways. Check fan motor
	Defective safety thermostat	Check with VOM on R × 1 while heating with match. Replace if does not open

be done since most of them are open-type controls. Since the thermostat settings are relative, however, calibration is seldom necessary.

Be sure to use heat-resistant wire for all connections inside the heater and an approved heater cord for replacing the cord. Don't try to repair an element by twisting it. Ribbons can be purchased as a set when replacing them in baseboard and other ribbon-element heaters.

Electric quartz heaters have found wide acceptance as energy-saving devices when used as spot heaters. They allow you to turn the thermostat of your central heating system down to a low level and use the portable heater for additional warmth only in the area you're inhabiting. Depending on the extent of the routine you're willing to follow, the savings potential of such a program can be significant.

Quartz heaters don't put out any more heat than any other kind. They deliver 3.412 Btu's of heat for every watt of power consumed, like any electric resistance heater. The difference is in the type of heat they produce. The quartz glass tube surrounding the heating element allows it to reach higher temperatures than conventional elements. This, plus a highly polished reflector (usually vertical), produces radiant heat. Unlike convection heat, which heats objects in a room indirectly by first heating the air, the heat energy from radiant heat travels through the air with little effect until it strikes an object, which it heats directly. That's why you can walk into a cold room, flip on a radiant heater and, if it's directed toward you, feel a pleasant warmth within seconds.

The reflector on a quartz heater is critical for proper operation because it directs this narrow (around 30-degree) beam of heat energy, and it should be wiped clean regularly. If stained or dirty, it can be polished lightly with the same type of metal polish you would use on silverware.

Most quartz heaters use a pulser type of control rather than a conventional thermostat, although some models have both. The pulser is a timer of sorts, very similar to the infinite heat control on an electric range. A bimetal heater inside the control cycles the elements on and off, increasing the length of the "on" periods toward the high position and making them shorter (and the corresponding "off" periods longer) as it is turned toward low. Contacts and internal heater can be checked with the VOM set to the $R \times 1$ position; if either is open, the control must be replaced.

Replace elements if the glass tube becomes cracked or if the element is damaged. Some models have plug-in elements, although most require removal of the top and bottom covers. Use care not to handle the glass with your hands when replacing an element since any oil deposit can etch and weaken the glass.

ELECTRIC KNIVES

An electric knife uses a universal motor to drive a worm gear that turns a pinion to which the blade sockets are mounted, one on either side. As the pinion turns, the rotary motion is converted to a reciprocal motion by the placement of the blade socket mounts. When the knife blades are slipped into the sockets, they move back and forth.

The blades are joined together, usually by a rivet, and are matched so they make a neat slice through the meat. The edges are rippled to aid cutting action.

The universal motor is usually powered by DC current, developed by a diode in the AC power supply. The diode acts as an electrical check valve, allowing power to flow in one direction but not the other. Cordless units use the same arrangement but have a battery pack in the handle. A charger built into the base keeps the batteries charged when the knife is not in use.

To check the batteries, test them with the motor running if possible. Use the red (+) lead on the positive end of the battery pack and the black lead on the negative end. The battery voltage should be approximately one volt or slightly more when the motor is running.

A GE electric slicing knife.

Close-up of drive assembly on this electric knife shows how worm drives gear to produce reciprocating motion at blade sockets. Drive gears are normally enclosed within housing.

QUICK-CHECK CHART FOR
ELECTRIC KNIVES

Symptom	Possible Cause	Remedy
Motor will not run (See Universal Motors in text, chapter 10)	No voltage to receptacle	Check with table lamp, replace fuse or reset circuit breaker
	Defective cord or terminal connection	Test and inspect with VOM on R × 1, replace cord if open or damaged
	Broken wiring connection	Inspect visually and repair as necessary
	Open switch	Test with VOM on R × 1 for continuity with switch in "on" position
	Brush sticking or brush holder binding	Inspect and repair or replace as necessary
	Open windings	Check with VOM on R × 1 scale
	Overloaded — motor or gear train locked or binding	Inspect by turning manually, locate and repair or replace damaged part
	Diode open	Check with VOM on R × 100 scale. Take reading, then reverse leads and read again. If no reading either way, diode is open; if reads both ways, diode is shorted. Either calls for replacement. If reads low one direction and high in the other, diode is good
Motor runs, blades won't reciprocate	Broken or stripped drive system	Inspect and repair as necessary. Lubricate when reassembling
Blades won't stay locked in	Worn or broken socket	Inspect for wear. If loose or damaged, replace sockets or pinion gear assembly
Lacks power	Brushes worn	Inspect and replace as necessary
	Brushes not making good contact with commutator or commutator dirty	Inspect brush condition and holder. Clean commutator and burnish
	Gearbox binding	Inspect and repair or lubricate necessary
Arcing at commutator	Brushes worn or not making good contact	See "brushes not making contact" above
Excessive noise	Damaged gear or motor	Visually inspect motor and drive train, repair as necessary

The handle is disassembled by removing screws, sometimes hidden under trim plates. Some units are sealed.

Don't try to straighten a bent blade. The blades are a precision fit, and must be replaced with a matched set.

A special lubricant is often recommended for the worm and pinion gears. Other lubricants may seep out onto the blade surface.

ELECTRIC HAIR CLIPPERS

Some professional hair clippers use universal motors to drive the cutting head, but most home models use a vibrator "motor." The vibrator is just what its name implies. A coil sets

QUICK-CHECK CHART FOR

ELECTRIC HAIR CLIPPERS

Applies to both universal motors and vibrators unless designated (U) or (V)		
Symptom	Possible Cause	Remedy
Motor will not run (See Universal Motors in text, chapter 10)	No voltage to receptacle	Check with table lamp, replace fuse or reset circuit breaker
	Defective cord or terminal connection	Test and inspect with VOM on R × 1, replace cord if open or damaged
	Broken wiring connection	Inspect visually and repair as necessary
	Open switch	Test with VOM on R × 1 for continuity with switch in "on" position
	Brush sticking or brush holder binding (U)	Inspect and repair or replace as necessary
	Open windings	Check with VOM on R × 1 scale
	Overloaded—motor or gear train locked or binding	Inspect by turning manually, locate and repair or replace damaged part
	Armature adjusting screw out of position (V)	Adjust armature screw until armature vibrates at normal speed
Not cutting well	Armature adjusting screw not set properly (V)	Adjust armature screw until armature vibrates at normal speed. Check by cutting pieces of small string
	Head needs cleaning	Clean according to manufacturer's instructions. Lubricate. if necessary
	Heads damaged or dull	Replace cutting head. Use matched parts only
Runs, blades don't revolve or reciprocate	Damaged gear train or parts loose	Inspect or repair as necessary

up an electrical field which attracts a spring-loaded armature. The push-pull effect of the magnetic field versus the spring vibrates the armature back and forth. While this motion is slight when compared to the rotary motion of a motor, it is sufficient to drive the blades. An adjustment regulates the amount of spring tension against the armature, which in turn regulates the length and speed of the stroke, within

limits. The adjusting knob or screw is located on the outside housing, where it is easily adjusted. The inner cutting head is attached directly to the motor armature; the outer (or lower) head is stationary.

The housing is easily removed by loosening screws normally found on the underside of the housing. The fields of the vibrator are checked with the VOM on the $R \times 1$ position.

ELECTRIC SHAVERS

The outer blade of an electric shaver serves much like a comb. As the whisker penetrates it, the inner blade (which is attached to a motor that causes it to revolve or reciprocate) comes along and slices the whisker off. The matching surfaces of the blades are critical, but once in use they are largely self-sharpening.

Some shavers use a universal motor to power the blades. It is similar to such motors

used in other appliances, only smaller than most. It is easily recognized by its brushes. Other shavers use some type of vibrator. A coil sets up a magnetic field which attracts a spring-loaded armature. The push-pull effect of the magnetic field versus the spring vibrates the armature back and forth. This is a tiny amount of motion as measured in distance, but the action is very fast and sufficient for the job. By using various linkages with the vibrator, a

Vibrator-type motor is used on this electric shaver. When coil is energized, armature vibrates back and forth. Pivot point of armature is arranged to gain maximum effect from movement. Blade attaches directly to fingers at top of motor assembly.

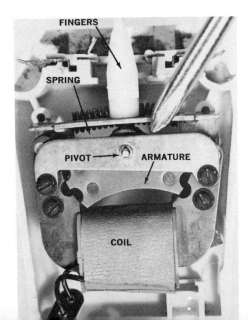

back-and-forth motion can be obtained at the blades.

A variation of the vibrator is the contact-point motor. This uses a coil, controlled through a set of contacts linked to the arma-ture. As the spring-loaded armature moves in one direction, the contact is broken and a quick return begins. As it moves in the other direction, another contact is closed and the armature moves again. Point adjustment is critical.

The armature in vibrator motors does not

QUICK-CHECK CHART FOR

ELECTRIC SHAVERS

Applies to both universal and vibrator types unless designated (U) or (V)		
Symptom	Possible Cause	Remedy
Motor will not run (See Universal Motors in text, chapter 10)	No voltage to receptacle	Check with table lamp, replace fuse or reset circuit breaker
	Defective cord or terminal connection	Test and inspect with VOM on R × 1, replace cord if open or damaged
	Broken wiring connection	Inspect visually and repair as necessary
	Open switch	Test with VOM on R × 1 for continuity with switch in "on" position
	Brush sticking or brush holder binding (universal motors only) (U)	Inspect and repair or replace as necessary
	Battery dead (rechargeable cordless shavers only)	Check on 24 volt DC scale on meter. Be sure that + terminal is matched to + (red) lead from meter.
	Open windings	Check with VOM on R × 1 scale
	Overloaded—motor or gear train locked or binding	Inspect by turning manually, locate and repair or replace damaged part
	Armature or contacts out of adjustment (V)	Adjust until armature vibrates at normal speed
Not cutting well	Heads damaged or dull	Replace cutting head. Use matched parts only
Runs, blades don't revolve or reciprocate	Damaged gear train or parts loose in gear train	Inspect or repair as necessary
Battery won't charge (cordless types)	Battery charger defective	If serviceable, check with VOM on R × 1 scale. Replace charging unit if open
	Battery dead	Check as above, replace battery if charger has DC output at terminal (+ is usually center post) but battery will not charge

rotate—it simply vibrates back and forth much like a buzzer. Some of these motors are started with a thumbwheel.

You may have to look closely for the screws or clips which hold the case of a shaver together. Often they are located in the head and are accessible after removing the blades. Always clean a shaver thoroughly when it is disassembled.

Cordless units have the same motor arrangements but have a built-in battery. A storage base has a built-in charger and keeps the battery charge built up when the shaver is not in use.

The batteries can be tested (if they are accessible) by using the 10-volt DC scale on the VOM. Test them with the shaver running, if possible. Use the red (+) lead on the positive end of the battery and the black lead on the negative end. The voltage should be one volt or better per battery when the motor is running.

The charging unit can be tested by using the 24-volt DC scale and measuring at the socket which the razor contacts when in the charger. The reading will depend on the rating of the battery pack. If no voltage is present, the charger base should be replaced.

ELECTRIC CAN OPENERS

Electric can openers use a shaded-pole motor to drive a sprocket gear which rotates a can under the cutting blade. It is similar in operation to a manual can opener except for the motor drive.

Since the shaded-pole motor is low in starting torque, a gear train is used to reduce the speed and increase the power to usable proportions. This is accessible after removing the cover. Screws which retain the cover are

Reduction gearing is necessary to gain power to open can from the low starting torque of the shaded-pole motor. If gears are damaged or broken, they must be replaced. Be sure to check condition of bearings on older units — wear can adversely affect gear alignment.

Grinding wheel attached to end of armature on this can opener makes two appliances in one. Housing is slotted to position knife correctly. Nut holds wheel on shaft.

located on the back or under the base.

The sprocket and cutter wheel should be cleaned regularly. A soap and water solution applied with an old toothbrush does a good job, although several applications may be required for sticky and gummy deposits. When either sprocket or wheel is replaced, be sure to note the positions of any spacers and reinstall them in the same order. If the cutter wheel is replaced, the larger of the beveled edges should be to the inside.

The motor can be tested by using the VOM set to the $R \times 1$ scale. If the coil is open, the motor should be replaced. Switches which control the unit are actuated by an extension of the handle or the drive assembly. When the can is open, the opener shuts off. The adjustment of these switches is made by moving the mount on an elongated slot.

The usefulness of many can openers is extended by mounting a sharpening stone on the rear of the motor rotor. A series of slots in the housing positions a knife correctly for a fine hollow-edge grind. The grinding wheel is held to the rotor shaft with a nut. Models with grinding wheel attachments should be cleaned more frequently than conventional models, since the filings can accumulate and find their way into bearings or motor windings.

QUICK-CHECK CHART FOR
ELECTRIC CAN OPENERS

Symptom	Possible Cause	Remedy
Won't run at all	No voltage to receptacle	Check with table lamp, replace fuse or reset circuit breaker
	Defective cord or terminal connection	Test and inspect with VOM on R × 1, replace cord if open or damaged
	Switch open	Check to see if switch is adjusted properly. Some models require can to be in position before unit will run. Use empty can to check. Replace switch if open when tested manually with VOM on R × 1 scale.
	Open windings in motor	Check on R × 1, replace if open.
Motor runs, sprocket-wheel won't turn	Gear broken or stripped	Replace gear
	Worn bearings prevent gears from meshing	Replace bearing (or casting if bearing is non-replaceable)
Not cutting cans	Sprocket gear worn	Inspect and replace. Install any spacer washers in same position as removed
	Cutter wheel damaged or worn	Inspect and replace wheel. Note position of spacers or shims. Larger beveled edge of cutter goes to inside
Abnormal noise	Damaged gear train	Visually inspect condition of gears, replace any that show signs of damage
	Loose fan on rotor of motor	Inspect and retighten fan or replace armature

ELECTRIC SHOE POLISHERS

A portable electric shoe polisher is much like a portable food mixer with one beater. It uses a universal motor, sometimes with a tapped winding to provide a second speed. The rotor has a worm machined into it which drives a gear that contains the socket for the shoe brush spindle.

The polisher is disassembled by "splitting" the housing. The retaining screws are usually located on the bottom side of the housing.

The driven gear requires replacement only if it becomes stripped or broken, or if the socket becomes worn. It may be held in place with "C clips" at the socket. When replacing the gear and parts, be sure to note the position of any washers or thrust bearings and reinstall them exactly as they were removed.

Stationary models have buffers at each end.

These use more powerful universal motors with dual shaft extensions, eliminating the necessity for a gear train.

A Sears electric shoe polisher.

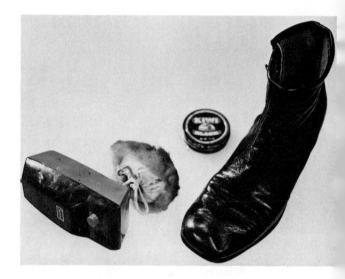

Universal motor drives single gear to turn shoe brush on Sears polisher. Ejector rod passes through center of gear to push brush spindle from socket. Motor's frame casting also incorporates gearbox into unit.

QUICK-CHECK CHART FOR REPAIRING
ELECTRIC SHOE POLISHERS

Symptom	Possible Cause	Remedy
Motor will not run (See Universal Motors in text, chapter 10)	No voltage to receptacle	Check with table lamp, replace fuse or reset circuit breaker
	Defective cord or terminal connection	Test and inspect with VOM on R × 1, replace cord if open or damaged
	Broken wiring connection	Inspect visually and repair as necessary
	Open switch	Test with VOM on R × 1 for continuity with switch in "on" position
	Brush sticking or brush holder binding	Inspect and repair or replace as necessary
	Open windings	Check with VOM on R × 1 scale
	Overloaded—motor or gear train locked or binding	Inspect by turning manually, locate and repair or replace damaged part
Motor runs, shoe brush won't revolve	Broken or stripped gear	Inspect visually, repair as necessary. Lubricate when reassembling
Shoe brush won't stay in place	Worn or broken socket	Inspect for tight fit with shoe brush spindle. If loose, replace socket
Lacks power	Motor brushes worn	Inspect and replace as necessary
	Brushes not making good contact with commutator or commutator dirty	Inspect brush condition and holder. Clean commutator and burnish
	Gearbox binding	Inspect and repair or lubricate as necessary
Arcing at commutator	Brushes worn or not making good contact	See "brushes not making contact" above
Excessive noise	Damaged gear or motor	Visually inspect motor and drive train, repair as necessary

CLOCK-TIMERS

A clock-timer consists of a small shaded-pole or synchronous motor that drives a face dial indicating the time, and a cam that operates a switch. The clock is often graduated into day-night intervals. It can be used to switch small appliances on and off (as can the timer on a range). It can also be used to control various lamps when you're away from home.

Some of these units are not serviceable. Others may be disassembled by removing screws from the rear of the housing. The motor may be tested by placing the VOM across the two motor leads with the function switch set to the *R × 100* scale. It should indicate continuity. The motor can be stalled by dust and lint, so be sure that the rotor is free.

The switching portion can be tested by using the *R × 1* scale and testing across the closed contacts. If the contacts are badly pitted, they should be filed with an automotive contact file and burnished. If they are in bad condition, the timer or contact section should be replaced. Since these units are relatively inexpensive, repair parts are not generally available. Often, however, no parts are needed; a simple cleaning and perhaps a drop of oil will

restore them to operation for many years.

Digital clocks are of two types: mechanical and electronic. Mechanical types use drum, flip-leaf, Ferris-wheel, and tape movements. Compared to conventional clocks, they have the advantage of large, legible, direct readouts. Electronic clocks use illuminated, segmented panels to display the time. They have no motor, but are controlled by an electronic-clock circuit that "counts" the individual pulses on the 60-cycle-per-second power supply. When used in conjunction with control circuits on appliances, they are often combined with light-touch switches for programming machine functions such as wash cycles and cooking times. Such clocks usually cannot be repaired unless the entire circuit board is replaced, but are very reliable and extremely accurate.

Digital clock from General Electric features Ferris-wheel mechanism that rotates readout numerals smoothly and slips them quietly into place. Plaques have numerals on both sides.

This General Electric clock-timer plugs directly into outlet, then appliance or lamp plugs into timer receptacle.

12
Understanding and Repairing Water Heaters

Water heater tanks are designed to work at a specific pressure, but for safety each one is tested at a much higher pressure. Note both of these pressure figures on the nameplate of your own tank. Most modern tanks are "glass-lined"—coated inside with porcelain for longer life. Tanks are wrapped in a blanket of fiberglass insulation and are placed within a cabinet for the sake of appearance. New high-efficiency types have very heavy high-density insulation to retain heat, and even have insulating pads at the bottom of the tank to prevent thermal contact with the cold floor.

Tanks usually have a faucet or plug at the bottom for draining if it is necessary to replace an element or otherwise enter the tank. The drain also makes it easy to flush sediment from the bottom at intervals. Do this at least once a year. Severe sediment or mineral buildup in the bottom can lead to loud popping or creaking noises from the tank.

WATER HEATERS AND ENERGY

Your home's water heater consumes more energy than any other device in the home except your furnace. That makes energy considerations important and worthwhile.

You have probably heard the admonitions to turn your water heater's thermostats down to a low level, 120 degrees being the most popular setting (155 degrees was the recommended setting in the days before the energy crunch). It's true that this will make a significant reduction in the heater's power consumption, but it's equally true that you will begin to encounter washability problems with your dishwasher. Many food soils and detergents won't dissolve at temperatures lower than 135 degrees. Your clothes washer may have the same problem to a lesser degree, since its warm water is a proportional mix of hot and cold. With the hot temperature lowered, the "warm" setting may be well within the "cool" or "cold" range, especially during winter months when incoming water temperature is low.

You can compensate for clothes washing by using a higher temperature setting when necessary (and you might be pleasantly surprised that you can use colder water quite satisfactorily for most loads), but the solution to the dishwasher problem is not so simple. At this time, the alternatives are to buy one of the few models that incorporate their own water heater into the dishwasher, or install an in-line water heater in the dishwasher supply line.

The best answer to the temperature controversy is to compromise and set your water heater at the lowest level that provides good dishwashing results. You also may need to set it higher to meet the daily needs of your household; also, since lowering the temperature effectively reduces the capacity of the tank in the sense that there is simply not as much hot water available to mix with cold for showers, baths, etc.

Another partial solution is to be sure that your water heater is as efficient as possible. You'll see all sorts of gadgets promoted to this end. Some are useful; if the cabinet feels warm to the touch, a supplementary insulation kit (available from most building supply firms) is worthwhile; adding insulation to your hot water supply lines can help prevent standby loss. Don't add a timer unless you dote on inconvenience or live in an area where you are charged for power on a time-of-day basis. By heating water during the lowest off-peak rates, a timer can save you money; otherwise, our tests have shown that they benefit you very little.

One new device that shows great potential is a new heat source—the heat pump water heater. This retrofit device is actually a refrigeration system that takes heat units from air in the basement or utility room and transfers it into your water system, using your existing water heater as a storage tank. The advantage is that it can provide almost three times as much heat per watt of power consumed as a conventional element.

CHECKING THE DIP TUBE

Since hot water rises, the hot-water line always leaves the tank from the top. Cold-water lines on many tanks enter at the bottom. In cabinet models the line may enter the side of the cabinet, or it may run through the cabinet alongside the tank to an inlet at the tank bottom. On some models both lines connect to the tank at the very top.

The cold-water line, however, continues as an internal passageway called a dip tube. This leads from the top, where the cold-water line connects to the tank, to a point a few inches above the bottom. It carries all cold water to the bottom of the tank. As the water heats, it rises to the top and is carried away into the home by the hot-water supply line.

From the standpoint of servicing the heater, the dip tube is important. It can lead to a problem called "bypassing," difficult to diagnose when a water heater malfunctions. Bypassing occurs when a dip tube breaks loose from its anchor at the top of the tank or leaks a large amount of cold water at its top seal.

There's an easy way to determine if dip-tube bypassing is limiting your water supply. When

HOW WATER HEATERS WORK

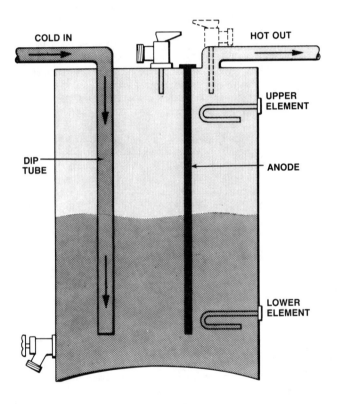

COLD IN

HOT OUT

UPPER
ELEMENT

DIP
TUBE

ANODE

LOWER
ELEMENT

This cutaway drawing illustrates the fundamental operation of a residential water heater. While electric heating elements are used as the heat source here, the operation of a gas burner would be the same except that the burner itself would be located below the tank and a flue would pass through the center or core of the tank.

Cold water flows into the bottom of the tank via the dip tube or into an inlet on the side near the bottom. As the water is heated by the element (only one of the two can be energized at any given time), it rises to the top of the tank. Since pressures are equal throughout the system, cold water automatically takes the place of hot water as it is displaced through usage.

The pressure-temperature relief valve should always be mounted so that its sensing element is exposed to the hottest water in the top of the tank. Most newer heaters have a threaded fitting expressly for this purpose. Lacking this, an alternate method is to install a T-fitting at the hot-water outlet, as shown in dotted lines, using a valve with sensing tube long enough to reach into tank. A drain line no smaller than the opening on the valve should be run to carry the water away from the heater, but not to the outside of the house (see text).

Many water heaters have concave bottoms as shown. This gives great strength and allows maximum flushing action when the drain is opened.

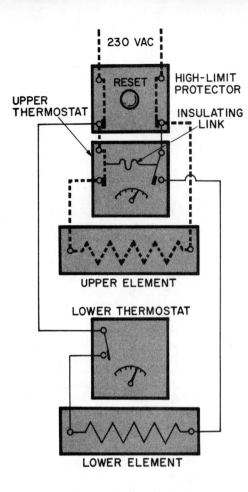

230 VAC

RESET

HIGH-LIMIT PROTECTOR

UPPER THERMOSTAT

INSULATING LINK

UPPER ELEMENT

LOWER THERMOSTAT

LOWER ELEMENT

This diagram is typical of the connections found in many currently produced water heaters. It shows how you may easily add a high-limit protector (available from your dealer) if your heater doesn't have one; it also shows how the two thermostats are utilized to prevent simultaneous operation of both elements.

In any electrical circuit, a path must exist between both sides of the line before current will flow. In this case, each line has a potential of 115 volts measured to ground, but 230 volts across the two lines. If you take this diagram and "draw in" a ground at any point on either element, it's easy to see how a heating element without the high-limit protector can continue to heat on 115 volts even when the thermostat contacts open.

Power flows first through the high-limit protector, a double-pole, single-throw (DPST) "snap-action" device. This means that it is designed to open both contacts of both lines at the same time when a predetermined temperature (normally around 180 degrees) is reached, interrupting all power to the heater. The reset button must then be manually depressed to restore operation.

At the output side of the high-limit protector, the circuit is "split" from each of the two sides, forming parallel circuits to each of the two elements through their respective thermostats. The upper thermostat is a double-pole, single-throw (DPST) bimetal type designed so that when one of its contacts is closed the other is always open, and vice versa. This thermostat is always in operation. Depending upon the demands of the water temperature, it will be furnishing power either to the upper element or to the lower element but *never to both at the same time.*

The lower thermostat is simply a single-pole, single-throw (SPST) bimetal-type thermostat which turns the lower element on and off. However, the upper thermostat must be "satisfied" before the element will be energized, even though the lower thermostat contacts may be closed.

Understanding this operation makes diagnosis of electrical problems easy. In this drawing, you can see that a circuit is completed to the upper element. Looking a little further you can also visualize, for example, that a problem of "not enough hot water" must relate to the lower element or thermostat circuitry—the upper portion would still provide half a tank. Conversely, if the upper element failed the heater would perform normally until the first heavy demand. As soon as the upper thermostat contacts switched to the position to energize the upper element (cold position), it would never transfer back to the lower element (hot) position since the upper element is inoperative and could provide no heat. The water heater would not operate again until the problem was found and corrected.

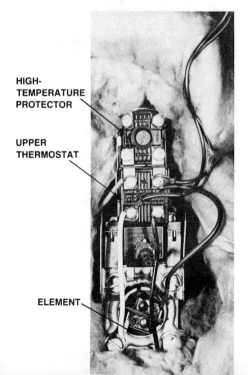

HIGH-TEMPERATURE PROTECTOR

UPPER THERMOSTAT

ELEMENT

bypassing occurs, the water doesn't become very hot. You may draw a large amount of *warm* water from any hot-water faucet because cold water entering at the top of the tank is mixing with the hot water there.

When a heater is operating normally, you can find a definite line between the cold water in the bottom of the tank and the hot water at the top. Check by turning off the power and turning on the hot water at any faucet when the tank is full. After letting it run for a few minutes, go back to the water heater. Remove the access panel and feel the tank at the very bottom. You should find it quite chilly from water entering from the main line. As you slowly move your hand up the tank, you will notice a definite line where the water turns hot. From this point up, the tank will be uniformly

hot to the touch. When by-passing is occurring, you will not find this stratification line. Rather, the entire tank will turn warm gradually.

When inspecting the dip tube, don't suspect it simply because you find a small opening about ⅛ inch in diameter near the top of the tube. This "bleeder orifice" is there as an antisiphon device to keep the tank from draining if the water system is drained or shut off—as it might be when a main is being repaired. If the tank were allowed to drain, the elements would immediately burn out if energized.

To cure bypassing, remove the cold-water line from the tank. If you have galvanized plumbing, uncouple the unit. If you have copper plumbing, cut the copper tubing about 6 inches above the tank. Remove the cold-water

Blanket of insulation often must be cut the first time that a heater is serviced. Be sure that all power is shut off before removing front of cabinet. Bracket at left top of cabinet holds indicator light.

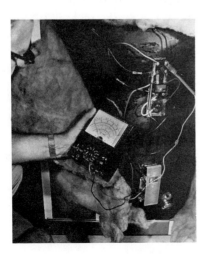

To verify that power is off, clip leads to incoming wires (here at input to high-limit protector), check meter reading on 250-volt AC scale. Also read from ground (any clean portion of tank or water pipe) to each lead.

Dip tube may be removed from cold-water inlet after water lines and fittings are disconnected. This plastic tube is capable of withstanding temperatures in excess of 400 degrees, and heater is so marked with tag. Don't use solder fittings close to tank as plastic components may be damaged by heat.

line. The dip tube may now be easily lifted from the opening at the tank top. If the tube is not there or if the seal is defective, a replacement dip tube may be obtained from your dealer or plumbing supply house. When you reinstall the dip tube, tighten all connections firmly. If it was necessary to cut the supply line to the water heater, use a solder-type coupling or two flare nuts and a flare coupling to reassemble the line.

In replacing a dip tube, you might also check the magnesium anode, a device found in most residential water heater tanks. This extends from the top of the tank to within a few inches of the bottom. An anode combats electrolysis if it occurs within the water-heater tank. Electrolysis erodes away the inner surface of the tank with a pitting action. You may have noticed the same action when two dissimilar metals like aluminum and steel are in contact with each other for any length of time. Electrolysis did not occur severely enough to

cause much concern until lined tanks were almost universally adopted by manufacturers. If even a pinpoint of surface inside the tank was left unglazed, electrolytic action concentrated there, causing a tiny hole in the tank—and a leak—after only a year or so of operation. The anode was the solution. The highly active metal of the anode flows to any unprotected area where electrolysis might occur and coats the surface of the tank and protects it from being eroded away. The anode is a sacrificial anode since it is itself eaten away by the electrolytic action. If your tank is several years old and you find it necessary to service it to the extent of removing the top cover, check the anode. In many areas you may find the anode in a like-new state—about ½ to ¾ of an inch in diameter. If your water has high mineral content or is highly acidic, you may find that only a thin wire rod remains. If so, the small cost of a new anode may delay tank replacement for several years. To replace the anode,

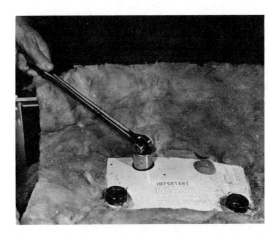

New anode is approximately ½ to ¾ inch in diameter. Old one would appear pitted, possibly as only a thin steel rod. New anode increases the life of the tank.

To remove magnesium anode, first locate plug in top of heater tank. Loosening plug reveals anode on bottom side. Use pipe sealer on threads when replacing.

look for a plug in the top of the tank. Remove this blank plug and you will find the anode attached to the underside. Simply screw the new anode in place, using sealing compound on the threads. If your heater is installed in a location that would make it difficult to install a replacement, you can obtain one from your parts supplier that is suspended from the heating element. It's worth considering in the event of element replacement.

WATER-HEATER CONTROLS

There's a vast difference between the controls used on gas and electric water heaters. Gas controls are basically part of a valve arrangement that opens and closes the source of supply to the burner. The tank of a gas water heater has a central cavity that carries away exhaust gases, acting as a flue. It also serves as a heat exchanger of sorts, transferring additional heat back into the central portion of the tank from the hot flue gases. The thermostat of a gas water heater is normally equipped with a sensing tube or bulb placed in a well, an enclosed section immersed within the water heater tank. Its proximity to the water allows accurate translation of water temperatures to the sensing bulb of the control. When water becomes cool from usage or from heat loss, the control mechanically actuates a valve seat within the gas burner, allowing gas to flow into the burner, where it ignites from the pilot or electronic ignition and heats the water until it has again obtained its required temperature.

Adjustments and calibrations by do-it-yourselfers are generally not recommended on gas water-heater thermostats or burners other than to set the temperature of the water to suit

Flue in center of gas water-heater tank incorporates an internal baffle which retains some heat from flue gasses. Remove vent periodically and clean and vacuum flue and baffle.

your needs. In most localities, a license is required of the technician or plumber who makes repairs or adjustments to the burner itself, and specialized equipment is necessary as well. If you pinpoint the gas burner as the problem area, call in a qualified technician to make the repairs—but give him an accurate description of the problem. This can reduce his diagnosis time and allow him to bring the proper parts to complete the job on the first call.

Thermostatic controls on electric water heaters are most often the bimetal type. Since most electric heaters have dual elements (one near the top of the tank and one near the bottom), two separate thermostats are required. In addition, in most areas the type of thermostat specified by utility companies allows only one element at a time to be energized. It works like this: As water is drawn from the tank for use, the tank begins to turn cold from the bottom up. When cold water reaches the lower thermostat and element assembly, about one-fourth the distance from the bottom to the top of the tank, the thermostat energizes the bottom element and it begins to heat. If water usage is relatively low, the energized bottom element alone will heat the cold water that has entered the tank, the element turning off when the thermostat is satisfied. But if water usage is high, the stratification line between hot and cold water will eventually reach the upper heating element. The upper thermostat (a single-pole, double-throw switch) then turns the lower element off and transfers the heating job to the upper element. This placement of the heating elements allows some gain in efficiency, for in periods of high hot-water usage the upper element heats water closest to the outlet.

Gas control may be threaded directly into tank or may be inserted into a "well" built into tank cavity. Servicing this component, as well as the gas burner, is best left to licensed experts. Faucet directly below control opening is to attach hose to flush sediment from tank regularly.

If heater tank is still hot, thermostat may be tested in place using $R \times 1$ scale on VOM after removing one lead. If tank is cold, slip thermostat from its mounting bracket, turn temperature adjusting dial to its lowest position, and warm back of control slightly with heat from match. Contacts should open cleanly and completely. Replace thermostat if terminals where wire attaches are burned or show signs of discoloration.

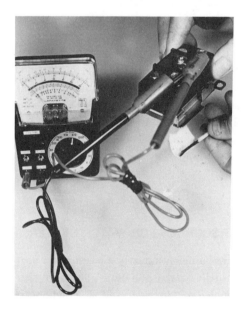

Electric water heaters must be serviced with respect and care. They operate from a 230-volt power supply, and cabinet and tank are grounded through the water lines to the system. Therefore, any slip could produce a dangerous shock if you touched the conductor and any part of the cabinet at the same time. *So make sure that all power is turned off before beginning any testing or checking procedure.* Don't guess. After turning off the switch, touch your volt meter leads to one side of the tank and then to each of the two line conductors in turn to make sure no voltage appears on either one.

Electric water-heater thermostats usually fasten to the tank with a bracket or snap, often mounted to the flange that holds the heating element. Water-heater controls are generally not repairable and need only be adjusted for proper temperature. However, a VOM check for continuity will often disclose burned or high resistance contacts when an erratic problem is experienced with an electric water heater. In this case, the thermostat must be replaced. A corroded wire terminal on a thermostat or one that appears to have been abnormally hot is a clue to this condition. A high resistance contact is normally caused by burning and pitting of the contacts within the thermostat.

HEAT SOURCES FOR WATER HEATERS

The gas burner commonly used on water heaters usually has a standing pilot and thermocouple-operated safety cutoff. You light the standing pilot with a match and it burns at all times. The pilot flame heats a sealed tube called a thermocouple. This heat energy, by action of the thermocouple, is transformed into a small electrical current that sustains a coil located within the valve. This coil is usually connected to the small button or plunger that you depress when lighting a gas appliance. As long as this coil is energized, the gas valve is free to open and close upon demand from the thermostat. But if the pilot should fail, which may happen if the orifice becomes clogged or if a draft blows out the pilot, the safety coil within the valve is released, shutting down the main burner and the pilot so no gas may flow until the pilot has been lighted again. Gas water heaters should always be vented with approved venting material to the outside of the home.

New high-efficiency water heaters may use electronic ignition. In this system, a spark is generated from a capacitor-discharge circuit in the vicinity of the burner orifice to cause direct ignition eliminating the standing pilot altogether. One disadvantage is that the heater may not operate during a power failure.

Two methods have been used to provide heat for electric water heaters. The most common is the immersion-type heating element, an enclosed sheath-type element mounted within the tank. This element fastens to a flange welded into the tank and water must be drained out before it can be removed. You can test the element by simply removing the access panel to the water heater. (Be sure the power supply is turned off before removing the panel.) When using your VOM, check for continuity and for grounds within the element. A grounded element can account for an overheating condition. Since both input lines to the heating element carry 115 volts each, a ground

Heating element is tested for continuity after first disconnecting one lead. Meter is set to *R × 1* scale for this check, then is switched to highest resistance scale for check to ground.

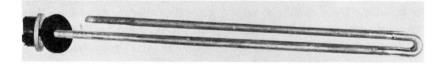

Immersible type element, removed from heater, is shown below. Some early high-recovery elements were noisy, due to rapidly boiling water surrounding their sheath. Newer elements, called "low-watt density" by manufacturers, spread the heat input over a larger area and eliminate the "singing." Don't change an element for this problem alone—the noise is only due to the high efficiency of the element, and won't do any harm.

IN CORRESPONDENCE RE-
GARDING THIS HEATER AL-
WAYS MENTION MODEL &
SERIAL NO'S.

(UL)

MODEL NUMBER			SERIAL NO.
153.312610			E73-

UPPER ELEMENT	LOWER ELEMENT	MAXIMUM	VOLTS
5500	5500	5500	240
WATTS	WATTS	WATTS	A.C. ONLY

Don't attempt to oversize replacement heating elements without first consulting nameplate, as shown in this enlarged section. Be sure to give supplier model and serial numbers when requesting components.

can result in this voltage being applied through the element to ground even though the thermostat is turned off. A grounded or open heating element must be replaced. When replacing an element, always obtain a new gasket as well as a replacement element. Torque each nut on the flange evenly. Be sure the tank is again filled before turning the power on. An element operating in air will destroy itself within a few seconds.

For the same reason, it is imperative that wrap-around elements—the second method of electric heating—be snug against the tank when they are replaced. There should be no insulation between element and tank, and the element should be tightly secured within its retaining bands. It's a good practice to pull the new element in as the old one comes out.

SAFETY DEVICES AND CONTROLS

These are of utmost importance. Paramount among the controls is the pressure/tempera-

ture relief valve. This is fitted into the top of the tank or into the hot-water line where it leaves the tank so the valve's sensing tube is located within the hottest water at the top of the tank. Some newer heaters have a threaded opening specifically for the installation of this valve. In the event of an extreme rise in temperature (to about 210 degrees) or pressure (to 125 or 150 pounds, depending upon local codes and the design of the tank) the valve will open and relieve pressure by allowing the hot water to flow from the tank.

Most newer combination pressure/temperature relief valves have a handle that allows the valve to be flushed. Do this at least twice a year. The valve should seat securely when it's released and should operate freely when the handle is pulled.

Water pressure increases at the rate of 10 pounds for each degree that temperature increases. If the temperature of water is increased from 50 to 150 degrees, the pressure reaches 1,000 pounds.

This amounts to a volume displacement of

one gallon in a 50-gallon tank. This volume has to go somewhere since water cannot be compressed. On a community water system, the extra volume backs up into the main; on a well system, it compresses the air in the top of the water-storage tank. If a check valve is used in either system (and it is usually required on a community system), the relief will come through the pressure temperature relief valve —and dripping will occur at the discharge outlet.

Since water is normally used in small quantities throughout the day, this expansion is negligible if a drain line is provided for the safety relief valve to carry this "bleed-off" water away from the electrical components of the heater. Expansion is greatest after the tank is quickly and completely emptied of hot water.

With a properly operating relief valve in place, there's little danger from a water heater. Without one, or with one that is improperly installed, you have real reason for concern if a malfunction such as a grounded heating element or a stuck thermostat occurs. Homes have been blown apart by an exploding water heater. The force is said to be equal to several sticks of dynamite. Since this threat is present in all of our homes, the first check we should make of any water heater is for the presence of this valve. A drain line commonly runs from the valve to floor level or perhaps to a drain in the floor because some water will flow from the valve due to normal expansion within the tank. This line must not run out of doors since freezing temperatures could cause ice to form at the outlet and block the flow of water.

A home plumbing system is basically a

Test pressure-temperature relief valve twice each year by raising handle to open valve and flush sediment. Shut-off valve in photo is on inlet line, a convenience when servicing. Open-end drain line will run from this valve when installation is completed.

Thermocouple, which is connected to the valve on gas water heaters, is easily distinguished from ordinary copper tube by its unique terminal connections. Connections must be firmly tightened in valve for proper operation.

closed system since most municipalities require a check valve at or near the water meter to eliminate the possibility of back flow into the main water line. If a quantity of hot water is drawn, for instance, at the beginning of the day, and then none is used for a number of hours, the water heater will heat the cold water introduced during the previous usage period. Naturally, expansion takes palce. The check valve in the cold-water line will keep this pressure increase from being relieved back in the direction from which the water came. But when buildup is sufficient, the pressure valve on the tank will open and relieve the pressure; thus the necessity for the drain line.

In the past, a pressure-relief valve was commonly installed in the cold-water line to a water heater. These valves contain no provision for relief in case of overheating unless excessive pressure builds up. Unfortunately, corrosion often set in before there was need for the valve to open; years later, when the long forgotten valve is called upon in an emergency, it doesn't function. If your system has such a valve, consider installing the newer pressure/-temperature relief valve. It not only allows biannual flushing through the manual operation of the valve but also provides over-temperature protection as well. These valves retail in most areas for approximately $10.

Another safety device worth consideration is an electrical shutoff mounted on the water heater immediately above the top heating element. This is a manual reset device that shuts off both sides of 230-volt power in the event of overheating. It is particularly helpful if an element on an electric water heater should become grounded. It can be wired as shown in

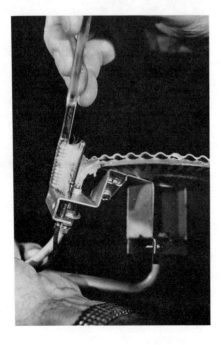

Pilot orifice and shield on gas heater can become linted, interfering with pilot operation. An old toothbrush can often be used to clean pilot assembly without moving burner.

the accompanying diagram. Installation is simple. It is standard equipment on many new models.

It should also be mentioned here that several years ago a number of manufacturers built water heaters that contained plastic dip tubes. In severe overheating it was possible for these tubes to melt, forming a colloidal suspension in the water. When the relief valve opened, the molten plastic would flow along with the water to the valve but would harden immediately when exposed to the cooler air outside the valve. In some instances, this blocked valve operation when it was needed most. The intention of the design, of course, was to further reduce electrolytic action. All currently approved water heaters have dip tubes capable of withstanding temperatures in excess of 400 degrees. If you have doubts about your own

heater, first look to see whether it has a dip tube. If so, jot down the model number and contact a dealer or write the manufacturer and inquire about the material used in making the original dip tube. To replace a dip tube, remove the cold-water inlet line and fittings. The dip tube may then be easily removed and reinstalled and the line coupled back together. If your water heater has a sticker or tag indicating that the waterways are approved for temperatures exceeding 400 degrees, there should be no reason for concern.

Preventative maintenance on water heaters is relatively simple. On gas models check the burner for linting and vacuum out the air passageways to the burner about once a year. If an electric water heater is protected by fuses rather than a circuit breaker, check the fuses in the circuit and be sure that they are tight.

If your fuse box for water heater is of this type, check for defective fuse holders if water heater appears to be blowing fuses regularly and no problem is found in the heater. Loose-fitting fuses cause insulator to overheat and rear contact surface loses its support, making proper contact impossible. Fuses may appear to be all right, but link will be melted internally as VOM check will reveal. Remedy is to replace fuse box. Be sure the power is switched off before touching fuse. Stand on a board, or other dry surface, when handling. Touch nothing but insulated surface of fuse.

A loose fuse can reduce voltage to the heater and overheating of the fuse itself can cause damage to the fuse box over a period of time.

Finally, with either gas or electric water heaters, attach a garden hose to the drain outlet at the bottom of the tank once a year and flush out any scale, rust, or sediment. Severe buildups of deposits can even cause noisy tanks, popping and crackling sounds, noticeable when the hot water supply is used. Also manually open the pressure relief valve, flush away any sediment that may have built up there, and check the valve for proper seating and operation.

RULES FOR THE USE AND CARE OF WATER HEATERS

- Water heaters should *always* be equipped with a pressure and temperature relief valve (or valves). It is best to use one which incorporates a handle to allow easy flushing and testing of the valve.
- The water heater should be located as close as possible to hot-water outlets for economy and efficiency. For some homes, two water heaters should be considered.
- The hot-water heater should be accessible for servicing and to permit good houskeeping.
- All water heaters should be installed in accordance with the manufacturer's instructions regarding clearances.

- Local plumbing codes should be carefully adhered to.
- Gas water heaters should be located as close as possible to a vertical vent for the combustion products, and where there is a free circulation of air.
- Water heaters should not be installed in attics or other areas where water leaks can cause damage in rooms below. All water heaters will eventually corrode because of water characteristics, and therefore must be replaced after normal life expectancy.
- Keep thermostat at desired temperature. Most water-heater controls will permit this setting to be between 120 and 160 degrees. Some heaters are certified for operation at up to 180 degrees.
- If you keep running out of hot water, check to see if your water heater capacity is adequate.
- Check dripping faucets. A constant drip could cause a waste of 300 gallons of water a month plus the energy required to heat this water.
- Drain the heater annually to flush sediment and rust from the bottom of the tank.
- A drain line must be run from the relief valve to carry "bleedoff" water (the result of normal expansion from heating) away from electrical components. It should *not* run outside, where it could become frozen and block water flow.

QUICK-CHECK CHART FOR

WATER HEATERS

Symptom	(E) - electric (G) - gas Possible Cause	Remedy
Won't heat at all	No power to heater (E)	Blown fuse in house circuit—replace
	Pilot outage (G)	Relight—be sure that no lint is near orifice and that covers and baffles are in place. Possible bad thermocouple
	High-limit protector open (E)	Check for cause, reset
	Upper thermostat open (E)	Check with VOM, replace if defective
	Upper element open (E)	Check with VOM, replace if defective
	Broken wire or burned contact (E)	Check with VOM, replace if defective
Overheating	Grounded element (E)	Check with VOM, replace if defective
	Stuck thermostat (E)	Check with VOM, replace if defective
	Stuck thermostat (E) control (G)	Turn temp. control down, listen for snap. If burner continues to operate, have control replaced
Insufficient amount of hot water, but temperature is normal until runs out	Lower thermostat open (E)	Check with VOM, replace if defective
	Lower element open (E)	Check with VOM, replace if defective
	Heater undersized (E or G)	Check capacity against usage
Insufficient hot water —temperature only warm	Dip tube bypassing (E or G)	Feel tank for presence of stratification line—replace dip tube if necessary
	Heater not recovered from previous usage (E or G)	Allow additional time for recovery
	Recirculation through automatic washer inlet valve	Feel both lines from washer. If both are hot, replace check valve(s)
Leaking	Check all elements and fittings where pipes enter	Replace leaking elements or fittings
	Tank leaking	Consider replacement of heater—check warranty status
Leaking from drain valve	Normal expansion (E or G)	One to three gallons per day normal
	Water pressure too high (E or G)	Check by placing pressure gauge (available at most plumbing supplies) on faucet—install pressure reducing valve on water system if above 80 psi
	Defective PT relief valve (E or G)	Replace valve

Symptom	(E) - electric (G) - gas Possible Cause	Remedy
Popping and cracking noises	Sediment In tank (E or G) Heater installed in twisted position (E or G)	Flush tank thoroughly from drain fitting—turn off electric power or gas supply first Check installation—shim or otherwise be sure that tank is firmly resting on floor
Shocking at faucets	Grounded element(s) (E or G) Ground fault in household electric system (E or G)	Check with VOM, replace—*see text* Have electrician check—*see text*
"Singing" noise	High watt density elements being used	Normal condition—replace with low watt density elements when original ones fail if noise distracts.

13
Keeping Clothes Dryers on the Job

The automatic clothes dryer has become standard equipment in American homes. *Merchandising Week* estimated a number of years ago that 25 million homes were equipped with dryers. That was almost 40 percent of the total wired homes at the time. Since then, sales of dryers have averaged around 4 million per year.

There are valid reasons for the popularity of the dryer. The savings in time are important to today's homemakers. The changes in clothing and in textiles make the dryer much more useful than ever before. The advent of today's sensitive controls and refined equipment allows you to take the clothes out of the dryer looking like new. A modern dryer actually treats clothes so gently that it's claimed the life of the fabric is actually prolonged.

The dryer is a pleasant appliance to work with. Most components are easily reached for servicing and testing, although there are a few little tricks that will help you through some seemingly rough spots, as you will see.

HOW IT WORKS

Regardless of the brand and type of machine you own, its components provide three functions common to all dryers—heat, air flow, and tumbling action.

Heating the air causes it to absorb more moisture. But heat must be carefully controlled. Too little will lengthen the drying time; too much may damage the clothing. An enclosed or open-type element provides heat on an electric dryer, while a burner, usually automatically ignited, is the heat source for a gas dryer.

Air flow removes the moisture-laden air from the machine. An exhaust fan accomplishes this by displacing air through carefully-arranged passageways. Ducts direct air into the heater box and across the heat source before it enters the drum. There the air absorbs moisture from the clothing before flowing through the lint filter and exhaust duct, through the exhaust fan, and out the vent. A

Modern dryers feature convenience, durability, and sophisticated control systems. Stationary rack in this Sears dryer allows shoes or other rigid items to be dried without tumbling.

Understand your dryer—and you'll have a good start toward repairing it. That's the first rule for any appliance. Here, technician holds Delrin drum bearing of a Sears dryer that has electronic control.

SENSOR   DOOR SWITCH   FRONT SEAL

belt may drive the exhaust fan or it may be attached directly to the motor shaft.

Tumbling action exposes all surfaces of the clothing to the heated air. Rotation of the drum provides the tumbling and baffles on the inner surface of the drum increase the action. The drum may be supported by a rear center bearing, rollers, slides, or a combination of the three.

A belt drives the drum from the motor. The most common current practice is to use a small-diameter Poly-V belt which completely encircles the motor pulley. Tension is maintained by using a spring-loaded idler, which also serves to keep the belt in alignment. In effect, this application uses the drum as a large pulley. You must remove the front panel of such dryers to replace a belt. You can easily tell if your dryer has this arrangement by raising the lid and examining the drum exterior. If a small, flat belt passes over the drum, as in accompanying photo, you can be sure that your dryer uses this system.

A second method of driving the drum uses pulleys at the rear of the dryer. A V-belt drives an idler pulley which in turn drives a pulley that is attached to the hub of the drum. Two belts are used with this method. The idler is spring-loaded to maintain tension on both belts. This arrangement must be serviced through a rear access panel.

Many dryers employing this system also have another belt to drive the blower. The blower bearing and shaft should be checked and lubricated with non-detergent SAE 30 motor oil or turbine oil. Since it is turning at almost 1800 rpm, it won't last long if its oil supply runs out. Many of these bearings have a large felt wick which can be saturated and will insure proper oiling for a year of normal use.

Some dryers have a Poly-V belt around the outer circumference of the drum to drive it. One example is the GE setup shown here. Note the electrical terminal board in the upper right corner. By consulting the wiring diagram, it's a convenient spot to make a number of important electrical tests.

Drum drive system typical of many dryers uses a belt through a spring-loaded idler pulley to maintain the necessary tension. Pulleys shown are in Westinghouse Laundromat model.

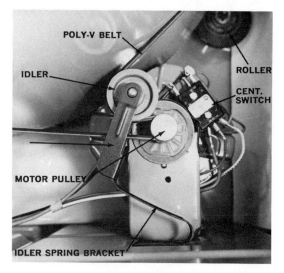

Note the relative positions of the idler roller and motor pulley, and how the belt loops through the idler bracket (arrow) in this Whirlpool arrangement. The bracket is spring-loaded to exert downward pressure upon the belt.

Air flow, heat, and tumbling combine to dry garments. In this GE dryer (equipped with air freshener), a blower draws air through toeboard openings, pulling it up the back through air heaters. The heated air, passing through small holes into and out of the revolving drum, picks up moisture on its way through the clothing. Passing through the lint trap, the moisture-laden air returns to the blower, which forces it out the exhaust duct. A thermostat in the trap duct turns the heaters on and off to control the temperature of the air.

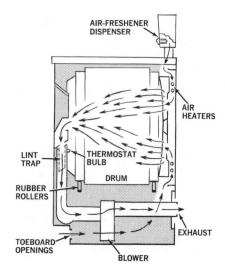

Replacing a Belt

When replacing a belt on a machine using the two-belt system, check the pulleys for tight fit and proper alignment. Check the condition of the idler shaft and bearing if it seems tight when you turn it with the belt off or if it has too much play. Be sure to look closely if a belt has to be replaced and see that all pulleys turn freely.

Be sure you obtain a belt that is an exact replacement. Poly-V belts vary in design. The wrong one could increase drum speed and prevent proper tumbling.

To check the speed, open the top of your dryer by removing the screws around the lint filter and any other screws anchoring the top. Turn the air/heat switch to *air* position. Press a piece of masking tape to the drum and turn the dryer on, avoiding contact with electrical connections. Count each revolution of the tape for a minute and you can determine the drum speed. It should be between 45 and 55 rpm.

Squeaks and thumping noises are signs of belt looseness or misalignment. Early inspection can often prevent failure.

Bearings are usually sleeve or roller, sealed and lubricated for normal use. Clean and lubricate them if removed for any repair. Follow the manufacturer's recommendations for lubrication of plastic or Delrin bearing surfaces. Plastic bearings which are used as support surfaces, at the front of a dryer drum for instance, are usually lubricated with Lubriplate 202 or its equivalent. Use special care when handling plastic or phenolic bearings, and make sure that no grit or residue remains when they are reinstalled.

When required, new motor bearings are best installed by a local motor-repair shop.

In today's dryers, one of three methods provides correct relationship of time and temperature. The oldest:

TIMER AND THERMOSTAT

The user selects the running time and temperature range when turning on the machine, and the timer turns on the motor and heat source. The timer usually consists of one or two cams, a motor (often without escapement) and two contact arms. An adjustable thermostat in series with the heating element or gas burner cycles heat off and on at a predetermined point, maintaining temperature level.

During the final ten minutes the machine operates in a cool-down period. The timer contacts open the heating circuit, allowing the motor to continue turning the drum and the blower without heat. This period lets the clothing cool before tumbling ceases, making handling easier and reducing the possibility of setting wrinkles in the clothing.

The time-temperature method of controlling a dryer is reliable, but it leaves much to guesswork. With the trend in recent years to clothing made at least partially from synthetics, which are much more sensitive to overdrying, it became evident that a better method was needed.

A more accurate means of control was found in what is commonly called the automatic control method.

AUTOMATIC CONTROL

In this system a single-pole, double-throw thermostat is connected to the timer motor

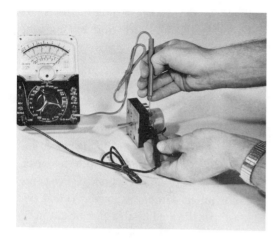 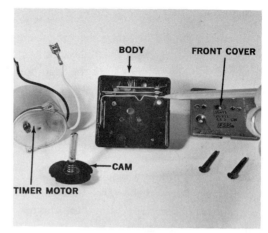

In testing timer, you test motor for continuity (left). Then, you test timer contacts for continuity from line to motor and from line to heat source. Use lowest resistance scale for contacts, higher scale for motor winding. In photo at right, lowest of three contact arms carries line voltage. Cam lobe raises it to contact middle arm and energize motor. As cam advances, both arms contact uppermost arm, energizing heat source.

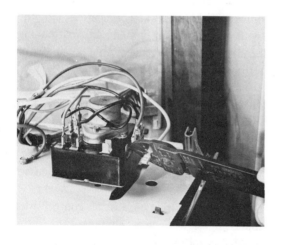

Dryer wiring carries high current loads, and connections must be secure and tight to endure. Wiring terminals and splices should be crimped with terminal crimping tool, then soldered.

and the heat source. With this arrangement, one or the other of the components is energized, but never both at the same time; when the heat source is off, the timer motor is on, and vice versa. By using a short-duration timer in conjunction with the thermostat, a time/temperature relationship is automatically established.

It works like this: The thermostat, which senses the temperature of the exhaust air, turns on the heating element or burner upon start-up. The timer motor is off, and the timer does not advance. The clothing is very damp at this point, and the heated air entering the drum from the heat source absorbs a great deal of moisture. Because of the evaporative process, the exhaust temperature remains fairly cool and temperature rise is rather slow.

As moisture is removed from the clothing, however, the "transfer" temperature for the thermostat is reached. Thermostat action now turns off the heat source, but turns on the timer motor. The cams and control knob advance slightly until the thermostat again turns on the heat source. After a number of these cycles, which increase in frequency and length of heat-off time, the timer cams have advanced enough to alter positions of the timer contacts. Until now, the thermostat has controlled the actions of the heat source and the timer motor. Now the timer takes command. The heat source is turned off, and contacts in the timer keep the timer motor energized to advance the timer. This is the cool-down period, and only the motor, fan, and timer are operative for the few minutes before shutoff.

The latest in dryer control systems, and the most accurate means of control, is the electronic control. This uses the wet clothing in the drum as part of the circuit. Sensing units are built into the revolving drum. One type consists of two metal bands that run around the inside of the drum. Others use an insulated plastic block, containing several copper fingers, fastened to the rear of the drum. In these units, the rear of the drum is stationary. This eliminates the problem of using slip rings or brushes to complete the circuit to a sensor that is moving with the drum.

As the drum revolves, clothes are jostled and tossed against these contacts. Each time a piece of wet laundry completes the circuit across the contacts, the dryer is held *on* for a few seconds. As the clothing dries, its resis-

Newest dryer control systems use "touch panel" instead of timer knob; induction or slight pressure of fingertip sets up complete cycle. "Ribbon" contains numerous conductors that lead to electronic control. Module at right is typical of "plug-in" functional parts of dryer control; other types may use enclosed components.

tance to electric-current flow increases. Finally, this resistance reaches a point at which it triggers a circuit that sends the dryer into "cool-down." A fixed thermostat controls heat at a moderate level during the entire cycle.

To check most electronic controls, start the dryer with no clothes load on the lowest (shortest) setting on the control. It should cut off within twelve to fifteen minutes. If it doesn't, unplug the dryer, remove the rear panel, remove and tape the wire(s) attached to the sensor band or feelers. If the dryer now shuts down within the proper time, the sensor is shorted or grounded. Look for foil, paper clips, or wire strands across the "feelers," or for a break in the insulating material.

If the dryer continues to run, the problem is most likely within the control. You may use your **VOM** to check further by testing the timer or relay contacts. Stuck contacts prevent the dryer from turning off. Open or high-resistance contacts prevent the dryer from running. If these components test okay, your problem definitely is in the control area.

Before condemning the control, however, check to see that a positive ground is provided by a wire attached from the cabinet to the cold-water line. Since the critical control current is fed to ground, this wire must be provided *in addition* to the cabinet ground provided to the neutral line of the power supply, used in most areas. While a ground to the neutral is acceptable for safety purposes, it is not sufficient to allow proper operation of electronic controls on many models. Consult the installation instructions that came with your machine.

THERMOSTATS

Thermostats are also of great importance in determining the time-temperature relationship, vital for good results in drying clothes. Those which control the operating temperature are referred to as operating thermostats, to distinguish from high-limit thermostats, used as safety devices to prevent severe over-

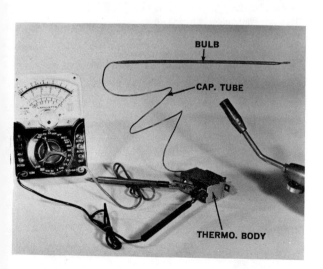

BULB

CAP. TUBE

THERMO. BODY

Adjustable thermostats are tested by placing VOM probes across switch terminals on lowest resistance scale, then heating (or cooling) sensing bulb while observing switch transfer on meter. As in any switch, closed contacts should indicate zero-resistance. Go easy on heat. Use low flame and keep your distance from thermostat. Don't use open flame near lint.

heating. Many operating thermostats are adjustable ones, controlled by the user when setting the heat range or temperature control. Typically, they consist of a liquid- or gas-filled thermal bulb, connecting capillary tubing, a closed expandable diaphragm, switch contacts, and a control screw. The thermal bulb is normally located in the exhaust air stream.

As temperature rises, the liquid in the sealed bulb vaporizes, exerting pressure in the diaphragm at the opposite end of the capillary tube connecting the two components. Pressure causes the diaphragm to expand, and the resulting movement opens the switch contacts, breaking the electrical circuit to the heat source. As the exhaust air cools, the diaphragm contracts and again closes the switch, resuming heat input.

Fixed bimetal thermostat is tested in same way as adjustable one. If terminals show signs of extreme overheating or if they are loose, thermostat must be replaced even if resistance tests check out. Defective contacts cause arcing and heat the thermostat bimetal strip, giving erratic performance. A thermostat won't last long in this condition.

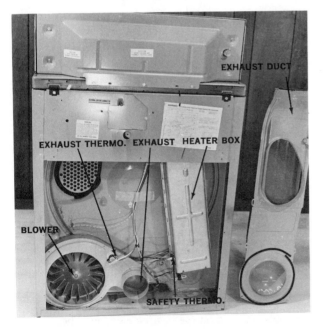

Typical location of exhaust thermostat is seen immediately above and to left of exhaust opening, while safety thermostat is mounted to heater box at right. Exhaust duct at right was removed for clarity.

This cycling action, which maintains desired temperatures, may occur many times during a drying period. The "temperature" knob or slide on the dryer turns the control screw, which places spring tension against the diaphragm, thus varying the amount of pressure required to activate the switch contacts and raise or lower temperature levels.

If your machine has no control knob with which you adjust the temperature, it likely uses fixed bimetallic thermostats. If several different heat ranges are desired, as in a multi-cycle machine, a timer switches in and out of the circuit fixed-temperature thermostats of differing temperature ranges. The thermostat is usually a bimetallic disc that snaps from its normal position when sufficiently heated. The snapping opens or closes electrical contacts to the heat source. When used as an operating thermostat, it's usually placed in the exhaust-air stream.

The fixed-temperature thermostat is also often used as a high-limit or safety device. Wired in series with the heat source, it is located on the housing of the heating element or burner. Fan-belt breakage, blockage of air flow, or any other condition that could contribute to overheating causes the high-limit device to open, breaking the electrical circuit to the heat source. This keeps the heat at a safe level.

SWITCHES

The motor centrifugal switch serves a dual purpose in a clothes dryer. It does the job of a centrifugal switch in a split-phase motor when it opens the circuit to the starting winding as the motor approaches full speed. In the dryer, an additional set of contacts closes the circuit to the heat source when top speed is reached.

There are two reasons for the additional circuit. First, most dryers use heating elements rated at 5600 watts or so (about 24.5 amperes). Add to this the motor-starting current and a 30-ampere fuse or circuit breaker doesn't stand a chance. With the centrifugal switch turning the element on after the starting windings are removed from the circuit, however, you are well within the limits of a 30-ampere circuit.

There's a built-in safety advantage here, also. If the motor fails to start for any reason, the heat source will not be energized.

The push-to-start switch is an innovation that has come into wide usage in recent years. It's a safety feature, requiring the push of a button to start the dryer at the beginning of the cycle or after interrupting the cycle by opening the door.

It works like this: Depressing the push-to-start switch completes a circuit to the motor through a set of contacts in the motor's centrifugal switch. As the motor reaches full speed, these contacts transfer to others that energize the motor directly from the timer. This action, occurring instantaneously, takes the push-to-start switch out of the circuit and acts as a holding circuit to keep the motor in operation.

Many electric dryers use relays, energized by the timer contacts, to control the heating element. The relay consists of a coil or solenoid and a set of heavy-duty contacts. When the coil is energized by the timer or thermostat, the resulting electromagnetic action causes a mechanical movement that closes the contacts, turning on the heating element. The

TESTING SWITCHES

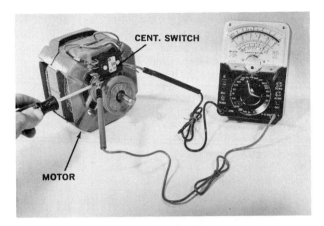

External centrifugal switch is used on the unitized motor to energize heater and disconnect starting windings as motor nears top rpm. Switch is being manually energized to test contacts to heat source in stopped and running positions.

External motor switches are easily replaced, but be sure to mark the wires before disconnecting from old switch. Adhesive tape with numbers or letters of corresponding terminals of switch marked on it, then wrapped around wire, is a good method. Tape switch together before removing it. Some fall apart when screws are removed.

Push-to-start switch is tested by placing VOM across terminals and depressing switch, using $R \times 1$ scale. Continuity should be observed only when switch button is depressed.

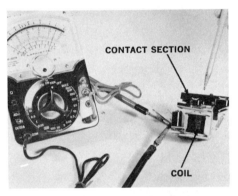

Switch contact section, indicated by pencil, is visible in photo of dryer relay. To test solenoid coil section, locate two small leads from coil and place VOM probes on these terminals. Use highest resistance scale. Solenoid coil section and switch contact section must be tested individually.

Dryer door switch is safety device that breaks circuit to motor and heater, may also operate light in some models. Linkages are usually mounted to door or hinge. Check for continuity with door in closed position, then open it and meter needle should fall to infinite resistance.

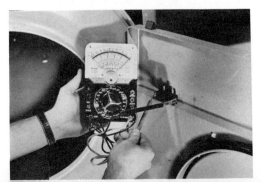

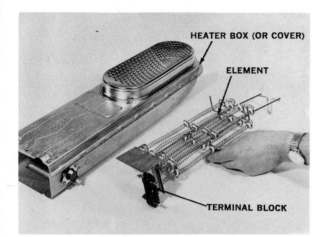

HEATER BOX (OR COVER)

ELEMENT

TERMINAL BLOCK

An open-type heating element is being inspected here for broken insulators. Before removal from heater box it was tested for grounds from both terminals in turn to the heater box, using highest resistance scale on VOM. Then it was tested for continuity, using lowest resistance scale. Always replace a defective element; it usually is stretched or expanded too much to permit a reliable repair. Twisting an open nichrome heating element wire together creates a high resistance connection and leads to early failure. Blockage of air flow is one likely cause of element failure.

purpose of the relay is to carry the heavy current load required by the heater, and not use the timer's lighter contacts.

HEAT SOURCE

The heat source in automatic dryers is provided by electric heating elements or by a gas burner. Heating elements may be either the enclosed-sheath type or the open type, but most often they are open. Test for continuity on the $R \times 1$ scale and for grounds on the highest resistance scale on your VOM.

Don't take an open element for granted. Before replacing it, look for signs of overheating which may have weakened the element and shortened its life. Typical causes of this are a blocked vent pipe or failure to clean the lint filter, defective seals which allow the air to be pulled in around the drum or door instead of across the heating element, and binding or slow-moving fans which reduce the air flow. When replacing the element, be sure that the

heater box which surrounds the element is in position and that air flow is unrestricted.

Servicing of a gas burner should best be left to a qualified technician—in many areas a special license is required. But it's likely that the problem is electrical rather than an internal problem with the valve itself.

To check the burner, turn the dryer on and observe and listen carefully. Burner operation is dependent on voltage supplied from the timer circuit. If there is any burner function—igniter or glow coil working, a gas valve snapping, even a hum from the transformer—you know that voltage is reaching the valve and you can eliminate the timer and thermostat as the culprit. If no function occurs, check back through the electrical circuit that controls the burner; this would include continuity checks of timer and thermostat contacts, wiring connections, motor centrifugal switch, and connecting wiring.

If the igniter tried to light the burner, but there was no flame, the problem is likely in the burner or in the gas supply. But if the igniter

Call a pro for repairs within the gas burner, but first be sure that that's where the trouble lies. Watching and listening can tell you if any burner function is present. If not, the problem is in the control circuitry. With VOM set to $R \times 100$, burner should indicate continuity at input terminals. If it does, and no function occurs, check back through the control circuits.

didn't work, the problem is still electrical. If a glow coil is used, check to see if it indicates continuity by removing the leads that attach to the transformer mounted on the burner, then read through the coil with the VOM set to the $R \times 1$ scale. If the glow coil is open, replace it. Trying to twist it back together is wasted effort. If a direct-ignition type igniter is used, look at the contacts carefully for signs of linting. If this is the case, a chattering noise will likely be noticed if it is the motorized-contact type that has a pair of contacts that chatter against each other. If it is the capacitor-discharge type, it will have an electrode mounted near the burner orifice. Check to be sure that all connections are secure.

If the burner is removed for servicing, be sure that the gas supply is turned off as well as the electrical supply. When it is reinstalled in the dryer, turn the gas on and check each joint with a solution of soapy water. A bubble indicates a leak. *Never, under any circumstances, try to locate a gas leak with a lighted match.*

You probably know that every dryer leaves the factory equipped for either natural gas, manufactured gas, or bottled gas (LP). If you should move or circumstances change, it may be necessary to use another type of supply. Manufacturers provide kits which allow the dryer to be converted from one to the other, but this should only be done by the use of this kit. Don't ever attempt to drill out orifices or tamper with the regulator adjustment, and don't let anyone else alter your equipment in this way. Not only is it a safety hazard, but such makeshift alterations can adversely affect the operation of the dryer. Your gas company should make the conversion for you.

HOW A TYPICAL GAS BURNER FUNCTIONS IN A CLOTHES DRYER

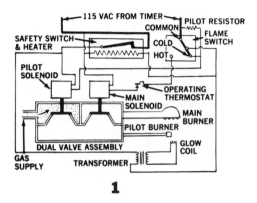

1

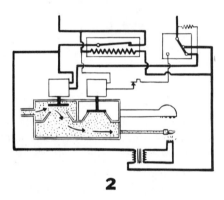

2

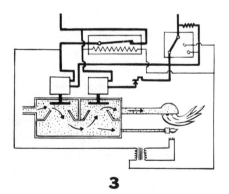

3

Most burners currently in use are of the "dual valve" type. The pilot and main burner passageways are interdependent and are cast within the same housing. Each has its own operating solenoid. In Fig. 1, the gas burner is in the *off* position. Both pilot and main burner solenoids are de-energized.

Turning the dryer on (Fig. 2) activates the pilot solenoid and the igniter. The safety switch and the *flame* switch must be in their closed (cold) positions, as illustrated. The heat from the *glow coil,* often a tungsten-rhodium filament, ignites the gas at the pilot orifice. The flame heats the sealed tube of the flame switch, causing a diaphragm to begin to expand; and a circuit is established to the heater within the safety switch, causing the contact arm to begin to warp open. If the flame switch contacts do not transfer to the *hot* side within approximately three minutes, the safety switch contacts warp open and the pilot coil is de-energized.

In Fig. 3, the pilot flame has caused the flame switch to transfer and the *glow coil* and safety switch heater are removed from the circuit. The main burner solenoid is energized through a circuit controlled by the operating thermostat of the dryer, which cycles it as needed. Both pilot and main-burner solenoids must be energized for the burner to operate. The pilot valve is held open through a circuit that includes the pilot resistor. The voltage drop is sufficient to hold the valve open, but not sufficient to raise it again. If it should drop, as it would if the door were opened, for instance, it would shut off all gas flow. When the burner cooled and the flame switch transferred back to *cold,* the ignition process would be safely repeated.

Many late-model dryers use direct ignition systems that conserve energy by eliminating the pilot flame and provide even faster safety shut-down. Some of these systems utilize the spark that occurs as two contacts "chatter" and arc when they interrupt an electrical current. Others use a high-voltage and/or capacitive-discharge arc between two electrodes mounted in the path of gas flow.

One of the trickiest problems when servicing electric dryers is also one of the most common. Let me explain.

The typical 230-volt, single-phase power supply to a dryer is carried by three conductors. The outer ones are electrically hot, the middle one electrically neutral. The two hot lines in the dryer circuit are protected by fuses or circuit breakers in your home wiring system.

Take a look at the wiring diagram of your electric dryer. Find the three lines representing the power supply and you will see that the motor and lights are connected from one side of the line to the neutral, and only the heating element circuit is connected across the 230 circuit between both hot lines.

The symptom of the problem—the dryer will run but won't heat or doesn't run at all. The cause: simply a blown fuse in one of the

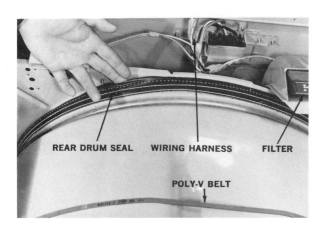

REAR DRUM SEAL   WIRING HARNESS   FILTER

POLY-V BELT

Drum seals insure that intake air is pulled from heater box, not from around drum. Replace seals if damaged or torn. Lint from some modern fabrics is flammable, should be removed with vacuum cleaner. Note position of lint filter on this Sears dryer.

Front view of this General Electric dryer shows position of front-mounted lint screen in door opening. Drum baffle may be seen inside door. This model uses magnetic latch to keep door closed.

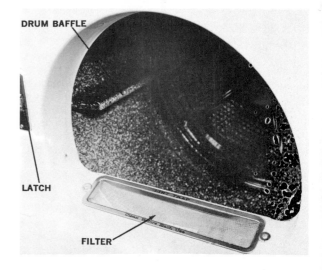

DRUM BAFFLE

LATCH

FILTER

outer conductors. It's very elusive but very simple if you understand how this typical 230-volt appliance circuit operates. To locate the defective fuse, test it for continuity with the VOM. Don't trust your eyes—you often can't see the break in the linkage.

And since you are now aware of this, you should make it a practice to automatically check the fuses first when an electric dryer exhibits one of the classic symptoms—it runs but doesn't heat or when it doesn't run at all

depending on which fuse is blown. This eliminates the need for making voltage tests altogether. Many dollars have been spent unnecessarily for service technicians to perform this simple task.

POINTS TO REMEMBER

With the basic operational concepts in mind, and following the illustrations and testing

Pilot and main burner coils may be replaced if open. Use $R \times 100$ scale on VOM to check for continuity. Flame switch unplugs from socket in burner.

A number of operating components are identified in the front view of this gas burner. If glow coil works but dryer doesn't ignite, or if pilot flame is yellow, look for lint accumulation in the area of pilot orifice just below glow coil.

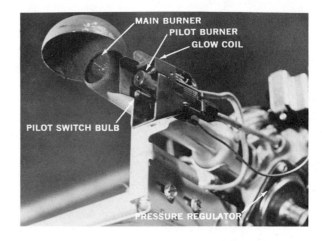

L-shaped terminal on dryer cords and receptacles is the neutral line. Outer (straight-terminal) conductors have voltage difference of 230 volts across each other, but only 115 volts to the neutral.

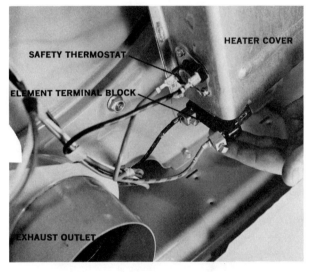

SAFETY THERMOSTAT

HEATER COVER

ELEMENT TERMINAL BLOCK

EXHAUST OUTLET

Good electrical connections are essential to proper operation of a clothes dryer—or any other appliance. In this photo heavy-duty clamps are used to attach the wiring harness to the heating-element terminals. The terminals and clamps must be clean and shiny before you reconnect them, and the wire must be in good condition. Otherwise, it should be replaced. In making repairs, take special care to tighten all connections securely.

procedures given here, you should be able to diagnose and repair most faults in your automatic dryer. A few other things to bear in mind:

When replacing electrical components, be sure that all connections are clean and tight. If terminals and disconnects are discolored, they've been hot. Replace or polish the connector in question. High current flow in electric dryers makes unacceptable anything less than a perfect connection.

Wiring used in dryers has a special high-temperature insulation and only this type of wiring must be used for repairs. It's available at appliance-parts dealers and distributors and at many electrical supply houses. Connectors and terminals should be both crimped and soldered to wires if they are replaced to insure a tight secure connection.

If it is necessary to replace the cord or "pigtail" on your electric dryer, take a close look at the plug configuration.

At one time it was standard practice to use electric-range cord sets for dryers, and these have a straight neutral blade (the middle one) at the plug end. In recent years, most codes have permitted the use of a cord set with slightly smaller conductors for dryers, and these are required to have an L-shaped neutral blade. The cord must match the receptacle, so be sure to check this before replacing yours.

In most localities, electrical codes specify that the dryer cabinet may be grounded to the grounded neutral line of the power supply. This is usually accomplished by a strap or wire connected to the middle terminal of the block where the cord set is attached to the dryer. It is a safety factor and should always be reconnected before you put the equipment back into use.

It is always wise to provide an additional ground by attaching a wire to a screw on the dryer cabinet on one end and clamping the other end to a cold-water line (never a gas line). If a ground fault should ever occur during use in a properly grounded machine, the current flows to ground and at most may blow a fuse. In an ungrounded piece of equipment, the entire cabinet could become "live" at line-voltage level—a very dangerous and undesirable situation. And remember, electronic controls require that external ground for proper operation.

VENTING

Venting is of utmost importance to obtaining maximum performance from your dryer. If you are moving your dryer or buying a new one, pay particular attention to the length and size of the exhaust vent—most manufacturers

Good grounding connections are essential for safety, sometimes for proper operation. In photo at right, neutral is grounded to cabinet by wire indicated, grounding cabinet through electrical system. Always put wire back before reconnecting dryer. Connection is at terminal block where dryer cord attaches to wiring harness. A separate ground wire to cold-water line is imperative on many dryers with electronic control.

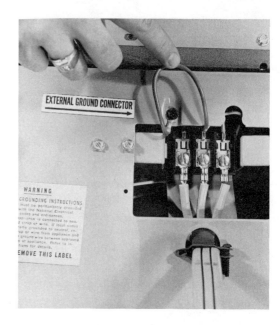

recommend a maximum length of around 16 feet for a rigid metal vent, including two elbows and exhaust hood. Deduct 2 feet for each additional elbow, and don't exceed four elbows. For flexible ducting material, where permitted, the maximum length should be about half that for aluminum. A few do's and don'ts to remember:

- The shorter the vent, the better—but always get the exhaust outside unless you're utilizing indoor venting to the living area to conserve energy in winter (explained later). All the moisture removed from the clothing is carried out in the exhaust air. If this is dumped into a restricted area such as a crawl space, it may eventually cause structural damage and/or other related problems, such as lint buildup, a potential fire hazard.

- A vent that is too long will restrict air flow, resulting in greatly increased drying times and requiring frequent clean-out to remove lint blockage.
- Don't use screws when joining sections of vent pipe—they, too, can contribute to lint buildup.
- Never try to get by without controlled venting. The lack of any vent will cause fast lint buildup within the machine and will greatly increase the humidity of intake air, reducing its ability to absorb the moisture from the clothing. This can also cause controls to sense incorrect temperatures, and in extreme cases the hot air pouring through the motor can cause the motor overload protector to open up.
- In a small utility room, it's a good idea to also provide a vent in the door to allow plenty of fresh air to flow into the dryer.

Venting is easy when you get one of the kits like this which includes all of the parts—flex metal tubing, vent hood, and clamps. Four-inch hole saw or a saber saw is needed to drill through wood, star drill for brick. Check local codes before using flex duct—it's approved in most areas but stick to the metal type, not plastic.

SEASONAL INDOOR VENTING OF ELECTRIC DRYERS

This practice has been frowned upon by manufacturers in the past, primarily for the good reasons stated above. However, tests at Oak Ridge National Laboratory, the Department of Energy, and at *Popular Science* all indicate that this can be a valuable concept for home energy conservation in winter months, and if properly done poses no problem in dryer operation.

Part of the reason for doing this is obvious —to reclaim the heat and moisture that is exhausted outdoors at a time when it could be utilized inside the home. But our tests indicate an even better reason. In a typical drying cycle, a clothes dryer that takes its intake air from the living area of the home can exhaust a volume of air equal to half the total volume in a 1500-square-foot home. In the winter, that's air that you have already paid to condition by heating and humidifying it.

Several commercially available devices are made for this purpose. Those that I have found to work best use a furnace filter to catch small

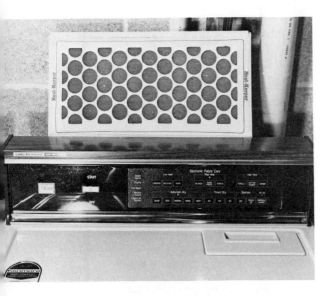

Dryer-Mate indoor vent system at left is readied for testing. Furnace filter in box screens air (standard dryer filter is left in place). Fan overcomes restriction offered by filter to insure that no back pressure occurs.

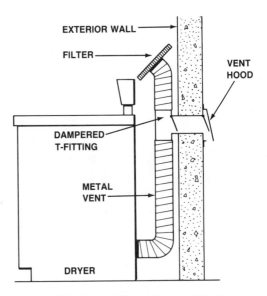

Dampered T fitting and filter holder, available from appliance parts distributors and some manufacturers, allow you to change from indoor to outdoor venting by flipping lever on T when installation is arranged as shown.

lint particles that the dryer's lint screen misses, and the outlet is designed so it can be installed near the top of the dryer away from the air intakes. This helps prevent problems of recirculation. A bypass valve can be installed in the duct to divert the air outside on warm days, and through the indoor system on cool days just by flipping a lever. Selective use of such a system can convert your dryer's operating costs from a deficit to an asset during winter months. Don't use indoor venting if you're not sure that your home has an adequate vapor barrier in the walls.

PERMANENT PRESS CONTROL

Minor modifications in time-temperature relationships have done a good job in caring for new fabrics and materials as they have been developed over the years, keeping the dryer modern without changing the basic layout or adding gimmicks. As an example of this, to care for permanent press it was only necessary to lower the operating temperature slightly and increase the length of the cool-down period at the end of the cycle.

Some models have carried this a step further

Two timers in one? The one on the left takes over after the normal cycle and turns the dryer motor on for a few seconds every five minutes, to prevent wrinkling permanent-press clothing. The other (main) section of timer controls the dryer during normal operation.

by providing an alternate timer which comes into play when the permanent-press cycle is used. This timer takes over after the drying cycle is completed. In a typical application of this concept, after the clothes have been left in the drum for five minutes, the timer activates the motor (no heat) and tumbles the clothes for a few seconds. When the machine stops, a signal (buzzer or bell—at one time one Westinghouse model actually used a music box that played "How Dry I Am") sounds. Five minutes later, if the clothes still haven't been removed, the process is repeated. This goes on for two full hours before the auxiliary timer finally gives up and the machine stops completely. Opening the door to remove the clothing deactivates the program at any time after the machine has initially stopped. It's a good feature—it allows you to go to the store and gives you some leeway without having to be concerned about your permanent-press items becoming wrinkled because you aren't there to remove them from the dryer as soon as it stops.

Dewrinkle cycles are short timed cycles which heat wash & wear clothing to remove the wear wrinkles. It should be removed from the drum immediately after cool-down. Fluff cycles provide tumbling with no heat, and are primarily intended for pillows, sleeping bags, etc.

The photos in this chapter illustrate practically all of the typical operations that you might encounter in your clothes dryer. By becoming familiar with your dryer and using these illustrations as a guide, you should be able to handle most repair problems as they arise.

PREVENTATIVE MAINTENANCE

A dryer responds well to preventative maintenance, and I want to emphasize some points that may prevent troubles before they start. Like most appliances, voltages at the receptacle with the machine running should be within 10 percent of the maker's rating.

Keep the machine lint-free. Remove the lint filter and clean it after each use. About once a year, disconnect your dryer and remove the service panels. Using a vacuum-cleaner crevice tool and brush, remove all lint accumulation, especially around the heater box and motor. This not only allows the motor to run cooler, but it also eliminates a fire hazard. Lint, especially from some synthetic fabrics now on the market, can be very flammable.

Inspect all belts for cracking. Tighten all wiring connections securely and look for signs of loose connections.

Check bearing surfaces and appliance motors for oil points, and lubricate with the lubricant recommended by the maker of the dryer. Often, for motors, this will be SAE 30 nondetergent oil. Plastic or Delrin bearings usually require special lubricants.

For most other purposes, or where no particular lubricant is specified, it's hard to beat turbine oil as a general-purpose lubricant for home appliances. It lubricates well even when used on bearing surfaces that are subjected to high speeds or high heat conditions. It can be found at most appliance parts distributors in a handy telescoping-spout container which is refillable. If you can't locate it in your area, write to P-G Assco Corp., 1395 Jarvis, Detroit, Michigan 48220, and they will send you the name and address of the distributor nearest you.

RULES FOR THE USE AND CARE OF A DRYER

- Locate dryer for shortest and straightest vent duct path.

- Clean lint filter after each use.
- Check dryer vent once or twice a year to make sure that it isn't clogged.
- Do not overload—this requires longer drying time and causes wrinkling. Dry no more than one washer load at a time.
- Remove clothes immediately at the end of cycle to avoid wrinkling. This is especially important for permanent press.

QUICK-CHECK CHART FOR

AUTOMATIC DRYERS

Symptom	Cause	Remedy
Machine will not run— no lights, no sound	Blown fuse or tripped breaker	Check both fuses in line to dryer— one or both may be blown; replace
	Open conductor in "pigtail"	Check with VOM, replace "pigtail"
	Open conductor in wiring harness	Check with VOM, repair break
	Open contact in timer	Check for continuity from line terminal to motor terminal on timer; replace if defective
	Open contacts in door switch	Check for continuity with switch depressed in "closed" position; replace if defective
Machine will not run— lights operate, no sound	Main motor windings open	Check with VOM, replace if open
	Motor centrifugal switch open	Replace centrifugal switch
	Push-to-start switch open	Replace PTS switch
	Motor contact in timer open	Check with VOM, replace if necessary
	Open conductor in wiring harness to motor	Locate with VOM and repair
	Connector loose or burned at timer or motor	Check visually, replace if needed
	Open contacts in door switch	Check with VOM, replace switch if open
Machine will not run— lights operate, makes humming sound	Broken or loose drive belt	Inspect and tighten or replace
	Motor centrifugal switch not energizing starting windings	Check with VOM, replace switch if bad
	Motor starting winding open	Check with VOM, replace motor if open

Symptom	Cause	Remedy
Motor runs, dryer will not heat	Blown fuse in **one** side of line	Check fuses in house with VOM, replace; check fuse box to see that fuse holders are not loose or corroded —have box replaced if bad
	Centrifugal switch contacts on motor not closing heater circuit	Check with VOM while holding switch in running position
	Open heating element	Check for continuity with VOM, R X I scale
	Safety (high limit) thermostat open	Check with VOM, replace if open
	Operating thermostat(s) open	Check with VOM, replace if open
	Corroded terminal at element	Inspect visually, clean and tighten
	Open contact in timer	Check heater circuit with VOM, repair or replace
	Gas burner inoperative	Check at terminals for timer voltage
	Relay inoperative	Check heater relay coil; switch contacts
	Air-heat switch open or set wrong	Check with VOM, repair or replace
Motor runs, dryer heats but clothing does not dry or drying time is excessive	Air flow inadequate	Check for clogged lint screen or exhaust duct, clean as necessary Check fan and fan bearings Check for broken belt to fan
	Loose drum seals	Inspect felt or plastic seals around outer drum area for proper fit; repair
	Operating thermostat defective	Eliminate all possibilities first; replace thermostat if necessary
	Clothing too damp when put in dryer	Check washer for proper spin speed.
	Drain speed too slow or too fast	Should be 45-55 rpm
	Dryer overloaded with clothing	Load with single washer load
Blows fuses	Wiring or component grounded	Check with VOM for ground in all components and wiring harness
	Defective fuse box	Inspect fuse holders—if loose, charred or corroded fuse box must be replaced. WARNING—NEVER TOUCH FUSE HOLDERS OR CONNECTORS AS THEY ARE "HOT" EVEN WHEN FUSES ARE REMOVED
	Improper fuse sizing	Check dryer nameplate for proper sizing—install time-delay fuse to allow for motor load
Drying temperature too high	Thermostat sensing portion insulated with lint	Inspect and clean lint from thermostat
	Defective thermostat	Check with VOM, replace as necessary
	Grounded heating element	Check with VOM, replace as necessary
Dryer runs with door open	Defective door switch	Check with VOM—also check linkages and mounts that actuate switch
Dryer is noisy	Loose panel or component	Locate and secure
	Foreign object in drum opening	Check while turning drum manually
	Lint in fan blades or blower	Remove and clean
	Belt or pulleys misaligned or damaged	Check belts and pulleys; align or replace
	Bearings binding or damaged	Clean and lube or replace

14
Keeping Your Automatic Washer Troublefree

The vast majority of service calls for malfunctioning automatic washers require only simple repairs ranging from adjusting a lid safety switch to replacing a belt. Only a small percentage of calls are in answer to difficult technical problems.

In fact, many of the calls are "instructional" in nature—but these are by no means limited to new equipment. A good example is a consumer who owned her washer for six years before she used the permanent-press cycle, and then called a technician because the water kept running out and then back in after the rinse. The instruction book which came with the machine (and which she had in a drawer beside the washer) explained the cool-down portion of this cycle in detail. Had she only remembered to look, she would have saved the price of a service call. So make it a point always to refer to the instruction book when you are putting new equipment into use or when you are using older equipment in new ways.

But even if there is a definite mechanical or electrical failure in the machine, the odds are very much in your favor that you will be able to remedy it, armed only with the tools that we recommended earlier in this book and with a basic understanding of how your machine operates.

One word of caution, however. Before you begin, pause to remember the points which will prevent this from becoming a "basket job" —where the service technician must assemble a box of parts before he can check for trouble. Washers are deceptively simple in appearance, and the rules which apply to all appliances are even more important here.

To prevent your project from becoming a "basket job," keep these points in mind:

- First, look ahead to the completed job before you begin work. Look at each component involved and plan each step you will take in disassembly and reassembly.
- Second, be sure of your diagnosis before you begin to dismantle the machine. Never take the machine apart with the hope of stumbling on the trouble.

Following these two rules will enable you to restore your machine to service a good part of the time. But you should also make it a rule to avoid two classes of repairs—dismantling the transmission (or replacing the transmission bearings) and repairs inside electronic controls or timers. Work in these areas requires highly specialized equipment and knowledge. You can, however, purchase rebuilt transmissions for some machines and install them yourself, resulting in a substantial savings.

TYPES OF WASHERS

Automatic washers vary in appearance and design, but they all wash, rinse, and spin-dry the clothes in much the same way. Top-loading washers are by far the most popular. Clothes are loaded through an opening or lid in the top of the machine into an upright basket. The basket fills with water, and a gear case or eccentric drive moves a vaned agitator or pulsator back and forth or up and down in the water. All washers clean clothing primarily by forcing water and detergent through the fabric, not just by contact with the fabric. Rinsing is provided by flooding fresh water through the washed clothing.

In the top loader, clothing is dried by spinning the basket and letting centrifugal force pull water from the cloth. Some top loaders drain water through perforations in the basket into an outer tub, from which it is pumped out before the basket begins to spin. Other models begin to spin the basket while it is still filled

Ease of servicing is major point to consider when buying automatic washer. Some manufacturers are designing serviceability into their equipment, as evidenced by this Maytag model. Removable front panel and hinged top permit servicing of most components without moving machine from wall.

with water. As centrifugal force mounts, water flows to the top of the basket and out into a tub formed, in many cases, by the outer cabinet itself. From here it is pumped out of the machine through the drain line and the standpipe installed at the rear by the wall.

In top loaders, the drive mechanism, motor, and pump are suspended under the tub, and are accessible through panels either at the front or rear of the machine. The timer, water temperature switch, and often the water level switch are located in the console, the operating panel which projects above or is formed from the top. This is the section where the dials and knobs are placed. On most newer machines, the components are accessible by removing several screws around the edge of the console and pulling it forward. Be sure that the machine is unplugged before the console or panel is moved.

On front-loading washers, tumble action moves clothing through the wash water. The force of the drop from the revolving drum and the water action remove dirt. Rinsing is provided by a series of fresh water changes entering and leaving the drum. The drum speeds up to provide centrifugal force for water extraction in the spin-dry cycle.

The controls for top loaders are usually located on the front panel of the machine, and are serviced and tested by first removing the top. This is done in most cases by removing the screws that attach the top at the back of the machine, lifting the top until it clears the cabinet at the back, then pulling forward to release it from clips at the front.

Wringer washers are still with us, although several manufacturers have dropped them from their lines within recent years. Since most of today's automatics evolved from the wringer, the drive system for the agitator is much the same. The wringer normally uses no belts, the motor being attached directly by a coupling and the pump engagement made through the use of a drive tread or rubber-surfaced wheel. This is possible because there is no alternate mechanism, such as the clutch necessary to spin the basket, as there is in an automatic. There is a power-take-off shaft to drive the wringer. The rubber rollers are turned through an "in-out" gearbox within the wringer head.

The newest thing in the home laundry field is the compact. Most are derived from both the wringer type and the automatic. They typically use impellers to circulate the water in the wash tub. Then, the clothing is moved to a separate basket for spinning and/or rinsing. Two separate controls, often spring-wound timers with a single set of contacts, cause either or both of the tubs to operate. The water is filled with a hose attached to a faucet, just as it is in the case of the wringer washer. A pump may be engaged to pump the water from either compartment. Semiautomatic compacts require attention during the course of the washing period to provide the manual needs of moving the clothing and adding water. But they require less space, they are portable and roll around easily, and require no special installation.

Yet another trend is in opposition to this. There is a demand for larger washers, primarily to provide greater capacity for large families where floor space is of no great consequence. Most lines have one or more large capacity washers available to meet this demand.

HOW MODERN CYCLES
MAKE YOUR WASHER MORE VERSATILE

FILL　　WASH　　DRAIN　　RINSE-SPIN　　DEEP RINSE　　RINSE-SPIN　　SPIN DRY

The basic format which has been almost universally adopted for automatic washer cycles is a very versatile program. Through the use of timer modifications and a multi-speed motor, it can be made to provide specialized care for practically every fabric. This basic format consists of a fill period followed by a period of washing (agitation with water). The dirty water is then drained and the clothes are spun with the basket to extract even more water, while a spray of water removes any remaining detergent. Then the tub is again filled with fresh water (deep rinse), agitates for a short time, drains, goes through another rinse spin, after which the water spray is shut off and centrifugal force removes much of the remaining water from the fabric.

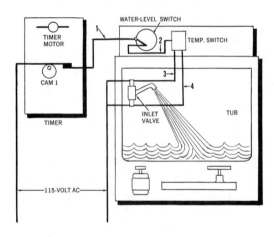

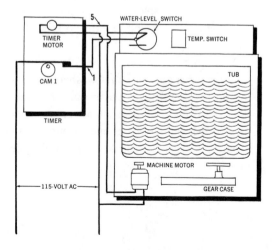

1. Fill cycle. By closing a contact that applies voltage to the float or water-level switch, the timer commands the machine, through wire No. 1, to fill. Since the machine is empty, the float switch does not override the command but transfers it to the temperature switch through wire No. 2. The temperature switch, previously told by the user what temperature to select, then transfers the command to the inlet-valve solenoids through wire No. 3 for cold water, wire No. 4 for hot water, or both for warm water. The solenoid then raises a plunger inside the valve, allowing water to flow into the machine. *Alternate methods:* Some machines use a "timed fill" method which allows water to enter the machine for a certain length of time.

2. Fill cycle continued. As the water in tub approaches the correct level, air or water pressure builds up and acts on the diaphragm of the float switch. The timer still gives its command through wire No. 1, but the movement of the diaphragm has shifted the switch to wire No. 2, releasing the temperature switch and the inlet switch from the command. Instead, the command is transferred to the timer motor and the machine motor, causing the cams within the timer to advance approximately six degrees every two minutes, and causing the machine to start running. *Alternate methods:* Some machines use a diaphragm located in the bottom of the tub to energize the water-level switch, which is located under the tub also. This arrangement does not provide automatic water-level control.

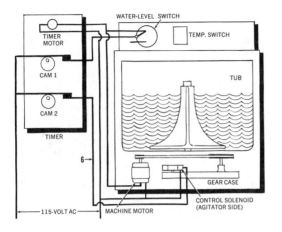

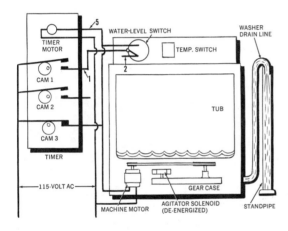

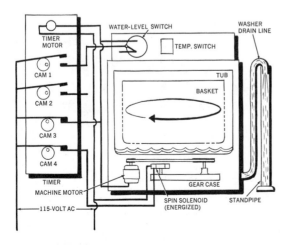

3. Agitation. As the machine begins to run, another cam is brought into action. It gives a command to another solenoid device through wire No. 6. This solenoid in effect puts the machine into gear, and the agitator moves back and forth in the water. In a tumble-type or front-loader, this cam would control a switch that would select the correct speed for basket movement, allowing the clothes to tumble in the water. *Alternate methods:* Some machines use the motor-reversal method of selecting either agitation or spin rather than the solenoid. In this case, the timer would control motor circuitry rather than the solenoid operation.

4. Pump-out. To pump the water from the machine in order to bring in fresh water for a rinse or to prepare for the final spin-dry, cam 2 has raised its movable contact, breaking the command to the agitate solenoid. This puts the agitator out of "gear" again and moves the pump valve into the open position, allowing the pump to force the water out the drain line. To prevent the machine from filling again, the cam controlling wire No. 1 has moved this contact to break the circuit and another contact (cam 3) is added to keep circuit No. 5 energized. Thus, a "bypass" circuit is established and the motors can operate the machine. *Alternate methods:* Machines which use motor reversal usually reverse direction of pump rotation to determine if the water flow is directed to the filter (during agitation) or to the drain (during spin-dry).

5. Spin-dry. The bypass circuit remains in action, and cam No. 4 now closes a timer contact commanding yet another solenoid device to move a mechanical linkage that operates a clutch, allowing the basket to rotate at high speed. The pump also remains in action as centrifugal force causes the water to leave clothes; water must also be removed from the machine. After the spin operation continues for a predetermined time, all cams open their respective contacts and machine operation ceases. *Alternate methods:* Some machines use the motor-reversal method of selecting spin function or agitation. Timer would control motor circuitry rather than solenoid operation.

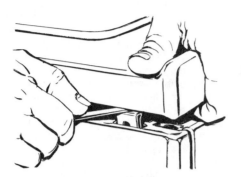

Top may be snapped up with ease in most cases by depressing the locking clips with a thin-bladed screwdriver.

Filter is built into the agitator in this Maytag. Water is forced through filter when the agitator is in motion. It is removed and rinsed off at the end of each cycle.

Hinged tops on most newer automatics like this Sears model allow easy access to many components. The inlet valve, snubber or friction pad, lid switch, and many terminals in the wiring harness are serviceable from above, thus speeding repairs.

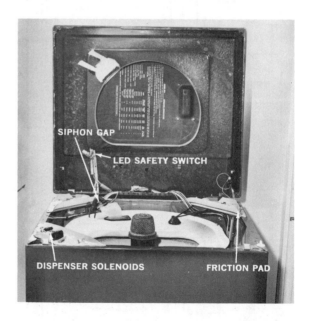

SIPHON GAP

LED SAFETY SWITCH

DISPENSER SOLENOIDS

FRICTION PAD

Semiautomatic compact models utilize two controls in many cases. The timer is often spring-wound with a single set of contacts to energize the machine motor. It controls the agitator or impeller in the wash compartment or the basket in the spin compartment.

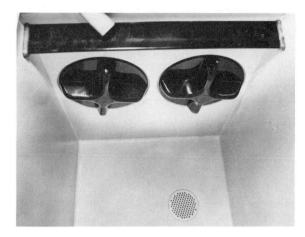

Maytag Porta-Washer uses dual impellers in wash compartment which reverse every half minute.

Today's market makes it necessary for me to simplify the service demands of wringer washers, compact twin-tubs, compact semiautomatics, standard automatics, and large-capacity automatics. The wringer is a simple version of the automatic, consisting of a gearbox to drive the agitator, a direct-drive pump and motor, and another simple gearbox for the wringer. The compact twin-tub is a simple mechanism without the accessories which make the automatic washer capable of carrying out a cycle without attention from the user. By planning your moves carefully and determining how the various components operate in an automatic, it should present no servicing problems. Many compacts can be placed on a table for ease of servicing. The compact automatics, the standards, and the large-capacity machines differ primarily only in physical size. Often the mechanisms and components used in each are identical except for the cabinet and basket.

In addition to the basic drive mechanisms and the basic components necessary to carry the machine through the washing cycle (such as water inlet valves, timers, motors, etc.), there is a myriad of other components which are found on many washers. These are "accessory" parts which give the various models the capacity to do more than others or to give special treatment to certain fabrics. Examples of these components are dispensers, signals, and special containers or baskets. Such accessories will be discussed after the basic drive mechanisms and their related problems.

HOW WASHERS WORK

Many have asked me about combination washer-dryers, the single-cabinet, space-saving machine described in the first edition of this book. These combos never caught on in the numbers their manufacturers hoped, and they have not been manufactured since the early 1970s. Those that remain in service are orphans. Major repair parts are no longer available. Consequently, when a breakdown occurs you may have no alternative to junking the machine.

Washing clothes efficiently requires a combination of chemical action and mechanical action. The chemical action is provided by the water and detergent (and often fabric conditioners and bleach as well). The mechanical action must be provided by the equipment. This consists of two separate and distinct movements—an oscillating movement of the agitator for washing and a spinning motion of the basket for extracting the water from the clothing.

On most washers, you will be able to visually separate the two mechanisms which provide these motions. To reduce motor speed and provide the proper movement for agitation, washers use a gearbox, often in conjunction with a belt or belts and pulleys. The gearbox may be called a transmission or gearcase. In the case of front loaders, it is usually called a speed changer since there is no need for the oscillating or pulsating motion of the agitator. Some Frigidaire washers have used a system of rollers rather than gears to provide the agitation function. These drive mechanisms are usually located directly under the agitator shaft.

There is also a need for another mechanism to reduce the motor speed of approximately 1725 rpm to the 600 rpm or so used by most manufacturers as the basket speed, and also to take up the initial load of bringing the basket up to speed. This is usually done by some sort of clutch, either centrifugal or disc type, and

by pulleys and belts as the means of reducing motor speed. A brake mechanism is necessary to bring the basket to a quick stop when the spin cycle is ended or when the lid is opened. Part of the spin mechanism may be inside the gearcase, or mounted to it so that it appears to be one unit. A close study will allow you to disassociate the components of each.

Finally, you should know that there are two methods employed by washer manufacturers to shift between the wash and spin functions of automatic washers. One method is to use solenoids to shift the mechanism, the other is to reverse the motor rotation. When the latter method is used, a torque spring is used to disengage the spin shaft during agitation. The torque spring is a heavy spring just slightly larger than the diameter of the shaft which it drives. When turned in one direction it loosens and does not grip the shaft; if it is turned in the opposite direction, it tightens and grips the shaft firmly. I won't list these machines by brand names, for some have used both methods during different times of production. But you can tell which method your washer uses by counting the number of wires going into the motor. If you count two wires for the normal speed of your washer and one for every additional speed (for example, a three-speed washer would have four wires) and this is the number of wires entering your motor, chances are that it is solenoid-shifted. If there are more wires than this, it probably is a motor-reversal mechanism.

If you have concluded that there are many differences among washers, you're absolutely right. There is more variation among brands of automatic washers than with any other appliance line. That's why it is important to develop

Spinner basket on Maytag's compact PortaWasher rotates at 2,000 rpm to provide fast water extraction. It won't operate unless lid is locked shut.

Drive mechanism uses O-ring type belt to drive impellers. Many portable units have small motor which drives pump only during pump-out.

that familiarity with your appliances that I mentioned before. But if you know what the differences are and understand that all machines aim to accomplish the same objectives in different manners, you should have no trouble diagnosing problems which arise.

DIAGNOSING THE PROBLEM

Since washers differ so much, we have to treat the analysis of them somewhat differently. The best way that I have found to do this is to make the diagnosis first from the symptoms of the machine, then from further tests in the areas where the particular problem is likely to occur. Symptoms are listed in the order they are most likely to occur in the cycle of the machine.

Symptom: Water Will Not Enter the Machine

Check the obvious first: An inlet hose may be crimped, or perhaps a faucet is turned off. Water-inlet hoses have filter screens at the couplings. Sand or rust scaled off within the water line may have clogged the screens. Another filter is located in the inlet valve at the point where the hose attaches to the machine.

Remove these screens and clean them under a running faucet, using an old tooth brush to remove all of the accumulation. Often these won't appear to be clogged—yet they won't pass water, due to a thin transparent film of algae. If cleaning doesn't remove all of the material, install new screens. Don't operate the washer without screens, as particles might

Frigidaire's Laundry Center combines functions of separate appliances in one machine. Removable front and top panels provide easy access to washer mechanism, dryer, and controls.

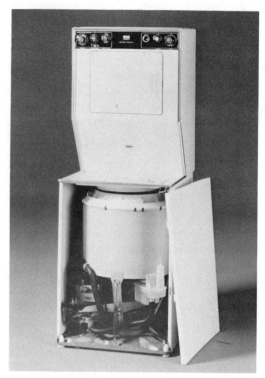

Another approach is to use special rack in conjunction with compact washer and dryer like the Whirlpool units shown. In addition to eliminating bending to place clothes in dryer, it reduces floor space taken up by laundry equipment.

Electronic controls haven't been overlooked by washer manufacturers. This Sears model can be programmed to perform any one of twelve washing functions at the touch of the panel.

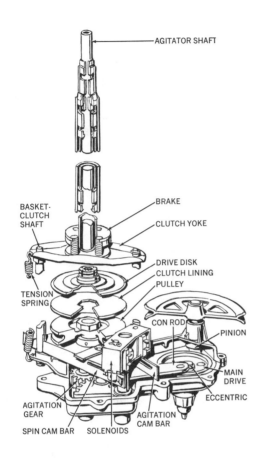

AGITATOR SHAFT

BASKET-CLUTCH SHAFT

BRAKE

CLUTCH YOKE

DRIVE DISK
CLUTCH LINING
PULLEY

TENSION SPRING

CON ROD

PINION

MAIN DRIVE

ECCENTRIC

AGITATION GEAR

AGITATION CAM BAR

SPIN CAM BAR   SOLENOIDS

Cutaway view of Whirlpool drive assembly (left) shows how agitator is driven through gear train at bottom of unit while spinning and braking action of basket is done through clutch assembly above. Tension spring must be removed and basket-clutch shaft freed from cam bar to change belt. Photo above shows assembly as viewed through the rear service panel. *Drawing courtesy of Whirlpool Corp.*

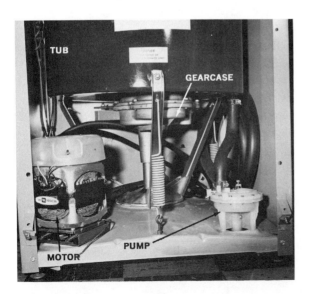

TUB

GEARCASE

MOTOR   PUMP

Pump, motor, gearcase and suspension system are clearly visible in this front view of Maytag washer. Suspension systems are important in standard and large-capacity dryers—baskets of this size can cause centrifugal force of up to 400 pounds when unbalanced. At 600 rpm, this load is experiencing 100 G's.

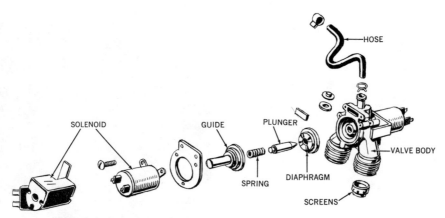

Exploded view of a typical two-port valve of an automatic washer shows order of assembly of components. Either or both solenoids may be energized, providing either hot water, cold water, or a mixture of both. Note positions of the plunger and diaphragm. *Courtesy of General Electric Co.*

lodge in the valve and prevent it from closing.

Still no results? Use your ears for a moment. Is there a low buzzing sound when the water should be coming in? If not, go to the water-inlet valve. To get to this valve you must raise the top of the washer or remove the valve mounting panel found at the rear where the inlet hoses attach to the machine. The tops of most washers are hinged at the rear. A slight forward and upward pull will release the top from its front holding clips and allow it to pivot. Others have screws at the rear of the top. Remove these screws, raise the top at the back, and slide it forward. Before exposing any electrical connections in this manner, *always unplug the machine.*

Water-inlet valves in automatic washers are operated by a solenoid. When current flows through this coil, a magnetic field is created, raising a plunger inside the valve and allowing water to flow into the machine. When the magnetic force is removed, spring action seats the plunger and the water flow is shut off.

Your washer will have one, two, or three of these solenoids, depending on the number of water-temperature selections. To check the coils, look for the wires leading to the water valve. Each coil will have two wires connected to its terminals. Check the coils for continuity and ground with your meter.

A deflection should occur when the meter leads are placed across the terminals of a solenoid, denoting electrical continuity through the coils of wire within. To check for a ground, touch one meter lead to the frame of the cabinet, the other to each of the solenoid terminals in turn. No meter deflection should occur, showing that there is no electrical leakage to ground. If either test shows that the solenoid is faulty, remove the screws that connect it to the valve and replace it with a new one obtained from your dealer.

If all checks well, refer to the wiring diagram on the machine for a component marked "water-level switch" or "float switch." This switch controls the amount of water entering the basket. The diagram shows one of the wires from the switch leading from the timer, and another leading to the inlet-valve solenoid or to the water-temperature switch. Continuity should be read across these two terminals with no water in the basket, and with one of the wires disconnected at the push-on terminals. Now go to the water-temperature switch, and check for continuity from the terminal

Console on this washer was lowered for servicing simply by removing four screws, two at each end. Here, water level switch is being tested for continuity using VOM on $R \times 1$ scale. Other contacts on any switch would be tested in the same manner.

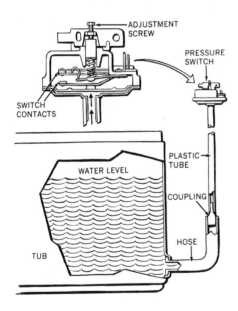

How a pressure switch works: As weight of water in tub increases, air pressure in sealed tub moves a diaphragm, which in turn activates switch contacts to control water level. Once set, the adjustment screw will rarely have to be calibrated. *Courtesy of Whirlpool Corp.*

from the water-level switch to the terminal leading to the solenoid in question.

Keep in mind the short cuts possible when you use one of the best test instruments available—your own ears. Listen to the machine. If you hear a slight hum, the solenoid is buzzing. This tells you that the solenoid, water-level switch, timer, temperature switch, and other electrical components are good. The problem is mechanical. Check for a restriction in the water line. By the same token, should no hum be heard, eliminate the mechanical operation of the water-inlet system and devote your time to testing the electrical components with your meter. Applying your efforts and thinking along this line makes your diagnosis more accurate and much quicker, and prevents traveling up many blind alleys. It's as easy as 1, 2, 3. Observe, listen, and analyze accordingly.

Symptom: Water Will Not Shut Off (Machine Overflows)

Unplug the machine. If the water flow does *not* shut off, the problem lies in the water-inlet valve. These valves depend on balanced water pressure on both sides of a neoprene diaphragm, which in turn is controlled by the solenoid-operated plunger. To allow pressure balance, small "bleed holes" are designed into the diaphragm. If a small grain of sand or particle of rust manages to escape the filters in the water line and lodges in these ports, the plunger is incapable of shutting off water flow. Small things like this can disable any washer.

On newer machines, a throw-away valve is used that is not serviceable, but to the manufacturer's credit, costs less than a major part of a serviceable valve. These have large bleed orifices, and internal problems are likely due to deteriorated parts. The only cure is replacement.

Most other valves, however, are assembled with screws and can be disassembled for cleaning. To clean the valve, remove it from the machine by uncoupling the fill hoses and any other connecting hoses. Remove the quick-disconnect wiring terminals, noting the color-coded wire for each solenoid. Then remove the two screws holding the valve to the cabinet. Disassemble the valve, observing the positions of diaphragms, plungers, and springs, and flush each part (including the valve body) under running water.

While the valve is disassembled, look for other signs of problem areas. Corrosion in the valve guides and on the plunger can disable the valve, as can broken springs and stiff or torn diaphragms. If everything appears to be all right, a good cleaning will probably restore operation. It's not likely that you will actually see the grain of sand which caused the problem.

Be sure to inspect and clean or replace the filters when the valve is disassembled. If a grain of sand passed both filters, they are in need of attention.

If the water flow *did* shut off when the machine was unplugged, check the solenoids on the inlet valve for a ground. There should be no indication that a ground is present. Then check the tube from the tub to the water-level switch to be sure that it is not restricted. If these checks fail to uncover the problem, the water-level switch is probably faulty and should be replaced.

Symptom: Machine Will Not Run at All

If the machine doesn't come on and no sound is heard or the light doesn't operate, use a table lamp to check for voltage at the receptacle—a fuse may be blown in the circuit or the circuit breaker tripped. If you find voltage here, check the two conductors in the power cord and plug. After unplugging the machine, follow the cord to the point where the leads connect to the terminal block or the timer. Check for continuity from each terminal to one of the blades of the plug. If the cord is defective, replace it with a heavy-duty appliance cord with a grounded-type molded plug attached. Be sure to follow the color code. Never use a small lamp-fixture cord or an extension cord on an automatic washer.

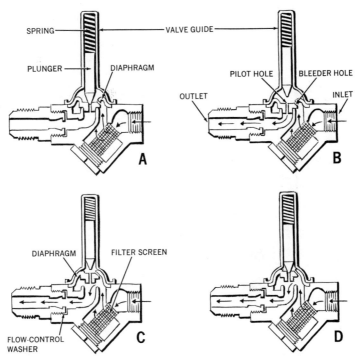

Water-inlet valve operated by a solenoid works as shown in this series of drawings. Starting with drawing *A*, you find valve in its closed position. In *B*, plunger has risen to open the pilot hole, and water in the valve guide escapes. In *C*, pressure of incoming water lifts the diaphragm and the valve opens. In *D*, dropping of plunger closes pilot hole, and pressure in the valve guide then closes the valve. Bleeder hole maintains balanced pressure on both sides of the neoprene diaphragm.

If your washer has no light, turn the water temperature selector switch to various positions and try several different timer positions. If one of the water inlet valve solenoids is open, turning the temperature selector will energize another circuit and should produce some action. During the initial starting period, only the fill circuit is energized on most machines. Open solenoids (check on the $R \times 100$ scale) and an open water-level switch (check on $R \times 1$) are suspect.

Symptom: Machine Will Not Run at All, Makes Humming Sound

Take a look at the motor after removing the access panel. Keep away from moving and electrical parts while observing. If the motor hums but isn't turning, remove the belt and see if it will run. If it does, check the other belt-driven components to see if one is locked or binding. If it does not, remove the motor and take it to a motor-repair shop for inspection.

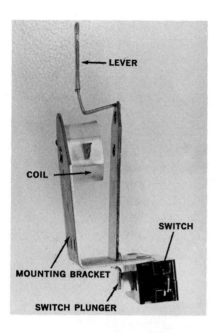

LEVER

COIL

SWITCH

MOUNTING BRACKET

SWITCH PLUNGER

Off-balance relay shuts machine down if clothes load causes chassis to move to the extent that it may strike cabinet. If chassis strikes lever, it closes switch which in turn energizes coil, causing lever to be attracted to coil because of electromagnetic attraction. Simultaneously, another set of contacts in switch has stopped machine action. Lever acts as buzzer until user resets it by turning timer off, then adjusting clothes load.

Many motor problems are due only to faulty centrifugal switches or capacitors, which may be replaced at a fraction of the cost of a new motor.

If the motor runs but does not drive the belt, the motor pulley may be loose on the motor shaft or the belt may be loose or broken. In either case, you will be able to see the problem area. A loose belt is tightened on most machines by loosening the bolts that mount the motor to the superstructure, and moving it back to reduce the slack. As a rule of thumb, most belt tensions are correct when the belt may be depressed about half an inch at midpoint between the two pulleys.

Some machines have a spring-loaded device, usually a pulley, to maintain constant belt tension. If the belt stretches enough to slip, it must be replaced.

If the belt is broken, or has a flat spot from slipping over a period of time, replace it. This may appear at first glance to be quite a job on some machines. Actually, it's usually simple. Always loosen the motor mount or idler pulley that applies belt tension. Then remove the belt from the pulleys. On General Electric machines you'll have to remove one of the clamps from the flexible coupling that drives the water pump. Do this with spring-clamp pliers if spring-type clamps are used.

On Whirlpool and Sears machines, a spacer is provided on one of the three studs that mount the gearcase to the superstructure. Remove this one spacer and the two bolts that hold the water pump in place. This will allow the belt to be removed from all but one obstruction—the basket-clutch shaft. Move the extractor cam bar toward the rear of the machine so that it is completely free from the shaft, drop the shaft down to free the belt, unhook the tension spring, pull belt free. Reverse this to install a new belt. Save the largest pulley for last—a new belt easily slips on if you turn the pulley with it in place. Some models have three braces between the gearcase and the superstructure. These are obvious if they are present, but they must be removed to install a new belt.

The belts used on automatic washers are sized and manufactured for this one specific purpose. Don't try to replace them with general utility belts. It's always best to use the manufacturer's own specified replacement for the job.

When you find a broken belt, check carefully for all possible causes. Some common ones are foreign objects in the pump or bad pump bearings, binding pulleys, or slippage due to failure to adjust the belt previously.

Symptom: Machine Will Not Agitate

Two methods are used to change from one cycle to another: by using solenoids to shift the mechanism upon a signal from the timer or cycle control, or by reversing the direction of motor rotation. A quick observation will determine which of these methods your machine uses. If solenoids are used, determine from the wiring diagram which one controls agitation. Watch its action when the timer is placed in the wash position.

If you can see its movement, you know that the solenoid coil is good and that the circuit through the timer is functioning. Check its mechanical linkage for a broken or binding link or a broken pin. If no movement is observed, move the solenoid manually to be sure that the armature or plunger is not binding. If not, check the coil for continuity, and also check each of the two wires back to the timer.

On some machines the solenoids move as the transmission is in operation. As they become older, the conductor may break inside the insulation of the wiring harness which goes to the solenoid. To check for this condition, remove the plug from the receptacle to disconnect all power from the machine. Then pull the connector from the terminal on the solenoid, grasp the wire about 6 inches back from the end, and pull on it firmly and steadily. If the conductor pulls out of the insulation or you feel a "give" in the wire, splice a new piece of wire into the harness at least 6 inches back from the terminal.

If yours is a motor-reversal-action machine,

Agitator is removed from standard Maytag washer by simply giving it a sharp pull upwards, exposing inner shaft which drives agitator. Basket is bolted to outer shaft which spins during extraction. Most standards employ this method. The outer shaft is often called the spin tube, the inner one the agitator drive shaft.

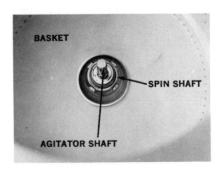

look to see if the rotation is actually reversing in the wash and spin cycles. Always check to see if the pulley driving the gearcase is turning the shaft to which it is attached. Most pulleys are locked to their shaft with Allen-head sets-screws. Check the belt or belts to be sure they are not slipping.

If these observations show that the external controls of the transmission are functioning, or that the agitator is engaging but slipping, then the problem lies in the gearbox itself. If your machine is less than eight years old, it is possible that you may be able to repair a broken gearbox. Usually, though, it's best to obtain an entire rebuilt drive assembly, available for many machines. The rebuilding of these assemblies requires special tools to properly align bearings and gears. Factory rebuilt units are available for many machines at a reasonable price. For Whirlpool and Sears machines,

it's necessary to install new spin tube bearings if the entire assembly is replaced. This requires special pullers and inserters, so you may choose to call a technician for this job. Luckily, though, the gearbox is not likely to require service until the machine has seen many years of hard usage. If the bearings become worn prematurely, evidenced by a rattling, knocking sound during the spin cycle, many appliance parts houses carry a special BK-1 bearing kit that can be installed by simply removing the basket.

Symptom: Timer or Cycle Control Will Not Advance

Check the control by turning it manually to be sure the timer shaft is not binding. If it is, apply a drop of oil carefully to the point that is causing it to bind. Never use more than a

Typical timer for automatic washer has three main parts (from top to bottom): knob, switch section, and motor. Some also have an external escapement mechanism located between the motor and the switch section. In most cases, the motor may be replaced. Burned switches usually call for complete timer replacement.

Timer motor is being tested for continuity in photo at far right. Replace it if circuit is open. Test on R × 100 scale of VOM.

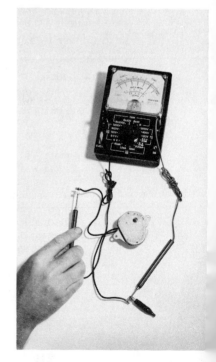

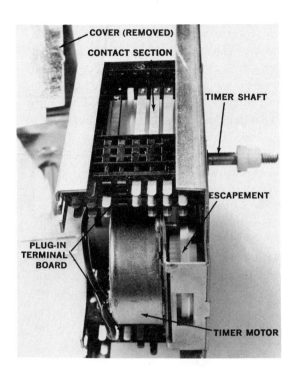

COVER (REMOVED)

CONTACT SECTION

TIMER SHAFT

ESCAPEMENT

PLUG-IN TERMINAL BOARD

TIMER MOTOR

Plug-in type timer motor is being offered in many newer machines. Wiring harness has molded plugs which lock onto terminal board at end of switch section. This is part of a trend toward making replacement of functional components easier for the owner.

Modern pushbutton mechanisms used on automatic washers are mechanical in operation, provide reliable means of selecting wash program. When pushbutton is depressed, actuator presses against actuating spring, which in turn spring-loads pin against disk, which is shown removed from pin plate. When timer knob is turned to start cycle, disk (which is mounted to timer shaft) turns freely until hole is opposite spring-loaded pin, which drops into hole and locks disk. When timer is depressed to start machine, pin releases—but timer is now set to exact spot for beginning of cycle selected.

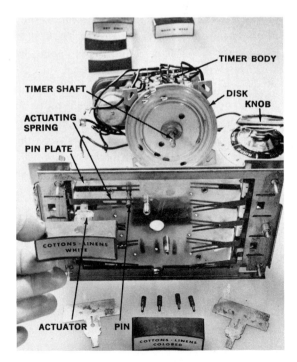

TIMER BODY

DISK

KNOB

TIMER SHAFT

ACTUATING SPRING

PIN PLATE

COTTONS - LINENS WHITE

ACTUATOR   PIN

COTTONS - LINENS COLORED

drop of oil, and never allow it to get near the electrical contacts in the timer.

Timers are driven by a small synchronous motor and a gear train, called an escapement, which advances the timer in sudden movements every one or two minutes, depending upon design. This reduces arcing at the contacts of the various switches by breaking them suddenly, rather than slowly. The timer motor is located in back of the timer in the washer console. It should be checked for continuity, and if faulty it can usually be replaced. If, however, your test shows that the escapement is broken or slipping, the complete timer assembly will have to be changed.

Symptom: Lint Filter Will Not Operate

Most late-model automatics have a filter in the water system to reduce the amount of linting from fabrics. Operating at all times when the machine is washing or rinsing, the system removes water from a tub outlet, pumps it through the filtering device and back into the washer basket. Valving devices in the pump control the water flow and direct it either to the filter or to the drain outlet. On motor-reversal types, the pump will discharge the water when turning in one direction to provide spinning action, and to the filter when turning in the opposite direction for agitation.

Naturally, if something happens to stop water flow through the filter, the filtering action will stop. On most machines, you can see the water flow back into the machine if it is functioning correctly. On others, you must visually check the components in the filtering system to be sure the passages are not clogged.

Some fabrics, such as terry cloth, flannel,

etc., give off large amounts of lint. Others, such as corduroy, hold lint. Lint givers and lint holders should not be washed in the same load, as the lint will become attached to the nap of the lint-holding fabric before it gets into the water stream where it can be filtered. If a problem with linting is encountered, a fabric softener added to the rinse water will do much to eliminate the condition, especially in the case of wash-and-wear fabrics.

As we noted, some automatics drain water through perforations in the basket before spinning. Others spin the basket while still filled with water, the resulting centrifugal force acting to force the water over the top of the basket and into the tub, to be pumped from the machine into the drain line. It sometimes happens that a small article of clothing goes over the top along with the expelled water and blocks the drain outlet.

When this occurs, it is usually first noticeable as a loss of filtering recirculation. To remedy, raise the top of the machine, push the basket to one side, and "go fishing"; reach into the tub and feel for the clothing at the outlet, or perhaps floating in the water, and pull it free. If a guard is present at the outlet, be sure not to remove it when the clothing is taken out. Of course, if the blockage is severe enough the pump-out will also be affected.

If this problem occurs frequently, check the manner in which your washer is loaded. Remember, it is water circulation through the fabric that does the cleaning. Therefore if the clothing is loaded correctly it will tumble and move through the water in the machine as it is circulating. If the machine is overloaded, the agitator will simply move in the middle of a pile of clothing, and little water action will be

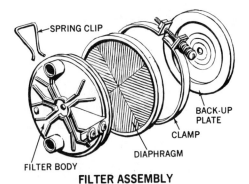

FILTER ASSEMBLY

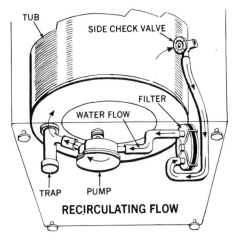

RECIRCULATING FLOW

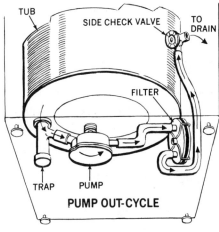

PUMP OUT-CYCLE

Self-cleaning filters on some newer washers offer high efficiency and convenience. In Whirlpool's Magic-Clean at top, diaphragm contracts during washing and rinsing as water is recirculated from side check valve through filter and pump and back into bottom of machine (middle drawing). Contracted diaphragm allows water to pass but traps lint contained in water stream. When valve in pump reverses water flow (bottom), diaphragm expands and releases trapped lint, which flows to drain. *Whirlpool Corp.*

observed. This is the easiest and most practical way to judge any clothes load.

The rating of washers in pounds is excellent as an industry standard, but is of little value in everyday washing. It's similar to the old riddle: "Which weighs the most, a pound of lead or a pound of feathers?" While 18 pounds of a heavy denim material may not reach the capacity of your washer basket, 18 pounds of nylon quilting may not even get into your washroom, let alone the washer. If you've any doubt about a particular load, observe the water circulation and clothes movement—if both are active, there is no need to be concerned about overloading.

If loading habits are correct, and a problem still occurs with clothing passing over the basket, consult the manufacturer. Most makers offer a guard for use on their commercial equipment which can be adapted to home washers. Others choose to pin small articles together or wash them in a net bag to prevent the problem.

If passageways to and from the washer pump are clear, and still no recirculation occurs, check the pump and its linkages. The pump is easily located by following the large outlet from the bottom of the tub. See if the pump coupling or belt is tight. The pump should turn easily by hand. If not, remove it by unfastening the attachment bolts, and remove the screws that hold the pump together.

Be sure no foreign objects have gotten into the pump and locked the impeller, which should turn easily. Impeller and pump body should be inspected visually for pitting and cracking. Valves should operate smoothly and positively. Whenever disassembling a pump, replace any seals that show a sign of leakage. Lubricate the impeller shaft and linkages.

Cork gaskets must be replaced—rubber O-ring gaskets may be reused if not damaged.

Symptom: Water Leaks from Machine

An axiom of washer-service technicians is that "leaks are where you find them." Since the appliance is using water in some manner during most of the cycle, notice carefully at what point the leak occurs. This will give a clue as to whether the leak is in the inlet system, the tub, or in the drainage system. Then, before the machine is moved, try to look under it with a flashlight to see the general location of the drip.

Check the inlet hoses before and after a fill period—heat expands the fittings and sometimes the couplings may leak only at this time. Also check the drain standpipe—it may need to be cleaned out. If you have an intermittent leak and suspect the standpipe, tie a rag around it. The next time an overflow occurs, the rag will absorb water and remain wet for several hours, while the hot drain line will dry very quickly.

Should the leak be in the machine, look for wet spots or a white stain left on the floor by detergent after the water has dried. If a hose is deteriorated it may be cut shorter and used temporarily. But replace it as soon as possible.

Many parts which were previously made from aluminum alloy—such as pump housings and valve bodies—are now made from newly developed plastics. If you find a leak where the alloy has become pitted from chemical reaction with detergents and bleaches, replace the entire component with its plastic counterpart. Chances are that you will never have to replace it again because of a leak.

Leaks sometimes develop around attach-

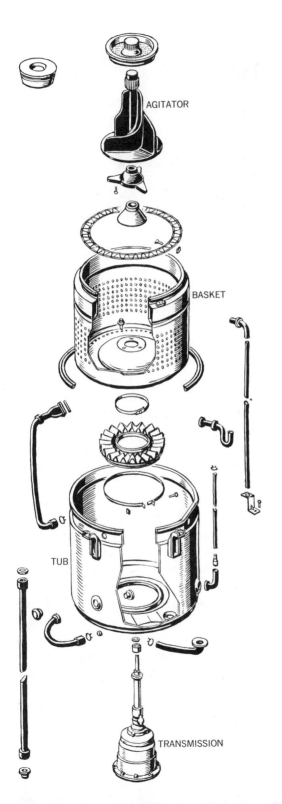

AGITATOR

BASKET

TUB

TRANSMISSION

Exploded view of tub and basket assembly shows much of
the water system of an automatic washer. To check for
leaks, all hoses, boots, and seals
must be inspected. It is important, especially in case of a
small leak, to locate general
area before moving machine.
Courtesy of General Electric.

General Electric Filter-Flo washer is serviced after removing screws which retain top. Basket is removed by loosening three bolts in bottom of basket under boot (removed in photo at left). "Horseshoe" into which bolts are threaded must be held in place when replacing basket on older models. One method of doing this is to saw the head off a bolt with the same thread size, and use this as a guide stud to position it until other bolts are started.

ment points in the porcelain-coated tub of the machine. If this occurs, check to see if the manufacturer doesn't offer a repair kit. These kits, sometimes consisting of brass bolts with large heads and neoprene gaskets, take the place of the old fastenings and cover the damaged area. For the small cost of the kit, they can give an old tub a new lease on life.

Symptom: Water Will Not Pump Out

Check to see if the filter water is recirculating. If not, check the same areas that you would for loss of filtration: pump, pump valves, pump belt, pump coupling, or restriction in water lines leading to the pump. When replacing the flexible pump coupling on GE washers, always install the new coupling with the fabric side out.

If water recirculation does exist, only two possibilities remain: The pump valve is not shifting from the recirculate position, or the drain line from the machine to the laundry tub or standpipe is crimped or clogged.

If you find that the pump itself is at fault, disassemble it to get at the root of the problem. A foreign object may have lodged itself against the impeller, preventing it from turning; or the pump bearings may be worn to the extent that the impeller shaft has "frozen." Bearing assemblies are available for many pumps which have plastic housings, and may be installed with only a screwdriver. For pumps with pressed-fit bearings, the best course is to replace the entire pump.

When reinstalling hoses, wipe any grit from the inside of the hose before putting it back in position. Check for leaks after it is installed. If you find one, it may be necessary to alter the position of the hose clamps. Be sure that all linkages are back in position when you are bolting the pump back in place, and readjust the belt when the job is done.

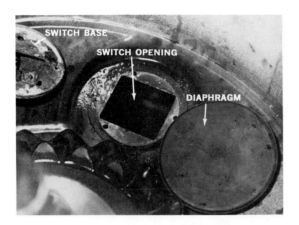

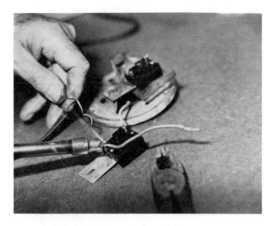

Diaphragm of water-level switch is being replaced in this photo. Retaining screws and switch are reached from bottom of machine, but washer basket must be removed to remove diaphragm.

Diaphragm switch has leads which are "pigtailed" to old switch and must be soldered to new one. Be sure that linkage works smoothly before reinstalling in machine.

Pump coupling (installed fabric side out) on a GE washer must be removed to service the pump or clutch, or to replace the belt. It is best to use hose-clamp pliers to remove the large spring-type clamps on older models.

GE pump assembly is easily serviced after removal from the bottom of the tub. Internal flapper valve, which diverts water flow either to filter or drain line, is controlled by direction of motor rotation.

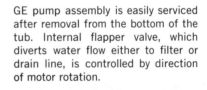

Symptom: Machine Will Not Spin-dry

Check visually to see that the motor-reversal or solenoid action is occurring to shift the basket drive mechanism. Inspect the linkages to see that they are not bent, broken, or rusted. If they are, replace or lubricate them so that they operate smoothly. Check the spin solenoid for continuity. If no solenoid action occurs, check the wiring harness for continuity, and then check the contacts within the timer as designated in the wiring diagram. The lid safety switch may be the culprit here. On some washers, it shuts off the entire machine when the lid is raised; on others, the spinning action only is stopped. To check it, locate the switch and check for continuity while holding it in the position it would be in with the lid shut.

If the basket spins slowly but does not pick up speed, see if there is water or detergent in the outer tub. If so, the braking action of the friction against the surface of the basket can slow the speed greatly. Oversudsing can be remedied by filling the machine with fresh water, then pumping the water back out. If oversudsing is extreme, this may have to be done several times. Also check for the possibility that clothing may have gone over the basket and wrapped around the basket hub. To detect this, you have to reach as far under the basket as possible, after first raising the top.

Another cause of slow spin could be a loose belt or slipping clutch. Automatic washers with a centrifugal-clutch mechanism (similar to that used on gasoline engines for power mowers, go-karts, etc.) generally provide no adjustment—the clutch linings have to be replaced if they are slipping. Those that use a dry-disc-type clutch to drive the basket provide an adjustment on the clutch linkage. There should be about ⅛-inch clearance between the lining and clutch pulley when in the agitate position.

Symptom: Excessive Vibration and/or Noise

Automatic washers are designed to absorb quite a bit of the shock of an unbalanced load without transferring movement to the cabinet, very much as an automobile is designed to absorb the impact of road bumps without transferring the chassis movement to the body structure. In both instances, however, if the movement is severe enough the suspension cannot absorb it all. Therefore, the first thing to do if vibration occurs is to rearrange the clothes in the basket. When washing heavy, highly absorbent items such as throw rugs, wash several at a time. Although the load itself will be heavier, the increased volume of several pieces will allow the water movement to place them around the basket for balance.

Inspect the leveling feet on the machine. It should be approximately level, and should rest solidly on the floor.

One of the most difficult problems you may encounter is trying to locate a noise when the machine appears to be functioning normally. The best clue will be to notice the point in the cycle where the noise occurs. Note whether it is pumping, spinning, or agitating at that point, thus at least eliminating components that could not be involved. Often it is helpful to use a makeshift stethoscope. Take a large screwdriver and place the driving end on the metal housing near the area where the noise seems to originate, and hold the handle near

Some washers are using adjustable agitators as well as varying water levels and motor speeds to customize treatment for small and delicate loads. Westinghouse approaches the problem by utilizing a hand-wash agitator that nests inside its heavy-duty counterpart when not in use. The outer agitator has deep ramps for normal and heavy fabrics, the hand-wash agitator has gentle sloping ramps. *Courtesy of Westinghouse Corp.*

your ear. This little trick has helped me pin down many evasive noises.

The suspension system of a washer, like an automobile, consists of springs or suspension bars and shock absorbers in the form of friction pads or snubbers. This system can be the source of associated squeaks and pops. The snubber pads should be dry and unglazed. If not, clean them and roughen the surface with a file or on a cement surface. Coil springs, which may develop a tendency to squeak, can be treated with a little grease.

Some squeaks or squeals can be traced to the belt. Check to be sure that there is proper tension, and if necessary, use a belt dressing. Never apply oil or grease to a belt or to a clutch lining.

Mastering the causes and effects of these basic symptoms will carry you successfully through most repairs that will arise with your automatic washer. In the accompanying dia-

gram, you will see how these basic functions are altered to give special care to particular garments. Most of these special cycles involve only changes in the timer programming, not in the basic mechanism itself except for the addition of motor windings to provide speed selection.

Dispensers have come into common use among the top lines of most automatic washers, and they serve a valuable function. They add the chemicals to the water at the proper time, and they dilute them as well.

The chemical action cannot be underestimated for its value in providing a clean wash. The detergent serves a dual purpose—it dissolves oils which help hold soil in the fabric and it holds the soil in suspension in the water. It also contains optical brighteners. Bleach negates some of this chemical action of the detergent, so it is usually added only during the last five minutes of the wash cycle. The rinse additive clings to the fabric to give it a softer feel —but if it is added at the wrong time, during the wash period for instance, soil may remain in the clothing.

Most of the early dispensers could handle only liquid chemicals. They usually consisted of a reservoir with a solenoid attached to a plunger in the bottom. When the timer energized the solenoid, it "pulled the stopper" from the bottom of the reservoir and the chemical flowed into the water. This served the purpose of dilution well, and it also added the chemicals at the right time. But the dispensers sometimes became clogged, especially if the chemicals were left in the reservoir for prolonged periods.

Newer types of dispensers recirculate water through the detergent dispenser, which gives it the capability of handling powdered detergents as well as the liquid type. This keeps the reservoir clean as well. Many are also simpler; an example is the dispenser being used on several brands where the rinse additive dispenser is mounted on top of the agitator. The additive stays in the chamber where it is poured at the beginning of the cycle until the machine begins to spin during the first rinse period. During the spin, centrifugal force pushes it into another chamber. From this chamber, it can pour into the basket when the agitator stops at the beginning of the deep rinse. It's simple and there is nothing to wear out. An occasional flushing is the only maintenance required.

If a dispenser fails to operate, or if it dumps the chemical as soon as it is poured in, visually check the condition of the plunger and linkage. Often a thorough cleaning and flushing is all that is necessary to restore operation. The VOM ($R \times 100$ scale) will check the condition of the solenoid.

Dispensers used on automatic washers are of the "one-shot" type which dump all their load into each wash when they are energized.

Never use the console or backsplash of a washer to move or handle the machine: this may chip the porcelain-enamel finish. Use an old blanket or quilt to protect the finish and the floor whenever it is necessary to lay the machine down. And remember; the better you understand your washer *before* trouble arises,

Wiring diagrams are your roadmap to proper diagnosis and repair. Here, a switch section of off-balance relay is identified for testing. Most such diagrams have been simplified so that all components are recognizable.

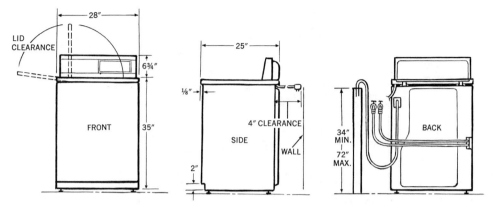

When buying a washer, compare dimensions with available space, otherwise built-in convenience may be lost. Supply faucets, drain pipe and the grounded receptacle should be close. Drain pipe should be approximately 34 inches high to prevent siphoning of water.

the better your chances of making the necessary repairs yourself.

RULES FOR THE USE AND CARE OF AN AUTOMATIC WASHER

• Locate the unit as close as possible to the hot-water source.
• Sort clothing according to color, fabric, and degree of soil.
• Clean lint filter regularly.

• Use correct temperature for type of fabric.
• Use correct amount of detergent, bleach, and rinse additive—this depends on hardness of water, load size, and degree of soil.
• Do not overload the machine. If in doubt, be sure that clothing circulates freely in the water during agitation.
• Use low-sudsing detergent for front-loading models. While top-loading models are not limited to low-sudsing detergents, under certain water conditions I've found that it is almost always advisable.

QUICK-CHECK CHART FOR

AUTOMATIC WASHERS

Symptom	Cause	Remedy
No water enters machine	Hose crimped; faucet off Filter screens clogged Inlet-valve solenoid open Water-level switch open	Correct as needed Clean or replace Replace Replace
Water will not shut off—machine overflows	Foreign particles in inlet valve Inlet-valve solenoid grounded Tube to water-level switch blocked Water-level switch faulty	Disassemble and flush with water Replace solenoid Clear tube of obstruction Replace switch
Machine will not run	Blown fuse Faulty power cord or plug Motor faulty Belt loose or broken	Replace Replace with heavy-duty cord Repair or replace Adjust or replace
Machine will not agitate	Agitate solenoid inoperative Loose drive pulley(s) Faulty transmission drive	Replace coil or repair linkages Tighten setscrews Refer to servicing organization
Timer will not advance	Binding Timer motor open Timer escapement inoperative	Lubricate carefully Replace motor Replace timer assembly
Lint filter inoperative	Tub outlet blocked Pump or pump valve inoperative Lint-holding fabrics being washed with lint-giving fabrics	Remove restriction—check washer loading Disassemble pump and repair or remove foreign object from pump Observe special loading procedure
Water leaks	Hose connections faulty or hose deteriorated Drainage pipe clogged Tub or pump housing pitted	Tighten or replace Clean drainage system Replace
Water will not pump out	Tub outlet blocked Pump or pump valve inoperative Pump coupling or belt broken	Remove restriction—check washer loading Disassemble pump and repair or remove foreign object from pump Replace
Machine will not spin-dry	Solenoid inoperative Water or detergent in outer tub Lid safety switch inoperative Clothing around basket hub Slipping belt Slipping clutch	Replace solenoid or repair linkages See "water will not pump out"; observe oversudsing precautions Replace or adjust linkages or brackets Remove and check loading procedure Check for proper tension Adjust or replace lining as necessary
Excessive vibration	Load out of balance Machine not level or solid on floor	Rearrange clothing in basket Adjust leveling feet to correct height; see that rubber boots are in place
Unusual noise	Assorted mechanical noises Sticking friction pads Springs squeaking Belt squealing	Use makeshift "stethoscope" Clean surface to remove glaze Coat with light layer of grease Adjust to proper tension

15
What You Should Know About Automatic Dishwashers

Chances are about 50-50 that your automatic dishwasher is not giving the service it could. It may be washing the dirty dishes, but not the way it should (or could). A representative of a top maker of dishwashers says their records disclose that 45 to 50 percent of all service calls involve factors not related to equipment defects or failures.

The faults are related to the environment in which the dishwasher operates.

The dishwasher is far more sensitive to outside influences than practically any other home appliance. The water may not be hot enough. There may not be enough of it. The detergent may have been on the shelf too long. Any or all of these can have a detrimental effect upon the operation of the dishwasher.

Testing the environmental factors ought to precede any repair. In fact, you may want to test your dishwasher even though it seems to be operating satisfactorily. First, however, you should understand the basic principles of automatic dishwashing.

A dishwasher works by making use of water pressure, heat, and chemical actions. An impeller or high-speed pump and spray arm produce the water pressure. The force of the water scrubs the dishes with hot water and detergent solution, loosening soil and flushing it away. A heating element, normally energized throughout the cycle, maintains the temperature. Detergent is added automatically during each wash period.

Dishes usually are dried by the heating element that maintains water temperature or by a small heater located outside the dishwasher tub within an air duct.

With the final rinse water pumped out, the heater raises the temperature within the machine and the heated air absorbs moisture. Since the dishwater is vented to room air, air flow occurs within the machine. Some machines have a small blower to increase air flow and speed drying action. On some new machines, an "energy-saver" switch turns the heating element off during the dry cycle, allowing the dishes to air dry or forcing air across them with a small blower. The heater is

244 AUTOMATIC DISHWASHERS

still energized in the wash cycles to maintain water temperature; otherwise, water striking the cool dishes and tub would quickly cool.

CHECKING PERFORMANCE

With the operating principles in mind, you can make sure you're getting all the performance your dishwasher will deliver. In the process you can eliminate causes of many service calls.

First, check the water temperature. Let the machine fill with water on a normal cycle. Then advance the timer by slowly turning its dial clockwise. This will pump out the machine and let it refill. With the second water fill in the tub, stop the machine, open the door, and insert a candy or meat thermometer in the water. Temperature need not exceed 160 degrees, but a temperature below 140 won't dissolve grease or detergent.

Wipe your fingers across the lower front corners of your machine if it's a front-loader. A greasy black film indicates that water temperature is too low. If your water heater is set to a higher temperature than that being delivered to the dishwasher, remember that a loss of one degree per foot of pipe is normal. This condition is much more prevalent these days since many of us have turned our water heater down to conserve energy. Some new models have built-in water heaters to heat their own supply; otherwise it may be necessary to install an in-line water heater to obtain good dishwashing results.

For the second test, observe the amount of water fill. The exact amount varies among different models of the same brand, but a good rule of thumb is that the water should reach the heating element. If it's low, be sure that you have adequate volume at the inlet line, or at the faucet if you have a portable model.

To do this, try filling a gallon container from the dishwasher supply. It shouldn't take longer than thirty seconds. If it does, you need to check the plumbing running to the dishwasher. If the supply is adequate, you should check the strainer in the faucet aerator of a portable machine and the one in the dishwasher's inlet valve. One or both may be restricted by foreign particles or by a thin film of algae. Remove and clean them under running water, using a small brush to be sure that every trace of foreign matter is removed. An old toothbrush is ideal for this purpose.

A small washer built into the inlet valve of many dishwashers serves as a water-pressure regulator, reducing the water pressure to a specific level to provide constant fills. This neoprene disc, usually called a flow washer, has a chamfered opening which constricts to reduce water pressure to approximately 20 psi (pounds per square inch), acting quite effectively in the 20 to 100 psi input range. If this washer is torn, damaged, or brittle it has an effect on the amount of water entering the machine.

Dishwashers use the "timed-fill" method for getting water into the machine; any water-level switches are usually intended only to prevent overflow. Don't attempt to adjust these to control water level.

Check your detergent. Dishwasher detergent is a highly alkaline compound formulated to loosen all types of food soil, to keep sudsing at a minimum, and to act as a wetting agent. It is quite unstable compared to other household detergents and has a short shelf life—as little as two weeks after the foil wrapper is broken, depending on temperature and hu-

Electronic controls on Whirlpool's latest dishwasher program wash cycles, also let you set wash cycle to occur at night to take advantage of low, off-peak power rates in some areas. By inputting special code, technician can get microprocessor to "tell" him where trouble is in equipment.

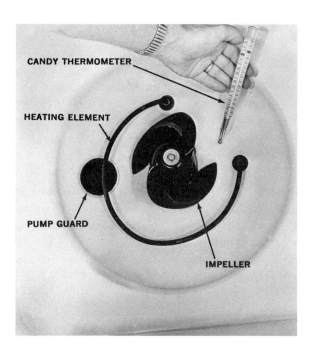

First checkpoint when a machine seems below par is water temperature. The magic number is 140 degrees. At lower temperature water action is greatly reduced. An ideal water temperature is 150 degrees— it shouldn't exceed 160.

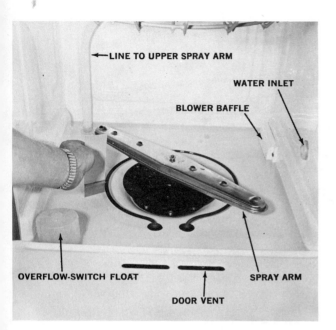

LINE TO UPPER SPRAY ARM

WATER INLET

BLOWER BAFFLE

OVERFLOW-SWITCH FLOAT

DOOR VENT

SPRAY ARM

Second check is water level. Does water reach the heater? If not, suspect low pressure or restriction in line.

midity. Watch for torn or cut outer wrappers when buying detergent. Close the pouring spout after using.

If detergent becomes caked it probably has passed its useful life. To test it, try the "two-by-two" test—place two teaspoons in a glass of hot water (not under 140 degrees) and stir for two minutes. If a gritty residue remains, the detergent is not satisfactory.

There's quite a bit of difference among various formulations of dishwasher detergents. If you're not satisfied with the washing results that you are getting, try another brand. Some brands work better in particular water conditions than others. Never substitute detergent made for dishpan or laundry use. A washing-by-hand detergent is much too sudsy for your dishwater (and dishwasher detergent much too strong in the dishpan).

Water conditions play a big part in the results that you obtain from a dishwasher. One directly-related problem that you may encounter is a filming condition that may show up on glassware. If it is a temporary precipitate, it can be removed by using a "stripping" cycle, using a cup of bleach (no detergent) in the wash water followed by a cup of vinegar in the rinse water. Then allow it to go through the cycle. This should remove the hardest film. To prevent it from reoccurring, be sure that you are using enough detergent in the wash water, and try using a rinse additive such as Jet-Dry or Dish-Dri. One of these can be a big help in obtaining good washing results, especially in hardwater areas. Primarily wetting agents, they reduce water surface tension, allowing the water to flow off the dishes.

This reduces mineral staining and spotting.

Most additive dispensers, injecting a few drops during the final rinse, hold about three months' supply. Check the level periodically. If your machine has no dispenser, additives are available in cake form for suspending from the basket. This works well. If the hard-water condition is severe, the only solution may be to install a water softener.

Another surface condition of glassware that usually occurs in soft water and which is often confused with filming is etching. In this case the damage is permanent. It is determined by the composition of the glass, and is primarily a reaction to water conditions amplified by the heat and strong chemical solution found within the dishwasher. It should be recognized that the same thing can occur even when the dishes are hand washed, but at a slower rate—and it is the heat and strong detergent which

allow a dishwasher to clean more thoroughly and efficiently than is possible by hand washing. As a rule, etching is more likely to occur on high-quality glassware than on the less expensive types.

Finally, check to be sure the dishwasher is being loaded according to the manufacturer's instructions. The design of racks differs in each brand, but a lot of thought and effort goes into each one, providing the best placement for the particular water patterns of the machine. Remember that it's the water that does the scrubbing, and it has to be able to reach each part of the utensil or glassware before good cleaning results can be expected. Watch particularly for "blocking," placing a large platter or plate directly in line with a smaller one; and "nesting," placing a cup or saucer inside another without enough space for the water to

Load it right so dishwasher can do best job. Don't nest one dish in or against another, or block the water flow with a large dish. Note how arrangement of racks helps keep utensils separated.

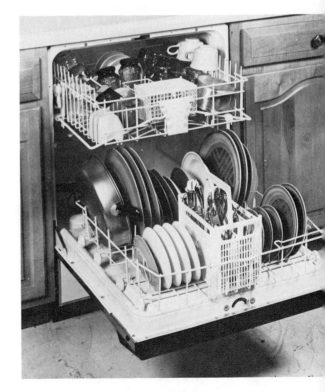

Even the portables are easier to load. Several models, like this GE Mobile Maid, have racks that lift with door and fold back into place.

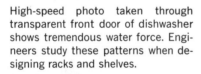

High-speed photo taken through transparent front door of dishwasher shows tremendous water force. Engineers study these patterns when designing racks and shelves.

Filters and protectors help prevent redepositing food particles on dishes as well as guarding the pump. Whirlpool's filter is easily inspected and is largely self-cleaning.

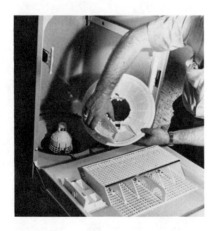

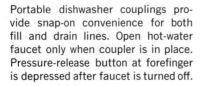

Portable dishwasher couplings provide snap-on convenience for both fill and drain lines. Open hot-water faucet only when coupler is in place. Pressure-release button at forefinger is depressed after faucet is turned off.

penetrate. Also be certain that no large items such as knives or spatulas project out of the basket where they might block the movement of the spray arm or impede a telescoping spray tower.

If you eliminate the environmental conditions that I have outlined as the cause of a dishwasher problem, you then must look deeper for any trouble that develops.

DISHWASHERS WITH OPEN IMPELLERS

As with any appliance, it's important that you understand how the dishwasher works before you begin to diagnose and make any repairs. Dishwashers can be divided into two categories. The first of these are primarily the older units which use an open impeller or paddle, spinning in the middle (sump) of the tub. This action slings water against the dishes with great force. I will refer to these as type-A units.

In these units the main motor turns in one direction only, and the pump is often powered by a separate smaller motor. Some models eliminate the pump, and use a solenoid-operated dump valve to empty the water into the drain by gravity flow.

Since mechanical components are usually mounted directly to the motor shaft, it's im-

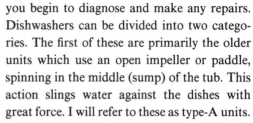

This type-A machine shows typical locations of impeller, heater, drain guard or pump protector, and vent opening. Stain at upper left is caused by high iron content in water. Stains can usually be removed by adding half a cup of citric acid crystals (available at drug stores) to clear water in longest cycle of dishwasher.

Give careful attention to the condition of the leading edge of impeller. Chipped and broken edges may cause erratic spray patterns and greatly reduced water action.

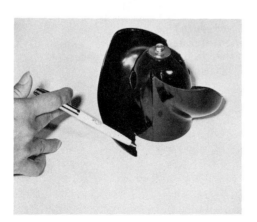

portant that you know how to troubleshoot the motor. First, look at the bell housing on the motor and determine whether it has a manual-reset protector—on type-A machines, many do. Push the reset button and listen. No hum or noise at all? Check at the motor terminals with a volt-ohm meter (VOM). A short, relatively loud hum (less than four seconds) followed by the overload protector kicking out indicates that both running and starting windings are being energized; check for foreign objects jamming the impeller, or stuck motor bearings.

If it hums or buzzes for a longer period, chances are that the run winding only is being energized; check the motor centrifugal switch. Problems in this area require removal and disassembly of the motor. It's best to let a motor-repair shop replace the switch; it must often be fabricated to fit the motor.

The impeller itself is critical on type-A machines. Chips and breaks on the leading edge cause erratic spray patterns and greatly reduce washing efficiency. Damage to impellers is caused by foreign objects, primarily silverware, dropping into the sump. If confronted with this problem, inspect the silverware basket and be certain the machine is being loaded according to instructions.

The shaded-pole motor that powers the pump on type-A dishwashers is a rugged device. If water doesn't pump out, check to see that the pump is turning freely; you can often tell by turning the motor shaft with long-nose pliers. If it's binding, disassemble the pump and inspect for foreign objects.

Motor bearings are usually accessible and will seldom require more than cleaning and oiling if the motor shaft itself is binding.

A strainer, usually in the bottom of the tub, protects the pump. It's a compromise, however; its openings must be large enough to allow soft food deposits to pass and be flushed away, but small enough to stop bits of bone, glass, olive pits, etc. The problem lies in *small* pieces of hard material. Check the strainer carefully whenever a foreign object is found in the pump. It's a tough feeling when you reassemble the pump only to hear the "chunk" of another object lodging against the impeller.

If the pump turns freely, check the pump motor for continuity with your VOM. If okay,

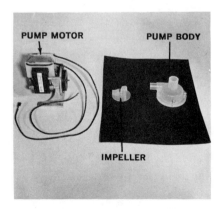

This pump assembly is typical of those found in older (type A) machines. Motor is mounted to pump housing and seal plate. Impeller threads onto motor shaft and pump cover bolts to the pump housing.

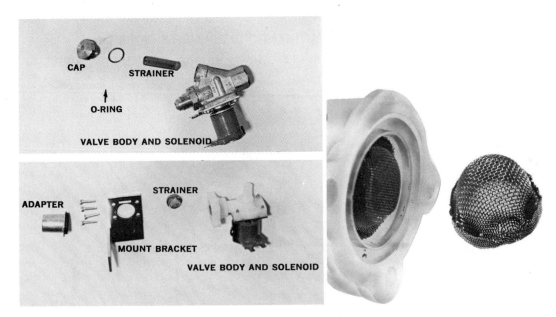

Disassembly of two common inlet valves for automatic dishwashers shows location of inlet strainer. Nylon-body valve at top requires removal of inlet line before removing strainer (right). Brass-body valve (lower) features strainer accessible by removing plug as shown.

you may find that the circuit through the timer contacts which supply voltage to the motor is open.

DISHWASHERS WITH SPRAY ARMS

A new breed of dishwashers is presently dominating the market. I will refer to these as type-B machines. You'll recognize a type-B machine by the absence of an open impeller at the bottom of the tub. In its place will be a stainless-steel or plastic spray arm, perforated with water-jet nozzles.

Water is directed from a high-speed, high-efficiency pump into the spray arm, making it revolve and direct its water jets to every inch of the tub. Some deluxe models use two arms, a spray tube and revolving rack or a telescoping tower, to accomplish two-level washing. In many machines, the motor turns in one direction to force water through the spray arms, and reverses to force it out the drain.

Checkout procedure for the motor is much like that for type-A washers, except that there is only one motor and there may be a current-operated relay rather than a centrifugal starting switch. It also may be reversible, and if this is the case, there will be four motor leads.

One lead is common to both windings, one energizes the running winding, and the other two energize the starting winding. Only *one* starting lead is energized at a given time, for this determines the direction of motor rota-

HOW A SPRAY-ARM AUTOMATIC DISHWASHER WORKS

Mechanical operations: Phantom view of a typical modern dishwasher illustrates common locations of major components.

The timer **(1)** is often located behind a bottom access panel under the tub, behind an access panel above the front-opening door. On some deluxe models, the timer is advanced to the beginning of various cycles by a pushbutton-actuated motor.

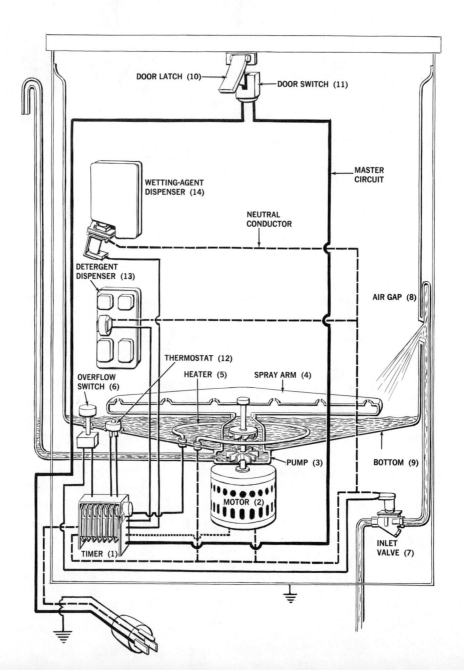

The machine motor **(2)** drives a high-capacity pump **(3)** that forces water jets from a revolving spray arm **4).** The motor may revolve in only one direction, with a solenoid-operated valve opening the drain line for the drain portion of the cycle; it may revolve in one direction to wash, in the other to pump out water; or it may utilize a separate, smaller pump motor. Bidirectional motors have four entering leads.

A heater **(5)** maintains water temperature and usually provides heat drying. In addition, many models have a small squirrel-cage blower under the access panel to force air through the tub during the dry cycle. At least one uses a separate air heater incorporated in the air-inlet duct. The newer models that incorporate an "energy-saver" switch turn the heating element off entirely during the drying cycle, relying on room air or air circulated by a small blower to dry the dishes. Without the resistance element energized, the overall energy consumption during the cycle is reduced considerably.

The overflow switch **(6)** provides a safety shut-off for the inlet valve **(7).** This switch may be float or diaphragm type. A built-in air gap **(8)** is always a required safeguard to prevent siphoning of tub water back into the fresh-water line in case of a pressure drop. Relative position of the tub-bottom within the cabinet is indicated at **(9).**

The door-latching lever **(10)** locks the door and activates the door safety switch **(11),** which controls all machine functions. A water-temperature-sensing thermostat **(12)** controls timer motor during sanitizing rinse cycle only, stopping timer until heater has raised water to 150 degrees in most machines. Detergent dispenser **(13)** releases detergent in each wash cycle, and wetting-agent dispenser **(14)** operates during final rinse. Components 11, 13, 14, and often 12 are located within the door on most front loaders.

Electrical operations: The electrical circuit shown by the broken-dash line is the neutral conductor, a grounded conductor which connects to each operating load in a 115-volt appliance and which serves to complete the circuit back to the power supply. This is not to be confused with the bonding conductor, a grounded lead that bonds each component and the frame of an appliance to ground through the middle (round) prong of a polarized line cord. The bonding conductor is a safety device and is not a part of the electrical circuit, while the neutral is. A neutral line should not be fused, nor should it be broken by a switch at any time.

The circuit drawn with a heavy line is the master circuit, providing the power supply from the AC plug, through the door safety switch **(11)** to the timer **(1)** from which it feeds all other operating circuits of the machine. The door must be shut and locked before the machine will function.

Circuit in dotted line is initiated from the timer **(1)** to operate machine motor **(2).** Reversible motors have four leads, usually with external relay. Direction of rotation of motor would be determined by the timer contacts.

Heater **(5)** is controlled by timer contacts, usually operating during wash, rinse, and drying. In models with a sanitizing-rinse feature, the auxiliary circuit, also shown, places the water-temperature-sensing thermostat **(12)** in series with the timer motor. When the timer reaches the final rinse cycle, the timer motor stops until heater has raised temperature to a predetermined level (around 150 degrees). Heat rise is usually one to two degrees per minute. Prolonged delay is an indication that the water supply to machine is too cool.

Timer energizes inlet valve **(7)** by way of the overflow switch **(6),** which must be closed to complete the circuit. Since water flow rate through inlet valve is constant because of action of flow washer, elapsed time of fill cycle determines the amount of water that enters machine. Overflow switch shuts off inlet valve in overfill conditions due to abnormally high water pressure (over 100 psi) or timer malfunction.

Dispenser **(13)** is actuated by timer during wash cycle. Most dishwashers empty one side of dispenser when door is shut at beginning of wash, uncover other side when unlatching solenoid is energized by timer during second wash period. Such dispensers are "one-shot" dispensers—they must be filled as a part of your routine for starting dishwasher.

Wetting-agent dispenser **(14)** is energized by timer during final rinse, injects only a few drops when energized. Storage reservoir holds three to six months' supply.

tion. Check the color-coding of these leads before disconnecting for testing, and be sure they are reconnected in the same manner.

If it is necessary to remove the motor on a dishwasher, it will usually be necessary to disassemble the pump section first. If the motor is mounted remotely from the tub, the pump and motor may be removed as an assembly. If the dishwasher is built into the cabinet, this usually means that the machine will have to be pulled out for servicing.

To do this, open the door and look for the clips or tabs which hold the top of the dishwasher to the underside of the countertop. Remove the screws, then remove the toe panel or lower dishwasher panel to gain access to the lower compartment. On some machines, it is necessary to remove the outer door panel before the bottom panel can be removed. Be sure that all power is shut off, then turn the threaded leveling screws to lower the dishwasher slightly. After the water line and power supply have been disconnected, you can pull the machine completely clear of the cabinet if necessary.

The pump assembly is mounted directly to the motor shaft. It's often located in the bottom center of the tub, the same location where the impeller was placed in older machines. Many dishwasher pumps contain two impellers—the upper one for the lower spray arm, the lower one for the recirculating system and the drain. This lower impeller circulates the water to the upper spray arm or spray nozzle when the motor is turning in the "wash" direction.

In other models, the pump is located in a remote location under the tub, and hoses connect the sump to the pump for water supply.

The pump discharges through a hose that leads to the spray arms.

Keep these tips in mind when servicing the type-B pump. The impeller is often made of aluminum. Electrolytic action may have frozen it to the steel motor shaft. If so, apply a few drops of penetrating oil to the top of the impeller; then drill a series of $\frac{1}{4}$-inch holes around the base of the impeller to (but not into) the motor shaft. A few light taps of a hammer should now loosen the tightest grip. Go easy with the hammer—don't risk bending the motor shaft.

Look closely for small brass washers used to shim impellers for proper clearance and retain these for use with a new impeller. Many firms furnish shims and an alignment gauge with each replacement impeller.

If an impeller is sheared, count the blades on the replacement and be sure that all pieces of the old one are recovered from the lines and pump housing. Any piece remaining may return to the pump and damage the new assembly. It's also a good practice to replace the pump seal when changing an impeller. The spring-loaded, carbon-faced seal is cheap insurance against leaks near the motor.

Finally, don't attempt to override the door safety switch to "see" if the pump is operating; you wouldn't believe that you could be so wet so fast. Clear-plastic doors and lids are used to study spray patterns in dishwashers; the water action is incredible.

LEAKS

If your dishwasher should develop a leak, the location and amount of the water can be a big

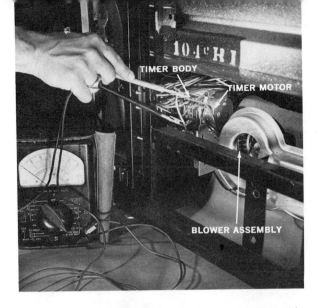

With side panel removed from this dishwasher, a continuity check is made through the timer contacts. Model has a remotely mounted timer with rapid advance drive. Power must be turned off before panels are removed. Use $R \times 1$ scale for testing contacts, $R \times 100$ to test timer motor(s).

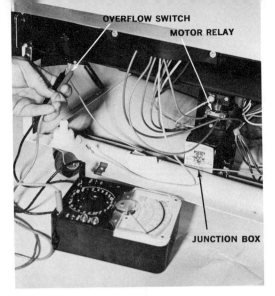

Contacts of overflow prevention switch are tested from front of this Sears machine. If float is raised by wedging with a piece of cardboard, contacts should open to shut off water flow. With switch in normal position, the contacts should indicate zero resistance with VOM in $R \times 1$ position.

Defective components were spotted by this test. Resistance reading on $R \times 1$ scale between contacts in timer indicated a fault. High resistance in switch contacts drops voltage to component, soon permanently damages contact itself.

Cleaning contacts restored continuity to the timer as shown. Cover plate was removed to expose contact arms within. Probes are attached to the same contacts which previously indicated resistance.

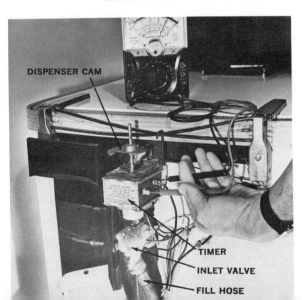

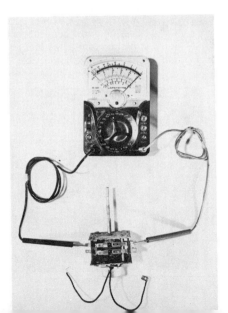

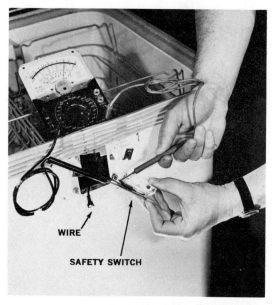

WIRE

SAFETY SWITCH

SIPHON BREAK

FILTER

INLET VALVE

Corroded terminals in interlock switch caused high resistance reading shown. Unlike the load, a switch should always show zero resistance. Switch contacts must be closed when tested. Switch plunger is shown being depressed in one hand while other hand holds test probe.

Siphon break and other components are accessible after this Maytag is pulled away from the cabinet. This is view from the left side. Bracket with multiple holes at bottom right of photo is for adjustment of door tension. If wooden trim panels are installed, the tension must be increased to compensate for the extra weight.

Two different approaches to two-level washing are seen in the two machines shown. The Maytag at left has spray arm in bottom and at top which are connected by recirculating hose. Dishes, silverware load into top rack; center tower helps reach lower portion of silverware. The Whirlpool machine at right uses no direct connection between two spray arms; a water jet from pump in bottom is directed into center of upper arm, causing arm to rotate and discharge upward into rack.

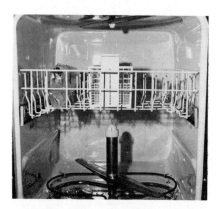

HEATING ELEMENT

FILTER

PUMP GUARD

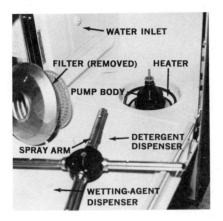

WATER INLET

FILTER (REMOVED)   HEATER

PUMP BODY

DETERGENT
DISPENSER

SPRAY ARM

WETTING-AGENT
DISPENSER

Pump is uncovered in the KitchenAid dishwasher by lifting the spray arm and removing the guard that protects the impeller. Both removed components can be seen in foreground.

High-speed pump used on newer (type B) washers mounts directly on main motor shaft. The diffuser is removed to uncover the pump's upper impeller in this photo.

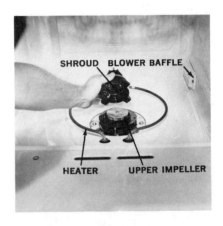

SHROUD   BLOWER BAFFLE

HEATER   UPPER IMPELLER

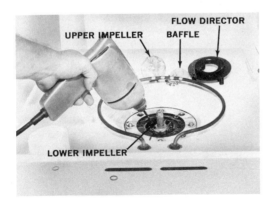

UPPER IMPELLER

FLOW DIRECTOR
BAFFLE

LOWER IMPELLER

Further disassembly allows access to lower impeller. Many dishwasher components, the impeller particularly, operate in hostile environment of heat and chemicals, sometimes making steps such as drilling this impeller necessary. Drill into circumference center of impeller until it can be released from motor shaft. Do not drill into motor shaft.

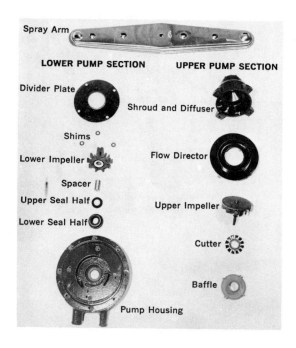

Here are components of pump assembly on a type B (Sears) machine. Lower section recirculates water to upper spray arm or to drain, depending upon motor rotation; upper section forces water through lower spray arm, which mounts to top of diffuser.

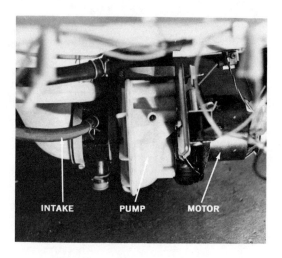

Motor and pump assembly in the GE machine shown here is remotely located under tub at rear of machine. This is view through front lower-access panel. Note large diameter of intake in this washer.

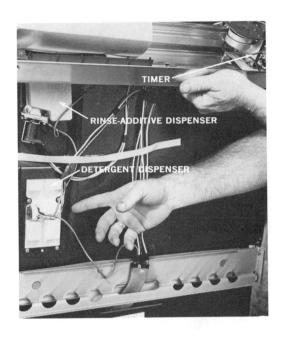

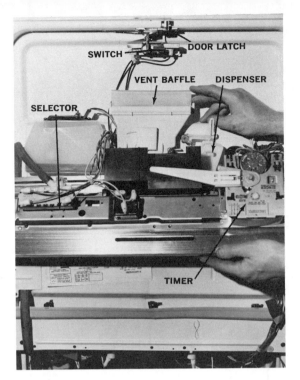

The door of a dishwasher holds many operating components. The outer panel is easily removed for access in Whirlpool at left and GE at right. Timer and selector switch are found in upper panel and rinse additive and detergent dispensers mount to inner door panel. Whirlpool dispenser is operated through action of bimetal arm.

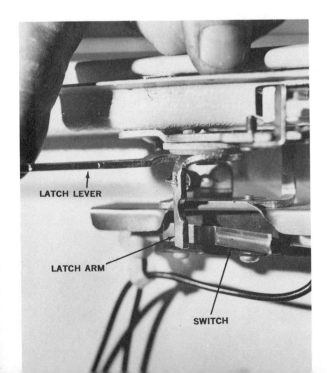

Door-latching mechanism is arranged so that latch from cabinet must be in position before lever will actuate safety switch. Examination of linkage with panel removed as shown will often reveal necessary adjustment

259

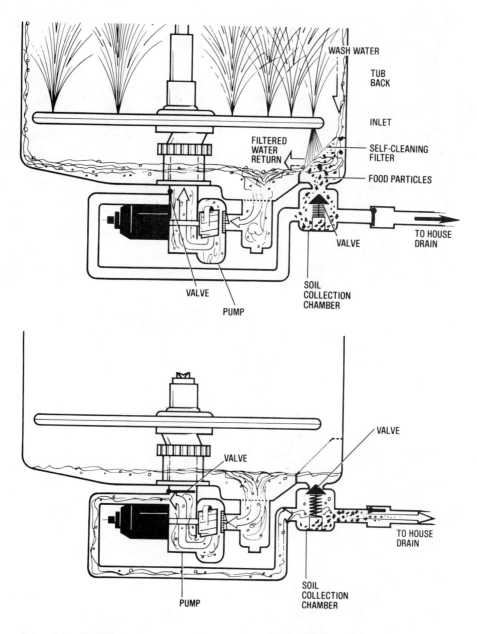

Some new dishwashers, like GE's Potscrubber III, dispose of food soils while washing and rinsing. Wash water runs down back of tub into filter where small food particles are trapped and settle into soil-collection chamber. A special water jet on the bottom of the wash arm cleans the screen on each revolution. During the drain phase, water is pumped out through the soil-collection chamber, forcing food soils down the drain.

clue in pinpointing the problem. The secret is to get where the action is. See if the water is sudsy or clear—this will indicate whether it came from the inlet side of the equipment or from the pump or drain hoses. Remove panels to expose every possible portion of the equipment and pinpoint the source while it's happening. Look closely around the area of the siphon break where the water enters the tub, and around the inlet valve, pump housing, and seal area.

Inspect hoses and clamps. Check the door carefully. Check all gaskets. If hardened or torn, replace them.

Water doesn't shut off? Suspect the inlet valve (if it continues to flow into the machine when the power is shut off or the plug is pulled, your suspicions are confirmed). The single-port valve (for hot water only) probably has foreign particles in the bleed ports of the diaphragm. Disassembling and cleaning, with particular attention to the filter screen, should eliminate the problem.

Remember that large amounts of water usually come from broken or loosened hoses or an overflow from the machine itself. A stand-pipe or trough is provided to direct water away from electrical components in the event that something prevents the machine from shutting off. If the machine has overflowed, the water will be found in the location of the overflow provision. Small amounts would primarily be seepage, and would likely be occurring around the door or gasket or from a crack in a hose.

When a small leak is encountered with a front loader, remove the outer door panel and inspect carefully the trough built into the inner door structure of most models. This "dam" is filled with water when the tub fills, but a leaking spray arm (which could cause surging within the tub), heavy sudsing from detergents, or leaking gaskets can cause a hard-to-find leak from this area.

DISHWASHER CYCLE

The dishwasher timer is similar to that on an automatic clothes washer (except for the sanitizing feature on some models). If the sanitizing cycle is selected, at a predetermined point, usually in the final rinse, contacts within the timer open and interrupt power flow to the timer motor. A thermostat outside the tub or in the door senses the water temperature.

When temperature is approximately 150 degrees, the thermostat contacts close and again supply power to the timer motor. Often a light is incorporated in the circuit to signal when the timer is not advancing because water is being heated.

Some of the more deluxe models use pushbuttons only to initiate the cycle—there's no knob to turn. In most of these machines, an auxiliary motor—often called a rapid advance motor—drives the timer at a higher rate of speed than the timer motor, and stops it at the place in the cycle corresponding with the depressed button. Other than the rapid-advance drive, the switch and timer motor would be tested as in any other timer. Such timers usually have a screwdriver slot in the shaft for manual adjustment.

A typical washing cycle includes the following stages (the figures show the approximate time that a typical type-B machine might devote to each stage):

First wash: Removes loose, heavy soil deposits. 4 minutes.

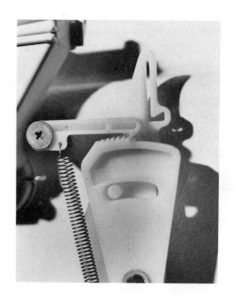

Solenoid trips cocked release to dump detergent on this dispenser. Most dispensers have an open bin for the first wash detergent, then uncover a second bin as machine reaches the second wash period.

Complete drain: 1 minute.

First rinse: Flushes detergent and remaining food particles from dishes and tub: 4 minutes.

Complete drain: 1 minute.

Second rinse: Flushes any remaining detergent.

Complete drain: 1 minute.

Second wash: Fresh change of water and detergent removes anything left from previous wash and rinse cycles. 6 minutes.

Complete drain: 1 minute.

Third rinse: Again flushes detergent and soil from dishes, tub. 3 minutes.

Complete drain: 1 minute.

Fourth rinse: Insures flushing of any remaining detergent or soils, prepares dishes for drying. Sanitizing cycle takes over during this rinse if machine is so equipped and/or selected, raising the water temperature to destroy bacteria. Wetting agent is introduced near the end of this rinsing period to reduce spotting as the dishes dry. 5 minutes plus sanitizing time (approximately one to two degrees temperature rise per minute).

Complete drain: 1 minute.

Drying: Heater(s) energized after all water is pumped from tub, raising the air temperature and, in some models, forcing air across the dishes with a blower. Air absorbs moisture and is vented into the room. 18 minutes.

Don't assume that the sanitizing feature on dishwashers which are so equipped compensates for low water temperature. This heating occurs *after* the wash water and detergent solution have done their job. A long delay period can in fact indicate that the water supply is too cool for good dishwashing. Most dishwater heaters raise water temperature only one or two degrees per minute, depending on heater size and voltage. A 30-minute delay could indicate that water entered the machine at only

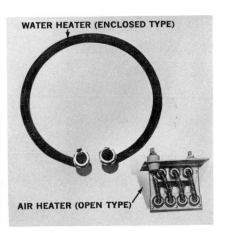

WATER HEATER (ENCLOSED TYPE)

AIR HEATER (OPEN TYPE)

Washed dishes are dried by a duct-mounted heater and blower on the KitchenAid (left). Finger points to heater in duct. Some KitchenAid models use a dual-element heater with two terminals (center). The sheathed heater (right) is similar to that used on most machines. The heater is usually energized throughout the cycle, maintaining the water temperature and drying the dishes in machine.

120 degrees, much too cool for proper washing. On the other hand, a slight delay or no delay at all means that the water temperature is well above minimum requirements.

There is some misconception regarding the term "sanitized." According to public health standards, it means that less than 100 bacteria per dish can be recovered. Dishes are not sterilized (*all* microorganisms destroyed), but it's the next best thing.

"Washability" is a dishwasher term with many connotations. From time to time washing problems may arise with certain dishes or tableware, or with certain other external factors. They are almost always due to area problems—water hardness, mineral content, etc. (See chart.)

One problem classified as a washability fault is redeposition, a condition where food parti-cles are left on dishes or the sides, wall and door of the dishwasher after the cycle is completed. Check first to see that you are using the correct amounts of detergent. Review your loading habits; heavy food soils should be scraped from the dishes before loading. You may need to vary them up or down to eliminate the problem. Many dishwashers have a filter which removes particles from the water as it is recirculated during the wash and rinse cycles—and this can total as much as 800 gallons during a single cycle! If the filter is clogged or damaged, however, food particles may get through and be redeposited on the dishes. At least one manufacturer, Maytag, has a self-cleaning mechanism that scrapes the trapped food particles from the filter at each pump-out and flushes them down the drain.

Other causes of this problem would be water

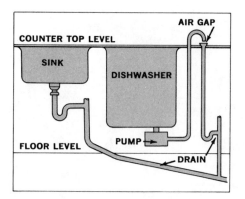

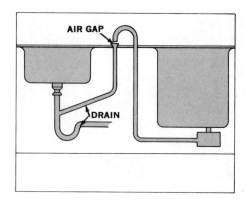

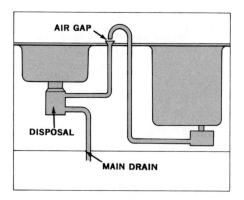

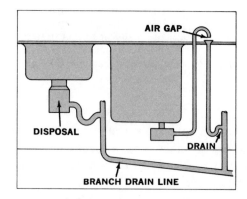

KEEP THOSE AIR GAPS IN YOUR DISHWASHER PLUMBING

Plumbing codes require an air gap in the fill system of dishwashers. This is simply a gap, vented to room air, across which water must pass. It is usually located where water enters the machine and is built into all dishwashers. This eliminates the possibility of dishwasher water flowing back into the home water system.

Air gaps are not always required in drain lines, but they should be considered in undercounter installations. They're preferred if the dishwasher is connected to a disposer. An air gap or siphon break in the drain system prevents reverse flow from the sink waste line or disposer back into the dishwasher. A deck-mounted air gap—a Pre San #12 or equivalent—makes a neat installation with minimum loss of counter space. Since the sink faucet is high in relation to the portable dishwasher, the hose coupling itself serves as an air gap for your dishwasher.

Some dishwashers have a solenoid-operated valve on the drain line, and these may usually be drained straight through the floor if necessary. Their instructions will point this out. Others have a built-in drain loop to help prevent draining from the machine except when desired. Remember this, for if you must remove the loop when servicing, you must reinstall it properly. Locate it as high as the cabinet allows. Some undercounter models provide a separate drain loop; this should also be installed as high as possible, even behind the countertop backsplash, if possible, and securely fastened.

temperature below 140 degrees, a binding or stuck spray arm, or insufficient water fill.

HINTS FOR BETTER WASHING

The quick-check chart and photographs accompanying this chapter should help you pin down dishwasher problems quickly and easily. Here are some other hints which can help you get better results.

Don't wash dishes during peak periods of hot-water use. Clothes-washing and shower demands can reduce temperature of incoming water. If you want to store used dishes in the machine and run the washer once a day, fine —but don't hold them longer than one day before washing. When loading large platters, keep them away from the detergent dispenser; they can obstruct water flow to the dispenser cups, and detergent must wash out easily as soon as the compartments open.

The power supply to your dishwasher should be within the 10 percent tolerance required for all appliances with the dishwasher in operation. As an example of proper operating voltage, a heating element rated at 1,000 watts at 125 volts delivers only 625 watts at 100 volts. Even worse, the load imposed upon the motor can lead to early failure.

The automatic dishwasher is an unusual appliance in many ways. It is one of the oldest home appliances, having been patented in 1850, but it took well over a century to begin to approach the status enjoyed by some of its more recent home appliance companions, and

the saturation in the market is still in its infancy. It's also unusual in its demanding requirements for proper operation. But I hope that you haven't gotten the impression that it is influenced by so many factors that you can't expect satisfactory performance. This just isn't so. Just meet its few relatively simple demands and it will be a faithful servant for many years.

RULES FOR THE USE AND CARE OF A DISHWASHER

- Make certain water temperature is between 140 and 160 degrees.
- Use soft water if possible.
- Use only detergents specified for dishwashers and use the recommended amount.
- Add detergent immediately before operating machine.
- If detergent becomes caked in box, throw it away.
- Wash only dishes, pans, silverware and cutlery that are approved for dishwashers.
- Use rinsing agent regularly in hard water areas.
- Properly load the machine—while this will vary from brand to brand, keep the following in mind:
Place metal items away from detergent cups;
Do not place large objects next to detergent cup or over smaller objects;
Rack lightweight items securely so that they cannot be displaced by water force.

QUICK-CHECK CHART FOR

AUTOMATIC DISHWASHERS

Symptom	Cause	Remedy
Water will not enter machine	Filter screen clogged	Remove and clean with toothbrush Remove screen on faucet aerator (portable)
	Inlet-valve solenoid open	Test with VOM—replace if open
	Interlock switch on door not making contact	Test with VOM—adjust or replace
	Overflow switch jammed or open	Adjust or replace
Water will not shut off	Foreign particles in inlet valve	Remove and clean
	Inlet-valve solenoid grounded	Test with VOM—replace if grounded
	Timer contacts stuck	Repair or replace timer as necessary
Motor will not run	Impeller or pump jammed	Inspect and clear, check for damage
	Manual overload kicked out	Check for cause and reset
	Centrifugal switch or relay out	Repair or replace as necessary
	Shorted or open motor windings	Replace motor
Water will not pump out	Type-B machines, see inoperative motor (above)	Repair inoperative motor as indicated
	Strainer clogged (Type A)	Remove and clean
	Line or passageway restricted	Inspect and clear
	Impeller sheared or loose	Repair or replace as necessary
	Impeller jammed	Remove foreign object
	Pump motor inoperative	Test with VOM—repair or replace
	No voltage to pump motor	Test timer and connecting wiring
Timer will not advance	Open windings in timer motor	Test with VOM—replace if open
	"Sanitize" thermostat open	Check stat with VOM, check water temp.
	Timer binding	Inspect and lubricate with care
Food particles left on glassware	Water too cool	Supply should be minimum of 140°
	Insufficient water charge	Should reach element
	Spray arm(s) not revolving	Inspect for binding and repair—may be caused by utensil protruding through rack
	Insufficient detergent	Fill cups full

Symptom	Cause	Remedy
Dishes not drying properly	Water too cool	Supply should be minimum of 140°
	Heating element open	Check with VOM—replace if open
	Blower motor inoperative (if so equipped)	Inspect for binding, test with VOM
	Wetting-agent dispenser empty	Refill—if not equipped, purchase solid type wetting agent available at markets
	Condensation	At end of cycle, open door a crack for 5 minutes before removing dishes
Leaking	Improper door adjustment	Inspect and adjust as necessary
	Hoses crimped or loose	Check and repair
	Sudsing	Check detergent and water temperature
	Split spray arm	Inspect and replace if necessary
	Gasket torn or hardened	Inspect and replace if necessary
	Leak in tub	Repair with epoxy
	Machine not level	Check and level as necessary
	Air gap splashes or overflows	Check for loose hoses or misalignment
Excessive noise	Foreign object in pump or impeller	Inspect and remove object
	Improper loading	Check for utensils striking arm or tub
	Loose sheet metal	Locate and tighten loose panel

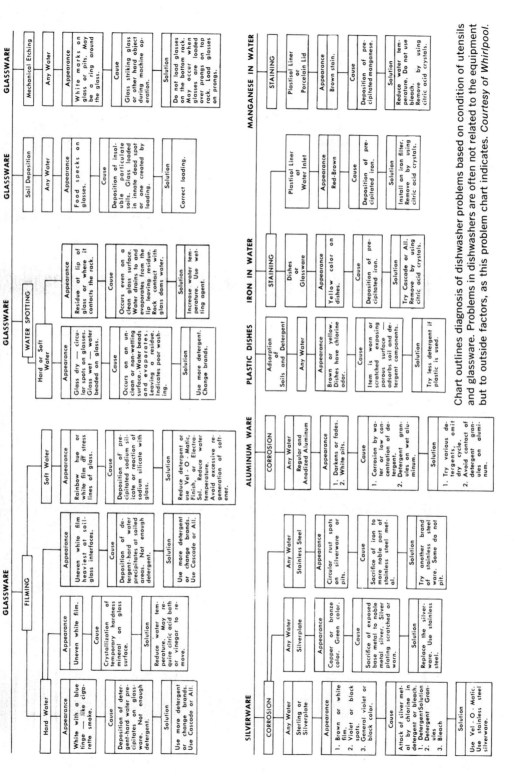

PROBLEM DIAGNOSIS — QUICK REFERENCE

Chart outlines diagnosis of dishwasher problems based on condition of utensils and glassware. Problems in dishwashers are often not related to the equipment but to outside factors, as this problem chart indicates. *Courtesy of Whirlpool.*

16
Troubleshooting the Home Sanitation System

In recent years, two modern appliances have been giving the old smelly garbage can a tough time. First, garbage disposers were developed for installation under the drain of the kitchen sink. These grind up food wastes into pieces fine enough to flush away through sewer lines. More recently, powered trash compactors have been making a good try at accepting almost everything that used to go into garbage cans—bottles, food wastes, cans, and plastic, paper, and cardboard packing materials. Some compactors even include a spray deodorant to control unpleasant odors.

In many of the newest kitchens the two appliances are installed together at the sink—and kitchen designers refer to the whole setup as the kitchen sanitary center.

Both appliances lighten the municipal job of waste disposal. One small compactor bag holds all the waste for which three 20-gallon garbage cans once were needed. Garbage men must handle less waste because some goes down the drain. Garbage trucks must haul away considerably less bulk. Consequently, the two appliances have attracted the interest of local government bodies.

TRASH COMPACTORS

A trash compactor is like a giant mechanical foot. A power-driven ram exerts great crushing force on waste dumped into a bag which is supported by a heavy-gauge steel container. The ram is the same shape as the container, only slightly smaller. The bags are plastic or plastic lined and some have a double paper exterior that remains strong even when wet. The ram compresses the trash to about one-fourth its original volume. When the bag is full, you lift it from the container, seal it and carry it to the garbage can for collection.

Some new owners of compactors have wondered whether there is *anything* that should not go into the appliance. The answer is "yes." Never deposit flammable materials in it. And

Compactor takes the place of the traditional garbage can in the modern kitchen. After trash is placed in container, drawer is closed, key switch turned to *on* position, and *start* button depressed. Compaction reduces trash to about one-fourth of its original volume.

never, never put in aerosol cans that have contained toxic spray materials, especially insecticides or paints.

Those who have contended that "the compactor converts twenty pounds of garbage to twenty pounds of garbage" miss the point. The basic purpose of the compactor is to provide a convenient method of handling garbage. It was developed after market research indicated consumers wanted it. The side benefits are secondary but nonetheless important. It saves daily trips to the trash cans, it keeps the kitchen neater and cleaner, and it makes for less clutter in the area where you store your trash. Manufacturers claim that a compactor will hold a week's worth of trash for the average family of four. The bag is about 18 inches deep, 18 inches long, and 10 inches wide. Manufacturers recommend that you run the

compactor each time trash is placed within the container. You'll also get much better "mileage" from compactor bags if you occasionally turn the compactor off just as the ram "bottoms out" and leave it overnight. This makes a surprising difference in the amount of compaction.

Though the compactor contains a myriad of safety devices, primarily to prevent children from being harmed, it is an easy-to-use appliance. On most models you lift the door slightly and pull it forward. Then you insert a key and turn a lock switch before a pushbutton switch starts the compaction cycle. With the drawer in the fully-shut position, the ram progresses downward to within about 5 inches of the bag bottom. It's a good idea not to place any cans within 5 inches of the bottom—"prime" the new bag with paper, etc. This provides a cushion of sorts at the bottom of the container to keep bottles and cans from puncturing the bag. Small tears won't hurt. Liquids are absorbed by the bag and the paper normally found as part of the trash from most households. In fact, it's estimated that paper comprises about 70 percent of the trash volume of the average family. Bottles, often broken by the compacting action, and other sharp objects, should go near the center of the bag to help prevent large tears in the inner liner and the bag itself.

Keep these safety points in mind when operating the compactor:

1. All compactors have a key lock that controls the electrical power supply. The unit cannot be operated unless the key is inserted in the lock and turned to the *on* position. Remove the key when the compactor is not in use, and place it where it is inaccessible to children.
2. The unit will not operate unless the drawer is closed.
3. The drawer can't be opened while the unit is operating.
4. Most units can be stopped at any time by pushing the stop switch. When the unit is restarted, the ram will travel upward to the starting (up) position, allowing the drawer to be opened.
5. Some drawers are deliberately designed to be difficult for small children to open.

When the key lock is turned *on* and the starting switch is depressed, the ram begins to travel downward into the container. This action is initiated by the motor assembly turning the power screws which are threaded through

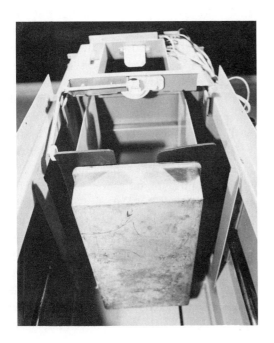

Garbage-eye view of descending ram reveals simple operating principle of compactor in this wide-angle photo from container position. Motor and drive mechanism are designed to exert 2,000 pounds of force.

a nut assembly at the top of the ram. The ram continues to travel downward, compressing the trash, until it reaches a point some 5 inches above the bottom of the container unless accumulated trash stops its progress further up. In either case, when the motor reaches a point at which it can no longer drive the ram downward, it stalls out as it was designed to do. The power screws and the motor capacity are engineered so the motor will stall at a predetermined amount of pressure. The ram actually exerts a force of some 2,000 pounds upon the compacted trash within the container. Since a split-phase motor is used in the trash compactor, its rotation is easily reversed simply by reversing the relationship of the starting and running windings. In most compactors, this relationship is determined by the contact positions of a switch located near the top of a stationary frame. As soon as the ram begins to travel downward, a linkage causes these contacts to change positions. Since by this time the starting windings have already been disengaged from the circuit by the relay, or centrifugal switch, it has no effect upon the rotation and the ram continues its downward travel. As soon as stallout occurs, however, the relay or switch is again called upon to try to restart the motor. Now, since the switch positions are interchanged, the direction is reversed and the ram immediately begins to travel upward. The same condition would occur if the ram were to stop for any other reason—pushing the stop button, trying to open the door, or even by power failure at any time during a downward movement of the ram assembly.

Compactors are of two basic types. In top loaders, the trash is put into the top of the compartment. In this type the ram retracts up into the top few inches of the machine and

extends down into the container only when compacting. The second basic type is the drawer-loaded unit. The drawer pulls forward from the base of the machine and you deposit trash much as you would in a garbage can. The drawer must then be closed before the compaction cycle can occur.

Regardless of type, little routine maintenance is necessary. Clean the machine periodically with soap and water, and replace disposable bags and deodorizer sprays (if used on your unit). Buy disposable parts from the dealer who sells the compactor unless your compactor is one that accepts ordinary garbage bags. Don't interchange parts among brands.

Servicing a Compactor

Unplug first, and check mechanical components if you notice any unusual noise. With a compactor, noise is a relative thing. It's not a quiet machine to begin with. For one thing, manufacturers have made little attempt to muffle mechanical noise from the drive assembly. The cycle is short, normally lasting only one to two minutes, and the noise does not become objectionable. Second, it would be next to impossible to hide the noise of bottles breaking, cans flattening, etc., and still maintain reasonable cabinet dimensions.

Most compactors are serviced either from the back or from the bottom. Those that are accessible through the back of the cabinet will have a service panel there. If a wrap-around cabinet is used, and no rear service panel is visible, the operating components will be serviceable from beneath. Turn the machine over on a quilt or pad and remove the bottom cover. If it should be necessary to service components

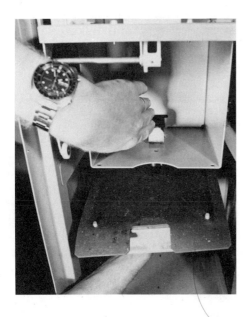

Ram head and wiper are easily removed for cleaning in most units. In this Sears model, drawer is removed and release lever pulled to allow ram cover to drop from the ram. Front is removed in this photo to provide visibility, but the operation is normally performed through access opening in front of compactor.

Ram had just begun downward travel when shutter snapped in this photo. Note the position of the directional switch and top-limit switch arms. Directional switch is actuated just prior to limit switch, when ram returns to top, insuring proper movement when new cycle is initiated.

Top-limit switch (facing camera) and directional switches are mounted "piggyback" style on this Whirlpool unit. Lower slot on mounting tab is elongated to allow for adjustment of actuating arms. Removing mounting screws and setting switch assembly back so that switch is not actuated, allows ram to "run off" the power screws when machine is turned on. Ram may then be lifted from top.

As ram travels down power screws (one side shown in center), it bottoms against rubber "buttons" fastened to frame members if compacted trash is insufficient to stop ram at higher point. This provides a cushion of approximately 5 inches in bottom of container.

With compactor placed on side, bottom is removed to reveal workings of drive train. Chain should have ¼-inch slack at midpoint of any span when properly adjusted. Drawer safety and tilt switches are mounted to tabs with two screws.

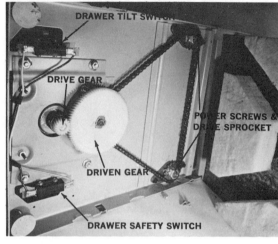

Motor mounting plate may be shifted to adjust chain after loosening four locknuts and sliding plate through travel allowed by elongated holes. Motor may be removed from bottom by removing the plate entirely.

Be sure to note position and order of wave and spacer washers when removing drive components, and replace in identical manner. Bolts extending through motor-mounting plate nearest drive gear secure motor to plate. Driven gear must be removed as shown to detach chain.

274

Power-screw drive sprockets contain needle bearings to absorb load and thrust of power-screw action. Note exact location of all components when disassembling. For power screws and pressure (guide) pads, most manufacturers specify extreme-pressure moly-lithium grease under their own part numbers.

Retaining clips for electrical components must be pried carefully from switch body; switch simply snaps back into place to reinstall. Insulator for terminals, shown removed and adjacent to switch, must be placed back over switch when component is replaced in compactor.

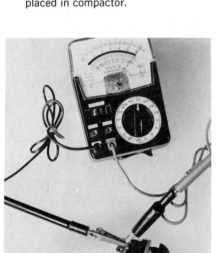

Start-Stop rocker switch is tested by fastening meter leads to appropriate terminals and depressing switch. No resistance should be present across switch contacts.

Defective switch was discovered when meter showed resistance of almost 10,000 ohms when switch contacts were open. Inspection revealed a cracked switch housing, allowing contacts to close erratically. Note action of lever against switch arm. This is the switch actuated by key, which is on other side of mounting plate in the rear view shown.

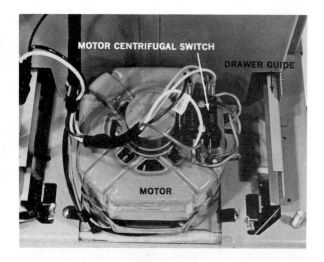

Externally mounted centrifugal switch is only serviceable part of this motor assembly. Actuating arms of drawer-tilt and safety switches are visible at the rear of each drawer guide in this view, taken from top rear with cabinet removed.

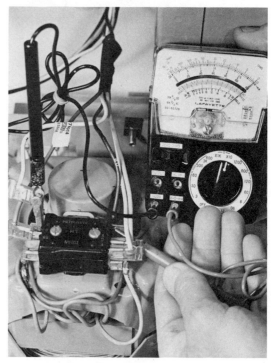

Centrifugal switch may be tested electrically without removing it. Governor arm, which may be depressed manually to test opening of contacts, is accessible by inserting screwdriver against button under U-shaped link seen toward center of motor behind switch.

Switch is removed by removing two mounting screws. Be sure to provide model number of compactor and all information found on motor when requesting replacement switches. Governor link and actuating button are seen at left of switch in this view.

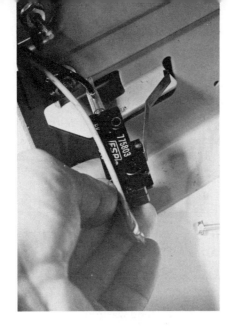

Drawer safety switch is removed from bottom of this Sears model. Use extreme care in handling compactor switches—actuating arms bend easily.

Switch is easily tested in or out of equipment by removing leads, hooking meter leads in their place. With meter set to lowest resistance scale, no resistance should be indicated when contacts are closed.

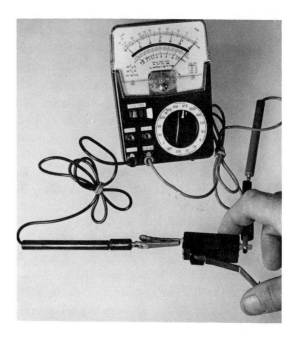

Container, drawer, and ram cover should be cleaned periodically. Latch at side of container may be released to make bag removal easier, Arm at opposite side of drawer releases aerosol spray each time drawer is closed.

277

near the top of the ram drive, such as the operating switches, remove the top as shown in accompanying photographs. Although it is unlikely that a situation will arise requiring removal of the entire cabinet, you can do this by removing the attaching screws.

When removing the power nuts or power screws for any reason, be sure to notice the position of all thrust washers and bearings. They must be replaced in exactly the same order, and the same number of spacers or thrust washers must always be used on the power drive. Power nuts are usually furnished in matching halves, and should only be installed in this manner.

Motor components are critical, and only those specified for the equipment should be used. The relay or centrifugal switch must team up with the motor and should be obtained by model number, listing any information on the motor itself as well. Motors of a higher (or lower) horsepower should never be interchanged within a compactor as this will change the amount of force that is exerted upon the trash in the compartment.

Lubrication and adjustments are necessary only when the unit is being repaired. Use only the manufacturer's recommended extreme-pressure molylithium grease for bearings and power screws. Motors are normally sealed and require no lubrication. Chain lubricant is usually not needed unless noisy operation develops. Use SAE 30 oil at power nuts and drawer rollers if it is needed.

When in proper adjustment, the chain should deflect about ¼ inch across any span. If a cogged belt is used rather than the chain, it should deflect only about ⅛ inch. Both directional switch and top limit switch should actuate before the ram comes off the power

screws, with the directional switch actuating approximately ¼ inch before the limit switch (as measured by ram travel). When you finish a repair job, be sure that no grounds exist before restarting machine.

RULES FOR THE USE AND CARE OF A COMPACTOR

- To clean, remove the ram cover and wipe. Wash periodically in warm, sudsy water.
- Wrap soft food waste in newspaper or cover it with several thicknesses of paper toweling before it is compacted.
- Place glass bottles, metal cans, etc. in the center. This reduces the possibility of a fragment penetrating the bag.
- If the compactor does not operate, check to see if the drawer is firmly shut, trash is lodged behind or under the bin, the lock is not in the *on* position, the *start* button was not depressed, or the latches which secure the steel container are not fastened. In some cases the unit may not start because it isn't one-third full as required.
- Occasionally stop the compactor by turning the switch off just as the ram reverses direction. This will result in greatly increased compaction and prolong use of the bag.

SAFETY NOTE: Grasp the filled bag only at the top when emptying the compactor. Glass chips can come through the bag and cause injury if the bag is not handled properly and with caution.

QUICK-CHECK CHART FOR

TRASH COMPACTORS

Symptom	Possible Cause	Remedy
Compactor will not run — no sound	No power to receptacle	Check with table lamp — replace blown fuse or trip breaker
	Key switch turned off (models with electrical type key lock)	Check position of controls
	Drawer slightly open	Close drawer — unit should restart and return ram to *up* position
	Drawer slightly open — won't open	Hold start switch down to return ram to top-open drawer & reposition load
	Drawer slightly open-won't open or close, start switch won't cause motor to run if depressed and held	Remove top-using yard stick, depress actuating lever of drawer safety switch while holding start switch in *start* position. Ram should return to top. Reposition load. On models with plunger type switches, use same procedure, only actuate plunger with table knife inserted between plunger tip and door.
	Open safety switch, tilt switch, start switch, key lock switch	Test with VOM, replace if damaged or defective
	Open motor windings	Test with VOM, replace if defective
Compactor will not run — humming or buzzing sound	Defective motor relay or centrifugal switch	Test with VOM, replace as necessary
	Drive gears or power screws locked	Disassemble and replace or lube as necessary
	Motor "start" winding open	Test with VOM, replace if defective
Motor running, no compaction, ram doesn't work	Drive chain or belt broken	Repair chain with master link provided by manufacturer or replace belt.
	Drive gear or driven gear broken or loose; drive sprocket loose on power screw	Inspect and repair or replace as needed. Check roll pin in drive sprocket.
	Stripped power nuts	Inspect and replace as needed
Compactor noisy (check to be sure that noise is not due to content of trash being compacted-glass, aerosol cans, etc.)	Belt or chain too loose or too tight	Inspect and adjust belt to 1/8 inch, chain to 1/4 inch slack. Lubricate with specified grease
	Power screw drive assembly or power nuts need lubrication	
	Drive gears damaged	Inspect and replace as necessary

Chart cont. on next page.

TRASH COMPACTORS *(cont.)*

Symptom	Possible Cause	Remedy
Not compacting sufficiently	Not enough trash in container	Compaction doesn't reach full capacity until compacted trash is at least 5 inches above bottom
(Check by placing two bricks, one atop the other, in bottom of container. Place two empty cans on top of the bricks. Cans should be mashed practically flat after compaction cycle.)	Motor windings shorted, causing premature stallout Drive train binding	Test motor and replace if necessary. Test by turning manually. Lube or replace components as necessary

GARBAGE DISPOSERS

A garbage disposer may or may not be permitted in your community. This useful home appliance made news some years ago when a number of municipalities banned it by ordinance, claiming it created problems in their sewage disposal systems. Now, however, disposers are *required* in all new construction in an increasing number of communities because the appliance lessens the burden of public waste disposal. As sewage treatment plants are updated in more and more communities, it is expected that many of the present bans will be removed.

You may have wondered whether a disposer can be used with a septic system. After considerable study, engineers have concluded that a disposal unit can actually be beneficial to the action of a septic tank. However, you should usually install a larger tank. The engineers recommend a 750-gallon tank for two to three persons with disposer, 500 gallons without. For four persons, a 1,000-gallon tank should be used rather than 750 gallons; for six persons a 1,500-gallon tank rather than a 1,000-gallon tank. The disposer may also increase the frequency of tank cleaning. On the average a tank will have to be cleaned every seven or eight years. With a disposer it may have to be cleaned every six or seven years, or an increase of about 10 percent.

There are two basic types of disposer, and the differences between the two should be considered when service is necessary. The continuous-feed type has a wall switch to control the disposer motor. The batch-feed type has the switch within the sink stopper, and you must place the stopper in a certain position and turn it before the disposer will operate. Other than the switching action, however, there's little difference between the two. Batch-feed units are somewhat more expensive, but installation may be less expensive since no separate switch is required. These are considered somewhat safer, but less convenient than continuous-feed disposers.

Except for the midriff bulge created by a

band of sound-deadening insulation on many new models, disposers still look much the same as they did when the first ones appeared just after World War II but the inside story is another matter. Improvements in materials and designs have been rather drastic. Today's disposer is more serviceable, has a longer life, is quieter in operation, and is much more efficient in waste grinding than early ones.

Proper usage of the disposer may add years to its life. This is even more important than with most appliances. Check the owner's manual to see what you can or cannot dispose of in your particular equipment. For the most part, though, a modern disposer is used for any wet garbage, the term generally applied to food scraps, meat scraps, corn husks, even the bones that usually are discarded in a garbage can. As materials have improved, so have the number and types of items a disposer can handle. This benefits the owner and adds to the life of the disposer. An example is a buildup of citric acid that commonly occurs from grinding fruits in the disposer. However, an occasional bone run through the cutting element cleans this acid from the body of the disposer before it can do damage. Not so long ago some service technicians cured similar problems by running a pop bottle through the disposer. It took manufacturers considerable time to convince them this really wasn't the thing to do. Actually, in most cases, the practice may not harm the disposer unless the disposer utilizes plastic shields and components. But the glass particles tend to build up in traps in sewer lines, making it necessary to call a plumber.

As food enters the hopper or mouth of the disposer it falls upon a rotating impeller driven directly off the motor shaft. The impeller forces the food outward toward the outer edge of a disc that has a number of cutting elements. As the food slams into the side of the disposer, these teeth grind it into particles fine enough to be safely carried into the drain by a flow of cold water, always necessary when using the disposer.

Servicing a Garbage Disposer

The most frequent disposer service problem is jamming. Unjamming can often be accomplished by reversing the motor, a feature on many disposers. Some reverse automatically if the motor stalls for any reason. If jamming can't be cured by reversing the motor, you must approach the problem in another way.

The first rule in servicing any disposer: Be sure power is turned off. Disconnect it from the power supply by unplugging from a receptacle or pulling the circuit fuse and disconnecting the wiring within the junction box if the disposer is connected permanently. Never insert your hand into the opening of a disposer.

Use a flashlight to look into the disposer and locate the object that has caused it to jam. Take a close look around the edges of the shredding disc next to the shredding ring. If you can locate the object, it's often possible to pry it loose with a large screwdriver. If this fails, try to rotate the disc with a broom handle or other wooden object. Some disposers come with an unjamming wrench. This can be inserted into the bottom end of the disposer to force the motor shaft to turn in either direction. (It's easy to make a heavy-duty unjamming tool from a piece of flat-steel stock. The accompanying drawing shows you how.)

In extreme cases you may have to disassemble the disposer to remove the foreign object. Only two or three other reasons would require

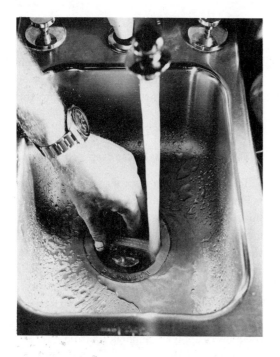

Where's the disposer? The sink flange and stopper are the only normally exposed components. The rest is accessible under the sink. Special stopper of batch-feed model activates switch when rotated in position. Stopper must *always* be in position, even on continuous-feed models, to prevent bone shards and other sharp objects from being thrown from hopper. Lots of cold water must be used to flush ground food wastes through drain and to harden grease so that it is finely ground and passes through system.

disassembly. The first would be for replacement of the shredding disc (flywheel) and shredding ring. This normally is needed only after years of hard service. Second, it may be necessary to replace the seals. Always do this when replacing the shredding ring. High-quality neoprene seals in modern disposers last for years and normally are good for the life of the appliance. Finally, in case of motor failure, the disposer would have to be removed from the sink and the housing assembly would have to be removed. Accompanying photographs show you how. But be forewarned that on many older disposers motor housings were sealed and are not serviceable. For the most part these were covered with long-term warranties.

Other components are easily serviceable from outside the cabinet. These include the motor starting relay, overload protector, and reversing switch. Often a capacitor is used with a split-phase motor to provide more starting torque, a highly important requirement for an appliance in this type of service. The VOM quickly pinpoints problems in these areas. Check for grounds after reassembling.

Buying and Installing a Disposer

Are you planning to buy a new disposer, replace an old one? Shop carefully. Prices range from the area of $50 to $225—quite a difference. There's a big market today for inexpensive disposers, primarily in tract homes where the builder wants to include a disposer

Flywheel

Here's an easy way to make an unjamming tool for those hard-to-budge jams in a disposer. Using a piece of ¼″ × 1″ steel stock, measure the distance from the center of the flywheel nut to the edge of the ear found on most such units (dimension X in the drawing). Grind or cut a notch in the end of the stock to fit the ear, then bore a hole slightly larger than the flywheel nut as indicated. Finally, bend the stock to form the L-shaped tool.

To use tool, unplug the disposer and insert it so that the nut is within the hole of the tool and the ear is in the notch. Now, with a crescent or other suitable wrench, force can be easily applied to the disk to loosen all but the most stubborn jams.

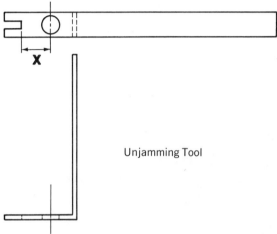

Unjamming Tool

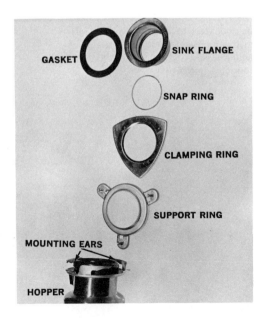

Mounting system of this GE model practically "falls into place." Sink flange is mounted above sink, then fastened to clamping ring and support ring with the snap ring. Mounting screws draw system together into leakproof fit, and ears of garbage disposer lock entire assembly together when they are twisted to mate with support ring.

This photo shows mounting system in place on GE Twistop batch-feed model. Safety switch is activated when stopper handle is turned to correct position. Switch is removed for servicing by removing one screw. Note single screw which holds retainer band together. Removing band allows hopper to be separated from motor shell.

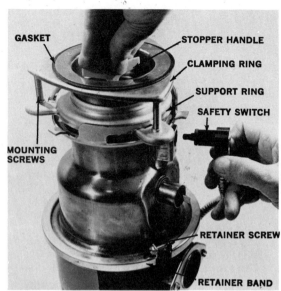

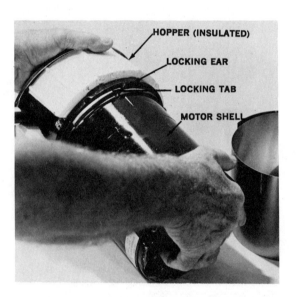

Motor shell is separated from hopper by twisting in opposite directions to release locking ears and tabs. It may be necessary to tap ears carefully with drift punch and hammer. Note ring of sound-absorbing insulation foam surrounding hopper.

Photo of KitchenAid disposer (left) and General Electric (right) illustrates two common variations in design. KitchenAid utilizes a fixed, porcelain-coated impeller to force food to cutting ring at outer circumference, while GE uses swiveling impellers mounted to a stainless-steel plate. When it is necessary to remove hopper from motor shell, always use a new gasket when reassembling.

Cutter rings are often pressed into motor shell, and require heat and patience to remove. Holding cutter ring (top of photo) with pliers, gently heat top of shell assembly with propane torch, rotating shell slowly to distribute heat evenly. Then tap motor shell in vicinity of locking tabs while suspending weight of motor from cutter ring. Use wooden block to protect shell from hammer blows.

When loosening impeller retaining nut, make use of ears cast into impeller to lock in place. Don't try to insert punch or screwdriver into holes; sumps of modern units are often coated or lined with plastic materials to prevent corrosion, and sharp instrument could damage this finish. If much force is required to loosen nut, use steel stock rather than screwdriver.

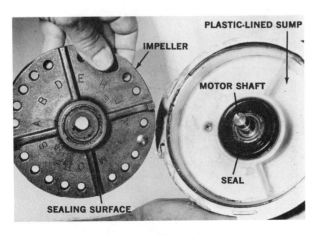

Seal is accessible after impeller is removed. Seal must always be replaced when removing impeller, and care must be taken to keep all sealing surfaces clean when reassembling. Use only seal specified by manufacturer, and replace at the first signs of leakage—any water seeping past seal can quickly damage motor winding.

Current-type starting relay is used in many disposers, serves to disconnect windings of split-phase motor as rotor approaches full speed. Details of checking are identical to relay in dehumidifier chapter.

Remove old seal with screwdriver. Lubricate new seal before reinstalling. If it cannot be pressed in with hand (after thoroughly cleaning seal cavity), measure the outer circumference of seal and use pipe of same dimension to tap into place.

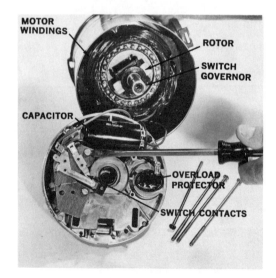

Some manufacturers prefer centrifugal switch rather than relay. Remove four throughbolts to remove bottom of this Sears unit. Remove switch by removing two screws that mount the switch-insulating board to the bottom casting. Always check to see that governor springs are in place if switch doesn't function.

Centrifugal switch is tested by (1) setting VOM to lowest resistance scale; (2) removing one lead from switch assembly; (3) connecting leads; and (4) checking for continuity while depressing actuating arm manually. Meter should indicate 0 ohms resistance when switch is closed, infinity when switch is open.

Capacitor is tested (left) by (1) discharging with a 20,000-ohm, 2-watt resistor, available at radio-TV parts suppliers; (2) using mid-range *(R × 10, R × 100)* resistance scale, connect VOM leads across capacitor terminals; (3) note meter reading. Meter should rise toward full scale, then fall back as meter's battery charges capacitor. Reversing leads should repeat the reading. Overload protector is tested for continuity (right) using lowest resistance scale on VOM. Reset button (manual reset type only) should be depressed before testing. Meter should indicate continuity through reset.

Starting and running windings of split-phase motor are tested for continuity, shorts and grounds using lowest VOM scale. To understand meanings of test readings (and to help you identify leads to each winding) see the chapter on basic electricity.

If disposer is equipped with reversible motor, reverse motor direction about once a week. Arrow in window of large reversing ring on unit below indicates direction of rotation. To reverse, slide ring opposite arrow.

but sees no point in paying for a top-of-the-line model.

Most improvements in disposers in recent years have come in the better models. Higher quality materials naturally cost more. Sound deadening insulation is not a feature of the lower line of disposers and may not be important to you, since they are only operated a few seconds at a time. But high horsepower motors, often as much as ¾ horsepower, are desirable for making sure food wastes are completely and quickly ground up. Consider these points in addition to the fact that the better disposers may last many years longer.

Installation charges can add significantly to the cost. Once you've selected your disposer, you can often save by making the entire or at least partial installation yourself if local codes permit. Installation generally requires removal of the original sink ring and drain trap from one side of the double sink and replacement with a special ring contained with the disposer. The new drain line components can usually be found at any plumbing-supply store. Use a hacksaw and a large wrench to tailor them to match your existing plumbing and take the place of the drain line removed prior to the disposer installation.

It is recommended that disposers be operated on a separate 115-volt circuit. If you replace an old disposer, the wiring most likely is already there. If you're installing a continuous feed model, be sure that the existing wall switch is rated at 15 amps or more. If not, change it. If you are making a new installation, check to see if a feeder is available nearby. If not, you may want to call in an electrician to run the circuit. In either case, you'll save substantially even if you install only the disposer unit yourself.

RULES FOR THE USE AND CARE OF A GARBAGE DISPOSER

- Grind all waste immediately.
- Always use cold water and the recommended water flow rate.
- Make certain water is running *before* grinding the food.
- Grind fibrous matter in small amounts with other food wastes.
- Do not grind metal, glass or china, unless otherwise indicated in your instruction book.
- Never pack waste in—this causes jamming.
- Be sure that disposer is empty before operating dishwasher.
- If dishwasher drains into disposer, run disposer for a short time after dishwasher is used.
- If odor appears, run through a tray of ice cubes and several orange or lemon rinds.
- Never put your hand into a disposer at any time. If necessary to probe, use a wooden spoon.
- If deflector allows water to pass through it, leave it in place during grinding to avoid splashback and to keep foreign objects from dropping into disposer.
- Avoid drain cleaners—they may be harmful to the disposer.

QUICK-CHECK CHART FOR
GARBAGE DISPOSERS

Symptom	Probable Cause	Remedy
Won't run—no sound	Fuse blown Overload protector tripped	Test for voltage, replace fuse Push reset button (manual type); Wait 30 minutes, try motor again (automatic resetting type); check hopper for binding impeller, overloaded condition
	Defective wall switch (continuous feed models)	Disconnect power, check on R × 1 scale. Should be rated at 15 amps or more.
	Defective stopper switch (batch feed models)	Test on R × 1 scale after disconnecting wiring, replace if defective.
Won't run—motor hums (may trip overload after few seconds)	Impeller binding	Check for cause of binding— usually foreign objects between impeller and cutter ring
	Defective relay or centrifugal switch	Test with VOM, repair or replace as necessary
	Open starting capacitor	Test and replace if necessary
	Open motor winding	Test with VOM—if winding open, replace motor as an assembly
	Motor bearings frozen	Check to see that rotor turns freely—many bearings are replaceable
Leaking water	Sink flange loose or not sealed (Leaks around outside of disposer)	Tighten, apply plumber's putty Also tighten mounting screws
	Impeller seal leaking (leaks from inside motor shell)	Disassemble disposer and replace seal
Excessive vibration	Loose mounting system	Inspect and tighten
	Loose impeller	Inspect and tighten
	Foreign object in hopper	Remove object and recheck
Water won't flow through drain	Line clogged	Clean and check—always clean line before installing new disposer
	Insufficient slope on drain line	Check before installation— should be *at least* 1 inch per 4 feet
	Insufficient flow of water during grinding	Open faucet to allow more water to flow when using disposer; remove and clean faucet aerator
	Impeller and/or cutting ring worn, not grinding food sufficiently	Inspect and replace if necessary

Chart cont. on next page.

GARBAGE DISPOSERS *(cont.)*

Symptom	Probable Cause	Remedy
Motor won't reverse (on models with reversible motor)	Defective reversing switch (manual reversing types)	Test switch for continuity with VOM, replace if open
	Defective transfer switch (automatic reversing type)	Switch is located by motor shaft, in conjunction with centrifugal starting switch. Test with VOM, inspect visually
Noisy operation	Foreign object in hopper Defective bearings	Remove object Inspect and replace as necessary
	Loose impeller	Inspect and tighten

17
Understand Home Refrigeration for Top Operating Economy

Mechanical refrigeration is the heart of most of our modern home refrigeration appliances. Gas absorption units are the only major exception—and these now are found primarily in recreational vehicles. Any mechanical refrigeration system does its job by removing heat units and transferring them elsewhere. To understand heat transfer, remember these three facts:

1. When a liquid reaches boiling point, heat units change into nonheat energy.
2. Altering atmospheric pressure raises or lowers the boiling point of a liquid.
3. Heat units always transfer from a warmer to a colder surface. The greater the temperature differential, the faster the transfer occurs.

In modern home refrigeration, one of two refrigerant chemicals is used—either R-12 or R-22. R-12 has a boiling point of −22 degrees F and R-22 boils at a temperature even lower: −41 degrees F. These chemicals are colorless, odorless, and nontoxic under normal condi-

tions, making them ideal for use in a home refrigerator.

As liquid refrigerant enters a low-pressure area, called the evaporator in every refrigeration appliance, heat is absorbed from adjacent air. The vapor passes on to a compressor from which it is discharged into a condenser.

Now the heat-laden vapor is concentrated under high pressure and, as it is cooled by the air passing over the condenser, it gives up the heat units which were absorbed within the evaporator coils. As the vapor cools, it condenses to a liquid state. Finally, it enters a metering device that regulates the flow of the liquid into the low-pressure area.

This metering device may be in the form of an expansion valve incorporating a needle and orifice to meter the refrigerant into an air conditioner's evaporator, but in all other home appliances (and in most air conditioners) it consists simply of a length of extremely small-diameter tubing carefully designed to provide the restriction necessary on that particular system. Without some means of restricting the flow of refrigerant between the high and low sides, there would be no pressure differential and the compressor would simply circulate the refrigerant.

The pressure-temperature relationship charts for various refrigerants point out the importance of this differential. An example: R-12 boils at −65 degrees F under a 20-inch vacuum; at 181 psi pressure, it boils at +130 degrees F.

As the liquid spills from the metering device back into the low-pressure area in the evapora-

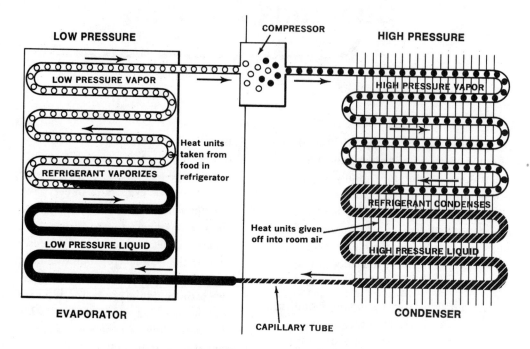

HOW A REFRIGERATOR DOES ITS COOLING JOB

All home refrigerating appliances, except gas-absorption units, operate on the principle that a liquid absorbs heat when it vaporizes. In the refrigerator, a refrigerant is alternately condensed into a liquid and then is permitted to expand into a gas. A compressor pumps the refrigerant through the system, which is sealed into a "closed circuit" by welding. In the condenser the refrigerant is converted to a liquid under high pressure. As it flows onward, it comes to a control device, such as a capillary tube, which restricts flow and thereby reduces pressure at its opposite end. Entering the low-pressure area in the evaporator (or freezing unit), the liquid refrigerant becomes a vapor or gas again, taking heat units from within the appliance and the foods stored there. At the condenser, the refrigerant gives up these heat units to air surrounding the appliance.

tor, the cycle is complete. In practice, this is a continuous effect so long as the compressor is running.

The compressor used in these systems is basically a pump. It is often a piston-type pump, especially in the larger air-conditioning units. In most refrigerators, freezers, and small air conditioners it is usually a rotary compressor. In these, a rotor is mounted off center within a cylinder. As it spins at high speeds, vanes attached to the rotor wipe the cylinder walls. Centrifugal force adds to the effectiveness of the seal between wall and vane. A system of valves, usually of the reed type, allows the refrigerant vapor to enter at the low-pressure area. As the rotor turns, the "section" which encompasses the refrigerant becomes smaller and smaller, and the refrigerant exits at another port under high pressure.

Regardless of the type of compressor that you have in your appliance, you'll see only a black steel cylinder or ball if you look for it. The reason for this is that the pump and motor are combined into one assembly and then sealed into a steel housing. The only components accessible are the electrical terminals. We use the term "hermetic" compressor to describe such compressors. They are used almost exclusively in small (less than 10 horsepower) refrigeration systems. They greatly reduce service problems and add years to the life of a refrigeration system. It has been said that rotary hermetic compressors don't wear out, they wear in. There's a great deal of truth in that statement.

The home refrigerator and freezer is a basic application of the refrigeration principle. Fundamental components—evaporator, condenser, compressor, and capillary tube—are sized and matched to maintain a particular temperature level. Most systems of recent years—many utilizing high-speed rotary compressors—maintain their design temperatures at approximately 70 percent running time. A simple thermostat cycles the compressor on and off to maintain the temperature level. It has a single pair of contacts and its sensing element is clamped to the evaporator. The demand upon the system and the amount of running time required will vary the load, the amount of usage, and the ambient temperature.

The simplest refrigerator of all is the one many of us grew up with. In these "standard" refrigerators, the evaporator forms a freezer compartment, always at the very top of the appliance. The rest of the refrigerator is cooled by the chilled air currents that fall from the evaporator above. Placement of a drip pan under the evaporator is critical. You may think that the sole purpose of this tray is to catch the water that results from refrigerator defrosting. Actually, its most important purpose is to act as a baffle for the natural air currents within the refrigerator. Many such trays have a flap for restricting air flow even further. Under normal conditions, this should be closed in winter when the load on the refrigerator compartment is light, and open in summer for increased cooling capacity. Don't remove the tray completely. This causes freezer temperatures to rise sharply and may reduce the efficiency of the entire system.

Condensers used on home refrigerators and freezers are classified as static and forced air. A static condenser, found on standard refrigerators, is one mounted on the back of the refrigerator or freezer cabinet, consisting of tubing with fins or wires to help dissipate heat efficiently. Air flows around it easily and heat is given off into this air within the room. There are no moving parts. Another type of static condenser is used on some freezers. In this application, the condenser tubing is attached to the inside of the cabinet. The warming effect in the cabinet helps reduce condensation. The forced-air condenser, however, has come into wide use in recent years. In this design the condenser coils are manufactured in a shape and size to fit under the cabinet. There, a cool-

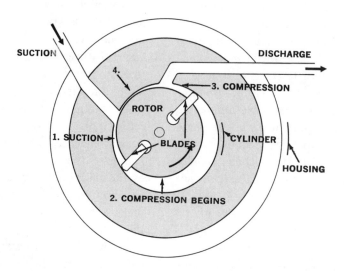

HOW A ROTARY COMPRESSOR MOVES REFRIGERANT

As heat-saturated vapor enters from the evaporator via the suction line, it enters a chamber which is increasing in size as the rotor spins. In the drawing, this is occurring at point 1. The negative pressure created by the enlarging chamber pulls the refrigerant into the chamber until the opposite blade passes the suction port.

At point 2, the refrigerant is being squeezed into an area which is decreasing in size. As the leading blade passes the discharge port, this compressed vapor can be sent out the discharge port, as shown at point 3.

Oil is pumped through the center of the shaft which drives the rotor, thoroughly lubricating all of the components of the sealed assembly. This oil pressure plus the centrifugal force from the spinning rotor (as fast as 3450 rpm) keeps the blades held tightly against the cylinder wall. The oil also acts as an effective seal at point 4, preventing "blow-by" of the pressurized refrigerant into the low-pressure suction area.

The all-important oil is sealed into the compressor along with the motor windings and pump assembly. If you should encounter a refrigerator which has been on its side for any reason (moving, etc.) allow it to stand upright for at least twenty-four hours before starting it, to be sure that sufficient oil has returned to the compressor. Otherwise, damage might occur to the highly polished surfaces and the compressor would shortly fail.

ing fan pulls room air across the coils, removing the heat that allows the hot refrigerant vapor to condense into liquid.

It is imperative that a free air flow be provided through the condenser, regardless of type. On a static condenser, a yearly dusting with the brush of a vacuum cleaner is sufficient. Forced-air models are *much* more critical. The increased air flow across the fins accelerates a buildup of lint and dust. These should be cleaned more frequently—at least every month or two. The housekeeper should make it a habit to vacuum accumulations away each time she vacuums the house. Follow the instructions that came with the refrigerator and be careful not to kink or bend any refrigerant tubing while cleaning.

Air blockage of a forced-air condenser can be a serious matter. If the coil becomes completely blocked, the refrigerant is unable to condense back to the liquid state. It re-enters the evaporator as a warm vapor. Evaporator temperatures rise and food thaws. In severe cases the compressor may become so hot that the overload protector will cycle it off. If this continues over an extended period, insulation on the compressor motor windings may be damaged. The result is an expensive system repair or possibly even a compressor replacement.

Defrost water from refrigerators and frostless freezers is carried to evaporation pan under cabinet (left), where heat from condenser and room air evaporates it. Pan should be cleaned every three to six months to eliminate odors from food particles which may find their way into defrost water. Pan placement is critical in "standard" refrigerators (right), since it acts as air baffle in addition to its duty as a container for defrost water. Recreational vehicles make wide use of such designs.

Lint on condensers, whether static or forced-air types, is an enemy of the system—and may result in severe damage to the compressor in extreme cases. The best preventative is a periodic schedule of cleaning.

GAS REFRIGERATORS

Most basic type refrigerators today are compact models for apartments and recreational vehicles. Those used in RVs often have a gas-absorption system. In a gas refrigerator, it is very important that passageways for fresh air flowing into and around the condenser be kept free from restrictions. The gas burner must also be free from lint and dust. A yellow flame is usually the first indication of linting around the burner orifice. Two thermostats may be employed on these models. One thermostat controls gas flow to the burner, increasing or decreasing the flow to provide the correct heat input. The second thermostat controls the system in the electric operational mode. At this time an electric heating element, rather than a gas burner, is acting as the heat source; the thermostat simply cycles this heater on and off

Compacts have gained a strong foothold in the market within recent years. Many units like the 4-cubic-foot model shown here are found in apartments, offices, dormitories, and as a second refrigerator around the home. *Courtesy of Frigidaire.*

as required. Checkout procedure for the electric thermostat is the same as for thermostats on electric refrigerators. For the gas thermostat, check as you would for an oven thermostat on a gas range.

AUTOMATIC DEFROST

Most refrigerators sold in recent years are either automatic defrosting or frost-free. The refrigeration system is basically the same as in a standard unit. The advantages of automatic defrosting systems are gained primarily through the control system and the placement of refrigeration system components. Frostless types also add an air-circulation system.

The early automatic defrost system was, for all practical purposes, a basic system utilizing a single evaporator with a heating element clamped to the evaporator. A timer was connected in series with the element and the compressor. At predetermined intervals it interrupted the circuit to the compressor and turned on the heater. This, of course, raised temperatures in and around the evaporator to a level somewhat above freezing, causing the freezer condensate to melt and run into a trough where it was collected and carried away to a pan located under the unit compartment at the bottom of the refrigerator. In this condensate pan, heat from the condenser (or in some cases, from a low wattage electrical heater) caused the water to be evaporated into the room air.

Manufacturers employ various methods of timing the interval of this defrost cycle. Many units use twenty-four-hour timers. These can be identified by the "day-night" markings on their dials. These timers initiate the defrost cycle during the wee hours of the morning (usually around 2:30 A.M.), a time when the refrigerator would not likely be in use. If a twelve-hour timer is used, it will defrost twice each day: usually at 2:30 P.M. and again at 2:30 A.M. Some manufacturers connected the timer motor to the thermostat so that it ran during the same periods that the compressor was op-

Dual thermostats regulate gas and electrical heat inputs to the gas-absorption system on this RV refrigerator. Mercury switch mounted on rear of gas valve automatically switches electrical mode on as the gas is turned off. If electric operation seems insufficient, switch to gas mode for a few hours; correction of problems by use of gas burner usually indicates low voltage in the campground supply.

HOW A GAS-ABSORPTION REFRIGERATOR
USES HEAT TO COOL

Before a gas refrigeration system leaves the factory, it's charged with hydrogen gas, water, and ammonia. The flame of a gas burner heats the mixture of ammonia (*A*) and water (*W*) present in the generator. This perco-

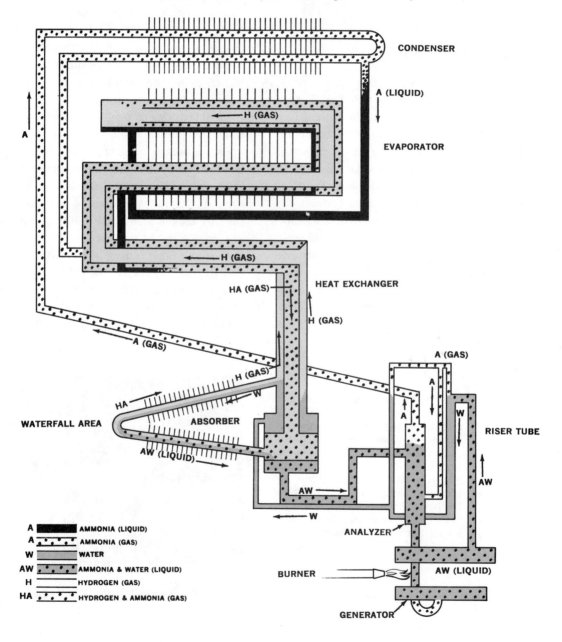

CONDENSER

A (LIQUID)

EVAPORATOR

A

H (GAS)

H (GAS)

HA (GAS)

HEAT EXCHANGER

H (GAS)

A (GAS)

A (GAS)

HA

H (GAS)

W

A

A

W

RISER TUBE

WATERFALL AREA

ABSORBER

AW (LIQUID)

AW

AW

ANALYZER

W

BURNER

AW (LIQUID)

GENERATOR

A		AMMONIA (LIQUID)
A		AMMONIA (GAS)
W		WATER
AW		AMMONIA & WATER (LIQUID)
H		HYDROGEN (GAS)
HA		HYDROGEN & AMMONIA (GAS)

lates up through the riser tube (very much like the water in a coffee maker), some of the liquid turning to ammonia gas since ammonia has a lower boiling point than water.

The gas generated passes through a liquid mixture in the analyzer, which cools it enough to remove any water present. It now rises to the condenser, where it cools and condenses to liquid ammonia.

The liquid ammonia drains out of the condenser and falls by gravity to the evaporator, where it meets with hydrogen gas (H). The hydrogen causes the ammonia to evaporate very rapidly, and as it does it absorbs heat. The hydrogen-ammonia gas (HA) leaves the evaporator carrying the heat which it has absorbed, and flows downward since it is heavier than the pure hydrogen entering the evaporator. (The evaporator is formed as a "tube within a tube.")

In the absorber section, the hydrogen-ammonia gas mixture is made to pass through several "waterfalls" created within the tubing by the water percolated from and flowing back to the generator (only one waterfall is shown here for simplicity). The ammonia is absorbed by the water and the ammonia-water liquid flows back to the generator, where the cycle begins all over. Since the water already contains all of the hydrogen that it can hold, the light gas is free to return to the evaporator from the absorber. When the thermostat determines that the evaporator is cold enough, the burner flame is reduced to a "holding" point which is sufficient to maintain evaporator temperatures.

A malfunction within such a unit is nonrepairable. The refrigerator must be returned to the factory. But the vast majority of problems are outside the system, so look closely before condemning the sealed unit. Because of the operating principles, leveling of the unit is critical. This is a major cause of operating failure, especially in recreational vehicles where the gas-absorption system finds its widest use today.

erating. The defrost cycle then occurred after a certain period of elapsed running time of the compressor. Still another method was to connect the timer motor in the circuit with the door switch so that the timer motor ran during the periods that the door was open and the interior light was on. Then the defrost period occurred after a certain accumulative length of time that the door had been open. There's more logic to this than you may think, for the purpose of defrosting is to remove the frozen condensate from the evaporator. This occurs most rapidly when the door is open, allowing warm, moist air to enter the freezer.

The heaters in these systems are enclosed with heavy electrical insulation and water-proof connections and wiring. They are clamped to the evaporator and often contain a fusible link to protect against overheating. Look for this link near the heater and check it for continuity with your ohm meter before condemning the heater. When replacing a link, heater, or making any repair involving the wiring harness, be sure that all connections are tight and waterproof and wrapped thoroughly and tightly with tape.

Manufacturers have used an alternate method of defrosting in some models. By using a solenoid-operated valve placed on the condenser section of the refrigeration system, they have eliminated the electrical resistance heater and call upon the hot gases within this system to warm the evaporator coil. A quick glance at the wiring diagram for your equipment will tell you which type you have. The same testing principles apply—the solenoid is energized by the timer and is usually controlled by a limit thermostat or by the cold control (thermostat) on automatic defrosting models.

Split-evaporation System

A major disadvantage of early auto-defrosting systems was that when the heater warmed the evaporator to melt the condensate, it could also partly thaw any frozen food within the evaporator, especially if the food was in direct contact with the evaporator plate. A major advance to eliminate this condition was adoption of the "split-evaporator" system. In this system the freezer evaporator is separated (and often insulated) from the refrigerator compartment which contains another "section" of evaporator surface. Often two separate doors are used, one for each compartment. The refrigerant first enters the freezer evaporator, and only after this evaporator is sufficiently cooled does the liquid refrigerant flow to the refrigerator compartment evaporator. The freezer section evaporator is often designed in a forward-opening U-shape to cradle the frozen food. Or a horizontal, O-shaped evaporator may completely encircle the food. The refrigerator evaporator may take the form of a fin and tube arrangement at the upper rear of the compartment, a serpentine coil across the top of the compartment, or a flat, expanded aluminum plate on the rear wall of the

Split-evaporator construction, with expanded plates, is used in this Philco model. Trough under lower evaporator carries defrost water to pan under condenser, where it is evaporated.

Serpentine coil in this GE refrigerator is located across top of refrigerator compartment. Tall cartons (and hands) can leave oily film, making washdown necessary (see page 294).

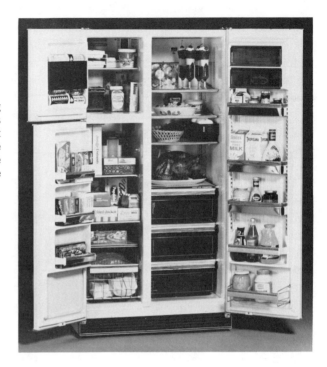

Configurations vary greatly among frostless refrigerators. Ice maker is contained in separate compartment with its own door on this Frigidaire model. Frequent openings for ice usage don't interfere with storage compartment temperatures.

compartment. These plate evaporators are interesting in that they are made from two sheets of aluminum plate bonded together except in certain areas where the refrigerant passageways will be formed. When high pressure is applied, the aluminum sheets are forced apart in areas where they were not bonded, leaving a precise pattern of passageways to contain the refrigerant.

With separate evaporators it is possible to defrost the refrigerator evaporator without affecting the more critical freezer temperature. The most common method of defrosting a "split-evaporator" system is the cycle defrost method. With cycle defrost the sensing bulb of the thermostat is attached near the end of the refrigerator section evaporator, the last point of the evaporator to be cooled by the refrigerant. The thermostatic control is so designed that it will cut the compressor off at some point, depending on the setting of the control knob, allowing you to raise and lower average temperatures within the compartment just like a conventional thermostat. Unlike an ordinary stat, however, regardless of the cut-off temperature, it will not cut on again until the temperature has risen to a predetermined point, normally 36 to 38 degrees. Since this is several degrees above the freezing point, it allows the frost that accumulated on the evaporator during the *on* cycle to melt and run off the evaporator. This occurs each time the refrigerator cycles.

Defrosting Problems

The most common problem of cycle defrost systems is a buildup of frost or ice due to foreign matter on the surface of the coil. Often, this is wax residue from wrapping paper or cartons. Also, these coils are "untouchable"; the oily film left when the tubing or plate is touched allows water droplets to remain, and these rapidly "snowball" to an ice accumulation after a few cycles. If you suspect such a condition, find an automatic dishwasher detergent marked "will not harm aluminum," mix up a mild solution in a cup of warm water, and wash the evaporator thoroughly. Do not use regular detergents, soaps, or detergents intended for hand washing. These products will often tend to make the problem worse by increasing the surface tension of the defrost water.

FROST-FREE SYSTEMS

These are not as far removed from the other methods as you at first might believe. They do offer quite a few advantages. But they really aren't frost-free—they might be more accurately described as "hidden frost" systems. In these units the evaporator is placed behind a wall or between the two compartments. The air within both refrigerator and freezer is circulated throughout the compartment and across the hidden evaporator, where the heat is removed from the air.

In most applications the chilled air from the evaporator is discharged directly into the freezer compartment. When more cooling is called for in the refrigerator compartment, it takes this air from the freezer compartment. In a typical application the refrigerator thermostat would open and close a baffle to admit air through a duct from the freezer compartment.

If enough chilled air is removed to allow freezer temperatures to rise, the freezer thermostat turns the compressor on to provide more cooling to the freezer. Thus a chain reaction effect is created. The thermostats used normally sense the *air* temperature within the compartment rather than the temperature of an evaporator plate. This method of control, combined with the forced air movement found within these systems, produces more even and consistent temperature than was previously possible.

This "frostless" operation is possible because of a phenomenon known as *sublimation,* by which some substances can pass from a solid to a gaseous state without going through an intermediate liquid state. In this application it works this way: when the door to a freezer compartment is opened, water vapor in the air condenses upon the much colder surfaces inside, just as it does on a glass of iced tea in the summer. In the freezer compartment, this moisture freezes to the inner door panels, compartment liner, and even food packages, forming a very thin film or coating each time the door is opened. Through sublimation this moisture will migrate to the coldest surface within the compartment, the evaporator coil itself. The process is greatly speeded up by the constant flow of air across the packages and surfaces of the compartment. This deposit of frost builds up on the evaporator until removed during the defrost cycle at regular intervals. If you'd like proof of the effectiveness of this system, take a frozen fruit-flavored ice confection, such as a Popsicle, remove the protective paper wrapping, and place it in the freezer compartment of your frostless refrigerator. In a couple of weeks, there'll be nothing

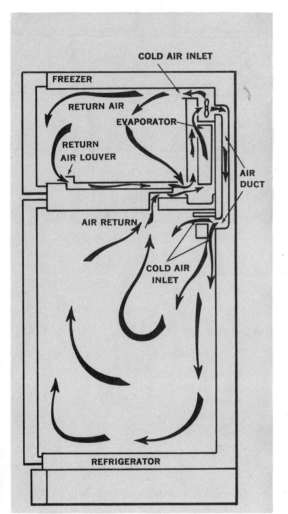

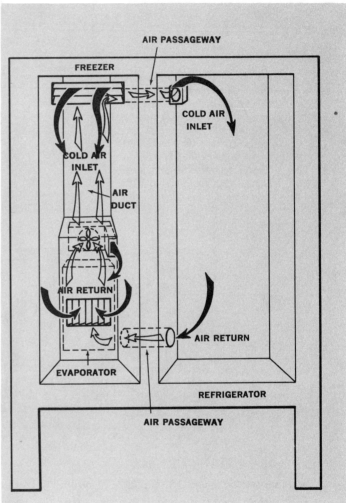

HOW AIR CIRCULATES IN FROSTLESS REFRIGERATORS

Follow the arrows to see how air circulates in two popular models of frostless refrigerators. In the top-freezer model (left), the fin-and-tube evaporator is located on the back wall of the freezer liner. The air moves from the evaporator through the air duct in freezer bottom. In side-by-side model, a thermostatic damper is often used to regulate amount of chilled air which enters refrigerator compartment. *Courtesy of Whirlpool Corp.*

With cover panels removed, location of evaporator and heater can be seen on frost-free system (above). This is a side-by-side model. Below is a top-freezer unit with a horizontal finned evaporator. In many top-freezer systems the evaporator is located at the rear, in a vertical position.

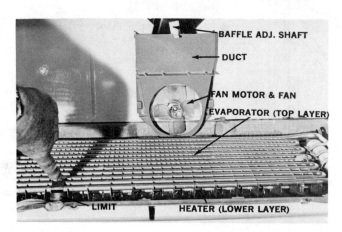

left but two sticks and a little puddle of syrup.

Frostless freezers operate in the same manner as frostless refrigerators except that they have only one compartment and the evaporator plate may cover the entire rear wall or may form a double-bank fin-and-tube arrangement around the bottom of the compartment.

The refrigeration system and the controls are altered to attain the colder temperatures required in a freezer. The evaporator surface is larger, and the thermostats are calibrated to maintain a near-zero temperature. The larger ducting passageways in frost-free models often cover the entire rear wall of the single compartment.

Symptoms and repair procedures are much the same as for refrigerators, but there are a few exceptions. There are also certain limitations to a home freezer which you should understand.

First, the home freezer of today is a storage freezer. This means that food placed in the freezer should be pre-frozen or it should be placed into the freezer in small quantities. A rule of thumb for warm food is never to put in more than 10 percent of the capacity of the freezer at one time. An 18-cubic-foot freezer, for example, would freeze properly about 1.8-cubic feet of food at any one time. Greatly exceeding this amount causes temperatures to rise quickly and lower slowly, and a great deal of flavor is lost in the process. In extreme cases, the temperatures may rise to the point that the entire freezer load of food may thaw and spoil.

Some freezers have a portion of their compartment designated as a "fast-freeze" section. Additional coils of evaporator tubing or close proximity to a frigid air outlet make this an excellent method to quick-freeze foods before moving them to another area of the freezer for storage. Some makers also add a push-button device to lock in thermostat contacts until the freezer has reached a colder-than-normal temperature.

RULES FOR THE USE AND CARE OF REFRIGERATORS AND FREEZERS

A question often asked goes something like this: "Why does my new refrigerator run so much?" Or: "What can I do to keep my refrigerator from using so much power?"

The average new refrigerator purchased today contains 17 cubic feet of storage space. The one replaced may have contained only 10. The new appliance is cooling almost as much

storage space as two old ones. Also the added conveniences such as frostless refrigeration and automatic ice maker increase power consumption. You can't do anything about reducing power needs for these conveniences, but you can easily keep power consumption to a minimum by using the appliance in the most efficient manner.

Keep air circulating as it should. Keep the condenser clean and make sure there is plenty of room around the refrigerator or freezer. Check your instruction manual for front, top, and side clearances and be sure you adhere to them. Keep all food covered and wipe up spills quickly. Replace any torn gaskets and remedy any other causes of air leakage into the cabinet. Keep controls set no lower than is necessary to keep foods properly chilled. This should normally be within a range of 35 to 40 degrees in the refrigerator compartment and 0 to +10 degrees in the freezer. Basic refrigerators do not have freezer compartments capable of maintaining such a low temperature. They range normally from +5 degrees to +20 degrees.

Probably the most important power-saving tip is to keep opening of doors to a minimum. Each time you open the door, heavy cold air inside the compartment flows out to the floor of the room. As soon as this occurs, warm damp air rushes in to take its place. This increases running time.

Other use and care pointers:

- Make certain the unit is reasonably level to insure proper operation of the defrost water-drainage system.
- Operate at recommended control settings for proper temperatures. When varying these for unusual needs or conditions, allow

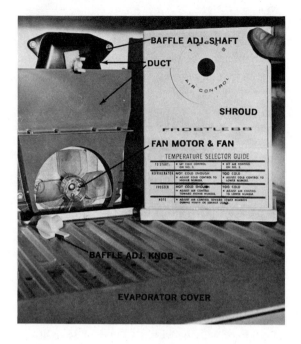

Duct seen at rear of evaporator incorporates an adjustable baffle to control the volume of air entering each compartment from evaporator. Packages must be placed so air flow remains unrestricted. Shroud snaps off duct after knob is pulled from shaft.

twenty-four hours between changes for system to comply.

• Never let frost in freezer compartment build up more than ¼ inch.

• Clean interior regularly with a solution of baking soda and water; clean exteriors with lukewarm sudsy water. Occasionally use wax on painted exterior surfaces.

• Vacuum the condenser as frequently as advised in the instruction manual, using the crevice tool attachment of your vacuum or a long-handle brush. Clean more frequently if house has unusual dust conditions or shedding pets. Signs of dirty condenser coils are: temperatures inside refrigerator begin to rise; running time increases; vibration noises increase; or the cabinet exterior becomes warm.

• Cover foods tightly to prevent drying and spreading odors.

• Refrigerate foods as soon as possible after preparation or purchase.

• Use special storage areas for their intended purpose.

• Do not overload a freezer at one time with unfrozen food. This slows the freezing process. A good guideline is never to add more than 10 percent of freezer's capacity at a time.

• Defrost nonfrost-free freezer models before more than ½ inch of frost forms.

SAFETY NOTE: When disposing of an old refrigerator or freezer, be sure the door or lid is removed as soon as it is taken out of service to avoid child entrapment.

18
Troubleshooting Home Refrigerators and Freezers

Use care in handling and working with any refrigeration appliance, especially when it's necessary to move components and bend tubing. A kink or split in the refrigerant tubing can damage the appliance and require an expensive repair job by a refrigeration technician.

Should a leak develop in the system, there are certain precautions which should be taken. While the refrigerant itself should be nontoxic in such small concentrations, it can form phosgene, a poisonous gas, in the presence of an open flame. Under such conditions, the highly irritating odor will give you plenty of warning to leave the area. Be sure to shut off pilot lights on gas dryers or ranges, or any burning pilots on gas appliances. Open windows for ventilation. As a gas, a refrigerant is heavier than air and would remain close to floor level. If you should detect a leak from which refrigerant is escaping as a liquid, as it might from a broken condenser line, just unplug the refrigerator or freezer. Never attempt to stop the leak—the

extreme cold of the evaporating liquid can give you frostbite.

Any repairs within the refrigeration system itself require a great deal of expensive and specialized equipment to do the job correctly. But this is a problem you're unlikely to encounter when a piece of refrigeration equipment fails to function. You should be able to handle any other job yourself.

Before attempting any repair, unplug the appliance.

TEMPERATURE TESTS

When diagnosing a fault in a refrigerator or freezer, take exact temperature readings of the sections that seem too warm or too cold. Check them carefully with an accurate thermometer. A dial thermometer is easy to use.

To make temperature readings in a refrigerator compartment, place the sensing end of the thermometer in a glass of water that has been

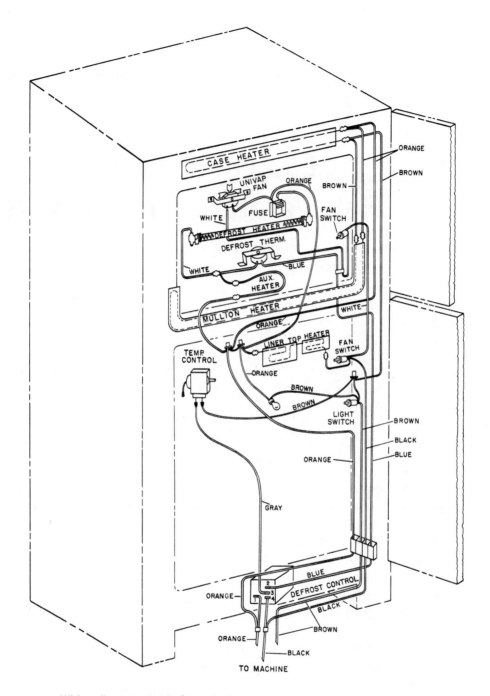

Wiring diagram of this General Electric refrigerator is excellent guide to diagnosis. Pictorial diagram shows locations of components and their connections, while schematic diagram simplifies each circuit. Compressor representation shows wiring harness connections in unit compartment. *Courtesy General Electric Co.*

308

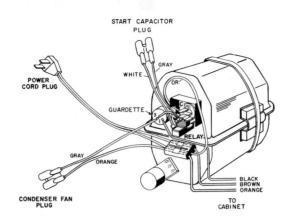

START CAPACITOR
PLUG

GRAY

WHITE

OR

POWER
CORD
PLUG

GUARDETTE

3

R

RELAY

GRAY

ORANGE

BLACK
BROWN
ORANGE

CONDENSER FAN
PLUG

TO
CABINET

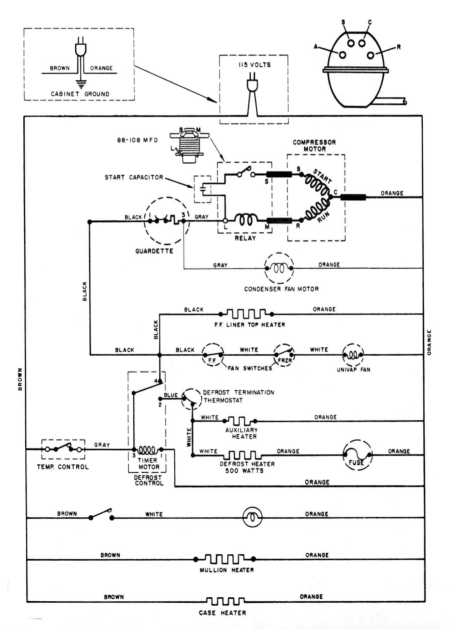

BROWN   ORANGE

CABINET GROUND

115 VOLTS

S   C

A   R

88-108 MFD

S   M

L

COMPRESSOR
MOTOR

START CAPACITOR

S   S   START

C

ORANGE

BLACK   3   GRAY   L   M   R   RUN

GUARDETTE

RELAY

GRAY   ORANGE

CONDENSER FAN MOTOR

BLACK

BLACK   ORANGE

F.F. LINER TOP HEATER

BLACK

BLACK   BLACK   WHITE   WHITE

F.F.   FRZR

BROWN

FAN SWITCHES

UNIVAP FAN

ORANGE

48

BLUE   DEFROST TERMINATION
2   THERMOSTAT

WHITE   ORANGE

AUXILIARY
HEATER

WHITE

GRAY

TEMP. CONTROL

3

TIMER
MOTOR

DEFROST
CONTROL

WHITE   ORANGE   ORANGE

DEFROST HEATER   FUSE
500 WATTS

ORANGE

ORANGE

BROWN   WHITE   ORANGE

BROWN   ORANGE

MULLION HEATER

BROWN   ORANGE

CASE HEATER

309

Baffle which separates evaporator from food compartment must be removed to check icing condition. This evaporator is under bottom of top freezer compartment. It is called "mullion" type since it is located behind mullion, which serves to divide the refrigerator from the freezer.

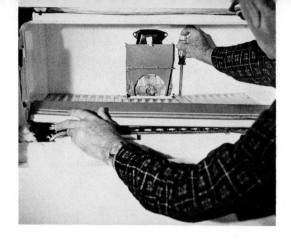

This dial pocket thermometer is typical of those used by many appliance technicians. Accuracy may be checked by immersing probe in ice bath, then adjusting dial to 32 degrees by turning hex nut on back side of dial. It is available from refrigeration and photographic suppliers.

Note method of clamping thermostat sensing tube to coil. If ice formation is constant problem at a particular place on evaporator, moving sensing tube closer to this point may help.

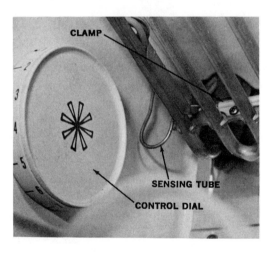

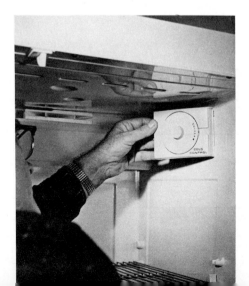

Air-sensing thermostats are easiest of all to replace. Sensing tube is arranged in control cover (often called an escutcheon). Be sure that tubing of replacement is arranged exactly as original and that plastic barrier tube is in place.

Contacts of air-sensing type are easily tested with VOM on $R \times 1$ scale. Continuity should be noted when thermostat sensing tube is warm. Meter should read 0 ohms when thermostat is calling for compressor to run. If compressor runs all the time and foods freeze, look for broken or damaged sensing tube or welded contacts. Replacement is necessary.

Automatic dampers utilize movement of diaphragm in thermostatic control to mechanically move damper rather than open and close an electrical switch. Testing is easily done by immersing end of sensing tube in ice bath (glass filled with ice cubes and then covered with water). Damper should barely be open at coldest thermostat setting. Refrigerator thermostat can also be tested this way—switch should be open under these same conditions. When tube is removed from water and grasped with fingers to warm it, damper should open wide (or switch should close) within a few seconds. Some adjustment is provided on most controls, and will be marked with arrow and often the word "colder." It's often necessary to adjust this for critical control at higher altitudes.

inside the compartment for at least eight hours. Simply placing the thermometer on a shelf is not a good test—it doesn't sense a true average temperature, and opening the door to read the thermometer can influence the reading.

In the freezer compartment you won't have water, of course, but you may have ice cream, the best medium for a sample temperature test. If there is none in the compartment, sandwich the thermometer between two packages of frozen food.

FROST BUILDUP

If a buildup of frost occurs on the refrigerator evaporator that uses the cycle defrost method, observe the frost pattern before making a diagnosis.

If the evaporator is evenly coated with frost before the compressor cycles off, the refrigeration system is operating satisfactorily. The problem is most likely in the thermostat. It could be turning on the compressor prematurely—before evaporator temperatures rise above the freezing point. Or it could be causing the unit to run constantly. In the latter case, you might find that temperatures within the entire compartment are too cold. First signs of foods freezing within the refrigerator compartment would be noticed in the vegetable bins at the bottom.

If the evaporator is only partly frosted and the unit is running constantly, there's a possibility that a slight leak exists somewhere in the refrigeration system. In this event, heavy frosting will most likely be noticed at the points where refrigerant enters the evaporator near the top. After a few ounces have escaped due to a leak, there just isn't enough liquid refrigerant to completely fill the bottom evaporator and reach the point where the thermostat sensing bulb is connected.

If the condition continues or is severe enough, the lower evaporator may not frost at all. In this case, the refrigerator section would be very warm, while the freezer section could be extremely cold. I've seen them as low as 25 degrees below zero. As the leak continued, even the freezer section would finally become warm.

If, after eliminating all other factors, you suspect a leak in the refrigeration system, it will be necessary to call a technician who specializes in this work, as noted previously. It takes a lot of special equipment and training to do system repair.

In frost-free models thermostat replacement is relatively simple, since the sensing bulb is usually housed within the same escutcheon upon which the thermostat is mounted. In many units only one screw holds the entire assembly in place. If it is necessary to replace a thermostat, note carefully how the sensing bulb is arranged before removing the old one. When you put the new one in place, be sure that the sensing bulb or capillary tubing does not come in contact with the compartment liner. A plastic tube, called a barrier tube, is often used on the sensing tube of such thermostats. This helps prevent short-cycling of the control when the door to the compartment is opened. Be sure this is in place on a replacement control if specified in the manufacturer's instructions. The barrier tube should extend ⅜ inch beyond the end of the thermostat sensing bulb.

Rising temperature in frost-free systems, in one or both compartments, is often a signal that the evaporator coil has somehow become frosted. By the time you actually see frost buildup on the cover or plate over the coil, you can be assured that the coil itself is completely blocked. When this happens, the frost acts as an insulation and chokes air flow across the coil. Since the operation of both compartments depends upon this cool air, temperatures begin to rise, slowly at first, then rather rapidly as the condition becomes more severe.

The first step, of course, is to find the cause of the icing condition. First, take a good look at the type of icing. It will be necessary to remove the cover to the evaporator coil. If the ice is clear and hard, this points to a possibility that evaporator frost has melted and the condensate water has refrozen before it could be carried away.

Check the drainage system from the evaporator. A food particle may have blocked the passageway, or maybe the tubing that carries the water from the evaporator to the condensate pan under the refrigerator has become blocked with algae. Bottom freezer models do not have the drain tubing running down the back of the refrigerator, but even they usually have a trap or float in the drain outlet at the bottom that can become clogged.

If at all possible, remove the obstruction before you try to completely remove the ice, as this will help drain the relatively large amount of water from the unit and make the job much easier. If algae in the tubing or trap proves to be the culprit, pour a tablespoonful of household ammonia down the drain line after you have finished the job. This kills any remaining spores and is good insurance against another buildup.

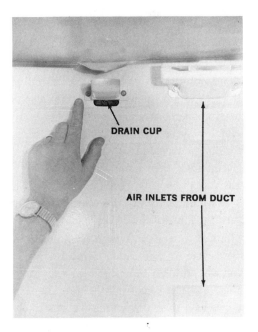

DRAIN CUP

AIR INLETS FROM DUCT

Drain line or cup blocked by algae is often the cause of defrosting problems. The cup shown above catches defrost water from mullion-type evaporator in Sears frostless unit. It is held in place by two screws. Remove cup and clean thoroughly, finish the job with spoonful of household ammonia poured into cup and flushed down drain tube which carries water to pan underneath cabinet.

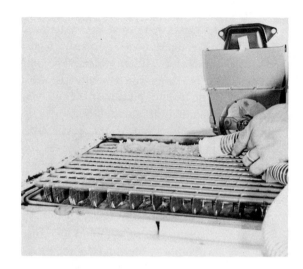

When defrosting an iced evaporator, use heat sparingly and carefully. Hot air directed from hose of hair dryer is good source. *All* frost must be removed before putting equipment back into operation. Even slight amount shown here would rapidly increase to original proportions.

Removing the solid ice is the hardest part of the job. It melts slowly and the temptation to apply excessive heat is great. Use caution here. Some plastic ducts and hidden baffles may melt at temperatures only slightly above 100 degrees. A good method of applying heat is to carefully direct air from a hair dryer on the ice and frost. Probably the safest method of all is to store the food in a freezer and let the compartment stand open until all the ice is melted. It is important to remove every trace of ice or frost that remains; otherwise the evaporator will almost surely become blocked again within a short length of time.

Another possible cause of such condensate ice buildup on some models is a faulty drain-trough heater. During the defrost cycle, this auxiliary heater warms the surfaces of the passageway which guides the water out of the evaporator compartment. A look at the wiring diagram of your refrigerator will tell you if such a heater is used and show you where to locate the leads. Use your VOM to test for continuity.

The Timer

If the frost is white and appears snowy but is hard to the touch, as it would be on the evaporator of a standard refrigerator, it's a sign that the defrost system is not working. These systems are normally quite simple. They consist primarily of a defrost timer, which on most refrigerators initiates a defrost cycle every twelve hours; a bimetal defrost termination limit switch to turn the heater off when the evaporator-plate temperature reaches a level above 60 degrees; and the heater itself, which may be embedded within the evaporator coil or located immediately adjacent to it. (Remember that some models use the "hot gas," as previously mentioned.)

An initial check of this system is to simply turn the knob of the defrost timer to the point where you hear the system click into the defrost cycle. If the heating element is working, you will probably be able to hear a slight "popping" as it expands from the heat, or perhaps a hiss as a drop of melting water strikes the

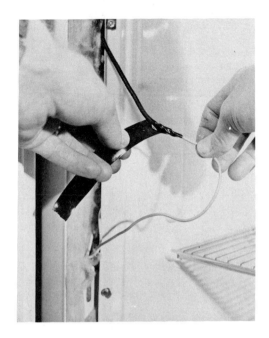

Splices in wiring of refrigerator should be wrapped tightly to provide moisture-proof connection. When at all possible, splices should be made in a location that will allow them to be pushed beyond the liner where there is less chance of moisture intrusion.

warm heater. If the heater sounds as though it is working, allow the timer to stay in the defrost position. It should end the defrost cycle and turn the compressor back on within a maximum period of twenty-five minutes. If it does not, suspect the defrost timer. The small synchronous motor may not be working. On many timers the motor movement may be observed through a small window in the back of the cover. Both motor and switch contacts may be tested with the VOM. A single-pole, double-throw switching arrangement is often used on these timers; a circuit to the compressor is established during the running cycle and a circuit to the heater during the defrost cycle. Both circuits should never be energized at the same time.

This brings up an exception to one of the principles that many technicians rely on for quick and proper diagnosis, and you should

know about it. When examining a refrigeration appliance, one of the first questions you should ask yourself is whether the problem lies in the refrigeration system or if the problem is electrical. If the compressor is running but not cooling, feel the condenser tubing. If it is hot or warm to the touch, you know that the refrigeration circuit is doing its job of removing the heat from the contents.

But in a frost-free system, there is a condition which causes the condenser to be hot, yet the evaporator is only cool (not cold) or even warm to the touch. This is caused by the compressor and the evaporator heater remaining energized at the same time, and the problem almost always lies within the defrost timer.

You can use the "hot condenser" principle to good advantage. If the system is running, and air passageways are clear but the evaporator is warm, a cool condenser means that there

One test necessary on a defrost timer is to check the motor for continuity ($R \times 100$ scale on VOM) or by observing whether the output gear or cam is rotating. Motor can usually be tested without disassembling timer by following motor lead wires to proper terminal. If connections are internal, look at wiring diagram to see at which terminals motor leads are attached. Many newer timers are sealed and disassembly is impossible. Reading is about 1000 ohms.

Next, timer contacts are tested for continuity. They should indicate 0 ohms resistance with VOM set to $R \times 1$ scale, indicating that contacts are not burned or welded together. To test in each part of cycle, turn timer knob manually as shown. Consult wiring diagram to determine which terminals control heater and which control compressor.

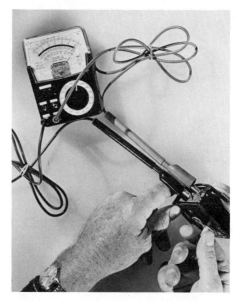

TERMINALS

CONTACTS

TIMER MOTOR (REMOVED)

DRIVE GEAR & CAM

Simple contact arrangement is seen in this view of disassembled timer. Motor drives cam gear shown through intermediate gear. Contacts are "stepped" or spaced so that circuit can be completed to either compressor or to heater, but not to both.

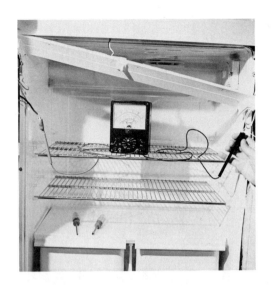

Continuity check of heating element is made at connectors or at terminal block. These connections were located behind refrigerator section breaker trims. Pictorial type wiring diagrams will show their locations. It's important to check for grounds in these heaters.

is likely a problem within the refrigeration system—probably a leak or restriction. It's time to call in a specialist. Don't forget, however, that your accurate description of the problem can save time and make the refrigeration technician's job easier.

The Heating Element

It usually is possible to check the heating element for continuity without removing the cover plate from the evaporator. Check the wiring diagram for the color coding and the location of the leads. Usually these will be accessible at a terminal block or at wire connections under one of the breaker trims, the plastic molding used between the compartment liner and the outer cabinet. When removing a cold breaker trim, first saturate a cloth with hot water and wipe it along the trim to be removed. This warms the plastic, making it more pliable and reduces the possibility of

cracking or breakage. Working from one end of the breaker, pull it away from the cabinet side first and then pull forward to remove it from the liner side.

Three basic types of heaters are used in frostless systems. The hardest to replace is one that is pressed into the fins of the evaporator coil. To replace this heater, remove the screws that hold the evaporator coil to the liner and carefully raise it so as to avoid bending or kinking any of the connecting refrigerant tubing. When the heater is accessible, pull the old heater from the fins. It is wise to use heavy gloves for this process to avoid cutting your hands on the sharp aluminum fins. Then, following the manufacturer's replacement instructions, carefully press the new heater into position. Avoid sharp bends of the heater sheath and avoid indenting it with a sharp tool, as either condition will lead to early failure. Try to make all electrical splices behind the liner if possible and wrap tightly with tape

Breaker trims are easily removed *if* you warm them first with rag soaked in hot water. Pull front side away from cabinet first, then pull forward to release from liner.

Heater replacement procedure varies widely. Here, heater embedded in evaporator coil of top-freezer model must be pried out and carefully pressed back into place (see text).

Radiant heater surrounding fin and tube evaporator in this upright freezer is a simple clip-in job. Drain trough below evaporator is also heated during the defrost cycle by the single heater. Trap under cabinet on many such models keeps air from entering through water drainage line, but it should be cleaned or flushed yearly to prevent blockage from algae or food particles.

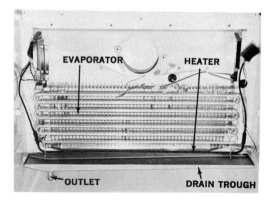

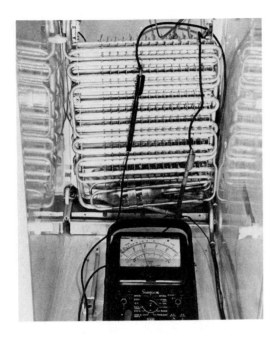

Look carefully at evaporator design before attempting heater replacement. This one is embedded between sections of fin and tube evaporator, which must be carefully pulled open to gain access to heater.

to make a waterproof connection.

Enclosed sheath-type radiant heaters which surround the evaporator are easier to change since they are simply clamped around the evaporator. Be sure that the heater goes back in the same position as the original and that all splices and connections are waterproof. Probably the simplest of all evaporator heaters to change is the enclosed radiant heater used on some models. Located just under and in front of the evaporator coil, this heater simply snaps in place and plugs into the wiring harness. After replacing a heater, be sure that all frost is removed from the evaporator.

The Defrost Termination Switch

This is possibly the hardest component of the electrical system to diagnose. Typically this component closes at a temperature of approximately 20 degrees and opens at 55 to 70 degrees. You can check with a VOM across its two leads and tell if it is opening by heating it and if it is closing by cooling it. It is hard to tell if the switch is erratic or if it is operating at something other than its designed temperatures; yet both these factors can have quite an effect on frosting conditions of the evaporator. Many technicians surmise that if you are positive that a problem exists in the defrost system and the timer and heater operate satisfactorily, then the defrost termination switch must be at fault. I do not endorse this theory completely, but it usually holds true. Again, when replacing a termination switch, be sure that all connections are tight and waterproofed, and that *all* frost is removed from the evaporator before putting the refrigerator or freezer back into operation.

Defrost termination limit switch provides high-temperature protection against overheating. Temperature range is difficult to check. This limit closes at approximately 20 degrees and reopens at 55 degrees; others vary up to 70 degrees. Erratic limit is often the cause of frosting conditions when both heater and timer are proved satisfactory.

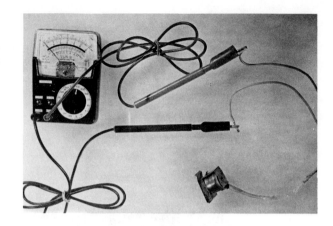

Appearances differ greatly between evaporator and condenser fan motors. Evaporator motor (right) is constructed for low ambient temperatures of freezing compartment; condenser motor (left) is designed for high temperatures of unit compartment.

Emergency repair for stuck condenser motor involves drilling hole into bearing cavity and lubricating wick with light oil. Also place drop or two of oil around front shaft and push and pull armature forward and backward until it is free.

Air Seepage

If the frost is snowy but soft, and rakes off easily, it's usually caused by large quantities of air seeping into the compartment. Check the door seals first. If your refrigerator or freezer is relatively new, it will probably have a magnetic latch or a magnetic strip built into the gasket. Look for tears and nicks in the gasket. If it is damaged, replacement is the only sure cure. Be sure to specify the exact model number and the door for which the gasket is needed when requesting a replacement part.

In the late fifties, regulations went into effect which set minimum limits on the amount of force necessary to open a refrigerator or freezer door. The object was to reduce the danger of children becoming trapped in them when the refrigerators were discarded. Of course, you should always remove the door completely before a junked refrigerator is taken out of service. But these regulations made a science of the study of door sealing. New door designs are such that they should seal well without a heavy force being applied to the door.

The "dollar bill" test is a good indicator of proper door seal. With a dollar bill inserted between the door and the gasket, a definite pull should be felt when you remove the bill with the door closed. Use this test in several spots around the door to determine the correct door-to-cabinet alignment.

If the door seals in one area but not in another, loosen the screws which retain the inner door panel and gently twist the door to provide proper alignment. Then retighten the screws. The door liners, made of a special plastic material, are designed to support the relatively flexible outer panel and to strengthen the door assembly.

To help maintain cold temperatures, freezers often use a twenty-four-hour defrost timer rather than the twelve-hour timer most often found on refrigerators. Sometimes, under conditions of high usage, numerous door openings may allow more moisture to enter than the system can handle. In a case like this, check all components thoroughly to be certain that no mechanical or electrical problem exists. Review your family's usage habits of the freezer. As a last resort you might consider changing to a twelve-hour defrost timer.

INSULATION

No discussion of refrigerators and freezers would be complete without a word about insulation and moisture migration. For many years now the standard cabinet installation for home refrigeration appliances has been high-density fiberglass. In many new high-efficiency models, urethane foam serves as the insulation as well as the support which holds the liner in place in the cabinet.

Regardless of the type of insulation used, it operates on the principle of providing millions of "dead-end streets" through which heat units must travel to get into the compartment. It is possible at some point between the liner and the cabinet to measure any given temperature between room temperature and the temperature within the compartment, and one of those given temperatures is the dew point—the point at which water vapor in the air condenses to the liquid state. Water is the enemy of all insulations. It closes the air passages and, being a much better conductor of heat than air, allows heat units to pass through easily. The moisture that can form in refrigerator-

Replacement magnetic door gasket may develop kinks in shipment. Low heat applied from hair dryer should straighten them out. Such gaskets normally require about two weeks to seat themselves properly. Strip of masking tape is suggested to prevent door springing open in the meantime. When properly seated and adjusted, gasket should compress only slightly when door is closed.

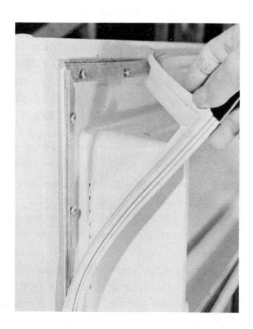

Door gasket replacement requires removal of door panel on most older refrigerators and freezers—newer ones use retaining band to hold liner and gasket in position. Easy method of replacement is shown in photo. Leaving door in place, remove screws from upper two-thirds of door liner. Pull old gasket out, slip new gasket into place and replace screws loosely around top and partially down side of door. Next, remove remaining screws, slip gasket around remainder of door liner and replace screws loosely. Adjust door by aligning with cabinet then loosening hinges to obtain correct door-cabinet spacing (see text).

freezer insulation comes from the same source as moisture that condenses inside the refrigerator—the air. The secret of retaining a good, efficient insulation barrier is to prevent air from entering the cabinet seals. Use a good sealer around all openings in the cabinet plugs, grommets, and even screws. Use care in repairing cabinets, in replacing gaskets, and in repairing door panels.

If you should become a victim of wet insulation, you will probably first notice a patch of moisture on the cabinet exterior. The only cure is to remove the wet insulation and repack it. Urethane is highly resistant to moisture retention, but if it should become wet it may be cut away and repacked with fiberglass or with a foam "repair kit" available from refrigeration parts suppliers. Fortunately, this will almost always be at an accessible point around the breakers. Foamed-in-place liners are not accessible or repairable.

Since "thin-wall" construction used in some models before the energy crunch taxes even the abilities of the newest, most highly efficient insulation available, most refrigerators and freezers use some sort of auxiliary heater to help warm the cabinet in spots where condensation is likely. These are located primarily around the door gasket and the mullion, the insulated dividing section between freezer and refrigerator. You can tell if they are working by feeling the cabinet at the points where the heaters should be in contact. Most refrigerators have a pictorial wiring diagram, and this will show the exact points.

If the cabinet does not feel slightly warm to the touch in these areas, remove the breaker trim and test the heater leads for continuity with the VOM on the $R \times 100$ position. Also check visually to be sure that these small heaters, usually with a foil backing, are in tight contact with the cabinet. If they pull loose, their thermal contact is lost and they are ineffective. They can be taped back into place with masking tape, since they are usually of very low wattage and give off little heat.

New energy-efficient models have a "power saver" or "energy saver" switch that can be used to turn these heaters off during periods when they aren't needed. In many locations, they may be required only during damp, warm weather; if the house is air conditioned, they may not be needed at all.

Door light switch may be the culprit when warm refrigerator compartment is noted. Reason may be a maladjusted door, a broken switch, or breaker trim not seated properly. Switch contacts are tested with VOM on $R \times 1$ position.

QUICK-CHECK CHART FOR

REFRIGERATORS AND FREEZERS

F—Frostless	C—Cycle Defrost	S—Standard
Symptom	Possible Cause	Remedy
Doesn't run at all—no sound	Blown fuse on circuit or tripped breaker in household circuit	See if interior light burns. Check wall outlet with table lamp. Replace fuse or reset breaker
	Defective cord	Check for continuity with VOM, replace cord and plug if defective
	Compressor overload open	Test with VOM, R × 1 scale. Should indicate 0 ohms resistance. Replace
	Relay coil open	Test with VOM for continuity, replace with exact specified part
	Broken wire in cabinet	Consult wiring diagram. Repair broken wire and tape securely
	Open running winding in compressor motor	Check with VOM in R × 1 position between C and R terminals
	Open thermostat	Check contacts with VOM set to R × 1. Replace control if contacts open while temperature at sensing point is warm

Chart cont. on next page.

REFRIGERATORS AND FREEZERS (cont.)

F—Frostless	C—Cycle Defrost	S—Standard
Symptom	Possible Cause	Remedy
Doesn't run, makes clicking sound at intervals.	Defective relay	Check contacts to start circuit. Replace with exact specified part if open. Use R × 1 scale on VOM
	Condenser air blocked, causing compressor to overheat. Clicking will be at long intervals, possibly as much as 30 minutes apart	Clean condenser coils thoroughly. Be sure that condenser fan motor is operative and turning at normal speed. Prior observation of fan motor during normal operation is a big help in diagnosing this problem
	Open start or running winding	Check with VOM on R × 1 scale. Test between terminals C to R and C to S
	Locked compressor	See patch cord diagram and warning
Runs, won't shut off —temperature too cold	Defective thermostat	Check with VOM on R × 1 scale. Replace if contacts will not open with bulb clamped to colder-than-normal surface (or in air temp. below normal limits for air sensing controls)
	Loose clamp on thermostat sensing bulb (C and S)	Check, position and tighten
	Chiller tray out of position (S)	Check and reposition
Runs, won't shut off —temperature normal	See "Excessive power consumption	
Runs, not cooling properly	Condenser air blocked	Clean condenser coils thoroughly. Be sure that condenser fan motor is operative and turning at normal speed
	Evaporator iced	Check door seal, door openings; see "Evaporator iced" below
	Excessive air leakage	Check door seal, review door opening habits
	Food overloading	Check amount of warm food placed in compartment
	Improper control setting	Check and adjust as necessary
	Leak in refrigeration system	Condenser will be cool, evaporator warm or partly frosted. Call for refrigeration technician
	Compressor not pumping	Very rare. Eliminate all other possibilities first

Symptom	Possible Cause	Remedy
Evaporator Icing (F)	Open heating element	Check with VOM on R × 1 scale. Replace if open or grounded
	Open defrost limit switch	Check with VOM on R × 1 scale while bimetal is at a temperature below +20 degrees. It should be closed at this temperature
	Inoperative defrost timer	Check timer motor and contacts. Use R × 100 or higher scale for motor, R × 1 for contacts. Replace if defective
	Hot gas defrost solenoid open (on models so equipped).	Test with VOM at R × 100 or higher. Replace if open
	Excessive air leakage into cabinet	Check door sealing and review door opening habits. Be sure that door has not inadvertently been left ajar.
	Clogged drain trough	Will usually be clear, hard ice. Check trough heater if so equipped on R × 100 scale. Check trough and lines for food particles
Evaporator icing (C and S) or frosting too quickly.	Coils need cleaning (serpentine)	Wash with dishwasher detergent solution (see text)
	Defective thermostat (C)	Test contacts with VOM on R × 1. Replace if contacts remain open with warm sensing tube
	Excessive air leakage	Check door seal and door openings.
	Excessive usage	Review usage habits.
	Food not covered carefully	Check food in storage
Water refrigerator compartment	Clogged drain cup or trough	Remove and clean, flush with household ammonia
	Clogged drain line	Remove line (usually found clipped to rear of cabinet), flush and clean. Final flush with ammonia
	Excessive air leakage into compartment	Check door seal
	Excessive usage	Review usage habits. Especially prevalent when humidity is high
Water on floor under ref. or freezer	Drain pan not in position (F AND C)	Check and reposition
	Drain tube out of place	Check and reposition
Noisy	Tubing touching in unit compartment	Check and reposition carefully
	Drain pan out of position	Check and reposition
	Cabinet not level	Check and level
	Fan blade out of position, striking shroud or baffle	Check and reposition. Forced-air models increase noise levels to some extent

Chart cont. on next page.

REFRIGERATORS AND FREEZERS *(cont.)*

F — Frostless C — Cycle Defrost S — Standard		
Symptom	Possible Cause	Remedy
Condensation on cabinet exterior (sweating).	"Anti-sweat" heater(s) open	Check with VOM, R × 100 scale. Replace if open, tape tightly to inside of cabinet
	Wet insulation	Remove wet insulation and repack — use high density fiberglass for refrigerator use
	Void in insulation	Pack insulation into void
	Extremely high humidity	Occurs in early spring and fall in some areas. Wipe away daily until weather changes
Excessive power consumption	Insufficient air flow around unit	Check owners manual for proper clearances
	Blocked condenser coil	Clean thoroughly, check condenser fan motor for normal speed
	Temperature controls set excessively high	Take temperature reading with thermometer, adjust accordingly
	Excessive usage	Review habits of usage and door openings
	Air leakage into cabinet	Check door seals and adjust as needed
	Partially frosted evaporator (F)	Check visually, refer to check-chart
	High ambient temperature (heavy summer usage)	Check usage habits carefully during exceptionally hot weather
	Grounded heating element (F)	Check with VOM — will usually also result in abnormally high compartment temperatures
	Heating element energized at same time as compressor	Check defrost timer — will usually also result in abnormally high compartment temperatures
Odors in compartment	Foods not covered	Check loading — be sure that all foods are covered and are air tight
	Drain pan needs cleaning	Check and clean as necessary
	Interior needs cleaning	Clean with warm water and baking soda — one teaspoon per quart. Do not use damp cloth around electrical components. Unplug refrigerator or freezer before cleaning

19
Repairing Automatic Ice Makers

An automatic ice maker is an appliance within an appliance. The refrigerator provides the environment necessary for the correct functioning of the ice maker. You should keep this important first fact always in mind, whether you are trying to spot troubles within this new home convenience or just want to understand how it works.

Ice makers differ in appearance, from brand to brand, and they make ice in different shapes —cubes, crescents, or rounded plugs—but they all operate in basically the same manner, although their physical appearance may vary drastically.

HOW ICE MAKERS WORK

A valve fills the ice mold with water, a thermostat senses when the water is frozen and initiates the ejection cycle: A heater thaws the ice just enough so that a motor-driven mechanism can remove the cubes from the mold and deliver them into the storage bin.

In some models the mold consists of a flexible plastic tray; in this case, the ejection cycle initiates a motor drive which advances the tray, inverting and twisting it so the cubes fall out much as they would from an ordinary ice tray. In either case, this cycle repeats until the storage bin has filled with cubes and a control arm stops the action.

To supply the ice maker with a constant supply of fresh water, a water connection is made with a saddle valve on a cold-water line that is as close to your refrigerator as possible. The connecting line runs to an inlet valve at the back or bottom of the refrigerator. A solenoid controls the valve.

In most cases, you buy an ice maker along with a new refrigerator. But some companies offer the ice maker as an accessory for a new refrigerator already equipped to accept it. In that case, you, your dealer, or your plumber would install it. If you move and take along your refrigerator, installation in the new house requires a water-line connection as well as the usual electrical plug-in.

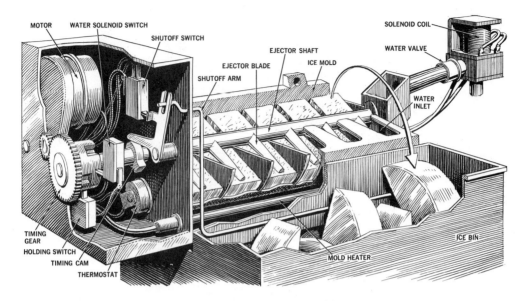

HOW AN ICE MAKER WORKS

Parts inside a typical ice maker are indicated in cutaway of a Whirlpool unit. Stall-type motor is geared to drive timing gear, timing cam, and ice ejector at about one revolution each three minutes. Timing cam has surfaces to operate shut-off arm, water fill, and holding switch. Solenoid operates at 105 volts because of voltage drop while in series with mold heater in fill cycle.

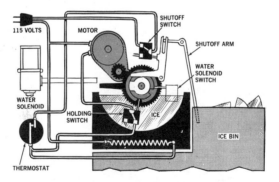

1. Ice has frozen in mold before stage represented by this drawing. When the mold temperature drops below 15 degrees F, thermostat switch sends current both to mold heater and motor. Motor turns the timing cam and ejector blades. Drawing shows only the circuits involved in this action. After a few degrees of rotation, the timing cam transfers holding switch (see next drawing).

Cont. on next page.

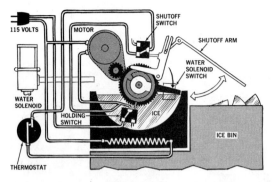

2. Motor stalls when ejector blades reach ice in mold, but continues to apply pressure until heater has loosened the ice enough so the blades can start the crescents on their way around to bin. Early in this cycle cam temporarily raises shut-off arm as shown. In a later cycle, the raised arm permits dumping of ice under it. Shut-off arm must be down for ice maker to work.

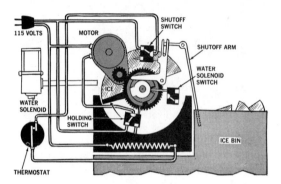

3. Ice has now loosened and ejector blades are carrying crescents around. Near completion of first revolution timing cam closes water-valve switch. However, no current is carried to solenoid since the thermostat remains closed, shunting the circuit around the valve. Therefore, no water enters. Ejector delivers ice to pan and blades begin second revolution.

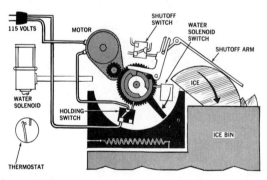

4. Mold warms up fast, since it has no ice, and the stat switch (at about 50 degrees) breaks the circuit to it. The holding switch provides current to the motor, however, and the revolution continues. Since mold heater has been deenergized, ice maker cools off. If bin is full of ice at this point, and the shut-off arm is held up, action would stop until ice is removed from bin.

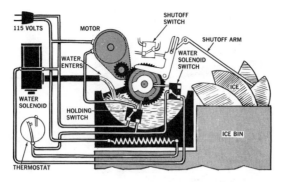

5. Mold now refills with water. Near completion of the ejector's second revolution, the timing cam again closes the water valve switch. This time a circuit is completed to the solenoid, through its switch, and the mold heater. The 105-volt solenoid operates the valve and water fills the mold cavities. At this point, all circuits are involved except those through the shut-off switch.

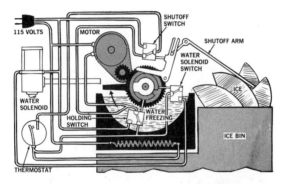

6. Everything's quiet now because bin is full and ice blocks up the shut-off arm. Timing cam has transferred holding switch to its normally closed position. When water freezes and mold temperature is about 15 deg., stat switch will operate but no cycle will begin until ice is removed from bin, and shut-off arm can drop. In this drawing, you can see all the wiring circuits.

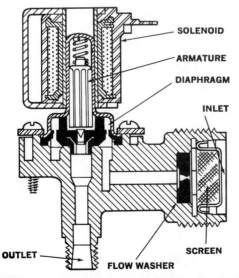

Cutaway drawing of automatic ice maker inlet valve illustrates its similarity to other appliances. Don't interchange these valves, however—internal porting and flow rate is different in most instances. *Courtesy GE.*

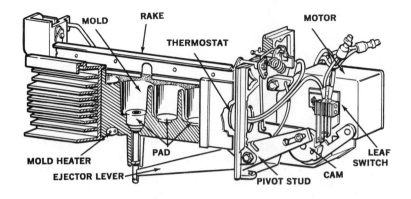

MOLD RAKE THERMOSTAT MOTOR

MOLD HEATER PAD LEAF SWITCH

EJECTOR LEVER PIVOT STUD CAM

While components in this Hotpoint ice maker look different in physical appearance, their function is very similar to "how-it-works" drawing. The pad serves same purpose as ejector blades, but pushes plugs to top of mold rather than loosening the crescents. In this model, the motor cam drives the ejector lever, which raises pad and actuates leaf switch as well. Thermostat initiates cycle when temperature is approximately 15 degrees. *Courtesy of Hotpoint Division.*

Ice shapes are not always cubes when they are delivered to you out of a modern ice maker. This General Electric ice maker turns out small rounded plugs, whereas the Whirlpool unit manufactures ice in crescent shape (see photo). You do get the usual cubes, however, from the Frigidaire Ice Service unit (not shown). All types operate on the same basic principles.

INSTALLATION

The installation of the ice maker consists of making the tap to the water line with the saddle valve (usually furnished with ice maker), running ¼-inch tubing (usually not furnished) between the tap and the refrigerator, and connecting the tubing to a stub on the refrigerator with a coupling. Be sure to use only the tubing specified by the manufacturer. A great deal of testing and research goes into any material which appears promising for ice maker connections, but only if it is tested and approved for use in the particular ice maker can you be certain that problems, especially tastes in the water, won't result.

You can often save a good sum by connecting your new refrigerator to the water line yourself. Begin by making sure that you tap a frequently used water line. One good practice, if conditions permit, is to connect it to the cold-water line under the kitchen sink.

This location will give you two other advantages, too: the installation of the saddle valve in a vertical run of pipe where sediment is unlikely to accumulate and where it is easily accessible for turning off the water supply to the ice-maker unit.

Some of the saddle valves furnished for ice maker installation are of the self-piercing type. If they are installed on copper tubing, it's only necessary to tighten the clamp and then screw the valve completely in to the shut position. Be sure that it is seated firmly, giving a full, clean cut. Now, the valve can be "back-seated" to open the line. Flush the connection into a bucket before attaching the tubing.

If you have galvanized plumbing or if the valve that you have is not the self-piercing type, it will be necessary to drill a small hole in the water line, usually ¼ or 3/16 inch. Use a hand drill, not (for safety reasons) an electric drill. Of course, the water must be turned off at the main supply line or at the meter before

If you install your own tubing to the ice maker, be sure to select a vertical run of pipe which is conveniently located for installation of saddle valve. Shut off water heater power supply, shut off main water supply, and drill 3/16-inch or ¼-inch (as specified for your unit) hole with *hand drill*. Leave coil of tubing behind refrigerator to allow room for servicing. If valve is self-piercing type, no drilling is necessary. Do not use electric drill because of shock hazard.

Saddle valve clamps tightly around tubing or pipe, providing leak-proof seal and convenient shut-off. Be sure to tighten packing gland nut as shown after job is complete. Follow manufacturer's instructions for proper tubing and check local codes before self-installing.

this type of valve can be installed. After either type of saddle valve is installed, be sure to tighten the packing gland nut to prevent leaking.

The copper tubing is attached to the valve using a ferrule or other fitting supplied with the valve. Make a clean cut with tubing cutters if copper tubing is used for the hookup. First "ring" the tubing, cutting almost but not completely through; then bend slightly until it snaps apart at the cut. Leave enough extra tubing behind the refrigerator to allow it to be pulled from the wall.

The coupling which attaches the refrigerator stub to the connecting tubing is usually also a ferrule type fitting. Before the final connection is made, it's a good idea to open the valve and flush the line with fresh water to be sure that all deposits and sediment are clear.

If your refrigerator was purchased recently, it likely has capabilities for adding an ice maker. If so, you will see various plastic plugs and perhaps a wiring connection in the freezer compartment. Should you decide to install

one, you should encounter no problem—but you should be aware of what is involved in tackling the job.

First of all, be sure that you purchase the kit specified by the manufacturer for your model refrigerator. Then remove the contents and match each part listed for your refrigerator so that you can recognize them. In most of these field-mount kits, a number of different models may use one basic kit, but only certain mounting parts of the kit are needed; the others will be discarded. Specific instructions are provided for each model.

No cutting of metal is involved, but be sure that sealer is applied around any opening where plugs are removed from the cabinet. Allow plenty of time for the job. And finally, follow each step in turn. In refrigerators with ice maker capabilities, the wiring harness is already in place—but be sure that it is plugged in at the inlet valve and the ice maker unit.

Some ice makers found in homes are separate appliances, serving only as an ice maker and not as a refrigerator or freezer. The majority of these intended for residential use function in exactly the same manner as the ones which are shown here—they have greater capacity because of specially designed evaporators which are in direct contact with the ice maker mold, causing it to chill faster and thus cycle faster. Some of the larger units (50 pounds and larger) often are based on the same principles as commercial units: they freeze a slab of ice which slides to a section of cutter grids, heated wires melt through the slab, and cubes are deposited in the storage bin.

SERVICING

When the time comes to service the ice maker, don't forget that most service calls stem from a failure to remember that the refrigerator creates the environment for the ice maker. If this environment is not up to par, the ice maker will not be able to operate properly since it is temperature actuated. So, the first rule when servicing an ice maker is always: check the temperature first.

Here's an example of the importance of this principle. Suppose the complaint is insufficient ice supply. The ice-making cycle is initiated by a thermostat at approximately 15 degrees F. If the freezer is operating at a temperature of 14 degrees, the unit will cycle slowly, if at all (such bimetallic thermostats may normally have a plus or minus five-degree tolerance).

A normal zero-degree freezer temperature would actuate the ice-maker thermostat quickly and cause faster cycling. If it's 10 degrees or above, adjust the refrigerator controls to provide a lower freezer temperature.

Unplug the refrigerator before servicing an ice maker.

If a lower freezer temperature proves unattainable, then look for problems within the refrigerator. A review of Chapter 18 should help you remedy the high temperature condi-

Inserting coin in slot removes cover of this unit. To keep out moisture, some covers require resealing with perma-gum, a sealer available at appliance or refrigeration parts suppliers. Most manufacturers market sealer under a part number for their unit.

tion, and this will likely eliminate the ice-maker problem as well. Blockage of the air flow across the condenser or problems within the defrosting system are typical causes of such temperature rises.

The shape and appearance of the cubes can tell you a lot about how the ice maker is operating. The molds of most units consist of cavities connected by tiny canals that allow water to flow into each cavity. When ice is ejected, the canal effect is noticed as a tiny bar of ice connecting the cubes.

When this bar is such that you can easily snap the cubes apart with your fingers, your water fill is approximately correct. Too heavy a connecting bar denotes an overfilled condition. Small cubes with little or no connecting bar denote an underfill. Keep in mind, however, that often the ice bar is shattered as cubes fall into the bin, and some ice makers have

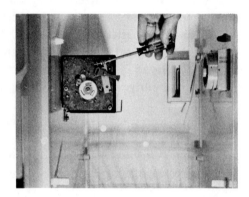

Water solenoid switch can be adjusted in many units to suit varying water pressure and to alter cube size. Lever at right allows limited adjustment without removing cover. Moving switch toward + mark increases size.

Loosening three screws on mounting clips and unplugging wiring harness at molded plug-in connector allows removal of complete unit. Note water inlet tube at rear of cabinet. Valve is located outside of panel to prevent freezing—usually behind panel on rear of refrigerator or underneath in unit compartment.

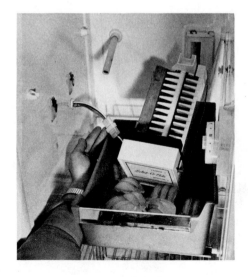

Rotate timing cam (center) manually before testing water switch for continuity. Note detached lead. Meter indicated resistance, disclosing pitted contacts. On some ice makers you can use an external lever (1) to choose cube size. Lever action is transferred by linkage (2) upon which water solenoid switch (3) is mounted. Relative distance between switch and timing cam determine length of fill period.

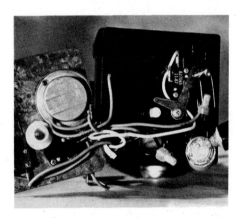

Disk-type thermostat senses mold temperature through direct contact with mold or with metal thermal slug. Replacing thermostat, apply conductive cement for positive thermal contact.

grids that cut the bar as the ice is ejected from the mold. You will still be able to see the approximate size of the bar before it was severed.

Would you believe hollow cubes? Or green cubes? They really exist, and you might find yourself faced with these problems.

Hollow cubes are usually the result of premature cycle initiation. They are released from the mold before they are completely frozen. Replacement of the ice maker thermostat is the probable cure.

First, however, verify if *all* of the cubes from a particular batch are hollow. If not, the ice maker may be unlevel, and the cubes with the smallest amount of water may form only a thin crust of ice. This can also occur with an underfill of water. In either case, the hollow cubes would be smaller than normal if lack of water caused the problem.

To check the amount of water fill, check the specification sheet which came with the ice maker. Then, hold a baby bottle calibrated in cubic centimeters (cc's) under the fill tube and test cycle the ice maker. The water level will indicate the amount which would flow into the mold with the ice maker in place.

Some typical amounts: GE ice makers require 80 cc's, Whirlpool-built units (recognized by the crescent shape of cubes, but found under several other brand names) with aluminum ejector blades require 140–150 cc's, and Whirlpool-built units with plastic ejector blades require 100 cc's.

If you are unable to determine the exact amount the mold should contain, remove the ice maker and fill it at the sink to the extent that a cube would appear normal in size. Then, empty this into a bottle or glass and mark the level. Connect the ice maker to the wiring harness and test cycle it, holding the empty marked bottle under the fill tube or remove the line on the rear of the cabinet and measure it there. Any large deviation from the approximate normal volume of water should be noticeable when the level is compared to the mark.

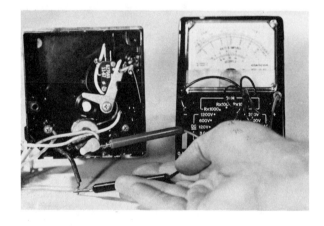

In testing mold heater with VOM, check for ground as well as for continuity. Detach lead from one side of heater; use connector as test point for other probe.

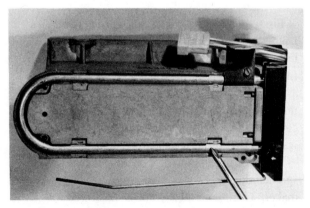

Mold heaters are replaceable on many ice makers. Check with manufacturer if in doubt. Replacement procedure for unit shown is to knock out stakes and remove old heater; apply Alumilastic conductive cement (from dealer) and place new heater in position, then retain it with self-threading screws furnished with new heater.

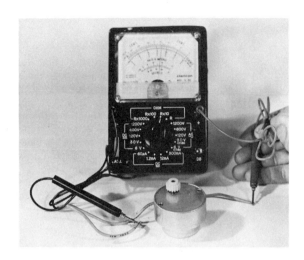

Motors designed to withstand prolonged stalling are used in ice makers. Never force drive gears. Test for continuity as shown.

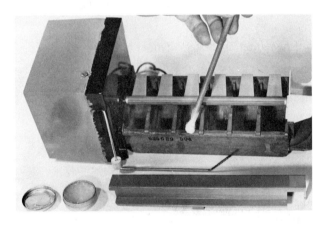

Icicles on outside of mold indicate water is being siphoned out by capillary action. Get silicone grease from your dealer; swab it on top edge of mold to stop this. Never touch hands to inside of mold.

Colored ice cubes are often pretty, but not very appetizing. I've seen green, blue, even yellow cubes; and I've sniffed cubes with every imaginable odor. The problem is environmental. Ice discolors from impurities in the water lines—often copper oxide from plumbing connections.

If you encounter a blue or blue-green ice cube, one of the first checks would be to verify that the refrigerator is properly grounded. If an inadequate ground exists at the receptacle,

the refrigerator will tend to use the ice-maker connecting tubing as the ground. The electrolytic action can lead to corrosion within the copper tubing.

When you encounter a problem with tinted cubes, recheck the supply connections. Make sure that the ice-maker line is connected to a frequently used water line and that it is connected to a vertical run. If it is near a joint of dissimilar metals (such as galvanized pipe and copper), a reaction could be causing the trou-

Disassembled ice maker indicates relative position of major components. Looking from front to rear we see (1) front cover, (2) front plate with holding and water solenoid switches and timing cam, (3) stall-type motor, (4) mold and mounting block, (5) ejector blade assembly, (6) stripper blade, (7) fill trough and bearing assembly.

ble. If you move the water line, leave the saddle valve connected and purchase a new one for the new installation.

If installation techniques check out okay, your servicing dealer can order an in-line filter to help remove unwanted foreign particles from your water supply. This filter uses a replaceable activated-charcoal element, and goes in the line between the refrigerator and the tap at the saddle valve. Most users report that the filters are of considerable benefit when a problem with water conditions is encountered. The frequency of replacement of the filter would depend on the type and severity of the condition.

Odors and tastes in cubes are as many and varied as the foods you keep in your refrigerator. That's where they come from. Modern frost-free refrigerators circulate a controlled supply of frigid air throughout the compartments constantly. This air also flows over and around the stored ice, which tends to absorb food odors easily.

Prevention is better than cure. Keep all foods covered tightly in both the refrigerator and freezer compartment. Don't store foods inside paper bags in your refrigerator; some bags have a high sulfur content.

Discard old ice. Examine a cube from the storage bin. If there's a snowy, frosty coating on it, that's a sign of aging, and the cube may have an off-taste. Ice that has been in the storage bin as long as two weeks should be discarded.

If it's necessary to clean the ice maker because you get abnormally heavy mineral deposits, obtain a small tube of silicone grease from the manufacturer or servicing dealer. Apply the silicone along the upper edges of the mold, after cleaning. If a spot of the original grease has been accidentally wiped away, you may find that a long icicle forms from the ice maker. A little silicone grease applied with a cotton swab in the troublesome area should solve this problem for you.

If a mold should become pitted or corroded

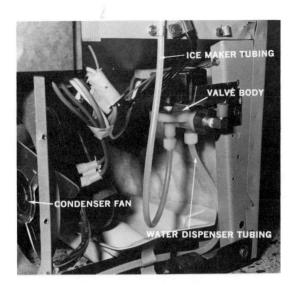

ICE MAKER TUBING

VALVE BODY

CONDENSER FAN

WATER DISPENSER TUBING

Water inlet valve for ice maker is located at rear of refrigerator. It's easily traced by looking for removable panel on rear of cabinet or by following water line from inlet tube at ice maker to the bottom of cabinet at unit compartment. Dual valve is used on the model in photo; one side provides water for ice maker, the other side for water dispenser chilling tank.

Filter screens should be removed and cleaned thoroughly if water flow into unit becomes impeded. They are located in inlet valve at entrance of supply line. Brush firmly to remove any traces of algae, which can form transparent film over screens.

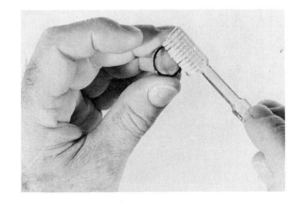

after a long period of use in extreme water conditions, it will be necessary to replace it. Most molds are furnished with the heater already staked in place. It is necessary to remove the front cover and drive assembly from the old ice maker at the front.

Make certain that all seals and gaskets are in place and in good condition when an ice maker is reassembled. When thermostats are removed or replaced, a thermal cement must be used to be sure that good thermal contact is made with the mold. You can get it from a servicing dealer or an appliance parts supplier.

Finally, don't remove the front cover from a cold ice maker within the room and immediately reinstall it. Condensation seeps into

Many new refrigerators have dispensers for convenient ice service through the door. This Whirlpool model also has Serva-Door door-within-a-door that allows easy access to often-used items without opening main refrigerator door.

Free-standing ice maker units are becoming popular for home use. Most use refrigerated cabinet with standard ice maker mechanisms—close proximity of coils in cabinet speed cycling time up. *Photo by Frigidaire.*

Test-cycling is done by (1) pulling metal ejector blades forward firmly but smoothly for about 10 degrees or (2) removing front cover (as shown), inserting screwdriver in slot of motor drive gear, and turning counterclockwise, or (3) using a jumper cord of #12 gauge copper wire with the insulation stripped from 1/2-inch of each end (for GE and Hotpoint models). A test receptacle is provided on these units, but be sure and replace rubber plug to seal out moisture.

every corner, and can form on switch contacts as well. The moisture will eventually block switch action if there is enough of it. Allow the unit to warm gradually, placing it in front of a heat register in winter or in the sun in summer. This will drive all moisture from the works. Then reinstall the cover and put the ice maker back to work in the refrigerator.

RULES FOR GOOD SERVICE FROM AN ICE MAKER

- Make sure installer allows enough water tubing to move refrigerator from wall.
- Store packages in freezer compartment so as not to interfere with delivery of ice into storage bin.
- Turn ice-maker switch off if ice storage bin is removed for an extended period, refrigerator is to be unused for a vacation or other long period, or water supply is shut off.
- Discard first batches of cubes when first connected or started up after a period of disuse.
- Keep ice maker in steady use. Throw away cubes that have been in storage bin for any time. They may be smaller, have off-flavor.

- Wash ice bin occasionally with mild soap or detergent in warm water.
- Unfamiliar sounds from the refrigerator are no cause for concern—water filling in, ice dropping into bin, ice maker turning on, etc.

QUICK-CHECK CHART FOR

AUTOMATIC ICE MAKERS

Symptom	Possible Cause	Remedy
Does not make ice (unit won't cycle)	Feeler arm switch open	Check with VOM on R × 1 scale while holding switch in both positions. 0 ohms resistance should be noted
	Holding switch open	Check with VOM in each position of switch. Usually marked C (common), NC (normally closed) and NO (normally open)
Continues to make ice when storage bin is full	Shut off arm switch closed	Check linkage and switch contacts
Ice cubes too small	Mold unlevel Inlet valve screens clogged	Level refrigerator and/or mold Remove screens and clean
Blue or blue-green cubes	Refrigerator not grounded	Check for proper ground at receptacle
Spills water from mold	Capillary action Water valve stuck Water level switch sticking Thermostat defective	Apply silicone grease around mold edge Remove and clean inlet valve Check with VOM, replace if contacts won't open Replace cycling thermostat (cycling too soon)
Hollow cubes	Mold unlevel Underfill	Level mold and/or refrigerator Check water level, see "ice cubes too small"

20
Solving Room Air Conditioner Problems

A room air conditioner performs four separate operations on the air in the room. It cools the air—by refrigeration. It removes moisture, thus lowering humidity and making you more comfortable. It circulates the air through the room, sometimes also providing ventilation. And it filters out dust.

When trouble occurs, you may eventually spot the cause within one or several of these four spheres of operation. So before you attempt a diagnosis, it will pay you to understand just exactly what takes place within this fine piece of home machinery—and how it's all done.

THE REFRIGERATION SYSTEM

The components of the basic refrigeration system are probably easier to identify in a room air conditioner than in any other refrigeration appliance. Because of the construction typically used in such units, you can readily see parts such as the evaporator and condenser

and can easily determine the heating and cooling effects which exist in various points.

Remember to transfer this knowledge to your work on refrigerators, freezers, dehumidifiers, and any other refrigeration appliance where the individual components may not be so accessible. The actual operating temperatures will vary among appliances, depending upon the design of the equipment and the use for which it is intended—you wouldn't expect the evaporator on a freezer, for example, to be as warm as the one on an air conditioner. But the basic principle is the same; it's still the evaporator where the heat is being absorbed and where the cooling effect is noted.

Many new air conditioners are designed as high-efficiency units, extracting the maximum amount of heat for every watt of power consumed. The ratio of Btu's of heat removed to watts of power consumed is expressed as the Energy Efficiency Rating (EER) and is used as a standard of comparison on energy labels of new appliances. The basic refrigeration system in high-efficiency units is unchanged, but com-

Basic refrigeration principle is easily traced in a room air conditioner, for all of the major components are quickly located. Note that the appliance makes use of two fans—one to drive off heat given off by the condenser and another to distribute the air that is cooled by the evaporator. But both fans may be driven by a single, double-shaft motor, Compare the diagram below with the one on page 292 and note similarity.

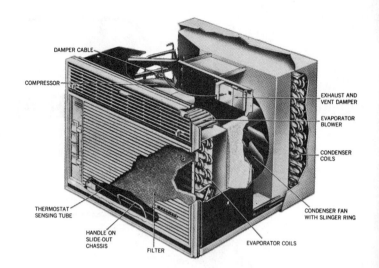

DAMPER CABLE

COMPRESSOR

EXHAUST AND
VENT DAMPER

EVAPORATOR
BLOWER

CONDENSER
COILS

THERMOSTAT
SENSING TUBE

HANDLE ON
SLIDE-OUT
CHASSIS

FILTER

CONDENSER FAN
WITH SLINGER RING

EVAPORATOR COILS

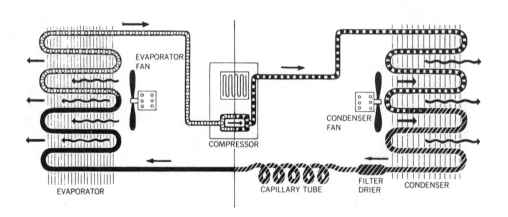

EVAPORATOR
FAN

CONDENSER
FAN

COMPRESSOR

EVAPORATOR

CAPILLARY TUBE

FILTER
DRIER

CONDENSER

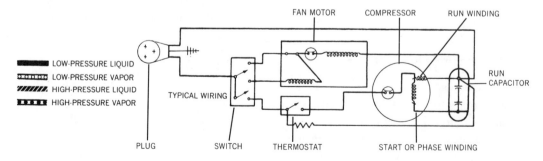

FAN MOTOR   COMPRESSOR   RUN WINDING

RUN
CAPACITOR

LOW-PRESSURE LIQUID
LOW-PRESSURE VAPOR
HIGH-PRESSURE LIQUID
HIGH-PRESSURE VAPOR

TYPICAL WIRING

PLUG

SWITCH

THERMOSTAT

START OR PHASE WINDING

ponents are modified; the evaporator and condenser coils are considerably larger than in standard units, and compressors have been improved to deliver higher capacities with reduced power consumption. Components outside the system are also very important. Suppose that air flow across the condenser is blocked because the fan motor has stalled, or because of an accumulation of lint or leaves on the fins, or even because of bent fins. When the air flow stops, enough heat units cannot be removed to reduce the vapor to the point where condensation occurs. The refrigeration stops.

Testing the System

Two simple tests will indicate whether a sealed system is operating efficiently.

1. Run the unit about ten minutes with the blower on high speed. Then, with a thermometer check the temperature of the air entering the unit, and that of the air coming out. You should find a difference of at least 20 degrees. Take this measurement after the air conditioner has been in operation for at least five minutes. This reading will vary with blower speeds, with the lowest

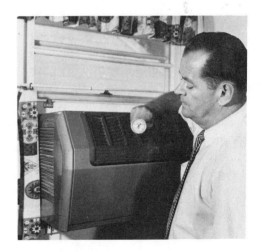

Testing temperature drop across evaporator coil of room air conditioner. Temperature at discharge louvers (shown) should be at least 20 degrees lower than that at air intake louvers (seen at left).

Electronic display on this Sears High-Efficiency room air conditioner keeps operating costs low by automatically changing temperature setting at night when room does not have to be cool, turning unit off during day when no one is home. In normal mode, display shows time of day.

temperatures being found at the lower speeds.

2. Block the air flow over the evaporator coil with a blanket. The evaporator should frost over within a few minutes. Remove the blanket quickly; operating the unit like this for any length of time might cause liquid refrigerant to slug back into the compressor.

If your system doesn't check out as above, call in a trained serviceman. Repair of a sealed refrigeration system requires special equipment and training. But most other functions of the air conditioner are fair game for home repairs.

Don't condemn the cooling system until everything else has been checked out. Remember what I've said before—it's the least likely source of a problem in a refrigeration appliance. A malfunction in many other components, such as a slow-turning evaporator fan or a clogged filter, will make their effects shown in the manner in which the refrigeration system operates; this does not mean, however, that the system is at fault.

If your air conditioner is less than eighteen years old or is a portable model, chances are it has a slide-out chassis, which can be pulled forward after you remove the front grille. Most components may be serviced by pulling out the chassis only partially. If yours does not have a slide-out chassis, you may have to remove the unit from the window and take apart the cabinet.

THE AIR-MOVEMENT SYSTEM

Many difficult-to-detect problems which arise in air conditioners can be traced to malfunctions in the air-movement system. An evaporator fan at the cooling coil draws warm, moist air from the room, forces it through the cold evaporator coils, where it is cooled and the moisture removed, and then pushes the air back into the room. A condenser fan at the condenser coil outside the house brings outside air in through the cabinet and forces it through the coils, thus cooling the superheated vapor within and forcing it to give up heat and revert to a liquid.

Slide-out chassis makes many servicing jobs easier on large room units. Chassis can remain in cabinet for most electrical checks near front of unit, making lifting unnecessary.

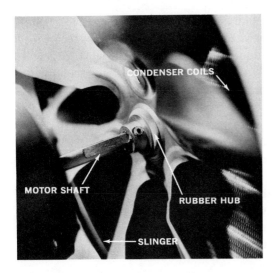

CONDENSER COILS

MOTOR SHAFT

RUBBER HUB

SLINGER

Slinger ring is evident in this photo of condenser fan. Rubber hub is used for isolation—it doesn't transmit noise and tolerates off-balance conditions.

The evaporator blower is usually of the "squirrel-cage" type to reduce noise, while the condenser fan is a simple fan blade with one difference—a "slinger" ring is incorporated around the outer circumference of the blades. This ring runs in a trough formed under the condenser, to which is diverted all condensate water off the evaporator.

If you listen closely on a humid day, you may hear the water spray being thrown against the hot condenser coils. This simple device not only reduces the amount of condensate that could drip from the outside but also increases the efficiency of the condenser. Depending upon the make and design of the unit, the condenser fan and evaporator fan may be mounted directly to opposite shafts of a single motor.

In investigating an air-conditioner problem, look and listen closely to determine its nature and general area. You may find as many as three motors running within a small area. Al-ways unplug the unit before exposing electrical connections. Do not operate it out of the cabinet with the fan blades exposed. Room air conditioners are heavy. Don't remove one from the window without someone to help.

Remember: The air-movement system is critical to the proper operation of an air-conditioning unit. If a blockage occurs in the air flow across the evaporator, the coil will tend to run too cold and the moisture will freeze, icing the coil and completely blocking air flow. Look for a clogged filter, a slow fan motor (usually caused by dry motor bearings or a defective motor winding), or determine if the air conditioner has been operated in temperatures below 70 degrees. Today's high-efficiency units often begin to ice if outside temperature drops into the sixties, and they shouldn't be operated in these conditions.

The condenser fan can also play tricks. If it turns too slowly, the pressure can become greater than normal, increasing the load on the compressor and causing it to shut down due to the action of the overload protector. Even a bush growing outside the window in which the air conditioner is mounted can grow enough in the early spring to block air flow. Look closely for these deceptive faults. I've known of compressors being changed for just such minor problems.

Directing the Air Movement

The components are relatively simple. They consist of the blowers, their motors, and dampers or louvers to direct the air and to admit outside air for ventilation. These dampers are mechanical, and their linkages are easy to locate and repair when trouble occurs.

A run capacitor is often used with blower motors also, and is tested just as the compressor run capacitor. If the capacitor fails, the fan motor will hum and may even turn at a very low speed. No attempt should be made to operate the fan motor in this condition.

A loud noise from the fan could be caused by worn or dry bearings or by a loose blower wheel. Tightening a squirrel-cage blower may require a long-arm setscrew wrench available from most automotive or hardware stores.

Cleaning or replacing the filter is one job (and a most important one) that everyone can do. Do this at the start and several times during the season. You can wash filters made of aluminum and some foam filters as shown in photos. If yours is a nonwashable filter, you can replace with one that is. Trim to size if necessary, as shown at right.

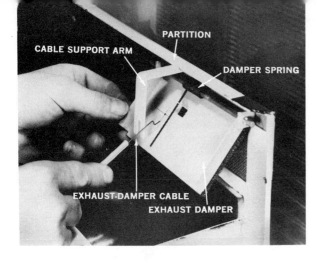

CABLE SUPPORT ARM
PARTITION
DAMPER SPRING
EXHAUST-DAMPER CABLE
EXHAUST DAMPER

Dampers divert air flow to provide ventilation and exhaust. Binding linkages and cables are easily detectable and repairable. *Courtesy Carrier Corp.*

Notch in squirrel-cage blower used for evaporator fan in this Sears unit denotes position of setscrew on shaft. Long-arm allen wrench is required to reach it. Blower must be loosened before motor can be removed. Loose, slipping blower wheels can be the source of noises and air flow problems.

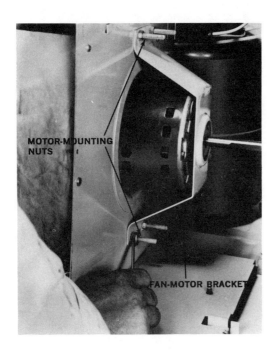

MOTOR-MOUNTING NUTS

FAN-MOTOR BRACKET

Fan motor is being removed from air conditioner after first removing condenser fan blade from motor shaft and loosening setscrew in evaporator wheel. *Courtesy Carrier Corp.*

351

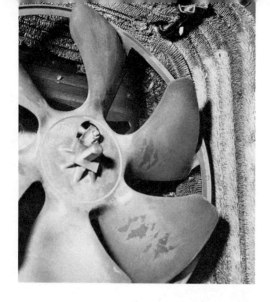

Retaining clip must be removed from motor shaft by loosening nut on units which are mounted like this. Note spine fins on condenser and slinger ring surrounding fan blade.

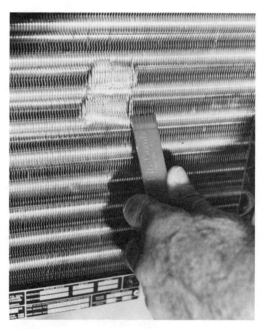

Fin comb straightens these bent fins easily and safely. They are available at any refrigeration or appliance parts distributor.

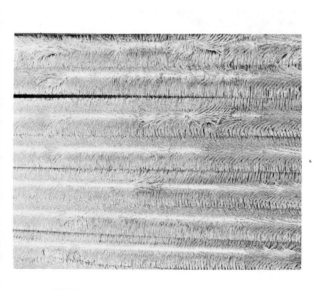

Spine fins on this General Electric model look like Christmas tree tinsel, but their many surfaces conduct heat very efficiently. Use care when cleaning to avoid flattening metal spikes.

Force of air leaving unit is put to use on this Sears unit. Wind turns "motor" which drives vanes to sweep air flow back and forth, or it may be locked in any position to direct constant flow.

You may not be able to see the setscrew itself. Look for a notch in one of the blades on the side next to the motor—an access opening directly over the setscrew.

If lubrication of dry bearings does not eliminate bearing noise, you'll have to remove the motor and take it to a motor shop for bearing replacement. To lubricate, look for a screw or a plastic plug on each of the motor's bell housings, and lubricate with a light, high-quality oil or SAE 20 non-detergent motor oil at the beginning of each season. Be sure to replace the screws or plugs.

Don't overlook the more obvious problems of the air-movement system—the cooling fins and the air filter. A tremendous volume of air moves through your air conditioner in a summer's operation. Check the filter every two weeks, and replace it when it can't be completely cleaned. Should the coils themselves become clogged, use a commercial solvent such as Aqua-Sol or Calgon coil cleaner, available from refrigeration-supply distributors.

Also available is a "fin comb" for straightening bent or damaged cooling fins. Any condition that retards air flow can cause the evaporator coil to frost over. This in turn blocks air passages and results in loss of cooling capacity.

Should the air conditioner leak water in the room area, check the passageways provided to carry the condensate away from the evaporator to the sump at the condenser slinger ring. If these are clogged, clean with a small brush and fresh water.

To help your air conditioner cope with its summer load, start it early in the morning on hot days before the house absorbs radiant heat from the sun. This allows it to keep up as the heat load builds up. Direct the cool air upwards for more efficient circulation. Keep curtains and other obstructions away from the air stream.

TESTING ELECTRICAL COMPONENTS

Many air conditioners operate on a single-phase 230-volt circuit. Two fuses protect this circuit. If either blows, the unit will not operate. In some units where this circuit is divided, the blower motors may be on a 115-volt connection. Should one of the fuses blow, the blowers may continue to operate but the compressor will not.

Often the fuses are of the cartridge type and give no visual indication that they are blown. So, remove the fuses, use the $R \times 1$ scale on your volt-ohm meter, and test for continuity. No deflection indicates a blown fuse that must be replaced. Use only time-delay fuses of a rating not greater than that on the air conditioner's specifications.

Using your meter, check each conductor of the power cord for continuity. Next turn to the selector switch. This serves as a master switch to provide either cooling or air circulation (blowers running with compressor off), and to select various fan speeds. To test it, unplug the unit, remove the quick-disconnect terminals from the switch, and test for continuity across the suspected contacts as indicated on the wiring diagram.

Control panel of many air conditioners may be swung away from cabinet after removing retaining screws. Switch, thermostat, and sometimes capacitor are accessible for testing or replacement when panel is removed.

15 AMPS –25 VOLTS   20 AMPS – 125 VOLTS   15 AMPS–250 VOLTS   20 AMPS–250 VOLTS   30 AMPS–250 VOLTS

Variety of plugs used for room air conditioners are shown here. The receptacles, of course, must match. Yours might be any of the five plug types shown here. You should never switch from one type of plug to another.

For instance, suppose you found that the compressor ran, the fan ran on high and medium speeds but not on low speed. The logical step would be to test for continuity between the line terminal and the terminal indicated for the low-speed fan winding. Always be sure that the fan-switch knob is turned to the position where the trouble occurs when making such tests.

While the selector switch determines the function of the room air conditioner, it does not determine the degree of cooling desired. This duty it delegates to the thermostat—simply a switch connected by linkages to a tube filled with refrigerant vapor. The tube has a flexible diaphragm at the switch end and is sealed at the other. Variations in temperature cause an expansion or contraction of the diaphragm. This mechanical movement activates the switch contacts, and the linkage is adjustable so that any normal range of cooling may be obtained.

The thermostat usually cycles the compressor only while the blowers continue to run in order to prevent stratification of room air. Since cold air is heavier than warm air, if the blowers shut down a blanket of cold air could form at floor level while at a height of 6 feet the air might be as much as 15 degrees warmer. Continuous air circulation keeps these layers from developing. In the interest of maximum EER ratings, many newer models are equipped with an "energy saver" switch that turns the fan off when the compressor cycles off. In many installations such a switch may cause stratification and the system may actually run longer. The best bet—try it both ways in your own installation.

The thermostat tube senses the temperature of the incoming air, and the coldest point along the length of the tube will activate it. For this reason, the sensing tube's placement is critical. It must not touch the cold evaporator tubing at any point, or the unit will "short-cycle"—cut off as soon as the tubing temperature is lower than the prescribed temperature,

Most newer units have switch diagrams in addition to the diagram for the entire unit, making testing of switch contacts a quick and easy job. Be sure to test with switch turned to each position, using *R* × *1* scale.

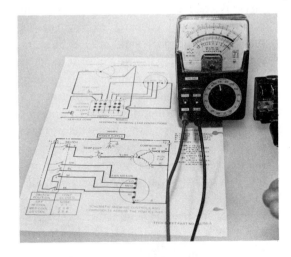

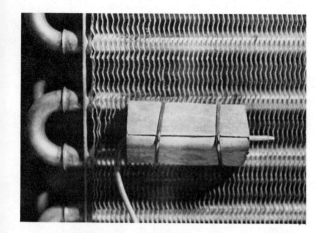

Rubber-like block which mounts this thermostat sensing tube to evaporator is "anticipator," and is necessary to provide proper differential and de-icing characteristics for control. It should be installed in same position as originally found.

which in this case would be long before the air temperature had dropped any measurable extent.

To test the thermostat, check for continuity across the switching contacts. Since the thermostat is designed to operate at normal room (ambient) temperature ranges of 75 to 80 degrees, the high setting should indicate continuity while the low setting should open the contacts. If you're in doubt about the ambient (surrounding air) temperature, the sensing tube may be cooled with an ice cube or warmed by grasping it firmly in your hand. A word of caution: If the compressor is running and it's necessary to turn the thermostat to a low position in testing it and the compressor shuts off, wait at least five minutes before readjusting the setting. This gives the pressures in the refrigeration system time to equalize and prevents trying to start the compressor under this load.

One of the primary reasons why refrigeration units are so dependable is the hermetically sealed compressor. Motor and pump are enclosed within the sealed housing. A centrifugal starting switch such as the one used for washer motors wouldn't do here since you could not replace it if it should fail. Many units have a starting relay outside the compressor operated by voltage induced in the starting winding of the motor after the compressor has approached normal running speed. Always install a replacement relay in exactly the same position as the old one (or in the position marked on the new relay). An improperly installed relay can cause compressor failure.

Most room air conditioners produced since 1960 use an oil-filled run capacitor to start the compressor. This has two distinct advantages: It eliminates the relay, and it also greatly improves the power factor of the compressor. This increased efficiency means that you get more cooling for less operating expense.

Here's how it works: When an electrical motor tries to start, a large current flows through the windings. The capacitor is in se-

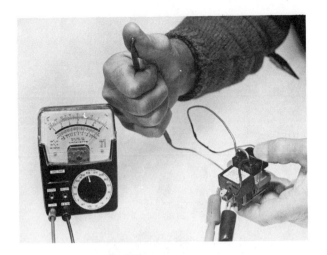

Thermostat contacts should indicate 0 ohms resistance when feeler tube is warmed by grasping in hand. Use $R \times 1$ scale on VOM. Be sure to mount sensing tube in exact position as it was when removed. If an enlarged bulb is found on the end of tube, it is a liquid-filled tube and mounting is even more critical.

ries with the start—or in this case, called the phase—winding. As the rotor picks up speed, the current drops and a shift in the phase angle of the voltage occurs. This has much the same effect as actually changing the physical location of the winding, and it becomes in effect a running winding.

Compressors for this type of operation are referred to as permanent-split capacitor (PSC) compressors. They should not be operated under severe low-voltage conditions (where voltage drops over 10 percent below rated voltage) as their starting torque is greatly reduced and, in fact, may prevent them from starting at all. Low-voltage kits, consisting of a starting relay and starting capacitor, may be added in some cases, but the correct solution is to correct the low-voltage condition itself.

The capacitor is a storehouse for electricity. It must be discharged before handling or testing, in order to prevent dangerous electrical shock or damage to test instruments. You may have seen this done by shorting the terminals

of a capacitor with a screwdriver. Don't do it! Most run capacitors now incorporate an internal fuse that can be blown by shorting the charged capacitor.

Get a 20,000-ohm 2-watt resistor (available from any radio-TV parts supplier) to discharge the capacitor. A resistor costs from 50 cents to 1 dollar; a replacement capacitor may cost $25 or more.

Test the capacitor with the meter set on a high-resistance scale. The needle should sweep up and then drop back when probes are placed across the terminals. Reversing the meter leads should produce the same effect. Apply your diagnostic skill here before you test.

If the capacitor is shorted, the compressor will start when the thermostat is turned up, but since the phase winding continues to act as a start winding, the high current draw causes the overload protector to open within a few seconds, and the compressor shuts down. A shorted capacitor will often be visible as well, as the housing may be swelled noticeably. An

Capacitor must be discharged using 20,000-ohm resistor before handling or testing with VOM. This safely discharges capacitor and prevents damage to meter as well. When reading on $R \times 100$ scale, meter should rise to low resistance level, then fall back toward infinity. Reversing leads should repeat this action.

Fan motor uses tapped windings to provide three speeds. Each must be checked separately ($R \times 1$ scale). Fan capacitor may be separate or it may be part of compressor run-capacitor. Dual capacitors require two tests with VOM, and each side must be discharged separately before handling.

open capacitor would usually prevent the compressor from running at all, and again the overload would shut it down, though not as quickly as in the case of a shorted capacitor.

Often one of the terminals of a run capacitor will be marked with a dot, meaning that the internal connections of this terminal are closest to the metal housing. Always connect the wire from the start or phase winding to the *opposite* terminal, as the higher voltage induced in the start winding could conceivably damage the capacitor. Always test a capacitor for a ground with your meter. If it indicates a ground, replace the capacitor.

The overload protector is similar to that in an automatic washer motor. It is a bimetal disc which opens the circuit to the compressor if there's overheating or excessive current draw. It is usually on top of the compressor housing but may be imbedded in the motor windings in some larger units. If it tests open under normal ambient temperatures it should be replaced. Replace capacitors and overload protectors only with components of the same value as the originals.

Remember that everything you do to make your air conditioner operate more efficiently also reduces energy consumption. For the ulti-

Room units such as this GE "Carry-Cool" model are fast gaining in popularity. One reason is the ease of installation and the ability to move easily from one room to another. Small units don't have slide-out chassis, but their light weight makes this only a minor inconvenience. Screws in side of cabinet attach it to chassis.

Latest room air conditioners like the Sears unit shown have electronic controls that allow precise temperature and humidity control as well as temperature set-up for nights or for times when no one is home. Fluorescent display shows setting input or time of day.

mate benefit, take it one step further—make a study of the conditions existing in your home and in your living habits to see if modifications here will help. Adding additional insulation can aid you year around, as can storm windows and weatherstripping. Be sure that vent fans above ranges and in baths and showers are being utilized. Be certain that all openings and cracks are sealed.

Finally, place a thermometer in the room or rooms which are air conditioned. Under most conditions, 76 to 78 degrees is considered as the minimum temperature range. You'll find that at 80 and 82 degrees you'll be plenty comfortable when the outside temperature is in the 90s. Even though refrigeration equipment manufacturers are working overtime to develop means of squeezing every possible BTU per watt of power consumed, until there is some still unforeseen breakthrough the maximum possibilities for economical usage of air conditioning lie with the user.

RULES FOR THE USE AND CARE OF A ROOM AIR CONDITIONER

- Correct location is very important—consider window placement and furniture arrangement.
- If the filter is washable, wash it periodically in lukewarm, sudsy water. Rinse and wipe or shake dry, or change it periodically according to instructions in your owner's manual.
- To avoid freeze-up at night when temperature drops, raise thermostat to middle setting and to medium or high fan speed.
- On hottest days, turn the unit on early before temperatures begin to rise, or even let it run continuously.
- Turn the unit off if fan motor fails to operate.
- Do not attempt to install the unit yourself unless you have access to manufacturer's instructions and he provides a kit. Read the instructions carefully before beginning.
- After the unit or compressor has been shut off or the temperature control setting has been changed, wait at least five minutes before restarting. Quick restarts force the compressor to attempt to start under the load of high-pressure refrigerant, and may cause a fuse to blow. A short wait allows system pressures to equalize.

QUICK-CHECK CHART FOR

ROOM AIR CONDITIONERS

Symptom	Possible Cause	Remedy
Will not run at all	No voltage to receptacle	Replace fuse; check both fuses in 230 circuits
	Defective power cord	Test cord and molded plug with meter; replace only with factory specification cord and plug
	Selector switch open	Test and replace
	Loose or broken terminal	Solder new terminal to wire
Blowers run, but compressor does not	Open circuit to thermostat from selector switch	Test for continuity with meter; replace switch if open
	Thermostat contacts open	Test for continuity with meter; be sure that ambient temperature is high enough to require cooling. Replace if defective, giving careful attention to placement of sensing bulb
	Run capacitor open	Discharge capacitor, then test with meter. Replace if open with component of identical rating. Replace wires in same position
	Compressor overload protector open	Test for continuity with meter, replace if necessary. Use identical replacement.
	Compressor motor windings open	Refer to authorized service agency
Blowers run; compressor starts, quickly shuts off	Shorted run capacitor	Discharge capacitor, test with meter. Would usually be visible by swelled housing on capacitor
	Relay contacts (if used) fail to open	Test with meter or examine visually; replace only with identical part and mount in exact position as indicated
	Shorted compressor windings	Refer to authorized service agency
	Short-cycling	Check location of thermostat sensing tube. Be sure it is not touching evaporator tubing
Compressor runs, but blowers will not operate	Selector-switch contacts open	Test for continuity with meter across suspected contacts, replace switch if open
	Blower run capacitor defective	Test with meter for open, shorted, or grounded capacitor. Replace only with one of identical rating. Blower motor may turn slowly in this condition
	Blowers or motor shaft binding	Check for foreign objects around blades by turning manually. Remove any object present, or adjust mounting to clear housings if binding occurs
	Frozen motor bearings	Lubricate or replace as necessary
	Open motor windings	Test with meter and replace if open
Compressor and blower motors operate, but little or no cooling is evident	Air flow restricted	Check to see that filter is clean; check to see that evaporator fins are not blocked or bent; check for evaporator icing condition—may result from either of above or from operating under low ambient temperatures (below 70°)
	Ventilation damper open	Remedy binding linkage or binding damper
	Blower wheel loose	Tighten setscrew
	Refrigerant charge low	Refer to authorized service agency
Water leaks into room	Condensate drain clogged	Locate restriction and clean
	Improper installation	Poor sealing—recaulk; improper slope to outside—should be approximately level to $\frac{1}{8}$" maximum drop toward rear of cabinet
Noise	Compressor mounts vibrating	Check to see that springs and washers are not creating vibration on "floating" types; rubber mounts on other types should be snug
	Blower blade loose or hitting housing	Tighten or align; also check for bent blade
	Refrigerant tubing vibrating	Move carefully to avoid contact with other tubing or with cabinet
	Improper installation	Check for weakened sash or support and brace

21
Keeping Central Air Conditioners Troublefree

A central air-conditioning system operates basically like a room unit. In a split (or remote) system, the evaporator is located at a distance from the condensing unit, which consists of compressor, condenser, and condenser fan. In a package unit, condenser and evaporator are contained within the same cabinet. Cool air is directed into a system of ducts, in many cases the same warm-air ducts which supply the house with heat in the winter. With remote systems the evaporator is often placed within the supply plenum of the furnace.

A remote thermostat much like the one on a furnace controls a central air-conditioning system. A 24-volt transformer supplies power for the control circuit. A fan relay works in conjunction with the transformer to energize the blower motor on high speed when the thermostat turns on the condensing unit to provide cooling. Most thermostats have an *automatic* and an *on* position. In the *automatic* position, the fan cycles with the condensing unit. It comes on when the condensing unit is turned on; when the thermostat turns off the condens-

ing unit, the fan turns off. In the *on* cycle, the fan runs constantly.

Many experts advise you to run the fan twenty-four hours a day during the cooling season. Here's why: When cold, heavy air is forced into a room, it falls to the floor (unless it is kept moving) and air in the room stratifies, that is, it builds up in layers at different temperatures. I've seen differentials of 15 degrees between floor level and thermostat level. This means that your feet are bathed in cold air while your head may feel warm when you stand up. Running the blower constantly keeps the air circulating and greatly reduces stratification. There's little if any additional power used because the motor requires a surge of power to start. Running constantly it uses relatively little, and the additional energy will probably be more than offset by the greater efficiency of the air-conditioning system itself.

An important rule for maintaining central air-conditioning equipment is to keep the air filter clean. If a filter permits dust and foreign particles to pass through it, the evaporator coil

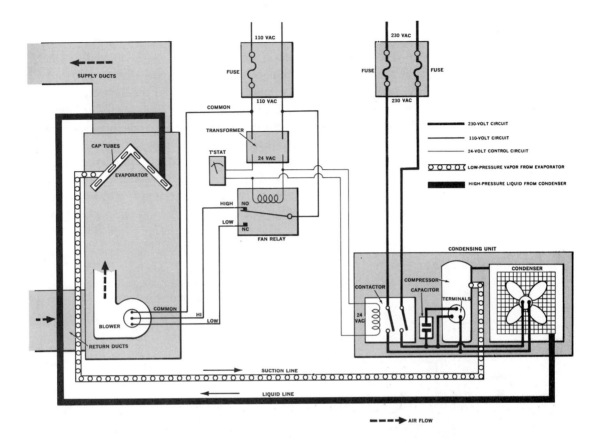

HOW A CENTRAL AIR CONDITIONER WORKS

Remember that three electrical circuits are used in many units: the 230-volt supply which feeds the compressor and condenser fan motor in the condensing unit; a 115-volt circuit for the blower motor and control circuit; and a 24-volt control circuit.

When the thermostat contacts close, a 24-volt circuit is completed to the coil of the fan relay and to the contactor in the condensing unit. When the fan relay contacts close, they complete a circuit to the high-speed winding of the evaporator blower motor. When the contactor coil is energized, the heavy contacts close and start the compressor and the condenser fan.

Two refrigerant lines connect the evaporator coil with the condensing unit. The large one is the "suction" line, carrying heat-laden vapor back to the condensing unit; the smaller of the lines is the "liquid" line, carrying high-pressure liquid refrigerant to the evaporator coil. When it reaches the evaporator coil assembly, it will pass through capillary tube (contained within the evaporator housing) before entering the coil itself.

The chilled air is carried into the house by ducts, often the same ones which carry heat in the winter.

In many newer systems, the lines connecting the two parts of remote systems are precharged and sealed at the factory. Connecting the couplings breaks the seal, but O-rings hold the refrigerant charge inside. This is a split-system or remote unit.

can become blocked. It's a good idea to have an access panel cut through the sheet metal of the plenum or duct so the evaporator can be cleaned and washed down when necessary. You must clean or change the filter monthly both summer and winter if the same ducts are used for both cooling and heating. Remembering to do this can increase the life and efficiency of your system.

The layout of the duct work has a great effect on how well a system operates. One thing you should look for is that the air intake or intakes, the return to the furnace, is supplied by an upper-level grill, one located fairly close to the ceiling. This tends to pick up the warmer air near the top rather than the cooler air near the bottom. Most heating systems use low-level returns to operate at greatest efficiency. Sometimes a section of wall has both a high and a low grill. The low one is closed and

Thermostat should be kept free of dust and lint. Be certain that all wires are in place and that movement is not restricted. Thermostat should be accurate when properly leveled by placing spirit level across top of housing.

High and low returns such as this allow return air to be sent to furnace from low grill during heating season, and from high grill when cooling. By keeping air flow more constant, this increases efficiency of system and also prevents uncomfortable stratification of room air.

the upper one opened for air conditioning. They are reversed when heating season comes. If you have a problem with stratification (uneven temperatures from floor level to ceiling) even with the blower running constantly and all your returns are low, adding a high return would likely be of great benefit.

A variation of the constant-run blower setup, one I've used successfully for a number of years, is easily arranged if your furnace and air-conditioning system has a multi-speed blower motor. By simply depressing the summer switch or constant run switch for the blower motor (if your furnace is so equipped) the blower will constantly operate on low speed, which is the normal heating speed. When the thermostat calls for air conditioning, the fan relay automatically disconnects the low-speed winding and connects the high-speed winding, so a two-speed constant air-

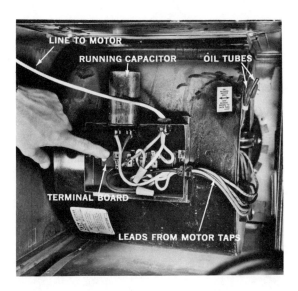

Direct-drive motor on this furnace has tapped windings to provide low speed for heating and high speed for cooling. Speeds are changed by altering position of wire on terminal board.

Belt-drive motors can also be used to vary speeds by using adjustable-sheave pulley as shown. Pulley is turned out to reduce diameter and lower speed for heating, turned in to increase diameter and raise speed for cooling. With this arrangement, sheave would have to be adjusted each season.

circulation system is put into operation.

One final tip for increasing the efficiency and ease of servicing your distribution system: If the filters on your furnace are hard to reach, filter grills are available which allow you to install the filters directly behind the return air grills. These, of course, are easily reached since they are right in the house. A simple twist of a coin in a slot lowers the grill and allows the filter to be taken out and replaced with a fresh one. With filter grills in place and filters checked constantly, you can eliminate the filters in the furnace and assure a good supply of filtered fresh air. But be sure that all return grills in your house are fitted with filters. You can measure the size of the opening and a heating supplier can likely furnish a filter grill from stock.

If filter accessibility is poor on your installation, consider the installation of filter grills like this in the living area. Grill is hinged at bottom. After lowering grill, just unclip filter and change. All return grills must be equipped with filters before removing filters at air handler or furnace.

Snap-on plastic diverters such as this used on supply grill can greatly increase efficiency in many installations. They are available for wall and floor registers. By directing flow of air upwards, they take advantage of the natural air flow to give more even cooling.

SERVICING THE SYSTEM

Switches, capacitors, and relays are serviced much the same as they are in a window unit. However, you may find some additional switches. One of these is a contactor, a relay which uses the 24-volt control circuit of the thermostat to energize a high-voltage circuit to the 230-volt compressor.

Low- and high-pressure controls are often used in central air conditioning also. These controls are connected directly to the refrigeration system, and any change which may cause damage will operate a diaphragm linked to a switch, shutting the unit down. If these switches have to be changed it's usually a job for a refrigeration technician, as some of the refrigerant charge is lost when changing them. But you can check to tell whether they're bad by using your VOM in the $R \times 1$ position. It should indicate continuity. Some of these pressure controls are manually reset by depressing a pushbutton. Look for it.

When testing central air-conditioning units, remember that several electrical circuits are involved. Be sure that all are turned off before you begin working. They include the 230-volt circuit to the condensing unit, the 24-volt control circuit, often the same circuit which controls the furnace, and, in a remote system, the 115-volt circuit which operates the furnace blower. Remember to disconnect all three circuits before attempting to service a central air-conditioning unit.

Remember, too, that the distribution system should push supply air upwards as much as possible since its natural tendency is to fall downward, and to take return air from as high

Running capacitor, shown below right in comparison with a starting capacitor, is like that on room units, only larger. Discharge with resistor before handling; capacitor can then be tested on $R \times 100$ scale. Needle should rise, then fall to lower level, and repeat this action when leads are reversed. If needle doesn't move, capacitor is open; if it shows continuity and indicates 0 ohms resistance, the capacitor is shorted.

Some air conditioners have fan and running capacitor combined in single housing (note terminals at top). Each side must be discharged with resistor as shown and tested as if they were separate capacitors.

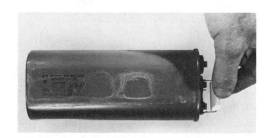

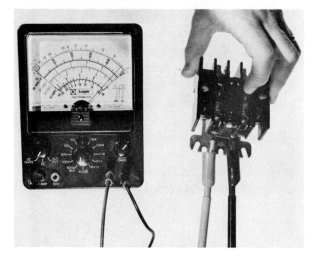

Two tests must be made when checking contactor. Coil is tested on $R \times 100$ scale. Contact terminals which control compressor should be tested on $R \times 1$ scale. Many contactors can be manually closed for testing by depressing contact retainer as shown.

Condenser fan motor is located in center of this semicircular condensing coil. Other units may be mounted behind coil. Some condensing fan motors are multi-speed to reduce noise when temperatures are cool and little air flow is needed; if yours has more than two leads, check between each one for continuity on the VOM.

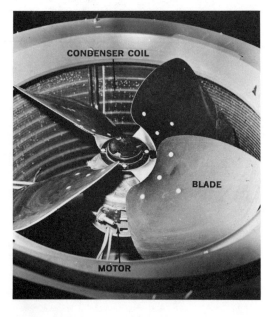

CONDENSER COIL

BLADE

MOTOR

◀ Condenser fan control controls speed of motor on multi-speed units, increasing fan speed as temperature of condenser increases. This control provides infinite speeds through solid-state circuitry. If open, control must be replaced as a complete unit.

Access panel to condensing unit is removed by loosening sheet-metal screws and pulling panel from lips on cabinet. Be sure that all power is turned off before opening panel.

With most units, cabinet can be removed by loosening screws that retain it to base. Here, most operating components of condensing unit are visible.

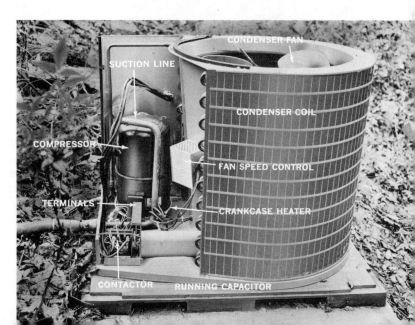

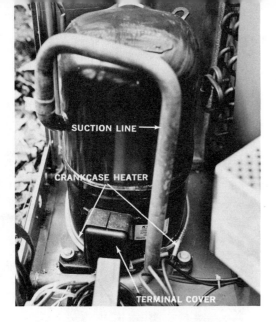

Crankcase heaters are visible in this photo of compressor. Heaters are important for prolonging compressor life when operated in cool weather, and at beginning and end of season. Check for continuity on $R \times 1$ scale, for grounds on $R \times 1000$.

Compressor terminals are exposed after terminal box cover mounted to compressor is removed. Most of these large compressors have internal overload imbedded in motor windings; be sure that motor is cool before testing, or false open readings can result. Read from C (common) to R (run) and from C to S (start). Open reading indicates failure in motor windings, and compressor will have to be replaced by refrigeration technician.

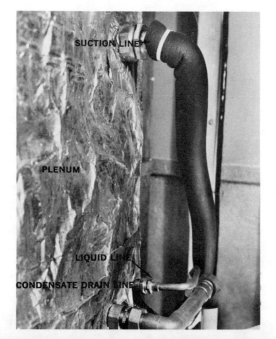

In this split system, evaporator is contained within furnace supply plenum. Refrigerant lines carry refrigerant to and from evaporator coil, while condensate line carries condensate water outdoors. Supply plenums and ducts must be insulated for air conditioning to prevent heat gain and "sweating" of lines and pipes.

a point as possible since this will be the warmest air within the room.

The same pointers which improve the efficiency of your heating system in winter also work in summer for air conditioning, especially such things as adequate insulation and sealing all cracks where air can enter the house. One accessory which can greatly improve the efficiency of your air-conditioning unit is a powered roof ventilator. These units use a small motor to exhaust air from the attic. One of them can make quite a difference in the temperatures near your roof. If you are a reasonably good carpenter, you can install one yourself. Many come with flashing kits and even mastic to seal around the opening cut in the roof. In addition to greatly increasing the ability of your central air-conditioning system to cope with hot weather, the reduced roof temperatures can add years to the life of the shingles.

Many central air-conditioning compressors are equipped with crankcase heaters which are constantly energized. The heat keeps the compressor oil free-flowing, and it also keeps the refrigerant from combining with the oil during long *off* periods. If you turn the power supply to your central air conditioning off during the winter, be sure to turn the power back on at least twenty-four hours before restarting the unit in the spring. This will allow the heaters to dissipate the refrigerant from the oil, and the oil will be warm and ready to protect vital areas as soon as the compressor begins to run.

RULES FOR THE USE AND CARE OF A CENTRAL AIR CONDITIONER

- Keep filters clean. Check and change them regularly. This keeps the evaporator coil and blower clean as well.
- Use constant air circulation to keep air moving within the house. Using magnetic "clip-on" baffles on registers often helps to push air to high levels where it can take advantage of natural circulation.
- Turn the switch to the condensing unit on at least twenty-four hours before starting the unit at the beginning of the season. This allows the crankcase heaters to warm the oil.
- Keep all obstructions such as drapes, furniture, carpets away from return and supply grills. They restrict air flow within the system.
- Keep shrubbery, leaves, and trash away from the condensing unit. Restriction of air flow through the coil causes insufficient cooling of the refrigerant within the system at this point.
- Set air handler or furnace blower to highest possible speed without causing undue whistling or cavitation, recognized by a pulsating sound.

QUICK-CHECK CHART FOR

CENTRAL AIR CONDITIONERS

Symptom	Possible Cause	Remedy
Condensing unit won't come on (no fan, no compressor)	Blown fuse in house circuit or tripped circuit breaker	Check with VOM on R × 1, replace fuse if open or reset breaker
	Thermostat open	Check across contacts or mercury bulb with VOM, clean or adjust if open
	Transformer open	Check primary and secondary windings of 24-volt transformer for control circuit. Use R × 100 scale on VOM after power has been turned off
	Contactor open	Check coil (R × 100 scale) and contacts (visually or R × 1 scale)
	High- or low-pressure switches tripped	Check and reset switches. Check for cause. High switch tripped indicates blockage of air at condenser section, low pressure switch blockage of air at evaporator section or problems in refrigeration system
Runs, won't cool	Iced or blocked evaporator	Locate cause (stopped-up filters, dirt on coil) and remedy. Check to see that fan motor is not slipping at belt
	Blocked filters	Replace
	Open condenser fan motor (compressor only runs)	Check with VOM, also check switch that controls motor when two-speed units are used. Use R × 1 scale on VOM
	Shorted or open compressor running capacitor (condenser fan only runs)	Test with VOM *after* discharging capacitor with 20,000-ohm resistor. Use R × 100 scale. Needle should rise then fall, repeat when leads are reversed
	Open compressor windings	Check with VOM. Be sure that compressor is cool. Many newer units use internal overload to open circuit if windings over-heat. Use R × 1 scale
Runs, partial cooling	Blocked filters	Replace
	Clogged evaporator	Clean and remedy cause of clogging (usually related to dirty filters)
	Insufficient air flow	Belt slipping on evaporator fan motor (may be the same one which is used for heating)
	Evaporator blower dirty	Check and clean as necessary
	Clogged condenser coil	Check and clean as necessary
	Low refrigerant charge	Look for partially iced evaporator. Call technician if refrigeration system problem is suspected

Symptom	Possible Cause	Remedy
Evaporator fan motor won't run	Fan relay open	Check coil and contacts with VOM. Use R × 100 scale for coil, R × 1 for contacts. Replace if open
	Fan motor capacitor open or shorted	Check as indicated above after discharging
	Fan motor windings open	Check with VOM on R × 1, replace motor if open
Fan runs, compressor cuts off before thermostat opens	Low voltage	Check at condensing unit with compressor running. Disconnect power, connect test leads with meter set to 250 volts AC, reconnect power and take reading. Must be within ten per cent of rating on nameplate
	Dirty or blocked condenser	Inspect and clean
	Shorted or open run capacitor	Test as described above, replace if defective
	Fan running slow	Check closely for normal operation. See that fan revolves easily without binding
	Defective compressor	Check with VOM on R × 1 scale. Be sure that unit is cool before reading continuity
Operates continuously	Defective thermostat	Check contacts or mercury bulb. Adjust or clean as necessary. If symptom continues, replace thermostat
	Defective contactor	Check with VOM on R × 1 scale. Contacts to condensing unit should be open with coil deenergized
	Clogged filters, evaporator coil or condenser coil.	Check and clean as necessary

22
All About Humidifiers and Dehumidifiers

Moisture control in your home is a year-round proposition. It plays a major role in your personal comfort and in the maintenance and upkeep of your home and its furnishings. Air is like a sponge. When dry, it absorbs moisture from any surface it touches; when saturated, it dampens every surface.

In winter months, heating systems dry out the home atmosphere. The moisture-hungry air then absorbs what it wants from furnishings and woodwork, resulting in cracks in paneled walls, flooring, and wooden furniture. Dry air also evaporates moisture from your skin, making you feel so cool that you run to move the thermostat up a few notches. You note it too in dry nasal tissues and membranes.

During the summer, a completely different situation exists. The warm air becomes saturated, and moisture is assimilated into every absorbent surface; primarily, again, wooden objects and furnishings. While the symptoms are not as noticeable, they may be even more detrimental. Mold and mildew form under carpets, rugs, and furnishings; furniture and wooden materials warp, metal equipment rusts, and an unpleasant damp and musty odor prevails.

An effective solution to these very different problems is found in two very different appliances—the humidifier and the dehumidifier. There's hardly a home that doesn't need one or both.

DETERMINING RELATIVE HUMIDITY

Moisture in the air is referred to as humidity. Air soaks up water like a sponge. And, like a sponge, air can hold just so much of it. When the air will hold no more, it is said to be saturated, or at 100 percent humidity.

The percentage of moisture actually present in the air as compared to the amount required to saturate the air is known as relative humidity. Heated air will hold more moisture than cold air. Air heated to 75 degrees will hold 20 times more moisture than the same air at zero temperature.

The chart below shows what happens when cold outdoor air is heated to room temperature.

What equipment does your particular home need for moisture control? An accurate means of determining the relative humidity of the air in your home is essential to proper selection and servicing of such equipment. For this consider buying a hygrometer, the humidity indicator found in most department stores, often in conjunction with other "weather instruments" such as barometers. Don't rely on its accuracy, however, without first calibrating it.

One method of calibrating a hygrometer is to place it outside in the shade for a few hours. Then check with your local weather bureau to find the exact relative humidity in the area at that particular time. Calibrate the indicator accordingly.

A more precise method of determining the relative humidity in a given area (or to calibrate a hygrometer) is to buy or build a sling psychrometer. This is an instrument engineers and technicians use to determine exact relative humidity. It consists of wet- and dry-bulb thermometers cradled in such a manner that

Outdoor Relative Humidity	Outdoor Temperature		
	0°	+10°	+20°
90%	5%	8%	12%
70%	4%	6%	10%
50%	3%	4%	7%
30%	2%	3%	4%

Indoor Relative Humidity at 72° Room Temperature

Courtesy Herrmidifier Co., Inc.

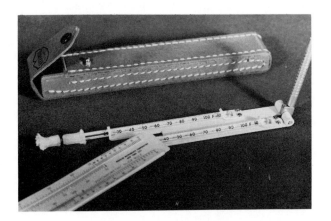

A professional sling psychrometer such as this may be purchased for $10 to $20. It comes with carrying case and tables. Slide rule for computing temperature relationships is an inexpensive and convenient option. Note dry-bulb and wet-bulb thermometers mounted to common support.

they can be twirled through the air within the area being tested. The rate of water evaporation from the wick of the wet bulb is dependent upon moisture content of the air. The evaporation has a direct cooling effect upon the thermometer. By comparing this wet-bulb temperature with the dry-bulb temperature, the exact relative humidity is found.

You can make your own sling psychrometer. Start with an accurate mercury thermometer. Epoxy the end opposite the bulb to a flat stick (you can be as elaborate as you wish, but even a Popsicle stick will do). Then drill a hole in the other end of the stick and insert a nail large enough to pass freely through the hole without the head going through. Hold the assembly by the pointed end of the nail and whirl it above your head about ten times. Note the reading at once. This is the dry-bulb temperature of the air.

Next, loosely wrap several layers of gauze bandage around the bulb and hold this in place with a small rubber band. Dampen this wick with water and repeat the whirling procedure. This gives you the wet-bulb reading. Subtract the wet-bulb reading (always lower) from the dry-bulb reading. This gives you the "depression." Apply these figures to the accompanying chart, and you will have the exact relative humidity of the air.

Even experts don't agree on the ideal relative humidity for most human activities, but they do concur that a range of 35 to 55 percent, maintained at all times, should eliminate humidity problems in the home. In very cold weather, the humidity should be toward the lower end of this range. Too much moisture can penetrate into the inner wall structure unless a good vapor barrier is present in the wall.

HOME HUMIDIFIERS

A humidifier may be portable, intended to add moisture to the air in one room or area, or it may be a permanently mounted unit located to discharge moisture into the warm air stream of the heating system and thus maintain the desired humidity throughout the house.

Take a close look at conditions that prevail in winter and you will have a better understanding of the task required of a humidifier. If you take outside air at a temperature of 20 degrees Fahrenheit and a relative humidity of 100 percent and raise the air temperature to 68 degrees (normal room temperature), you then have only 9 percent relative humidity. If the temperature is zero degrees at 100 percent relative humidity, the drop is even more dramatic; to 4 percent at 68 degrees.

These conditions are not extreme. In many parts of the country, they are found on many days each winter. If the inside humidity is maintained at the 35–55 percent level, however, the midwinter blues of creaking floors and furniture and cracked flooring won't be around. You may realize an appreciable savings in fuel as well since you will be able to turn the thermostat down and still remain comfortable.

If you install and maintain the humidifier yourself, it's not an expensive addition. However, it is important to select the right humidifier for your needs *and* for the water conditions that prevail in your area. There are two broad classifications of residential humidifiers: evaporative and atomizing.

The evaporative type of humidifier forces dry air across media pads saturated with water and into the supply plenum (the large metal

DETERMINING RELATIVE HUMIDITY
Air Temp. Depression of Wet-Bulb Thermometer (t-t')

t	0.5	1.0	1.5	2.0	2.5	3.0	3.5	4.0	4.5	5.0	5.5	6.0	6.5	7.0	7.5	8.0	8.5	9.0	9.5	10.0	10.5
70	98	95	93	90	88	86	83	81	79	77	74	72	70	68	66	64	61	59	57	55	53
71	98	95	93	90	88	86	84	81	79	77	75	72	70	68	66	64	62	60	58	66	54
72	98	95	93	91	88	86	84	82	79	77	75	73	71	69	67	65	63	61	59	57	55
73	98	95	93	91	88	86	84	82	80	78	75	73	71	69	67	65	63	61	59	57	55
74	98	95	93	91	89	86	84	82	80	78	76	74	71	69	67	65	63	61	60	58	56
75	98	96	93	91	89	86	84	82	80	78	76	74	72	70	68	66	64	62	60	58	56
76	98	96	93	91	89	87	84	82	80	78	76	74	72	70	68	66	64	62	61	59	57
77	98	96	93	91	89	87	85	83	81	79	77	74	72	71	69	67	65	63	61	59	57
78	98	96	93	91	89	87	85	83	81	79	77	75	73	71	69	67	65	63	62	60	58
79	98	96	93	91	89	87	85	83	81	79	77	75	73	71	69	68	66	64	62	60	58
80	98	96	94	91	89	87	85	83	81	79	77	75	74	72	70	68	66	64	62	61	59

t	1	2	3	4	5	6	7	8	9	10	11	12	13	14	15	16	17	18	19	20	21
80	96	91	87	83	79	75	72	68	64	61	57	54	50	47	44	41	38	35	32	29	26
82	96	92	88	84	80	76	72	69	65	61	58	55	51	48	45	42	39	36	33	30	28
84	96	92	88	84	80	76	73	69	66	62	59	56	52	49	46	43	40	37	35	32	29
86	96	92	88	84	81	77	73	70	66	63	60	57	53	50	47	44	42	39	36	33	31
88	96	92	88	85	81	77	74	70	67	64	61	57	54	51	48	46	43	40	37	35	32
90	96	92	89	85	81	78	74	71	68	65	61	58	55	52	49	47	44	41	39	36	34
92	96	92	89	85	82	78	75	72	68	65	62	59	56	53	50	48	45	42	40	37	35
94	96	93	89	85	82	79	75	72	69	66	63	60	57	54	51	49	46	43	41	38	36
96	96	93	89	86	82	79	76	73	69	66	63	61	58	55	52	50	47	44	42	39	37
98	96	93	89	86	83	79	76	73	70	67	64	61	58	56	53	50	48	45	43	40	38
100	96	93	89	86	83	80	77	73	70	68	65	62	59	56	54	51	49	46	44	41	39
102	96	93	90	86	83	80	77	74	71	68	65	62	60	57	55	52	49	47	45	42	40
104	97	93	90	87	83	80	77	74	71	69	66	63	60	58	55	53	50	48	46	43	41
106	97	93	90	87	84	81	78	75	72	69	66	64	61	58	56	53	51	49	46	44	42
108	97	93	90	87	84	81	78	75	72	70	67	64	62	59	57	54	52	49	47	45	43

This chart will enable you to determine the relative humidity in your home, using a psychrometer. The difference between the dry-bulb and wet-bulb readings is called the "depression." On this chart, the depression is given between the two sets of horizontal ruled lines. For air temperature (same as dry-bulb temperature) read down the left-hand column. When you have determined both the depression and the dry-bulb (air) temperature, use the chart to find the percentage of relative humidity. For example, if the dry-bulb reading is 100 degrees F. and the depression is 10 degrees, the relative humidity is 68 percent—reading down from 10 and across from 100, as the chart indicates. *Courtesy of Whirlpool Corp.*

box atop your furnace from which the warm-air ducts exit) or, in the case of a portable unit, directly into the room. Water evaporated into the room air is essentially pure. Minerals and impurities in the original water remain behind in the humidifier and must be cleaned out. Some humidifiers are equipped with a bleed-off drain and flush automatically during operation. These units need only a seasonal clean-out and replacement of the media pad. While extremely hard water may dictate more frequent clean-outs and possibly require more service, an evaporative humidifier is still a good choice for hard-water areas. If you select a unit with bleed-off drain, servicing will be reduced to a minimum.

Atomizing humidifiers are the second broad type. These inject tiny droplets of water vapor into the air stream and depend upon the heat to finish the evaporative process. They often have greater capacity than evaporative humidifiers and are a good choice where soft water is available (under eight grains hardness). With the atomizing humidifier, there is no actual chemical change in the water itself. The mineral content tends to settle out as dust in the air stream as the water evaporates. Under extreme conditions of hard water, this may be seen as a grayish white dust or flake with the general appearance of a slight ash residue.

The increasing popularity of heat pumps and solar heating systems complicates the business of humidification because these are low-level heat sources—they operate at much lower temperatures than ordinary gas or oil furnaces. One design that overcomes this is a "hybrid" system that combines the principles of atomization and evaporation. The water is

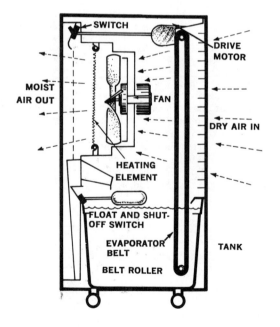

SWITCH
DRIVE MOTOR
MOIST AIR OUT
FAN
DRY AIN IN
HEATING ELEMENT
FLOAT AND SHUT-OFF SWITCH
EVAPORATOR BELT
TANK
BELT ROLLER

In console evaporative-type humidifier, motor-driven evaporator belt slowly passes through water in bottom tank. Highly absorbent media is saturated before reemerging. Dry air, drawn through wet belt by fan, absorbs moisture (and is filtered at same time). This unit also reheats air to room temperature before discharge into room. Other evaporative humidifiers, such as duct-mounted units, use variations of this principle. Wetted media may be in form of drum, when it revolves through sump formed by tank, or it may be stationary pad saturated from sump or inlet valve.

sprayed onto a media pad that is in or close to the air stream. Water that is not caught up in the air stream is carried away through a drain line.

Don't make the mistake of connecting a humidifier to a line carrying water from a water softener. A softener removes calcium salts from water, but replaces them with sodium salts at a ratio of about five parts sodium to four parts calcium by weight. Softened water, therefore, may make it necessary to clean a humidifier more often.

Humidifier capacity depends upon many things—the type of construction, the amount of wetted surface exposed to the air stream, the amount and temperature of the air passing through the humidifier. Most manufacturers now rate their units in pounds per hour capacity or in gallons per day capacity. Consult the accompanying charts to compare performance characteristics of various units and to help you select the size unit that best fits your needs. Be sure to take into consideration the amount of floor space, and the design temperature of

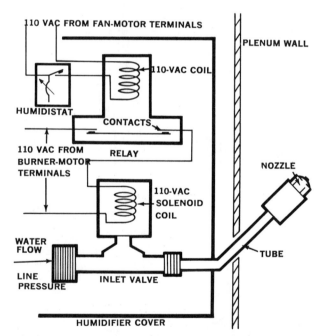

In this atomizing humidifier, voltage from fan motor is applied across relay coil when fan motor is turned on by fan switch on furnace and humidistat contacts are closed. Inlet-valve coil, however, is energized only when relay contacts are closed and burner motor (or gas valve) is operating. With such a hookup, droplets spray from nozzle when fan runs, but spray turns off with burner. Fan continues to run, so warm-air flow through ducts evaporates remaining moisture. Since nozzle design and orifice size determine capacity, capacity may be changed by replacing the nozzle.

your heating equipment. This should be at least equivalent to the lowest temperature normally reached in your area during a winter season.

Sizing a Humidifier for Your Home

The capacity of a residential humidifier is determined by several factors. In atomizing types, it's the size of the nozzle or pump. In evaporative types it's the amount of air, the temperature of the air, and the amount of surface presented by the media pad. Since this capacity is designed into the humidifier in many cases, it's important to choose the correct size. A talk with your dealer will usually help. If you want to go prepared with a "ball park" figure, take a look at the following chart:

SIZING RESIDENTIAL HUMIDIFIERS

Capacity required is determined by cubic feet of heated air space to be humidified and estimated air changes based on construction.

For 10,000 cu. ft. — TIGHT CONSTRUCTION
(one-half air change per hour)

With Outdoor Design Temp.	Lbs/hr Capacity for 72° indoor temperature at percent relative humidity desired					
	30%	35%	40%	45%	50%	55%
−10°F	1.6	1.9	2.2	2.5	2.8	3.1
0°	1.4	1.7	2.0	2.3	2.6	3.0
+10°F	1.2	1.5	1.8	2.1	2.4	2.8
+20°	.8	1.1	1.5	1.8	2.1	2.4
+30°	.4	.7	1.0	1.3	1.6	1.9
+40°	—	.1	.4	.7	1.0	1.3

Adjust capacity found on above chart to cu. ft. of heated air space in home.

    Example: For 14,000 cu. ft. home—
               multiply capacity by 1.4

               For 18,000 cu. ft. home—
               multiply capacity by 1.8

Correct adjusted capacity for type construction.

    Average Construction (one air change per hour)—
        multiply by 2

    Loose Construction (two air changes per hour)—
        multiply by 4

NOTES:

1. Fireplaces without dampers or when frequently used will add at least one air change per hour.
2. Humidifier capacities are based on operating time of the units. When connected electrically to warm air system blowers, operating characteristics of the heating system must be considered.
3. It is better to put in a unit with excess capacity and controlled with a humidistat than to install a unit with too low a capacity to do the job adequately.

Courtesy of Herrmidifier Co., Inc.

Note that the chart gives you the required capacity in pounds per hour, but some equipment is rated in pounds per day or even gallons per day. To correlate your figures, multiply pounds per hour by 24 to arrive at pounds per day. Divide this figure by 8.33 to determine gallons per day.

The outdoor design temperature shown in the chart is usually the lowest normal temperature reached in your area in a normal season. At this point, your furnace would be running constantly. If you're unsure of this figure, any heating contractor in your area can give it to you—it's the figure that he uses to determine proper furnace sizing.

Adjust the figures in the chart for the size of your home as shown. To find the cubic feet contained in your home, multiply the square footage by the height of your ceilings (in most cases this will be 8 feet). Figure tight construction for insulated ceilings and walls with wood siding, average for insulated ceilings and walls with brick veneer, and loose for no insulation. Did you realize that the average home has a complete change of air twenty-four times a day?

Don't add a humidifier if your home doesn't have a vapor barrier. Most homes built since the early fifties have one.

Installing a Humidifier

Happily, the humidifier is an appliance which is easily installed as a weekend project. To prepare for the job, take a close look at the location of your heating system. Quarter-inch copper or plastic tubing is normally used to connect the humidifier to a convenient water line. This tubing may or may not be supplied with the humidifier. If it is, make sure you have enough to reach the water line. If not, measure the amount you will need and allow a few additional feet so that the humidifier may be removed for servicing and cleaning. Also check the location of the blower motor and fan switch on the furnace, and obtain sufficient wiring to reach. Check your local codes to be sure you're allowed to do this part of the job. If you don't already have small tin snips, buy or borrow a pair. A small hand drill (not an electric drill) will be needed if the humidifier does not have a self-piercing saddle valve to make the water connection.

Follow the installation instructions supplied with your unit step by step. Accompanying photos show a typical installation.

A humidistat controls the degree to which the air in your home is humidified. This control is important. It is sometimes necessary to adjust the humidity to outside temperature conditions. While experts agree that 40 to 50 percent relative humidity in a home is ideal under normal conditions, on extremely cold nights you may wish to loweer the percentage to reduce condensation on windows. Here's a good rule of thumb: Determine the lowest temperature expected, add 15, and set the relative humidity at this figure. For instance, if the lowest temperature expected during the night is 10 degrees, 25 percent may be sufficient.

The humidistat is also necessary to prevent excessive moisture levels within the home. When the outside temperature goes down, condensation occurs. Some condensation is normal on windows within a humidified area and is almost impossible to avoid if you maintain proper humidity. However, an extremely high relative humdity within a home can cause excessive condensation on interior wall surfaces or between walls. This may lead to struc-

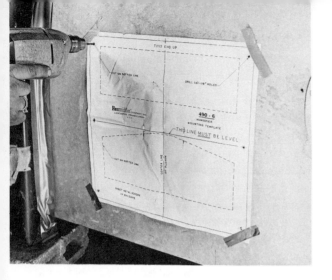

INSTALLING A HUMIDIFIER IN SIX EASY STEPS

1. Locate the supply plenum of your furnace by turning the furnace on and touching each of the plenums in turn to find the warmest one. Using a spirit level, sight across one of the horizontal lines on the template supplied and tape the template to the plenum. Drill holes marked on template. Don't install near smoke pipe or into air-conditioning coil; place humidifier *above* coil.

2. Next, use tin snips to cut out openings in plenum as indicated on template. Use file or hammer to remove burrs and sharp edges. Then use sheet-metal screws to fasten adapter plate provided with humidifier. Check with level before tightening screws.

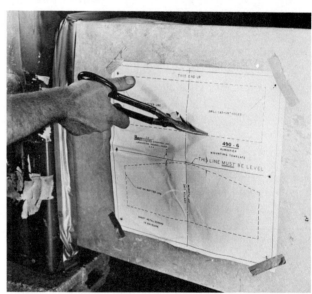

3. With adapter in place, humidifier mounting is easily accomplished. This Herrmidifier evaporative type pushes into upper groove of adapter and then seats into bottom groove. Clips keep the unit in position.

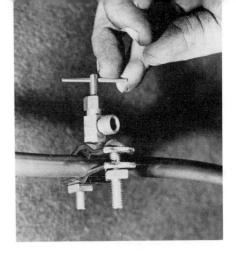

4. Locate a cold-water line and install saddle valve furnished with humidifier. The self-piercing type pictured here is simply clamped to copper water line and a threaded shaft is turned down to the normal "closed" position to puncture tubing. When it is necessary to drill water lines, the use of a hand drill (*not* an electric drill) is recommended.

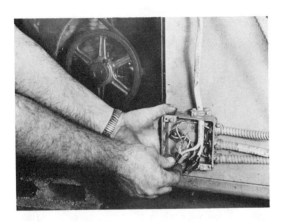

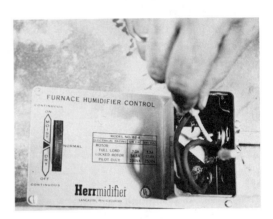

5. Locate the junction box or the fan switch of the furnace. Be sure all power to the furnace is turned off. Connect wiring to the leads which energize the furnace blower motor (consult the diagram accompanying your humidifier carefully here). If you have central air conditioning, consult the diagram which came with your furnace; on some types which utilize multi-speed motors, a relay must be installed in the circuit to prevent damage to motor windings. If a humidistat is used (see inset), be sure to connect "hot" side of line from furnace to humidifier through the humidistat contacts.

6. Finally, make water and power connections to the humidifier. If flushing system is used, run the bleed-off tube to a floor drain (don't run it outside—freezing will quickly block the flow). Turn furnace on and adjust controls; check to see that humidifier turns off when fan is off and when humidistat contacts open.

tural damage over a long period of time.

There are two common locations for humidistats—in the living area or on the return-air duct or plenum. A different type of humidistat is needed for each. One of the two may be furnished with your humidifier. If not, either location is acceptable. If you locate the humidistat within the living area, be sure to place it away from such sources of moisture as kitchen sinks, dishwashers, etc. Locate it where it can record average humidity for your home. Installing the humidistat on the return-air duct or plenum enables it to respond to air from serveral locations within the home and, theoretically, adjust to an average humidity condition. But this location has the drawback that you must go to the basement or crawl space to make adjustments.

Servicing a Humidifier

In servicing a humidifier, distinction must be made between the two types. In the evaporative type a fan forces dry air across media pads saturated with water. The air absorbs moisture and is discharged by way of the supply ducts into the living area. Atomizing humidifiers inject tiny droplets of water vapor into the air stream, depending upon the heat to finish the evaporative process.

The electrical system of a residential humidifier is relatively simple. At most, components consist of an on-off switch, easily tested with a VOM; a motor, used to drive an evaporative media belt through the water reservoir (evaporative type), or a solenoid which operates a water-inlet valve, allowing water to flow across a stationary media pad (evaporative type) or pass through the nozzle (atomizer), or

into a pump impeller (atomizer); and in many models a small fan motor. These small synchronous motors and solenoids should be tested on a high resistance scale ($R \times 100$) on the VOM. If open, they should be replaced. Be sure to check the mechanical gear train of the motor as well as the motor windings. Do not attempt to manually turn the wheels or rollers attached to the motor. This may damage the gear train and make replacement of motor components imperative.

If the humidifier doesn't operate at all, check to see that power is being supplied at the proper time. If not, test the contacts within the humidistat. They should read zero ohms resistance when closed. Many duct-mounted humidistats won't close at all when humidity is above 40 percent unless a test position is provided on the control. On some newer solid-state controls, voltage must be applied to the humidistat before the contacts will operate. Such controls are usually equipped with a pilot light to tell you when they are closed. If the light is on, the humidifier should be operating. Remember that in most cases humidifiers operate only when the blower is operating (although some suppliers of evaporative humidifiers now allow their equipment to be connected directly to line voltage, operating at all times that the humidistat calls for increased humidity). Atomizing humidifiers often turn on with the furnace and off with the burner or gas valve of the furnace. In either case the blower would be operating before voltage will be supplied to the humidifier.

If your furnace or heating system is equipped with central air conditioning, the humidifier should be shut off whenever the air conditioner is in use. On hot, muggy summer days you're more interested in removing moisture from the conditioned air than adding it.

The amount of service that your humidifier will require will likely depend upon water conditions prevalent in your area. Soft water will cause little problems with mineral and lime deposits but may form algae within the reservoir which must be removed periodically. This condition will show up as a green or brownish scum within the reservoir. Some manufacturers furnish chemical tablets to help eliminate the condition. A teaspoon of chlorine bleach, such as Clorox or Texize, added to the humidifier at intervals may help.

If you live in a hard-water area, mineral deposits removed from water during the evaporative process will build up in the reservoirs. This is not corrosion and won't damage the reservoir—but heavy deposits may damage the motor or moving components. The deposits can clog media material on evaporative types, clog nozzles and impellers on atomizing types, and clog water valves on both.

When disassembling a water valve, be sure to note the proper location of each component.

It's a good idea to lay out the parts on a counter in the order removed. Clean each part thoroughly with an old toothbrush before reinstalling. A pipe cleaner, too, is handy for cleaning small passageways and orifices. Be sure all parts operate freely. On equipment using a float valve, look closely at the rubber button and orifice that admits the water. Some models have buttons which may be reversed when worn (wet soap rubbed on the button makes it easy to snap in place). On older humidifiers, water may have eroded the orifice to the point that the button will no longer make a tight seal when the float is raised. In such cases, consider replacing the entire float-valve assembly.

If you remove rollers or media wheels from motors, be sure the small rubber "slinger ring" on the motor shaft is reinstalled. It prevents water and mineral deposits from creeping up the motor shaft and into the bearings. In hard-water areas, a humidifier with a built-in flushing system will help keep mineral deposits to a minimum.

Wash the evaporative belt or pad

Console humidifiers can fit in among room furnishings. Check water level daily and fill as necessary, unless an optional connection is made to water supply. Unit shown humidifies up to 2,500 square feet and has a discharge capacity of up to 18 gallons of water per day.

Control panel displays (from left to right) humidistat, selector switch, refill indicator light, water-level gauge, and *on* indicator light. *Temp* selection energizes heating element along with low fan speed and media motor, raising humidified air to room temperature before discharging it.

After you have removed the front grill, front panel drops down to allow testing of components. Heating element is visible in discharge opening. Unplug humidifier before removing panels.

Fan motor, media track, and motor are serviceable from rear after access panel is removed. Plug (in hand) allows quick disconnect of assembly from humidifier. Rod seen extending into plastic tank is attached to float in tank and to water-level indicator at opposite end.

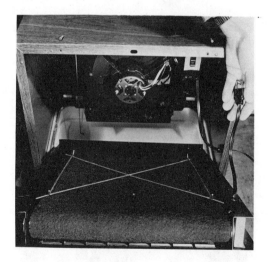

Four-point fan mounting is rubber cushioned to reduce vibration and noise. Fan motor is removed by removing blade, then loosening screws which clamp it to mount.

Belt is easily removed from assembly by removing end caps on two rollers. Handle belt carefully, especially when dry. Clean in manufacturer's cleaning solution or a 50 percent solution of white vinegar and water. Do not wring belt after cleaning. Just rinse thoroughly, drain and reinstall.

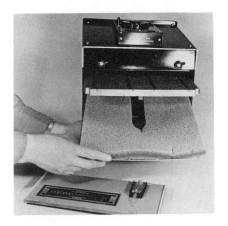

"Drawer" type evaporator pad and air filter on this evaporative duct-mounted unit makes cleaning and servicing easy. Door is removed by turning four latches one-quarter turn. Plastic gauge on door front tells you when pad needs cleaning.

Media is mounted on revolving drum in this evaporative humidifier. Float visible in sump (center) regulates amount of water which enters and a small synchronous motor, similar to appliance timer motors in appearance, is mounted in enclosure on right of sump and rotates drum. No fan motor is used. Humidifier is mounted to warm-air plenum and is connected on supply side to cold-air plenum. Resulting pressure differential between the two sections forces air through humidifier.

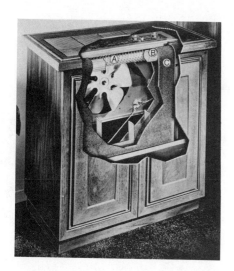

Arvin has developed a self-cleaning feature used on the evaporative model above. The plastic roller (**A**) has hundreds of blunt end projections which press pad (**C**) against fluted roller (**B**), breaking down mineral sediment. *Courtesy of Arvin Industries, Inc.*

Float and valve assembly is apparent in this top view of tank. Stub just above inlet valve fitting on side of tank is overflow drain, used only if float valve should fail to cut water off. Overflow drain line should *always* be connected when a humidifier is used in an area where overflow would cause property damage.

This atomizing humidifier is designed for through-the-wall mounting, allowing concealed humidification for homes without warm-air ducts. Unit is permanently connected and may be installed within a closet.

Components in this atomizing unit are rugged and noncorrosive. From bottom in a clockwise direction is the diffusing screen and retaining clips, motor, motor base, and impeller.

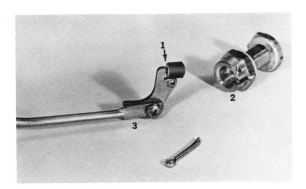

Most float-valve assemblies are easily disassembled for cleaning. Rubber plunger (**1**) closes orifice in seat (**2**) to shut off incoming water supply. Screw (**3**) allows adjustment of float height to determine water level in tank. Damaged seat or plunger requires replacement of valve unit.

This atomizing unit uses water line pressure to provide the force. Relay is designed to turn solenoid valve on with the blower and off with the burner of furnace when properly connected. This provides a "purging" action which dries moisture from ducts before end of heating cycle.

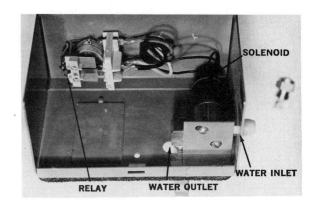

Business end of the Aqua-Mist unit shows specially designed nozzle which provides such a fine spray that it resembles a cloud. For remote mounting in confined spaces, nozzle adapter can be removed and a length of copper tubing attached between adapter and control panel.

Wall-mounted humidistat (left) would be installed in area of home where it would be subjected to average humidity conditions. A hallway is often a good choice of locations. Duct-mounted humidistat (right) is mounted on return air duct where it will sense an average of the humidity being returned to furnace from living area.

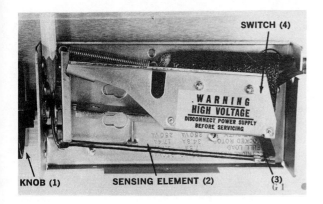

SWITCH (4)

KNOB (1) SENSING ELEMENT (2) (3)

This closeup reveals typical workings of humidistat. Knob (1) turns screw indicated by pencil which determines amount of tension placed upon sensing strand (2). Moisture in surrounding air allows strand to stretch, and when spring tension exerted at (3) causes enough motion, switch (4) is deenergized. Nylon ribbons and strands of human hair are common materials used for the critical sensing element.

Switch unit of any humidistat is easily tested with VOM. Connect on $R \times 1$ scale, turn humidifier indicator to any position above room humidity level, and needle should sweep towards 0 ohms resistance.

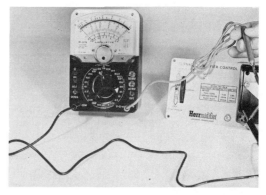

thoroughly in a vinegar solution, rinse thoroughly (don't squeeze), and allow to drain. If the belt has stretched and isn't fitting its rollers or wheels snugly, it's time to replace it. Rollers and fans should operate smoothly—lubricate slightly if necessary. Be sure that

float valves are operating smoothly and that the button completely seals the orifice when the float is raised. When reassembling, be sure that all rotating parts (wheels, rollers, and fans) have sufficient clearance.

RULES FOR THE USE AND CARE OF A PORTABLE HUMIDIFIER

- Manually fill reservoir every few days or as needed to maintain proper level.
- Clean water reservoir frequently to guard against buildup of bacteria. It is wise to use a bacteriostatic agent, which is sometimes available for purchase through the manufacturer.
- Clean media pad monthly—possibly replace yearly.
- Make certain that humidistat is set for proper humidity level. "Sweating" windows are a sign of too much humidity.
- Do not place unit near any source of concentrated heat such as registers or radiators.

QUICK-CHECK CHART FOR
HOME HUMIDIFIERS

Symptom	Probable Cause	Remedy
No humidification or low humidification (also check calibration of instrument used to diagnose problem)	Dirty media pad, clogged nozzle or impeller	Remove and clean as necessary
	Clogged float valve or inlet valve	Disassemble and clean
	Binding media or pump motor	Remove, clean and oil
	Open windings in media or pump motor	Replace
	Open contacts in humidistat	Calibrate or replace as necessary
	No power supply to humidifier	Check for voltage with VOM—check for open fan switch on furnace
	Furnace fan not operating long enough	Check setting of fan switch on furnace
	Binding media wheel or pad	Check for mineral buildup or mechanical binding
	Undersized humidifier	Check sizing of equipment
Excessive humidification	Humidistat contacts stuck closed	Calibrate or replace as necessary
	Humidifier improperly connected to power supply	Check by diagram furnished with equipment
Humidifier overflowing	Stuck inlet or float valve	Remove and clean mineral deposits or replace components
	Clogged drain	Clean
	Capillary action siphoning water over case	Remove and clean mineral deposits from case
Noisy operation	Loose or binding bearing surfaces	Inspect or lube as necessary or use silicone grease
	Interference caused by mineral buildup	Check and clean humidifier

DEHUMIDIFIERS

The work of a dehumidifier is exactly opposite that of a humidifier. It's easy to see why. The moisture conditions that usually exist during warm summer months are the opposite of those that occur during the winter months. A dehumidifier, therefore, is mostly a summertime appliance. Most of them are portable. In all but the most severe cases one unit is sufficient to control humidity in an average home. To do this, rotate it on a regular basis from one problem area to another.

Basically, a dehumidifier is a refrigeration appliance. To determine if you have a need for it, check humidity levels with your sling psychrometer or humidity indicator regularly. During damp periods, it's impossible to keep humidity at optimum levels in summer, even with a dehumidifier. But be on the lookout for the symptoms of excess humidity—the mold, mildew, and other symptoms mentioned at the beginning of this chapter. Keep in mind also that air conditioning removes significant amounts of moisture from the air as well as cooling it. If you are plagued with a moisture problem and are considering the addition of air conditioning to your home, it would be wise to evaluate the situation again after the air conditioning is in operation. Chances are that it will provide all the moisture-removal capacity that your home needs.

If you already have an air conditioner and still have suspicions that there's too much moisture in your home, take the moisture-content reading after the equipment has been turned on for at least two hours. Keep in mind that this action occurs only when the compressor is in operation, and not at all times that the fans are running. For this reason, it's unwise to greatly oversize an air conditioner with the hope of gaining increased cooling capacity; the "short-cycling" of the cooling system in moderate weather will do little to lower humidity. Since cooling and moisture removal are both important for summer comfort, it's a signifi-

Dehumidifier blends well with room furnishings, and protects them from excess humidity. Condensate pan slides from rear of unit to empty.

cant point to remember if you're considering the purchase of an air conditioner this season.

Eliminating moisture that originates within the house will assist your dehumidifier and in extreme cases might even allow you to get along without one.

Consider first the range, sink, and dishwasher in the kitchen and the shower in the bathroom. Use your ventilators if you have them; if not, consider installing them. Clothes dryers should always be vented to the outside of the home.

An often overlooked source of summer moisture is a basement crawl space. Moisture problems there are doubly important, since darkness and dampness can be prime contributors to structural damage as well as affecting comfort in the living area above. The problem is easily resolved, however, by placing strategically located strips of four mil (.004 inch) polyethylene, 10–12 feet wide, directly on the ground. Enough material for an average house will cost around twenty dollars at any builders supply. Don't try to cover the ground area completely. Leave openings between the strips and along the foundations. It may even be necessary to expose ground area in winter if humidity levels drop too low.

The typical dehumidifier consists of a basic refrigeration system, but differs from most refrigeration appliances in that a fan pulls the room air across both the evaporator and the condenser coil simultaneously. It's a logical approach. The cold evaporator (often referred to as the collector coil in a dehumidifier) extracts large quantities of moisture from the air much as a glass of ice tea "sweats" on a hot, muggy summer day. The evaporator also chills the air as it passes. The warm condenser coils reheat the air before it is discharged into the

room; this avoids the possibility of chilling the room uncomfortably on mild days.

A humidistat, usually adjustable, controls the system by turning the compressor and fan on whenever moisture levels rise above the relative humidity selected.

A dehumidifier is one of the simplest appliances to use, requiring only that you set the humidistat at the desired level of humidity. The humidistat knob usually has an "off" and a constant "on" position, although some use push buttons for these functions.

Under certain conditions of low temperature and high humidity, it's possible for the evaporator coil to ice over when the unit is first started. This frost will usually disappear after the first thirty minutes of operation. Some models incorporate a deicer into their electrical circuitry to automatically defrost the unit under a severe icing condition. This deicer control is a bimetal thermostat tightly clamped to the tube carrying the refrigerant from the evaporator back to the compressor. If the icing becomes so heavy that it reaches the control attachment point, which is at the very end of the evaporator tubing and would not normally be cold, the compressor shuts off. Since the fan continues to run, the coil quickly defrosts. When this occurs, the coil senses the warmer refrigerant line and restores the compressor to normal operation. Most manufacturers do not recommend operation of dehumidifiers in ambient temperatures below 65 degrees.

How to Select a Dehumidifier

All dehumidifiers for homes use the same basic principle of cooling humid air to condense the moisture it contains with the cooling

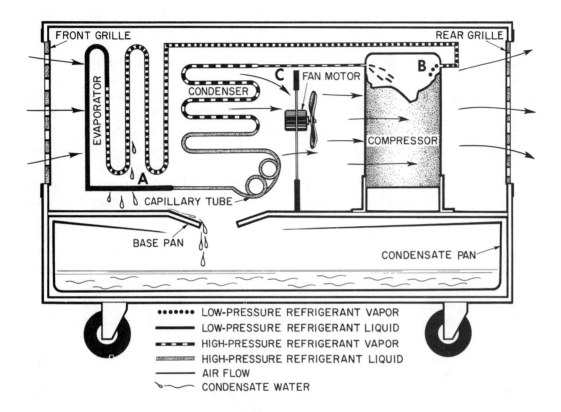

•••••• LOW-PRESSURE REFRIGERANT VAPOR
―――――― LOW-PRESSURE REFRIGERANT LIQUID
▬ ▬ ▬ ▬ HIGH-PRESSURE REFRIGERANT VAPOR
▨▨▨▨ HIGH-PRESSURE REFRIGERANT LIQUID
―――――― AIR FLOW
〜〜〜 CONDENSATE WATER

HOW A DEHUMIDIFIER WORKS

When the humidistat turns the unit on, a fan pulls room air through front grill, across the evaporator and condenser coils, and past the compressor before it is discharged back into the room through the rear grill.

At the same time, the compressor pumps refrigerant through the system. Liquid refrigerant enters the evaporator from the capillary tube at a lowered pressure. There it evaporates and takes heat from air passing through the evaporator coil. Refrigerant 12, the most commonly used in this application, has a boiling point of approximately 21 degrees below zero. The heat-laden vapor then flows to the compressor (**B**) where it is pumped into the condenser (**C**) under pressure. There, high pressure and the cool air passing over the condenser coil causes it to condense back into a liquid state. The liquid enters the capillary tube (**D**). This tiny tubing serves as a restrictor and metering device, thus lowering the pressure of the refrigerant as it is discharged again into the low-pressure area within the evaporator tubing at (**A**). The cycle continuously repeats itself.

Moisture condenses on the cool evaporator coils much as it would on a glass of iced tea. The condensed water drips from the evaporator coil and flows through an opening in the base pan into a collector pan or through a drain hose. The condenser warms the air before it is discharged through the rear grill.

Components are easily reached when cabinet is removed. Clean yearly with vacuum and damp cloth, lube fan motor with SAE 20 motor oil if ports are provided.

Evaporator (collector) coil is always first component in air stream, followed by condenser which reheats air. Air also flows directly over compressor, which cools the motor somewhat and adds some heat back to room air. Compare this photo with drawing to understand how a dehumidifier works.

(evaporator) coil of a simple refrigeration system, then reheating the dried air with the condenser coil before circulating it out into the room again. The actual physical arrangement of the components may vary with different manufacturers.

Dehumidifiers are rated on their water-removal capacities at standard rating capacities of 80 degrees Fahrenheit and 60 percent relative humidity by the Association of Home Appliance Manufacturers (AHAM). Capacities range from around 11 pints to 32 pints per day. Be sure that the AHAM certification accompanies the appliance.

The size you will need for your home is dependent upon many conditions, such as the area to be dehumidified, the climate, the type of construction, and the presence or lack of vapor barriers. As a basis for sizing your system, figure that you will need one pint of water removal capacity for each 1,000 cubic feet of space in your home. Example: A 2,000-square-foot home with 8-foot ceilings would contain some 16,000 cubic feet. You would need at least a 16-pint-per-day capacity to dehumidify the area. Increase the figure if there's no vapor barrier, if water seepage is present, or if doors and windows are regularly left open. Unlike an air conditioner, the dehumidifier can be oversized with no detrimental effects. If in doubt, select a higher-capacity model.

An automatic shut-off device and an adjustable humidistat are desirable features when selecting the equipment. Also be sure to determine if the manner of condensate disposal (collector pan or bucket, drain hose, etc.) suits the location of the unit. It's also wise to check the length of the cord; extension cords are not recommended on any appliance.

If the unit is to be placed in a living area, appearance, noise levels, and the presence of wheels or casters become important considerations.

Last but not least, ease of cleaning and servicing may greatly increase your enjoyment and usage of the dehumidifier. See that the coils are accessible, the cabinet removable, and the pan easily removed for emptying—a job you may perform twice a day.

Installing a Dehumidifier

The area of dehumidifier coverage is limited, but since the appliance is portable you can place it where moisture problems develop. For example, if moldy shoes are discovered in a bedroom closet, place the unit in the bedroom. If mildew is found under the living room rug, use the unit in that area. While severe conditions may require several units, a single portable unit will usually suffice if left for several days at a time in each problem area.

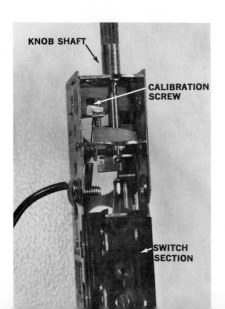

Humidistat operates like thermostat but senses air moisture rather than temperature. It should be accurate to within 10 percent relative humidity, but calibration is not critical—the knob can be set to a higher or lower level to compensate for inaccuracies. Clean burned contacts with striking surface from book of matches if switch is not sealed type.

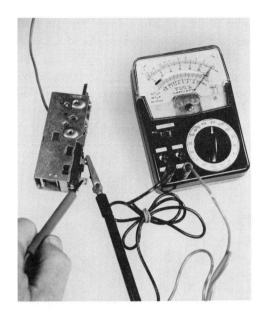

Humidistat contacts are tested like any other switch with $R \times 1$ scale of VOM. Most have constant *on* and *off* positions, and should indicate 0 ohms resistance in the *on* position. Replace control if mechanism is binding or is not operating.

Running controls for compressor are bimetal overload protector and starting relay (indicated by finger). Run to line terminals of relay will indicate closed circuit on current-type relay shown here, since relay coil is part of this circuit. The start contacts will be open unless circuit is energized.

Measure continuity from *L* (line, possibly marked *C* for common) terminal to the *R* (run) terminal to test the relay coil. Set your VOM to $R \times 1$ or lowest scale. If the coil is open, replace the relay. As in the case of the faulty humidistat, it just doesn't make sense to repair a relay that's gone bad.

The presence of a suitable drain must also be considered in locating a dehumidifier. While most portable units have self-contained collector pans, they seldom are large enough for 24-hour capacity in damp weather. For instance, a unit capable of removing 22 pints of water a day may have only a 12-pint container, requiring you to empty it twice daily. Most units can empty into a floor drain (or into a sink if the dehumidifier is placed above the sink drain) simply by removing the pan. Some models incorporate a fitting for a garden hose to carry the condensate water to a remote location, but be sure that the hose has no kinks and that the outlet is low enough to permit proper drainage.

To test the starting contacts of current type relay, first test from *L* to *S* (start) with the relay in correct position (relay will be marked at top). No continuity reading should be obtained. Then invert the relay and needle should sweep to 0 ohms resistance. Both tests are made on *R* × *100* or lowest scale on meter.

Overload protector opens circuit to compressor if excessive current flows or if temperature reaches abnormal limits. The device can prevent compressor motor winding failure due to a malfunction of other components, such as a stuck starting relay. If it fails, it will usually be open, and the compressor will make no sound or hum. It should read continuity as shown above.

Don't overlook the possibility of "recycling" the condensate water. It's practically as good as distilled water for use in steam irons, automobile batteries, etc. (but don't drink it). Before using the condensate water, filter it through a clean cloth to remove any lint.

Be sure the area being dehumidified is isolated from outside air as much as possible; otherwise, moisture may flow into the treated area as fast as it is being removed.

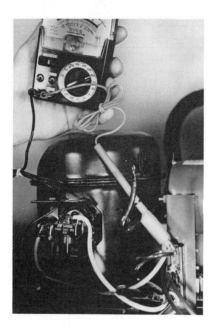

Adjust diaphragm switch for water level control by turning knob to alter spring tension. More tension raises level, less tension lowers it.

To test compressor and overload, unplug dehumidifier and set VOM to $R \times 1$ scale. First place one meter probe on line going to overload, other on terminal where line from overload attaches to compressor. Meter should sweep to full-scale reading; if not, overload is open and should be replaced. If reading is okay, leave probe attached to compressor terminal. Remove leads from other two terminals and touch meter to each in turn. If meter sweeps to full scale, internal windings have continuity; if not, compressor is bad. Final test is to set meter to highest resistance scale and read from each terminal to metal shell; if reading is noted, compressor is grounded and must be replaced.

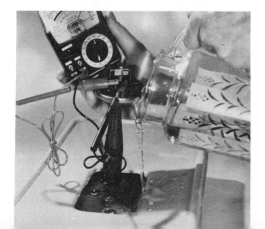

Overflow prevention switch shuts unit off if pan is full. Some models also use switch to turn indicator off. Test for continuity with VOM while operating linkage manually. Sealed diaphragm shown here is tested while slowly immersing open end of sensing tube in full condensate pan. Switch contacts to unit should read open when held at a normal level above pan.

Accompanying photos show you how to handle most problems you might encounter in maintaining a dehumidifier. Probably the only tools you'll need are a VOM, Phillips and standard screwdrivers, and possibly a soldering iron. Repairs within the refrigeration system are best left to a specialist.

RULES FOR THE USE AND CARE OF A DEHUMIDIFIER

- Locate the unit in an area closed to outdoor air and in an area where air flow in and out of the unit is unimpeded and the dehumidified air can circulate freely within the room.
- If the unit is equipped with a manual drain pan, empty regularly to avoid overflow.
- Do not place unit directly on damp floor areas or where water is likely to accumulate.
- Operate on a level surface for proper function of drainage system.
- Use as needed. Usage will vary depending upon conditions and geographical location, but it will seldom be required when the heating system is in use.
- Do not operate when surrounding temperature falls below 60 degrees.

PREVENTATIVE MAINTENANCE FOR HUMIDIFIERS AND DEHUMIDIFIERS

Most manufacturers recommend inspecting a humidifier every four weeks. Since water conditions play such a large part in the frequency of cleaning, use this as a starting point. If water hardness is severe, the checkup may need to be more frequent; if water is soft, less frequent. Always check and clean the unit at least once a year. It's good practice to clean the reservoir at the end of each season and shut off water and power supply for the summer. Next winter the equipment is off to a clean start.

Be sure that all power to the heating system and humidifier is turned off before beginning your checkup. Turn off the water, then remove the cover from the unit. Wash all parts thoroughly with the manufacturer's recommended cleaning chemical or a 50 percent mixture of water and white vinegar. Check nozzles, pumps, screens, and filters for deposits.

Preventative maintenance of the dehumidifier is simple but important. Before each season begins, remove the cabinet and wipe the collector coil with a clean cloth. Then vacuum the condenser coil and the remainder of the unit. This removes lint accumulated from the large volume of air which passed through the unit during the past season.

Oil the fan motor if it has oil ports. Most manufacturers recommend a few drops of SAE 20 oil in each port. If a sealed motor is used, it's still a good idea to clean all lint from the motor shaft and apply a few drops of oil on the shaft close to the motor housing. If necessary, work the motor shaft from end to end to help the oil reach the small sleeve bearings.

QUICK-CHECK CHART FOR

DEHUMIDIFIERS

SYMPTOM	PROBABLE CAUSE	REMEDY
Unit won't run	Humidistat open	Check humidity level and setting of humidistat. Check switch section with VOM. Replace if defective.
	Overflow switch open	Check level in pan. Check for binding linkage. Check switch section with VOM, replace if defective.
	Selector switch open (if so equipped)	Check with switch in ON position. If VOM doesn't read continuity, replace switch.
	Fuse blown	Test for voltage at receptacle by plugging in table lamp.
	Defective power cord or wiring harness	Test for continuity with VOM. Repair as necessary. Use only polarized-type plug or cord.
Fan runs, compressor off	De-icer open	Normal if evaporator coils are frosted. If coils are warm, test bimetal de-icer with VOM for continuity, replace if open.
	Compressor overload open	Check for cause (blocked airflow, defective relay). If okay, check for continuity with VOM; replace if open. Use only OEM replacement for compressor.
	Relay run circuit (coil) open (current-type relay)	Test for continuity from C to R, replace if open.
	Compressor windings open	Test from C to R and from C to S for continuity. Replace if open (refer to qualified technician). Also check from each terminal to ground, replace if continuity indicated.
Fan runs, compressor buzzes	Compressor bearings locked	Test with starting cord (see photo). Refer to refrigeration technician if faulty.
	Compressor-relay starting circuit open	Test with starting cord. Test relay contacts with VOM. Use only specified replacement relay if defective.
	Compressor start windings open	Check compressor terminals C to S for continuity. Refer to technician if faulty. Also test for ground.
	Compressor starting capacitor open (if so equipped)	Test for continuity with VOM on RX 100 scale. Needle should rise, then fall back toward zero. Reversing leads should repeat reading.
Fan won't run, refrigeration system operating	Fan motor open	Test for continuity on RX 100 scale, replace if open.
	Fan motor binding	Clean and lube as necessary. If armature still isn't free, replace motor.
FULL indicator light doesn't go off	Switch linkage binding	Check manually, clean and lube as necessary.
	Switch open	Test for continuity while operating manually, replace if necessary.
FULL indicator light doesn't come on	Switch linkage binding	Same as above.
	Lamp burned out	Test for voltage at lamp terminals, replace lamp if voltage reaches terminals but lamp doesn't burn.
Unit runs, doesn't dehumidify sufficiently	Area being dehumidified not sealed off from outside air	Close doors or isolate area.
	Airflow through unit obstructed	Move unit away from walls, etc. Clean vacuum coils.
	Equipment too small for area being dehumidified	Close off part of area, dehumidify each section at different times.
	Low refrigerant charge in system	See if cooling effect is evenly distributed across evaporator coil—symptom may result in partial frosting of coil. Refer to refrigeration technician.

23
At Home on the Kitchen Range

The range may appear to be just a simple appliance that serves as a heat source. In reality it's called on to do much more. It must deliver controlled amounts of heat to the right places at the right times on the cooktop or surface units and to the oven. Within the oven, the heat must be even and the oven walls must be capable of containing the heat to prevent the outside from becoming dangerously warm and to minimize heat loss.

Gas and electric ranges are much alike in the basic construction of the cabinet, oven cavity, and insulation procedures; the works are entirely different because of the two energy sources involved. The two are practically even in sales.

ELECTRIC RANGES

The power supply for most electric ranges in the United States is a three-wire, 115/230-volt circuit, very much like the one used for automatic clothes dryers, except that the range circuit must use heavier wiring because of the higher current flow when it is in full use. The third (middle) conductor is grounded, and often serves as a portion of a 115-volt circuit used to power burners on low heat and the timer motor and lighting circuits. The oven elements and surface units on high heat (and, with infinite-heat switches, on all heat settings) make use of the 230-volt circuits only.

(In some sections of the country, particularly in New York City, 208-volt power supplies are sometimes used for home ranges. The ranges designed for this condition are basically the same as 230-volt ranges except that the elements are rated for use at the lower voltage. The 208-volt rated elements have a heat output comparable to the 230-volt elements when both are operated at their rated voltage. It is possible to use 230-volt elements on a 208-volt power supply, but cooking time will be reduced substantially. It's not wise, however, to substitute 208-volt units when 230-volt units should be used, for the higher voltage will lead to early failure of the element. It should also

Is this a stove or a dishwasher? It's both. Modern Maid's combination unit illustrates versatility found in modern ranges and solves many remodeling problems as well. Top oven is continuous cleaning.

Another versatile design is shown on this Jenn-Air drop-in unit. Stones contained in cages under grill are heated by electric element. Drippings from meat fall upon the hot stones and the resulting smoke gives meat an outdoors flavor. Grease is trapped in throw-away container underneath grill and smoke is carried to outside by powerful blower built into oven.

GRILL   BLOWER INTAKE   CAGE (REMOVED)

Ceramic cook tops have heating element underneath patterned area. Top must be lifted for servicing. Use care to prevent clipping or breaking.

be noted that in most instances a separate grounding conductor should be used from the frame of the range to a cold-water line. The National Electrical Code allows grounding by connection to the grounded circuit conductors —if they are not smaller than No. 10 AWG— on a 115/230-volt, single-phase, three-wire circuit or on a 115/208-volt, three-phase, four-wire circuit. If you don't know which of these you have—and the three-phase power supply is not common in residences—a check with your power company will bring a quick answer.)

When the combined 115- and 230-volt circuits which can be obtained from a 230-volt power supply are used to vary the heat of the surface units, a five- or seven-position switch is often used. The switch may be a rotary or pushbutton type. You can recognize this type of circuitry because the element itself will have two separate and distinct coils, a small one (referred to as the inner coil) and a large one, referred to as the outer coil because of the location of the outermost rings. Each element will have three leads—one to the outer element, one to the inner element, and one to a double terminal connected to both sections.

Newer electric ranges carry the heat control for surface units a couple of steps further. A switch with a bimetallic element is used to provide a timed power input into the burner. On the high selection the 230-volt power supply is fed constantly to the burner. On a medium setting, however, or as the switch progresses toward the low setting, the bimetal unit cycles the power input on and off. This reduces the amount of *on* time and increases the amount of *off* time as the switch approaches the low setting. At the low setting the *on* periods are timed at their shortest point. This has the advantage of providing any in-between settings between high and low; for this reason it's

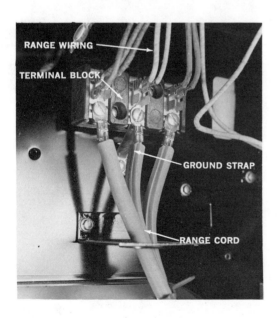

Terminal block on range connects pigtail (range cord) to range wiring. In most localities, middle (neutral) conductor is fastened to cabinet as shown to provide positive ground. Check with your local power company if this is not permitted in your area. Cabinet *must* be grounded to neutral wire with ground strap or to cold-water line with external ground wire, or by using both methods.

Access to control panel can be gained from front in many cases. In this photo screw is being removed from trim to service top oven controls. Opening is provided in trim at bottom, indicated by arrow, so retaining screw can easily be reached. Power must be turned off before panels are removed.

Plug-in burner, used with infinite heat control, is tested across both terminals with VOM on $R \times 1$ scale, then tested for grounds on highest resistance scale as shown.

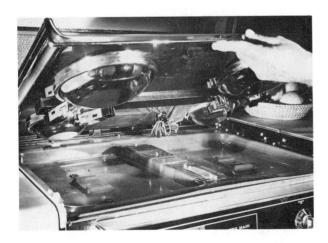

Snap-up top featured on many ranges allows easy access for both servicing and cleaning. Be sure the power is turned off before opening top or otherwise exposing any wiring connections.

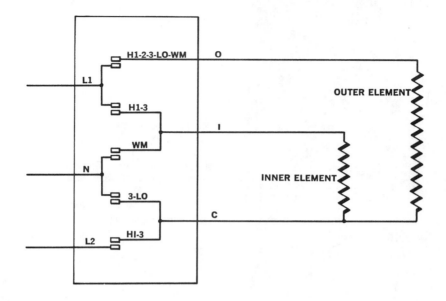

HOW FIVE-POSITION RANGE SWITCHES WORK

In this drawing, typical circuitry through a five-position switch is shown. Each set of contacts is marked with the position in which that contact will be closed. By putting this together, it's easy to see that the following combinations will be provided to control surface unit heat output:

HI   230 volts across *C-I* (inner element) and across *C-O* (outer element).
2   230 volts across *C-O* (outer element only).
3   115 volts across *C-I* and across *C-O*.
LO   115 volts across *C-O*.
WM   115 volts across *I-O*. If both elements are of the same resistance, this would be approximately 58 volts across each. The elements are in series with each other at this setting.

This can be varied further to provide additional positions, but the basic format of changing the voltage and element circuitry at each position remains the same. Some ranges use seven positions instead of five.

To test surface-unit element on this model using five-position switch, check from common terminal to each of the other two in turn, using $R \times 1$ scale on VOM. Then check from each terminal to ground using highest resistance scale. If element is grounded or open, it must be replaced.

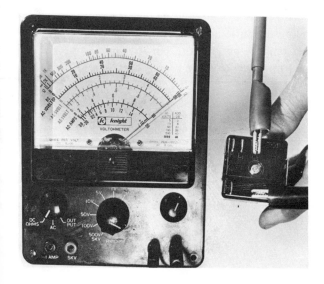

To check five-position switch, check wiring diagram and test for continuity across closed contacts with switch in each position. Since switches are sealed, and cannot be repaired, defective switch must be replaced.

Many surface units simply unplug from their receptacle. By raising unit in front and pulling away from receptacle, unit is easily removed for testing with the VOM.

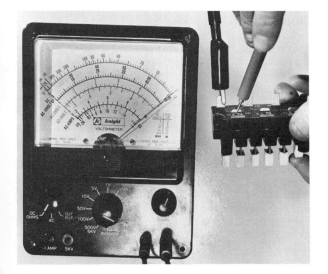

Infinite heat controls require testing of contacts and heater with switch in *on* position and VOM set to $R \times 1$ scale. If either circuit is open, switch must be replaced.

commonly referred to as an infinite-heat type of control. The only disadvantage is that even on the low setting slight boiling of some sauces and other foods may occur during the *on* period. This stops of course during the *off* period of the power pulse into the burner. On some deluxe ranges one or more burners may be divided into two or three segments. If so, a

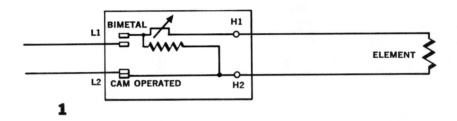

1

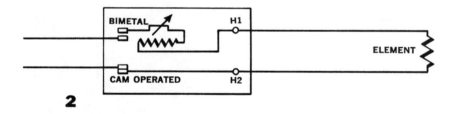

2

HOW INFINITE-HEAT SWITCHES WORK

There are two basic types of infinite-heat switches currently on the market. In the one shown in Fig. 1 the heater is connected across the line, and may be used with any wattage element. Turning the switch to any *on* position closes the contacts shown at *L2*, and presets a spring load on the bimetal arm at *L1*. 230 volts flow through the heating element and through the heater within the switch, which is close to the bimetal arm. As the heat is absorbed by the arm, it tends to bend upward until it breaks the circuit at *L1*, breaking the circuit to the surface unit and to the switch heater. As the bimetal arm cools, it again closes and the cycle is repeated. In the *HI* position, the switches are locked in a constant *on* position, while at the *LO* position the *on* cycle is shortest and the *off* portion of the cycle longest. As the knob is turned from *HI* to *LO*, the tension on the bimetal arm decreases and allows the heat to open the contact faster.

The heat control shown in Fig. 2 works in much the same manner except the switch heater is in series with the element. This means that this switch *must* be matched to the wattage of the surface unit for proper operation, and vice versa. Keep this in mind when replacing these components.

selector switch is provided to heat either the small inner coil, the middle coil, or the larger outer coil.

GAS RANGES

Before discussing these, we want to remind you that all safety organizations discourage do-it-yourself repairs to any home gas appliance. Because of the twin dangers of explosion and asphyxiation, this is a sensible precaution. But if you understand the operation of a gas appliance you can at least make certain it is being used in the most efficient manner—and know when to call your gas company for service.

In gas ranges the simplest and most common type of control device for the surface unit is a valve which has a plug between the manifold where the gas enters and the tube approaching the burner. At the full *off* position the hole between the two sections is closed. At the full *on* position it's completely open, simply a drilled passageway through the plug. As the burner is turned toward the lower setting, less and less of this passageway is exposed to limit the gas flow into the burner from the manifold. This, too, provides an infinite heat arrangement into the burner.

While the valve itself is simple enough, the flow of the gas from the orifice through the mixing chamber to the burner is somewhat more complex. Primary air is admitted through a shutter near the orifice to mix with the gas on the way to the burner, and at the burner itself; the burner is designed to admit secondary air to make the flame more efficient and concentrated in the right places. The ad-justment of the air shutter is quite important. Yellowness in the flame indicates an excess of carbon, usually caused by a lack of sufficient air. On the other hand, a hard flame which may even pull away from the burner ports is caused by too much air. The best way to set it is to open the shutter as far as it will go, giving a hard flame. Then turn the shutter in until the flame has a definite blue cone but a soft border with no traces of yellow. This should be the most efficient operating position for the gas burner.

Even with the correct amounts of gas and air mixture flowing to the burner, there still must be something to ignite it. Common practice in the past has been to have one or two standing pilots with small tubes, called "zip tubes" or "flash tubes," leading from the pilot to the burner. At the burner there's a small orifice at the opening of the zip tube. When the gas is turned on, the gas-air mixture flows into the tube toward the pilot at the opposite end. Then the tube is ignited, the flame flashes back to the burner, and the burner is ignited almost instantaneously.

If the pilot fails to ignite, check the zip tube to be sure that it's in position. A pilot is properly adjusted when the top of the flame height is just at the middle of the tube, approximately $3/16$ of an inch.

The orifice limits the amount of gas which can flow to a burner. Orifices of gas burners are both fixed and adjustable. They're very important in determining the gas-air mixture and have to be sized correctly. Orifices can be plugged by dust, scale, or grease. You can clean them by blowing through them or by carefully reopening them with a round wooden toothpick.

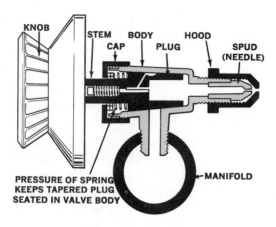

HOW GAS VALVES PROVIDE INFINITE HEAT CONTROL

By controlling the amount of gas which flows to a burner, the gas valve can control the heat output. The one shown in the drawing is one of the simplest and most common types of gas valves used on ranges.

The housing is threaded on the outlet end for an orifice or hood. The orifice shown here is adjustable; with the hood turned completely in toward the body, the output is correct for LP gas. As it is turned in the opposite direction, it can be adjusted for natural gas. The setting of such orifices should be checked with instruments for measuring the amount of gas flow to be sure that it complies with the nameplate rating.

On the opposite end of the body, threads hold a cap to retain the spring and plug in place. A stem on the plug extends through the cap and is provided with a flat surface for the knob.

The manifold is filled with gas from the supply. A bottom extension of the valve is threaded into the manifold. Here it's in the *off* position. *Courtesy Whirlpool Corp.*

This type of valve provides a positive *full on* setting. Other settings are obtainable by rotating the knob to expose more or less of the passage opening. In this manner, an infinite number of heats is available.

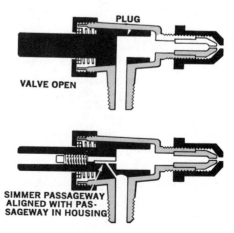

A small auxiliary passageway and an adjusting screw adjusts the *low-simmer* flame. From the *full-on* position, the flame decreases as the main passageway is closed, leaving only the simmer passageway to provide gas to the burner. *Courtesy Whirlpool Corp.*

Two types of orifices are used on gas-burner valves. Adjustable type shown here can be adjusted to vary gas output, allows use of natural L or LP fuel without replacing orifice. Fixed orifices should be removed with socket to avoid distortion of opening. Blow through orifice or use round wooden toothpick to clean it.

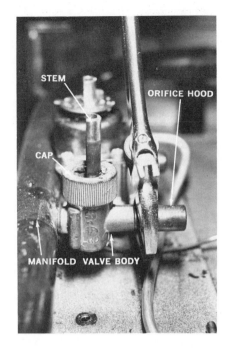

Air shutter adjustment is important for efficient operation of gas burners. Some slide and some turn, but they're always located near the orifice and their operation should be apparent.

Zip tube guides fuel from side tower orifice of burner to pilot when burner is turned on. When gas ignites, tube guides flame back to burner. In practice, ignition is almost instantaneous on properly adjusted burner.

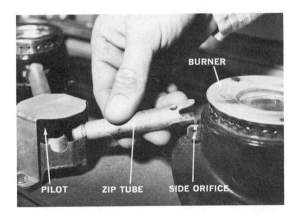

411

Many newer gas ranges incorporate an electronic capacitor discharge ignition. This has a small printed circuit board from which spark gaps or electrodes extend to the burners. When the burner switch is turned to the *light* position, arcing occurs at the spark gaps and the gas jet from the burner is ignited. When this arrangement is used, there is no pilot at the burner. Some ovens use this arrangement also; others use a glow coil for automatic lighting, and still others use a standing pilot. The advantage of the automatic ignition system is that no gas is being consumed when the appliance is not in use.

RULES FOR THE USE AND CARE OF A RANGE

- On electric ranges, cooking utensils should be essentially the same diameter as the top of the element used. The size of the unit is related to the size of the pan that goes on it and is *not* related to the speed at which it cooks.
- On gas ranges also, utensils of the proper size should be used and the flame adjusted so as not to extend beyond the utensil for best cooking results and proper safety precautions. Failure to follow this guideline increases the possibility of igniting clothing. Extreme care should be taken when wearing loose garments, particularly those with flowing sleeves.
- Make certain that gas or electrical installation is done by a competent technician and electric circuit is properly grounded.
- Use the ventilating hood at the beginning and throughout the cooking operation.

- Use cooking utensils which cook and heat quickly and evenly. Refer to the manufacturer's manual for suggestions. Smooth (ceramic) cooktops may require special cooking utensils.
- Use heat setting required for each particular food.
- Avoid blocking heated air circulation in oven when using aluminum foil. Do not cover any openings in the oven bottom and do not cover entire shelves.
- Make sure that range is level. If not, cakes will rise unevenly.
- To minimize spatters during broiling, use the broiler pan designed for that model's broiler—not disposable ones.
- Clean all ranges regularly for sanitary and safety reasons in accordance with manufacturer's instructions.
- Keep ventilating hoods and filters clean.
- Do not use oven or surface units for heating the home.
- Turn off surface units when cooking is finished or utensil is removed.
- Do not use oven door or range drawers as a step ladder or chair; be particularly careful that children don't climb on oven or range.
- Stand away from range when opening oven door and let hot air or steam escape before removing or placing food.
- Keep children away from oven door surfaces during cooking or self-cleaning operations.

OVEN AND CABINET

The oven and cabinet are critical parts in both electric and gas ranges. The correct amount of

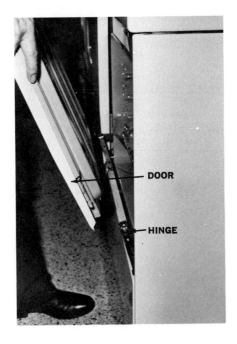

DOOR

HINGE

Removable door allows easy access to oven on many new free-standing ranges. Be sure that door is pushed completely back into position when reinstalling on range. Many hinges used with removable doors have a latch lever which must be unlocked before door can be removed.

insulation and the design of the oven tank itself determines to a large extent the cooking results that you can achieve with it.

One of the first things to check is that the oven is level. Place a level at least 12 inches long on the center oven rack. Level from front to back and from side to side by turning the threaded feet in or out.

Ventilation

Every oven has a vent which allows air to enter, usually around the door itself, and flow out an opening located near the top of the oven. The door vent is often incorporated into the door seal—it may appear as though part of the oven gasket is missing at the bottom of the door. The upper vent often exists directly under one of the rear surface units. This venti-

lation system must be clear before good baking results can be achieved. Check it at any time when you are investigating a complaint of unsatisfactory oven temperatures.

Door Seals

While this controlled air through the oven vent system is absolutely necessary for even heating and good baking results, too much air —or air entering and exiting at the wrong places—can have an adverse effect on baking qualities. If this occurs, the problem probably is caused by a poor door seal. The door should close firmly, but not smoothly; a cam is used to hold the door in the broil position in many ranges, to allow air to exit when broiling. You feel this as a "bump" when closing the door.

If the oven door isn't sealing evenly across

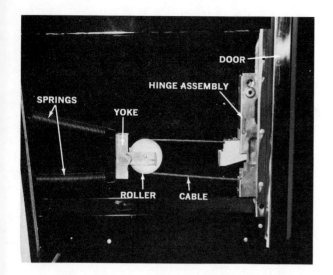

Built-in ovens and surface units are serviced much like free-standing ranges except they must be removed from cabinet for access to parts at rear. Door hinge assembly on this Frigidaire oven is easily reached by pulling forward. Note layout of spring mechanism.

its top surface, it will probably be necessary to align it. To do this, loosen the screws on the inner side of the oven door, then twist the door into position. Retightening the screws snugly (but not so tightly that the porcelain coating is chipped) will hold it in position. After the door is aligned, or if the door will not align properly, check the door spring tension. Look for the spring arrangement attached to the hinge. In older ranges, it is almost always on the sides of the oven cabinet or underneath beside the pull-out storage drawer. Sometimes it may be necessary to remove the range side panels to reach it. In many newer ovens, the springs may be inside the door. There are slots or holes provided to increase or decrease spring tension, which in turn will have the same effect upon the door when it is closed.

When adjusting a removable front door, be sure that it is in position before making any adjustments. Often the only problem is a latch which is not secured or a door pulled partially out of position. Pushing the door back in place should cure the problem.

If it is necessary to disassemble the door to reach the springs and the hinge mechanism, loosen the screws on the inside door panel. This will allow the outer panel to be removed. Be sure to note the exact placement of all insulation within the door. It may appear as though there are voids in the insulation, but this is often done to provide air flow through the door and actually keeps the surface cooler than it would be if packed with insulation. Be sure to keep insulation away from all moving parts of the hinges and cams. If it is necessary to use a lubricant on the hinge assembly, use that specified by the manufacturer. This will almost always be a special high-temperature type of lubricant.

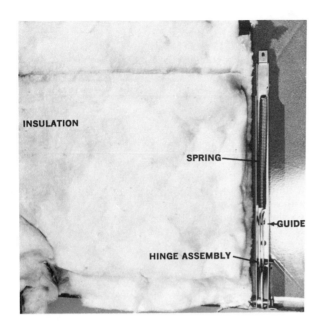

INSULATION

SPRING

GUIDE

HINGE ASSEMBLY

Some door-spring assemblies are located within the door. After removing screws on inner door panel, outer panel is free and spring assembly is accessible. Don't let insulation get into hinge mechanism when reassembling. Note that outer end of door is not insulated to allow air flow. Insulating this cavity can actually increase door temperatures.

Door gets its rigidity from inside panel. If adjustment is required for proper sealing, loosen screws slightly, twist door gently to desired position, then tighten screws snugly but not so tight that they can chop porcelain coating.

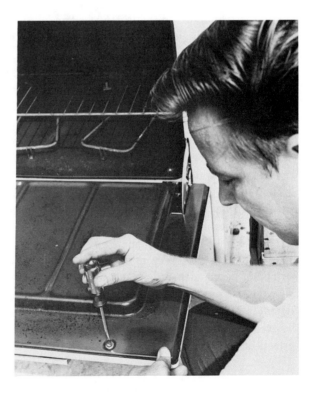

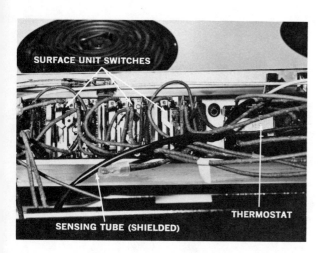

SURFACE UNIT SWITCHES

SENSING TUBE (SHIELDED)

THERMOSTAT

Console of this free-standing range is tilted forward to service switches. When replacing infinite heat switches, be sure that the same power supply line goes to all *L1* terminals and the opposite supply line to all *L2* terminals. With some switches, interchanging them can result in a short circuit. Note protective plastic shield covering thermostat sensing tube. This prevents damaging tube if it should come in contact with an electrical terminal. If tube doesn't have a shield, wrap it with electrical tape wherever there's a possibility of touching. Unplug range before removing panel.

The Thermostat

The thermostat which controls oven temperature is usually located with the other switches, but close examination will reveal a sensing tube leaving the thermostat switch and entering the oven compartment, where clips support it near the side or back. It is important that this tube not touch the side of the tank; otherwise erratic temperatures will result. (Be sure power is off before removing access panels.)

The tube is filled with a liquid or gas that expands when it is heated and contracts when it is cold. A mechanism much like the one used on a refrigerator causes a snap-action movement of the contacts, preventing arcing and burning of the contact section. Of course, this linkage is arranged in reverse of that in a refrigerator. When temperature drops, it turns the element on; when temperature rises, it turns it off.

Check Utensils

If baking results aren't up to par, check the utensils being used before proceeding. Modern ovens depend upon the reflected heat from pans and sheets to obtain the desired result, and a variation here can make a tremendous difference in the way that baked goods turn out. Review the owner's manual to see that the proper material and color of material is being used. As an example, a shiny aluminum sheet won't substitute when a dark tin sheet is called for; the shiny one won't retain much heat, and the bottom of a pie might not be done while the top may be burned. The reverse is also true if a shiny utensil is called for. As a rule, these guidelines will apply: for biscuits, cookies, or cakes an aluminum pan usually gives the most even browning. For pies, darkened tin, anodized aluminum, or stainless steel give good results. If you use ovenproof glass, reduce the oven temperature 25 degrees, since glass bakes

Bake unit can be removed after loosening retaining screws. (Be sure power has been turned off.) Unit will then pull forward sufficiently to loosen connecting wires.

Broil element is viewed from rear in this photograph. It can be tested in place after removing one lead, using VOM on $R \times 1$ scale. If it has to be replaced, it must be removed from front like bake unit in previous photo.

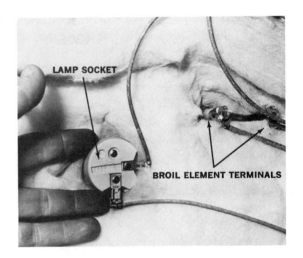

LAMP SOCKET

BROIL ELEMENT TERMINALS

faster than shiny metal pans.

Also check the method of pan placement in the oven. When baking on one rack, locate it near the center of the oven. When several racks are used, try to arrange the pan so that they are not directly over each other. Be sure to leave at least 1½ inches between the pan and the side of the oven. Never cover a rack completely with foil, and don't use it on the oven bottom unless the manufacturer recommends it.

Though it may not appear that this is related to appliance servicing, the fact is that too many thermostats are recalibrated (even by service technicians) for situations caused by a simple change in the owner's baking habits or utensils. It is important to avoid such a mistake by taking time to determine whether a baking problem is caused by something other than a malfunction in the range itself.

Calibrating the Thermostat

If you have determined that the temperature has indeed strayed from its proper setting, it can be compensated for by calibrating the thermostat. The secret to oven calibration is in the technique you use in obtaining your readings. Begin with an oven thermometer of known accuracy. This may be one purchased at a department store or appliance store for a few dollars, but be sure that it is accurate by comparing it against the settings of at least two other ranges or by placing it in boiling water and checking to see that it registers approximately 212 degrees.

To check the temperature of your oven, place the thermometer as near the center of the oven as possible, and turn the oven control to 375 degrees. *Wait at least twenty minutes before taking a reading.* The temperature often

"overshoots" at first, then settles down to a more stable level. If much variation is noted as the thermostat cycles, take an average of the high and low readings. Most manufacturers don't recommend calibration if the temperature is within 25 degrees of that indicated on the knob.

To adjust the thermostat, look for a screw on the thermostat body or knob marked "increase" or "decrease" with an arrow. This might be located under the knob (which on most ranges simply pulls forward), but in some cases it is necessary to remove the two front retaining screws. Be sure that power is turned off before attempting calibration. On several thermostat arrangements, temperature adjustments are possible simply by moving a retainer on the back side of the knob. On yet another variation, the calibration screw is located in the middle of the thermostat adjusting shaft, the one where the knob attaches. To reach it, simply remove the knob and look closely within the center of the shaft. This one will usually be unmarked, but move it one-quarter turn in either direction and check to see if you have raised or lowered the temperature. If you went the wrong way, it's easy to return to the

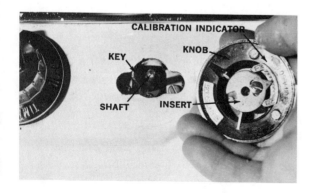

Thermostat calibration on this GE unit is adjusted by loosening insert at rear of knob. Major adjustment must be made by loosening shaft and positioning key.

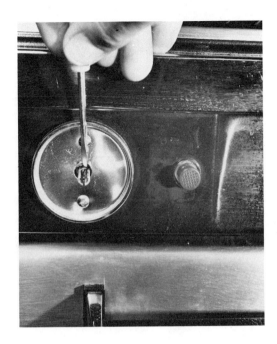

This thermostat is calibrated by turning tiny screw in center of hollow shaft, accessible when knob is removed. Check calibration after each quarter turn.

starting position and begin anew. If the adjustment wanders again shortly after calibration, or if the thermostat fails to respond to calibration procedures, the only recourse is to replace it.

Checking Heating Elements

Be sure to test heating elements for grounds when checking for continuity with the VOM. When an element fails, always find the cause. Often it is improper usage. Attempts to heat the kitchen with the range, pans which don't fit squarely on the element, and foil wrapped over the surface-unit drip pans without leaving an opening in the bottom all lead to overheating and premature failure. The last practice can also lead to poor baking results by blocking the free flow of air from the upper oven vent. Since these problems will result in

greatly increased service expense, it's wise to look for them at any time that an element fails.

When replacing an element, be sure that all connections are clean. Solder as well as crimp any replacement terminals because of the high current load. Tighten all connections securely, and use only high-temperature wiring for replacement purposes.

The Timer

Most ranges use a timer to make the oven capable of turning itself on and off at predetermined intervals. Many range owners never use their timer, yet it can be at fault when a "no heat" problem arises with an oven. The oven circuit passes through the contacts of the timer when the oven is in operation, unless the range has a "timed bake" setting which isolates the timer in other positions. If the timer contacts

Terminals in receptacle can be serviced by removing one screw when plug-in units are used. Solder and crimp terminals to wire when they must be replaced.

Components are visible in this rear view of timer. Motor and switch contacts can be replaced as component parts in many timers.

should fail, the oven won't operate. A resistance test with the $R \times 1$ scale of the VOM should quickly pinpoint the trouble. If the contacts are burned, many timers have component parts available and only the switch section would have to be replaced.

Many times an "oven won't heat" complaint is timer related but there is nothing at fault. Most timers have a *manual* or *on* position indicated. Unless the oven is being operated on a *timed* setting, the timer should always be in this position. It's easy, however, to move the set knob from the manual position when cleaning the range. Check this out.

While the fuses for electric ranges are usually part of the household circuit, the accessory circuits (lights, receptacles) must be fused within the range. The timer is also often connected to this circuit. When any of these circuits don't operate, check the range fuse or circuit breaker. The small "minibreakers" used on ranges are usually on the front panel, easily visible; to find the fuse, however, you

may have to look under the rear burners or inside the storage drawer door. When replacing the fuse, be sure to use one of the correct size (usually 15 amps) and tighten it firmly in its shell.

Since two fuses protect the 230-volt circuit to an electric range, it is capable of pulling the same stunt as an electric clothes dryer. If *one* of the two fuses blows, the range lights and clock would work normally. The surface units wouldn't work at all, unless the five or seven-

Accessory fuses are sometimes completely hidden, other times very obvious. The one in photo at left is located under the cook top. It's viewed from rear of range with servicing panel removed. Fuse in photo below is located on control panel. Well marked, it's easily accessible by pulling cover forward and turning.

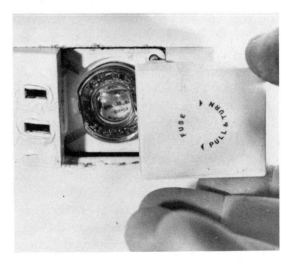

Many ranges now use "mini-breakers" rather than fuses to control accessory circuits. This combination has breaker, receptacle, and oven light switch grouped together in front.

position switch was used; the circuitry might then allow the units to heat on low settings. The oven would not work at all. It's a confusing condition since part of the range is operative thanks to the multiple circuits in the power supply. Don't let this one throw you.

CERAMIC COOKTOPS

Many top-quality ranges now have ceramic cooktops. They have become popular because of their clean appearance and the lack of cavities to entrap food particles. On the other hand, they present their own set of problems.

They are made of a special crystalline material which can be broken by the impact of a heavy object, so care should be exercised not to store such objects above the cooktop. Newer versions of this product change color when hot to provide a built-in warning system, and most are equipped with pilot lights as well.

While the greatest appeal of the ceramic cooktop is its clean look, cleaning is the biggest problem. To prevent staining, the surface should be cleaned daily by sprinkling baking soda onto the soiled areas and scrubbing with a moistened towel or sponge. Residues from burnt food spills can be removed with soda and rubbing with a soap pad, rinsing afterward to remove soap. Liquid dishwashing detergents may be used for light surface soil, but should be rinsed and wiped away completely to prevent discoloration.

For light stains, apply a cleanser such as Comet and rub with a moistened sponge or towel, then remove thoroughly before cleaning. An overnight treatment of cold chlorine bleach can be used for light-moderate stains, using no more than two teaspoonsful on the stained area, then covering it with oven-bag baking material and allowing it to soak without heat. For more persistent stains, one of the oxalic acid-base cleansers can be used following manufacturer's instructions, but with care.

Elements for ceramic cooktops are located under the panels and are serviced by raising the top. Use extreme care when working around the fragile material. Some ceramic tops use switches with sensing bulbs much like

Ceramic cooktop demands care to maintain clean appearance. Be sure that bottoms of utensils are clean before placing on cooktop, then clean cooking surface daily to preserve appearance.

those used to control the oven. Be sure they are repositioned perfectly before securing the top in place.

The other new appliance on the scene is the induction cooktop. The basic principle is simple, but controls and refinements become quite complex. A "power pack" converts line current to a 30–32 kilohertz pulsating DC power supply. When this is passed through a "work coil" located directly beneath a smooth glass cooktop, a strong magnetic current is induced above the coil. When a pan or utensil made of any ferrous material such as cast iron or steel is placed within this field, it acts like a shorted secondary winding on a transformer and it heats. The heat level is controlled by electronic controls. The advantages? It's fast, comparing favorably with the gas burner, it's responsive, and it's safe—the only heat on the cooktop surface is that transferred to it by the pan.

MICROWAVE OVENS

The other new development is strictly "hands off" at this state of the art. Microwave ovens require delicate, expensive instruments to test for leakage after any servicing operation.

Don't let anyone tamper with a microwave unit unless he has such equipment and is trained to use it.

Microwave ovens use electromagnetic radiation to cook the foods rather than thermal radiation, the principle best illustrated by the standard heating element. The frequency of the magnetron in the microwave oven is such that it causes the molecules of the food to tend to align themselves with the constantly changing field some 2,450 million times per second. The constant, rapid movement causes the food to heat.

Of course, there is concern for leakage of this energy from the cabinet of the range, hence the large number of safety devices built into the equipment and the required testing procedures. With the ever-increasing popular-

ity of the units and their wide availability in every style from compact portables to over-under ranges and even combination units combining microwave and conventional cooking in a standard-size oven, the servicing procedures and safety precautions have become strictly defined. Most of that work must be done by a technician; however, routine maintenance falls into your domain and is the best safeguard against expensive professional repairs.

The jobs that you can do include cleaning the filters, if present, and replacing lamps. These procedures should be clearly outlined in your owners manual—refer to it before attempting either job. Keep the interior of the oven, and especially the area where the gaskets seal around the door frame, free of spills and food deposits. Be certain that you don't close

It looks like a conventional range, but inside Tappan's Convectionaire Range a blower (inset) forces air over a special heating element, then channels it down over foods from vents located in top of oven. Air movement decreases cooking time and results in better browning.

Whirlpool eye-level microwave range offers speed and efficiency of microwave plus convenience of full-size self-cleaning lower oven. Fold-down cooktop cover gives extra workspace when surface units are not in use.

the door on any object, even paper—it can allow microwave energy leakage during cooking and possibly damage the door seals. Follow the manufacturer's instructions specifically concerning the type and position of utensils within the oven cavity.

In any event, call a pro if your microwave comes on at any time that the door is open; if the door does not appear to seal properly; if the door seal becomes damaged or broken in any way, or if any other malfunction occurs.

CONVECTION OVENS

Convection ovens are available in countertop, freestanding, and built-in models. They use a different air-flow system to help overcome the

"layering" of air patterns that occurs in a conventional oven. A motorized fan is used to circulate heated air from the element compartment into the oven and around the food, in much the same manner that a frostless refrigerator circulates the cold air in the food compartments. The more consistent heat patterns in the convection oven speed up cooking times by 30 to 50 percent.

Servicing procedures are much like a conventional oven except that the elements are usually located behind a divider plate and may not be visible until that plate is removed. The fan is energized whenever the oven is on. If it fails to operate, it can be checked for continuity with the VOM set to $R \times 1$, and should also be checked manually to be sure that the motor shaft is not binding. The fan motor should only be replaced with the manufacturer's correct part.

RULES FOR THE USE AND CARE OF AN ELECTRONIC OVEN

- Use cooking utensils made only from recommended materials. Do not use metal or aluminum foil, unless otherwise directed by the manufacturer.
- Always check the filter below the oven prior to use. Soiled or greasy filters can prevent

air from cooling the magnetron tube, which may stop operation.

- Never operate the oven without the filter in place.
- Do not operate the microwave oven with the door open. If, by chance, the oven operates when the door is open—call a service technician at once.
- Avoid any possible microwave loss or exposure. Never place anything between oven frame and door such as paper or cloth.
- Do not allow soil to build up on door seal, door surface or oven frame. Follow specific cleaning instructions.

QUICK-CHECK CHART FOR

RANGES

Causes apply to both electric (E) and gas (G) ranges unless indicated

Symptom	Possible Cause	Remedy
Won't heat at all— lights, timer don't operate	Fuse blown or breaker tripped	Check with VOM on R × 1 scale, replace fuse or reset breaker
	Broken wire or connector	Check at entrance of range cord. Check terminal block
	Gas supply turned off (G)	Check other gas appliances to see if they are operating
Won't heat at all— lights, timer operate okay	One fuse blown (E)	Check with VOM on R × 1 scale, replace fuse
	Gas supply turned off	Check other appliances to see if they are operating
Heats on low heat settings only (range has five position type switch arrangement) [E]	One fuse blown	Check with VOM on R × 1
	Broken wire or connector	Check at entrance of range cord and terminal block

RANGES *(cont.)*

Causes apply to both electric (E) and gas (G) ranges unless indicated

Symptom	Possible Cause	Remedy
Oven won't heat	Timer switch set to open position	Check and set properly
	Timer switch section open	Check with VOM on R × 1 with timer set to energize range circuit. Replace or repair contacts if pitted or defective
	Oven selector switch open	Check with VOM on R × 1 scale in each position of switch. Replace if defective
	Oven thermostat open	Check with VOM on R × 1 scale. Visually check condition of sensing tube
	Heating element open (E)	Check with VOM on R × 1 for continuity, on R × 1000 or higher for grounds. Replace if open or grounded. Clean wiring connections thoroughly
	Pilot or igniter not operative (G)	Check pilot and relight. Test igniter and transformer with VOM on R × 100 scale
	Wiring to element or gas valve broken	Check with VOM on R × 1, replace if broken. Use heat-resistant wire, clean connections thoroughly
	Open solenoid or thermal element on valve (G)	Check with VOM on R × 100 for continuity
Surface units won't heat — oven okay	Power supply to switches open (E)	Inspect and test L1 and L2 leads to switches with VOM
	Pilot flame out (G)	Relight and check adjustment of pilot flame and gas-air mixture to burner
	Zip tubes out of position (G)	Check to see that all parts are positioned properly
Individual surface units won't heat	Poor connection at burner receptacle (E)	Check to see that burner is in position
	Open switch	Check with VOM on R × 1, replace if open
	Open heating element (E)	Check with VOM on R × 1 for continuity, on R × 1000 for grounds. Replace if open or grounded
	Zip tube out of position (G)	Check to see that tubes are positioned properly

Chart cont. on next page.

RANGES *(cont.)*

Causes apply to both electric (E) and gas (G) ranges unless indicated

Symptom	Possible Cause	Remedy
Pilot goes out (G)	Overfired burner	Adjust air (see text)
	Improperly adjusted pilot	Adjust pilot flame to middle of zip tube
Oven not performing correctly	Improper utensils	Check owners manual
	Rack covered with foil	Remove foil
	Thermostat not calibrated	Check and calibrate (see text)
	Restricted vent flue	Check to see that vent passage-ways are clear
	Oven bottom not in position	See that all parts are in place

24
Repairing Self-Cleaning Ovens

Self-cleaning ovens are of two types—catalytic and pyrolytic. Catalytic ovens clean continuously while being used. A specially finished liner, rough in texture and dark in color, allows many food soils to decompose at normal cooking temperatures. Pyrolytic self-cleaners use intense heat to burn away the hardened grease spills and spatters, and the housewife decides when the cleaning job is necessary. Temperatures around 825 to 900 degrees and a controlled amount of air slowly burn away food soils. Smoke and odors are ventilated through a platinum-palladium screen that serves as a catalytic "afterburner." Both catalytic and pyrolytic ovens are made in your choice of gas or electric models.

Do they really work? Very well indeed—provided you don't expect them to do more than they were designed to do. In the catalytic system, the coating is fragile and must be handled with care—scratching reduces the catalyst's effectiveness. Major spills must be wiped away as they occur, or the catalytic coating might become smothered and ineffective. Sur-

faces that aren't treated—racks, windows, and often door liners—must be cleaned as usual. Since there's little to go wrong with catalytic cleaning systems, and their basic construction is the same as for other ranges, we won't treat them further.

Pyrolytic ovens have advantages over the catalytics. Their intense heat reaches all surfaces exposed to cooking spatters and greases—including racks and door glass. No supplementary cleaning should be required.

On the other hand, pyrolytic ovens require a complex control system and electrical circuitry to carry out their cleaning function. A locking mechanism is necessary to make cleaning a "no go" proposition if the door isn't securely latched—and it's impossible to unlock it until temperatures reach a normal level after cleaning.

As you can see, pyrolytics have a greater potential for trouble than standard ranges—there are more components and circuits involved. But before we consider their possible problems, let's review the costs involved in buying and using a range so equipped.

The initial cost of a range with pyrolytic oven may be anywhere from $70 to $150 more than a comparable range without a self-cleaning oven. But for this money you're getting more than the self-clean feature. You also get thicker, denser insulation, a special porcelain finish, better door sealing, and five to seven times as much chrome plating on racks.

A typical clean cycle can use from ten to twenty cents worth of electricity or gas per cleaning, depending on the length of the cycle and the rates prevailing in your area. On a cost basis, this compares very favorably with commercial chemical cleaners. Also, the lower heat loss during normal operation actually *reduces* operating costs as a whole in many cases.

Two facts must be emphasized about the cleaning operation. First of all, no cleaning can occur at temperatures below 750 degrees —and even at this temperature it's a slow process. Most self-cleaners operate within a range of 825 to 900 degrees F. Secondly, cleaning is equally dependent upon time. The correct amount of time depends upon the amount and types of soil in the oven. The burning, or oxidation, is purposely carried out slowly by the controlled application of heat and oxygen. One and a half hours is a minimum time required to complete the process, and that under light soil conditions.

With these basic operational factors in mind, you're ready to take a look at a malfunctioning pyrolytic oven. Remember that the appliance sleuth always applies the old rule of "Stop, look, and listen" before all else.

Oven door must be latched before cleaning cycle is initiated. In locked position latch finger protrudes through oven throat and engages oven door. Latch won't release until oven temperatures have cooled.

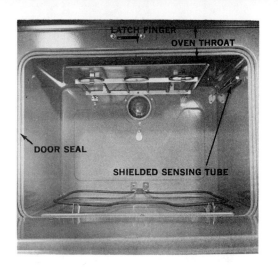

Visible differences between cavity of standard and self-cleaning oven include latch finger which locks door during cleaning, thicker oven throat to accommodate more insulation, fiberglass or heavy-duty door seal, and heavily shielded or solid-state temperature sensors.

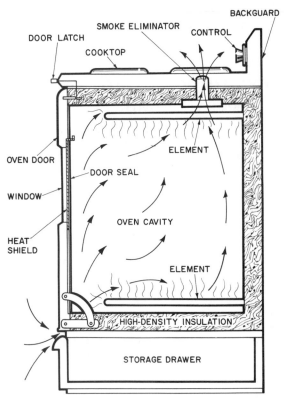

HOW AIR FLOW CARRIES SMOKE FROM OVEN

Typical air flow pattern while self-cleaning oven is in operation is illustrated here. Air enters at "gap" in door seal at bottom of door. Convection currents produced by oven heat carry it upwards until it is expelled through the smoke eliminator. If oven has window in door, heat shield must be in closed position before clean cycle may be initiated.

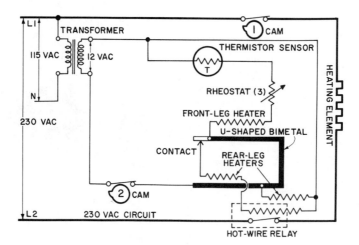

WIRING DIAGRAM OF A SELF-CLEANING OVEN
(SOLID-STATE CONTROLS)

This control, similar to one widely used for automatic surface units, was adapted for use in self-cleaning ovens because of its ability to withstand high temperatures. As shown in the diagram, when the control dial rheostat (**3**) is set to any baking temperature, the internal cam-operated contacts (**1**) and (**2**) close, completing the circuits from line 1 to the heating element and from the step-down transformer to the low-voltage circuitry. At the same time, a certain control resistance is set up through the rheostat which is dependent upon dial setting (**3**). A complete 12-volt circuit is established from the transformer through the sensor, the rheostat, the bimetal heaters and the hot-wire relay. The hot-wire relay is a device which uses a taut wire to hold a set of contacts apart. When voltage is applied to the wire, however, it becomes hot and expands, allowing the contacts to close and completing the 230-volt circuit from line 2 to the oven heating element. (You may detect a slight time lag while the relay is closing.)

Because of the U shape of the bimetal switch, the heaters on the back and front legs tend to oppose each other in trying to keep the normally closed contacts closed. The sensor, in series with the rheostat and the front leg heater, is actually a thermistor which changes its electrical resistance in proportion to temperature. As it becomes warmer, its resistance increases, reducing the current to the front leg heater, allowing it to cool slightly. In time, the hotter rear leg heaters overcome the force and break the contact.

This de-energizes the hot-wire relay and the rear-leg heater in series with it. As the relay cools, its contact opens and the heating-element circuit is broken. With the rear-leg heater off, the heater on the front leg quickly recloses the contacts and recycles the unit. Since the sensor is continuing to become hotter and thus offers more resistance, the front-leg heater becomes progressively less effective, and this unit cycling sequence eventually balances out to maintain indicated dial temperature.

DIAGNOSING SOIL

In the case of malfunctioning self-cleaning ovens, there is always a formidable clue which points you down the correct path of diagnosing the problem. That clue is the condition of the soil that remains in the oven. To diagnose food soils, simply apply what you know about pyrolytic ovens to what you see. If the food soil is brown and soft, possibly baked on, but still feeling greasy when you wipe your finger across it, it's a sign that no heat or only bake heat came on during the cleaning cycle. The soil would appear just as it did after normal usage. Check timer and control settings, and try again before condemning a component. Also check fuses in house and separate fuses for the oven circuitry contained in some model ranges. To find these, go back to your owner's manual for details, or contact a dealer giving the full model number.

If the soil is dark brown and hard, possibly appearing as black varnish, it's a sign that the oven wasn't hot enough during the clean cycle. Again, check the control setting. A selector or latch not turned *completely* to the clean position can cause this problem. Other possibilities are a torn door seal, a miscalibrated or faulty control, or an open element.

If the oven is partially cleaned, leaving no doubt that some cleaning has taken place but with some spots or areas not fully clean, you can generally assume that the oven reached cleaning temperatures but didn't stay there long enough. It's likely that the timer wasn't set to allow enough time to clean heavy soils. Try a longer cycle, and this will likely remedy the problem. Other possible causes are an open element or a poor door seal.

Now that you've made observations, you have a definite direction to follow in checking the components—if indeed you haven't already solved the problem. But by now you should have eliminated many components as being the culprit, and the field is narrowed down. Be sure to unplug the range before removing access panels or attempting servicing procedures.

TEMPERATURE CONTROLS

Two basic types of oven temperature controls are used. One is a solid-state control. Other thermostats may appear to be much the same as the liquid-filled bellows type used in ordinary ranges, but they're more complex. Their sensing tubes are heavy-duty or are wrapped in copper to shield them from high temperatures. These dual-range thermostats (DRT's) often contain several sections with several sets of contacts. For instance, one contact set may control the bake element in *bake,* the broil element during *broil,* and both elements during *clean*—at different temperature levels. Consult the wiring diagram to isolate the contacts to be tested.

Handle these controls with care. They are delicate and critical components, and in addition, the capillary tubes and sensing bulbs are easily broken. Use rubber gloves when handling them and avoid bending them repeatedly. After handling a broken capillary, wipe your hands with a *dry* towel and wash with soap and water immediately. Capillary bulbs on some temperature controls contain sodium and potassium hydroxide (lye). Helium is also used as an expansion agent in high temperature controls.

The thermal element of a typical bellows-type thermostat consists of a bulb and a metal diaphragm connected by a capillary tube. This is a sealed system filled with a liquid (or sometimes gaseous) substance. The sensing bulb is located in the oven at a point determined by the manufacturer. As the bulb is heated, the liquid or gas throughout the thermal element system expands, causing an increase in pressure on the diaphragm or bellows. This actuates a switch through a mechanical linkage that provides snap-action, necessary to reduce arcing of contacts. Self-cleaning gas ranges normally use the same control as the electric ranges, with electrical solenoids opening and closing gas valves. In standard gas ranges with mechanical thermostats, the movement of the diaphragm would move a valve disc towards the seat (in the closed position).

It's easy to see that the placement of the capillary has a direct effect upon oven temperature. Be sure that it is firmly in place in the clips or brackets provided. A tube touching an oven liner gives erratic readings and sluggish operation. Sharp bends in capillary tubing can prevent transmission of pressure change to the diaphragm. To calibrate the oven thermostat, follow the same general procedures that you would for a standard oven—but be certain that you turn the *bake* calibration screw and not the *clean* adjusting screw. Remove the knob from the front panel and locate the calibration adjusting screw *for the bake cycle*. If it's not readily apparent, look within the center of the control shaft or look for a movable skirt on the knob itself. You'll probably see an arrow marked *increase* and pointing in a clockwise or counterclockwise direction, indicating the direction you should turn to increase or decrease temperature. Proceed to adjust the temperature following the same general guidelines given for standard ovens in the preceding chapter.

Remember that some self-cleaning oven controls have separate calibration adjustments for the *clean* temperature. Normally, this never requires adjustment. If you suspect that

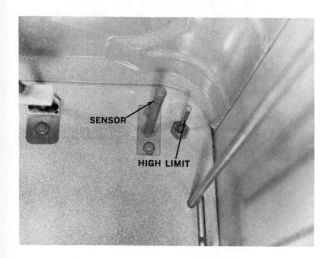

Solid-state oven controls have unique appearance. Sensor changes resistance with temperature change and controls bake cycle. High-limit control works during clean cycle.

Responder incorporates hot-wire relay in piggyback fashion. When low voltage current is applied, the thin wires, indicated by pencil, become very hot, expanding and allowing normally open contacts to close.

Relay is shown removed from responder body. Pencil indicates contacts, and taut wires are clearly visible. During clean cycle, relay is energized by high limit to cycle elements.

your oven system is not reaching cleaning temperatures, you can obtain a special temperature-indicating pellet from appliance parts distributors. It should be placed on a folded piece of aluminum foil in the center of the oven. If it melts during the cleaning process, the oven temperature has exceeded 800 degrees F. If adjustment is necessary, move the adjusting screw only about ⅛ turn at a time, then retest. A slight movement can make about 25 degrees difference in temperature levels.

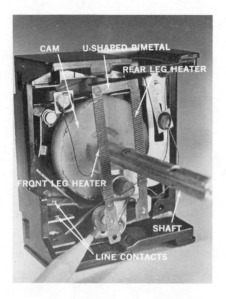

Control circuit to hot-wire relay during bake cycle is regulated by responder circuitry. Line switch contacts are indicated. Pencil indicates contacts of U-shaped bimetal, which are controlled by rear leg and front leg heaters. Cam actuates line switches and determines resistance of rheostat, which is under cam.

Sensor is tested with VOM on lowest resistance scale. At room temperature, resistance of most sensors should be about 18 ohms. Consult an authorized service department for exact specifications if in doubt. If sensor is open, elements won't be energized. If sensor is shorted, elements won't turn off. High limit is tested in the same manner but should indicate zero ohms resistance at room temperature.

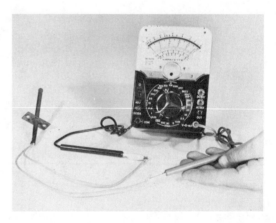

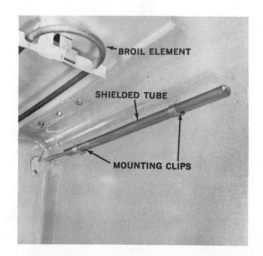

Sensing bulb of thermostatic control is well shielded in self-cleaners to give accurate calibration and protection from heat. Bulb should always be securely fastened in mounting clips in proper position.

Rear view of this control shows mechanism which prevents accidental engagement of clean cycle. Fork, indicated by pencil, moves with control knob. At broil or high temperature positions fork touches stop. To engage clean cycle, knob must be depressed to allow fork to straddle the stop and lock over it.

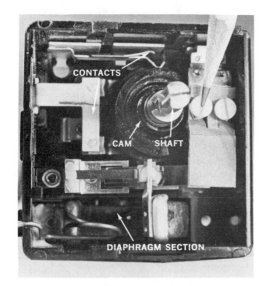

Numerous contacts in this control body regulate oven operation in various cycles. Diaphragm moves with temperature changes and cycles elements on and off. Position of cam, turned manually by knob, determines which contacts are actuated. Calibration screw, indicated by pencil, adjusts bake temperature. Other screw adjusts clean temperature; never try to raise this beyond factory setting.

Hot-wire relay in this oven is a separate component. Thermostat doesn't control element in oven; it controls only the small heater on this relay while heavier relay contacts cycle heating element. This arrangement prolongs thermostat life by reducing current through thermostat contacts.

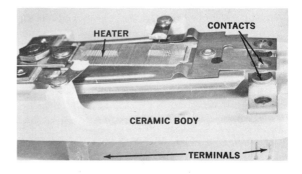

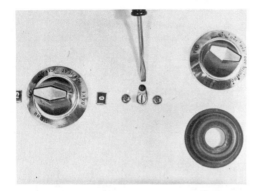

Bake temperature is easily calibrated on this responder by removing control knob and rubber splash shield, then turning adjustment screw in center of shaft. Two Phillips screws hold switch in position.

SELECTOR SWITCHES

These control circuitry in various selections after being manually set by the user. The wiring diagram is necessary to pinpoint the circuits involved. Check individual contacts for continuity with a volt-ohm meter. It might be helpful to know that I've observed that the selector switch often is blamed for many ills in self-cleaning ovens, but it seldom turns out to be the real culprit.

TIMERS

These are basically the same as standard oven timers with the addition of one or two sets of contacts. A clock mechanism mechanically activates the switches, depending upon the setting prescribed by the user. These contacts are often exposed, making visual inspection simple. Again, the timer is seldom the offender. On some models it disconnects a rear surface unit during clean cycles.

Some new models use digital electronic timers to control oven functions. On these systems, the timer energizes a separate relay rather than a self-contained switch like that in the mechanical timer. The relay coil can be checked for continuity with the VOM set to the $R \times 100$ position; switch contacts are tested on the $R \times 1$ scale.

LATCHING MECHANISMS

Self-cleaning ovens are fitted with a latching device to lock the door when temperatures rise above 600 degrees. This latch keeps the door locked until the oven has cooled down after cleaning. It's a safety device. You should *never* override or disconnect it.

But sometimes the latch may not close completely, and an electrical interlock prevents the range from going to *clean* temperatures unless the door is secured. Or worse, perhaps the door won't unlock at all. Before you remedy the problem, you must determine if the latch is mechanical (with a lever that you move manually to lock the door) or electrical (locks automatically when switch is turned to clean position).

When the lock handle of a mechanical latch is moved to *lock,* a latch finger moves from the top oven frame. The latch finger engages a slot in the top inner face of the oven door, pulling the door and fiberglass seal against the oven front frame and sealing the door. The latch mechanism and lock switch are accessible by removing the handle knob and raising the range top. The latch switch serves two purposes. At about 575 to 600 degrees, a bimetal moves a lock pin within the latching mechanism and effectively "jams" it. The lever can't be moved again until temperatures subside. At the same time a set of contacts close within the switch and turn on the *Locked* indicator light. Since the latch switch operates by conducted heat, it must make good contact with the top of the oven liner when it's replaced or repaired. With this type of latch, an actuating rod extends from the handle through the rear of the range, actuating interlock switches which insure that the range is in the *Locked* position before cleaning circuitry is energized. These switches are serviceable from the back

of the range. Elongated mounting holes allow adjustment of the switches.

General Electric ranges incorporate an electrical solenoid into the mechanism which must be energized by a pushbutton switch before the handle can be moved. At temperatures above 550 degrees, a thermal switch completes circuitry to the *Lock* light and the solenoid is inoperative even though the latch release button is depressed. The thermal switch closes, restoring the circuit to the solenoid, when temperatures are down to normal levels.

Other electrical latch systems have no latch handles. A latch finger engages a slot in the oven door just as it does in the mechanical latch, except that a rotisserie-like motor operates the latch finger through a rod linkage. This motor, located in the rear of the range, turns a cam that connects to the latch rod. The cam also actuates two switches, which act as limit switches for the motor, stopping it at the correct positions and providing circuitry to the lock light and oven temperature control.

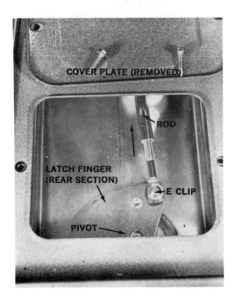

On this automatic electric latch, latch finger moves on pivot when motor-driven rod moves toward rear of range as indicated by arrow. Adjustment of latch finger is accomplished by removing E clip and turning threaded portion of rod. In case the mechanism malfunctions, the finger may be released by removing clip *after oven has cooled.* Pivot is accessible after removing cover plate.

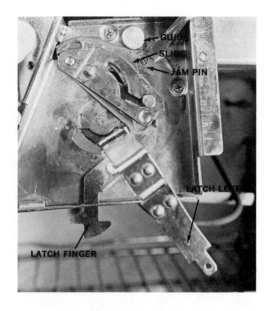

This mechanical latch mechanism engages door when latch lever is moved to *locked* position as shown. Jam pin is attached to bimetallic disk; it raises and jams mechanism in *locked* position as temperatures pass 550-degree mark. Pin should be .015 inch below surface of bracket at room temperatures. Be sure that bimetal on underside has good contact with top of oven body and that no insulation separates the two surfaces.

Close-up of mechanical latch mechanism in *jammed* position. Note that slotted upper portion of jam pin is now above surface of bracket, preventing any movement of the mechanism which must move across top of pin to unlatch door.

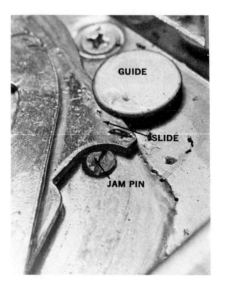

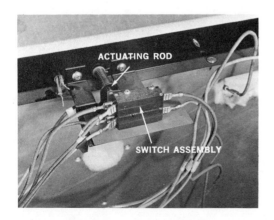

Mechanical latch also has interlock switches to control clean cycle. Spring-loaded rod from latch mechanism actuates switch assembly. Be sure the range is unplugged before exposing wiring connections.

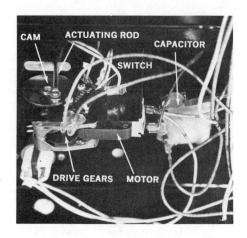

Actuating mechanism of electric latch is this rotisserie-like motor mounted at rear of range. Motor-driven cam moves latch finger and actuating rod, and activates switches. Switch acts as a limit to start and stop motor at correct position, also completes the circuit to controls to prevent use of clean cycle unless door is latched. Door switch must be closed before motor will operate.

Latch-limit switches are easily tested for continuity by removing lead, connecting VOM to terminals, and actuating plunger manually. Cam may also be rotated manually to check adjustment of switches. Meter should read zero ohms resistance with contacts closed.

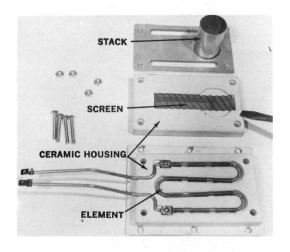

Element of powered smoke eliminator may be tested without disassembling, using lowest resistance scale and testing at leads from terminals. Platinum-palladium screen is shown. Stack at top of picture sits atop ceramic block and forms oven vent when in place.

SMOKE ELIMINATOR

Naturally, when food soils are burned away in the oven some smoke and odor must be present—an objectionable factor if something isn't added to remedy it. That something is an inconel screen which is coated with platinum and palladium and then oxidized. It's called the smoke eliminator. The coated screen acts as a catalyst which causes smoke to burn at lower temperatures.

Some manufacturers simply place the screen in the oven vent at the top of the oven. Others use an enclosed sheath type element or an open element encased in ceramic surrounding the platinum-palladium screen, giving an "afterburner" effect. These work amazingly well, but it is possible to overload them with heavy soils and greases with resultant smoking —another good reason for removing major spillovers before cleaning.

HEATING ELEMENTS

Heating elements, like other components on pyrolytic self-cleaning ovens, are heavy duty and heat resistant. Temperature must be brought up slowly to insure complete soil oxi-

dation. In some units, cycling switches are employed to continuously cycle the units at about 50 percent *on* time during cleaning. Cycle switches are located beneath the service panel and are connected in series with the heating elements. They are similar in appearance to "infinite-heat" type surface unit controls but are nonadjustable and must be replaced if faulty. Since the cycling rate depends upon the wattage of the element, be sure to replace with the *exact* switch specified for your range.

Another method is to connect the upper and lower heating elements in series during cleaning, dividing the voltage between them. This is accomplished by means of the selector switch. Once cleaning temperatures of 875 degrees or so are reached, the elements are cycled to maintain temperature by a high-limit control. This may be a separate switch, or it may be a set of contacts incorporated into the thermostat.

DOOR SEALS

The door gasket is made of a tough woven fiberglass material that withstands a good deal of abuse. Unless it's torn, it probably won't require replacement during the stove's life-

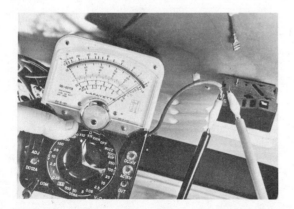

Cycling switch found on many self-cleaners is tested by removing lead and checking with VOM on lowest resistance scale. This switch cycles units *on* during approximately 50 percent of clean time.

time. If replacement should prove necessary, be sure to leave the specified gap across the bottom of the oven throat or door. This allows room air to enter the oven body during baking and cleaning. The oven is also vented at the top, usually under a surface unit.

The oven throat outside the oven door seal should be wiped with a damp cloth prior to cleaning the oven, since it isn't subject to the high heat of cleaning. This is usually easily done, since it isn't subjected to baking heat, either, and the foods aren't baked on. When cleaning extremely heavy soils, some smoke may escape around the corners of the gasket and should be wiped away when the cycle is completed. *Never* use a commercial oven cleaner on any part of a self-cleaning oven, pyrolytic or catalytic.

The oven door is adjustable by first slightly loosening the screws which hold inner and outer door panels together, then carefully twisting the door to the desired position. Tighten the liner screws, being careful not to chip the porcelain. Hinge screws are usually adjustable toward the front or rear of the range through the use of elongated slots.

To check the door seal, close the door on a shim made of construction paper, about one inch wide and eight inches long. When removing the shim, a definite drag should be felt between door and gasket. Try this in several strategic locations around the door's edge.

LOOK AND LISTEN

Become familiar with *the sights and sounds of self-cleaners.* The next time your self-cleaner is ready for a clean cycle, take a close look. Notice the appearance of the food soil before cleaning. See how the door latching mechanism works. Listen to the click of a solenoid, the whir of the latching motor, the feel of the latch as the door is closed. Watch the clean and lock lights sequence. On some models, you may hear a cooling fan quietly pulling fresh air under exterior panels, thus lowering surface temperatures. A few minutes spent in such observation may provide a hot clue to pinpoint a future problem.

QUICK-CHECK CHART FOR

SELF-CLEANING OVENS

Symptom	Possible Cause	Remedy
1. Oven won't clean, won't operate on Bake or Broil cycle	Blown fuse in power-supply line in home	Replace fuse after testing with VOM **Note:** lights may operate when only one of the two fuses is blown
2. Oven won't clean but Bake and Broil operate normally	Controls improperly set	Review settings, especially clock timer; be sure window heat shield is raised
	Door not shut completely	Close and reset controls
	Locking mechanism inoperative	See "Door won't lock" below
	Defective component:	
	Oven sensor ("solid state" models)	Check for continuity: If open, replace
	Transformer ("solid state" models)	Check primary, secondary sides for continuity; has 12V output on secondary. Replace if open
	Door latch switch	Should indicate continuity with door closed. Check linkages for proper adjustment
	High-limit	Should indicate continuity at temperature below 800°. Replace if open
	Timer contacts open	Check for continuity with timer in Clean position. If open, replace switch section
	Selector switch open	Refer to wiring diagram and test for continuity with switch in Clean position
3. Partial cleaning	Not enough cleaning time allowed for food soils present	Try in another cycle, allowing longer time for cleaning
	Temperature too low	High limit, bias resistor, or Clean t'stat section out of calibration. Check high limit for continuity, replace if open. Call technician to make other adjustments
4. Door won't lock	Latching mechanism inoperative (mechanical type)	Check solenoid or bimetal arm. **Do not attempt to force lever.** Check linkages
	Latching motor won't run	Check motor windings for continuity; open, replace Cam switch open or out of adjustment; test with VOM, replace or adjust
	Oven too hot from previous usage	At high temperatures (above 500°) the lock switch may close even though the selector is set at Bake or Broil. Let oven cool before initiating Clean cycle
5. Door won't open	Oven not sufficiently cooled after Clean cycle	Allow proper time for oven to cool; be sure that lock light is off
	Clean cycle selected momentarily during control adjustment prior to cooking	Turn selector to Clean position, leave for one minute, then return to Off position
	Latching motor or latching solenoid defective, or switch open	Test with VOM, repair component or replace as necessary; refer to wiring diagrams
	Latching mechanism binding	Check and adjust
6. Lock light glows during normal baking, broiling	Baking or broiling at high temperatures	Temperatures over 550° may transfer lock light bimetal—will not interfere with normal operation, but cool oven before cleaning
7. Smoking	Food soils overloading smoke eliminator	Remove or wipe heavy soils from oven before starting Clean cycle
	Element of smoke eliminator open	Check with VOM, replace if open

25
Keeping Your Sewing Machine in Action

The sewing machine is a precision-built piece of equipment. There are many things about it that you shouldn't attempt to service yourself. This includes anything to do with the timing mechanism—the timing belts and shafts and gears that make up much of the mechanical arrangement that is referred to as the "head." The same caution applies to the zig-zag mechanism. The primary reason that I advise you against this type of repair is that special gauges are necessary to set the close tolerances on many of these parts, and these dimensions vary with every brand and between many models of sewing machines. The electronics in some of the more sophisticated models require special test instruments and are also not within the realm of do-it-yourself repairs.

But don't think that this doesn't leave much that you can service yourself. Far from it! In fact, judging from the problems that exist with machines brought in for repair service in sewing machine repair centers, you should be able to solve about 90 percent of the problems that arise. That's about the proportion of calls that are answered for such things as adjusting the tensions, cleaning, and replacing belts and motors. All of these you can do, and even more.

First of all, you should understand how a sewing machine works. Two threads are used —the upper one, which passes through the upper tension device, the take-up arm, and the needle; and the lower thread, which is contained in the bobbin. This lower thread passes through the lower tension device, a spring on the bobbin case.

The needle brings the thread down to the shuttle, which carries the thread around the bobbin case. The take-up arm then pulls the

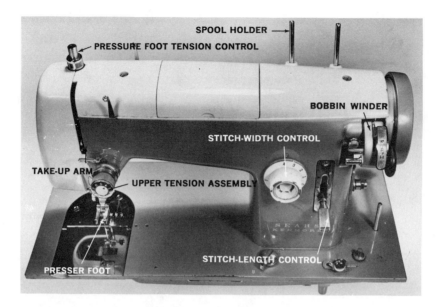

SPOOL HOLDER →

PRESSURE FOOT TENSION CONTROL

BOBBIN WINDER

STITCH-WIDTH CONTROL

TAKE-UP ARM

UPPER TENSION ASSEMBLY

STITCH-LENGTH CONTROL

PRESSER FOOT

Major components of typical sewing machine are shown in this photo. Access cover on top of head can be removed for cleaning and oiling.

thread up into the cloth, forming a knot. The tightness of this knot is controlled by the upper tension and the lower tension. The knot should be formed exactly in the center of the material.

ELECTRICAL PROBLEMS

When your sewing machine acts up, determine if the problem is electrical or mechanical. Electrical problems are fairly easy to pin down, because they are limited to problems with the universal motor that drives the machine, the speed controller, and the lamp or the cord assembly. The universal motor is subject to the normal problems that can arise with this type of motor (see Chapter 10).

The motor control may be an adjustable resistor, consisting of an open, wound resistance wire which is wiped by a conducting arm attached to it. The voltage of the output of the control is determined by the point at which the arm contacts the resistance element. As the pedal or arm is depressed, the resistance is lower and the voltage to the motor (and the motor speed) increases. A carbon-pile control accomplishes the same effect. In some newer machines a solid-state control uses a silicon-controlled rectifier to "clip" portions of the cycles of alternating current feeding the motor, thus limiting its speed. Solid-state controls are nonrepairable for the most part, and the controls and motors are matched in most of these machines. Don't attempt to substitute these components, as the wrong one may dam-

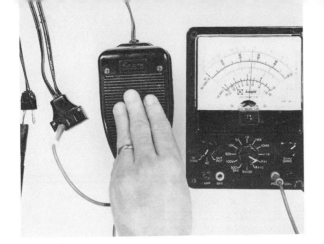
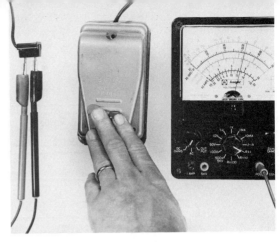

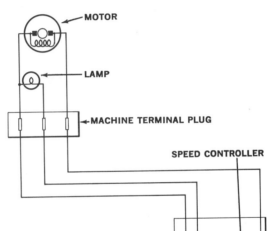

MOTOR

LAMP

MACHINE TERMINAL PLUG

SPEED CONTROLLER

Speed controllers are tested by setting VOM to $R \times 1$ scale and checking to see if meter deflects when pedal is depressed. It should indicate near 0 ohms resistance when pressed fully in. In plug-in arrangement shown in photo at left, one of the three terminals is connected directly to one side of the line at all times, even when pedal is not depressed; the other terminal is connected to the other side of the line at all times and serves to feed the light; the third terminal is fed from the speed controller, and is used to energize the motor. When testing, you first must place the VOM on the $R \times 1$ scale and check from each pin of the plug to the terminal; when you have isolated the two terminals which are connected to the line, you then must check through the plug to the other terminal while depressing the switch. With the arrangement used in photo at right, the leads can simply be clipped to the plug that enters directly into the machine.

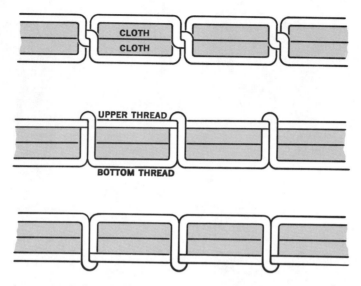

Here's a cross section of stitches as they might appear (much magnified) when viewed through the material of a test cloth. In the top drawing, the stitch is locked in the middle of the cloth, indicating that upper and lower tensions are correctly adjusted.

In the middle drawing, the upper thread lies on top of the material, while the loops from the lower thread in the bobbin are looped around it. When using two colors of thread, a condition like this is readily apparent. It's caused by the upper tension being too tight. If the loops protrude beyond the upper thread, it would indicate that the lower tension was much too loose.

In the bottom drawing, the thread lies on the bottom of the material, with the loops from the upper thread looped across it. This is caused by the lower tension being too tight. If the loops from the upper thread protrude below the lower thread and are not pulled tight against it, it would indicate that the upper tension was much too loose.

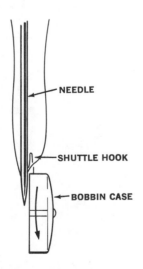

The relationship of the shuttle hook to the needle is very important. If the needle is not positioned correctly or is bent, it is impossible for the hook to pass between the needle and the thread, causing skipped stitches.

age the other. Use only specified replacement parts.

Sometimes the rheostat type of control can become linted or dirty. Open the control cover to clean it. Usually brushing the lint away and spraying the resistance windings with television tuner contact cleaner will eliminate the problem.

MECHANICAL PROBLEMS

If you diagnose the problem as mechanical, the first step is to get out the instruction book that came with the machine. Since sewing machines have so many varying tolerances between brands and models, this is the only way that you can be certain that it is properly adjusted.

Before proceeding further, make a test cloth of two pieces of cotton cloth about the thickness of cotton sheets. Put a new needle into the machine for testing. Sometimes this is the only

problem with the machine. In any event, this step will assure that you have an accurate test pattern. Use threads of two different colors, but of the same weight—a dark color in the bobbin and a light on top, or vice versa. This lets you differentiate between the two on your test pattern. With average stitch widths, sew for 5 or 6 inches along the cloth. Remove the pattern and look at it closely.

Observing the results will allow you to set the tension adjustments properly, and there is a very good possibility that this will solve the problem. If a thread lies loosely along the top of the material with the other looped around it, the upper tension is too tight. If the thread lies along the bottom, the lower tension is too tight. If both upper and lower threads are locked in the middle of the material, the tension is correct.

The upper tension is controlled by the upper tension device, which is calibrated and easily adjustable. The thread must pass between two discs, which apply pressure depending on the

Lower thread tension is adjusted by turning screw *slightly* that retains lower tension spring to bobbin case. For starting adjustment, tighten until bobbin case with full bobbin can just be lifted from hand by thread.

Upper tension is set by turning calibrated knob that adjusts spring loading on tension disks. This setting is often varied when differing weights of materials are to be sewn.

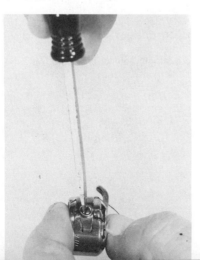

amount of springloading that is determined by the adjustment. This is often varied during use, depending on the weight of the material being used. It covers a wide range, and unless one of the springs becomes bent or damaged or the discs get clogged with lint, it's not likely to wander very far afield.

The lower tension, however, is not so easily adjusted. To set it, remove the bobbin case and bobbin. To make a preliminary adjustment which will give you a starting point, take a full bobbin of thread (the same weight as that on top of the machine) and put it in the bobbin case. Be sure that the thread is properly positioned under the lower tension spring, just as if you were going to use it in the machine. Then hold the loose end of the thread in one hand and the bobbin case and full bobbin in the other. When you lift the thread, the tension should be just sufficient to lift the bobbin and case from the other hand. When you jerk on the thread, it should slip slightly from the case. If you need to tighten or loosen the ten-

sion, look for a small screw where the tension spring is held to the bobbin case. Tightening the screw (turning clockwise) tightens the tension, turning counterclockwise loosens the tension.

With this adjustment made, install the bobbin case in the machine and make another test stitch with the upper tension set at the midway position. This should put you "in the ballpark" so that one or two fine adjustments will have the tension adjustments perfectly set.

While you are inspecting the bobbin tension, be sure to take a close look at the shuttle and race assembly. Some are machined together as one piece and cannot be separated. Others come apart quite easily, simply by slipping off the spring-loaded retaining clips. Be sure to remove all traces of lint and thread from the race and watch to see that it operates smoothly. It's also a good idea to take a soft lead pencil after the race has been cleaned and run the pencil around the polished surfaces of the race. The small quantity of carbon that is

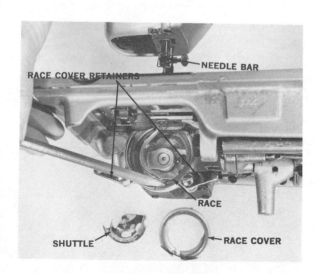

Lint and thread should be cleaned from race periodically. After removing race cover and shuttle, brush lint away using pointed wooden stick for stubborn areas. Before reassembling, go over polished surfaces with pencil containing soft lead to help lubricate and smooth race.

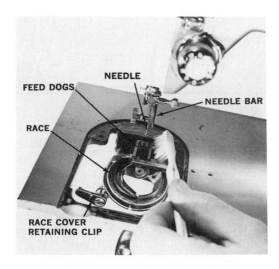

FEED DOGS

NEEDLE

NEEDLE BAR

RACE

RACE COVER
RETAINING CLIP

Needle plate must be removed to gain access to feed-dog assembly. Using an old toothbrush, remove all lint and thread, being careful to keep it away from the race. This is the first place to look if improper feeding occurs.

left serves as a lubricant, and won't collect lint or dust or get on the material.

Remove the needle plate periodically and brush the lint and thread off the feed dogs, the teeth that push the material past the needle plate when the sewing machine is in use.

There are many other jobs that you can perform easily enough on sewing machines. Replacing the rubber tires on the bobbin winder, belts, and motor pulleys is a part of long-term maintenance of the equipment. And don't forget to oil the machine regularly, but follow manufacturer's instructions and don't use too much oil. This can only serve to trap lint and dust where it isn't needed.

RULES FOR THE USE AND CARE OF SEWING MACHINES

- Oil the machine regularly according to manufacturer's instructions.
- Keep the owner's manual handy for reference; use it each time you change accessories or make adjustments.
- Let the machine move the material under the presser foot. Attempting to pull it through can bend needles and damage the needle plate.
- Clean lint from the shuttle and bobbin area regularly.
- Remove the needle plate and brush lint from the feed dogs at regular intervals.
- Start the machine at a slow speed with the take-up arm in the raised position. This allows smooth starts and helps prevent thread breakage.

QUICK-CHECK CHART FOR
SEWING MACHINES

Symptom	Possible Cause	Remedy
Breaks upper thread	Not threaded correctly—check owner's manual	Thread machine correctly.
	Tension too tight	Loosen upper tension
	Needle installed incorrectly	Check needle installation
	Defective needle	Replace needle
	Feed dogs clogged with lint, thread	Clean feed dogs after removing needle plate
	Needle plate hole or shuttle has sharp or rough edges	Inspect and smooth with emery cloth or replace
	Machine not started with take-up arm and needle at high position	Follow instructions for starting the stitch
	Shuttle clogged with lint and thread	Clean shuttle and race
Breaks lower thread	Not threaded correctly—check owner's manual	Thread bobbin case correctly
	Tension too tight	Loosen lower tension
	Bobbin case or tension spring has sharp or rough edges	Replace spring or smooth edges
	Bobbin case full of lint or thread	Clean bobbin case, shuttle, and race
Skips stitches	Needle bent or damaged	Replace needle
	Needle not installed correctly	Check needle installation
	Incorrect needle	Check to see that proper needle is installed
	Shuttle bent or otherwise damaged or loose, spacing needle too far from shuttle	Inspect and replace or adjust shuttle as necessary
Doesn't feed cloth correctly	Feed dog action blocked by thread and lint	Remove needle cover plate and clean feed dog assembly
	Feed dogs not correctly set	Be sure that they are set to the raised position if machine controls provide this feature
	Presser foot tension too loose	Increase pressure foot tension
	Teeth on feed dogs are dull	Replace feed dogs
Puckers and wrinkles material	Tensions set too tightly	Adjust tensions

SEWING MACHINES *(cont.)*

Symptom	Possible Cause	Remedy
Puckers and wrinkles material *(cont.)*	Using different sizes of thread	Be sure that both bobbin and upper threads are the same
	Presser foot tension too tight	Decrease pressure foot tension
	Defective needle	Replace needle
Irregular stitches	Tensions not properly adjusted	If loops at top of material, loosen upper tension or adjust bottom. If loops at bottom, loosen lower tension or tighten upper
	Lint and/or dirt buildup between upper tension assembly discs or in bobbin case and shuttle race	Clean tension devices thoroughly
	Defective needle	Replace needle
	Bobbin not wound smoothly	Rewind bobbin
Motor runs, machine doesn't operate	Belt broken or slipping	Inspect and adjust or replace
	Clutch slipping	Be sure that clutch (located within hand wheel) is tightened
Motor doesn't run	Brushes worn	Check and replace
	Commutator dirty	Polish with sandpaper & burnish with hardwood block
	Open motor windings or armature	Check with VOM and replace motor
	Open resistor in speed control	Check with VOM and repair or replace control. Check to see that resistor is clean and that connections are tight
Sewing machine noisy	Dirt and thread build-up under feed dogs or in shuttle	Check and clean feed dog assembly, bobbin case, shuttle and race. Use wooden stick to clean race
	Belt tension too tight or belt damaged	Check and adjust or replace belt as necessary
	Loose parts	Isolate noise by using screwdriver as "stethoscope." Tighten loose part as necessary

25
Keeping Built-In Appliances Accessible for Repairs

No kitchen is ever large enough to give storage and counter space for all the equipment and appliances we accumulate. No kitchen is ever small enough for the working convenience we want in having everything right at hand. You can achieve the best of both worlds by carefully selecting your appliances and then building some of them in.

I'm not thinking just of the typical built-ins —dishwasher, range, and wall oven. Portable dishwashers and many other appliances that gobble up floor or counter space can also be built in. But before you build, plan for future access, easily, without ripping cabinetry apart. As a person who repairs his own appliances, you will want to make certain you keep them all readily accessible. Removable panels attached with screws sometimes are the answer.

A microwave oven is a good example of an appliance that often robs a countertop of working space. Housewives have told me countless times that "I love my new microwave, but it takes up so much space." So let me tell you about some solutions.

In building a new home, I gave special care to planning the kitchen. I remember describing it with pride as "compact and convenient." But then the inevitable happened. The undercounter area, where an ever-growing array of small appliances was kept became a snake's den of cords. I renovated a used commercial food slicer. This gobbled up lots of countertop space. It was a long walk to the garbage cans, so a compactor joined the crowd. No problem —I placed it in front of three drawers that "I hardly ever use." I used them more than I thought I did. When a microwave oven took up the remaining countertop space, it was clear that something had to be done.

WHICH WAY TO GO?

The first step—and the most difficult—is to make a decision about what you can move where. The first thought, especially if your problem appliance is a large one, may be to build it into your present cabinets. That's not

The problem—accumulation of several large appliances plus numerous portable appliances severely limits usable space in compact kitchen. For solution, look at interior walls, over the range, and even outdoors for a spot to build them in.

"After" shot of this kitchen shows the big difference with compactor and microwave out of the way on the right. Small appliances, shown clustered around Food Center power unit on countertop, are compact and cordless, store easily in small section of cabinet below.

often the best answer because you'll lose cabinet space. Also, such an installation usually requires tricky cabinet work. Look instead to the walls of your kitchen. If there's one with a little-used area beyond it, perhaps a closet, that's the way to go.

If your problem appliance is a microwave only, look above your present range. One of the most innovative kitchen products in recent years has been GE's "Spacemaker" that combines microwave, range vent, and work light in one unit that replaces an existing range vent hood. It's available in several versions. Other manufacturers now offer some models based on the same concept or special housings to adapt their microwaves to such an installation. If you already own a microwave, you can get a combination microwave shelf and range hood such as the MicroMate to adapt it to over-the-range installation. This kit as well as over-the-range ovens and mounting kits are adaptable to outdoor vent systems or are available with a carbon filter for ductfree installations.

In my case, the problem involved more than the microwave and there was no way to expand into another interior room. The only way to go was out. The exterior wall was taken up in large part by a sliding glass door which opens onto a deck. I wanted to avoid a major renovation—doing away with a load-bearing wall or tying into the roof system.

My solution was what came to be called "the elbow room." I decided that a small offset

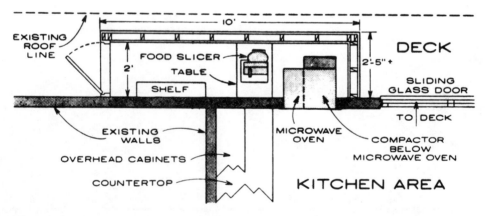

Diagram shows layout of "elbow room" that solved my problem; your solution should be tailored to suit your own needs. If you elect to go outdoors as I did, size your addition to the amount of roof overhang available. In some cases it may also be necessary to build a foundation for the floor.

on the outside of the house could protect the appliances. A wide, 36-inch overhang permitted making use of the existing roof without modification and allowed clearance to avoid blocking the continuous soffit vent. The new addition also provides room for a small table for the food slicer, used only a few times each month. On the higher portion of the inside wall there was room for a small shelf to store fruit in the fall. Finally, there was space in the addition to store items that tend to accumulate on the deck—cushions for deck furniture, an ice cream churn, etc. Inside dimensions of 24 inches by 10 feet were sufficient to accomplish all of this without infringing upon a major portion of the deck area.

This sounds like a major project, but it took only two evenings and a full Saturday to com-

plete. The same basic concept will work for most homes when there's no way to go but out.

INSTALLATION KITS

Some appliances, such as the compactor, require no modification to adapt them to built-in installation. Others, such as the microwave and some air conditioners, require a "sleeve." This is nothing more than a metal housing designed to provide proper clearance and ventilation for the appliance, and often includes a receptacle or adapter for connecting to the power supply. The manufacturer or a dealer can provide information concerning the availability of such a sleeve for your brand and model of appliance.

Amana's microwave oven build-in kit consists of galvanized steel sleeve (shown being assembled above) that contains receptacle for microwave and junction box for connecting to power supply. Kit also includes front-mounted grilles for air passage.

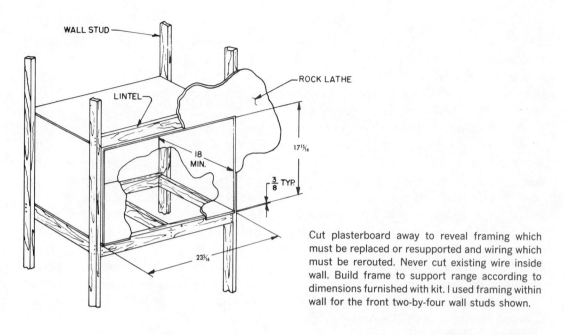

WALL STUD

ROCK LATHE

LINTEL

18 MIN.

$17\frac{15}{16}$

$\frac{3}{8}$ TYP.

$23\frac{3}{16}$

Cut plasterboard away to reveal framing which must be replaced or resupported and wiring which must be rerouted. Never cut existing wire inside wall. Build frame to support range according to dimensions furnished with kit. I used framing within wall for the front two-by-four wall studs shown.

Compactor requires no kit, and in this case I didn't have to remove existing top. After unit is installed in wall opening it can be positioned by adjusting leveling feet.

Outside view of wall before framing is enclosed shows appliances in position. Both can be pulled forward into kitchen area for servicing. I also put additional insulation around compactor, which is much quieter now than when free-standing.

With cypress planking installed, finished room blends well with existing wall of home. Avoid blocking roof ventilation when building such an addition; careful planning will let you place room to avoid modifications.

Here's a nice touch for built-in appliances—attach a wooden front to match existing cabinets. I gave the full treatment to compactor. First, top cap of front panel is removed by loosening three screws, then existing metal panel is lifted out. Quarter-inch birch panel, which I treated with stain and polyurethane varnish before installation, slides into position to replace it.

Microwave at eye level is much more convenient than before. Ordinary shop mull trim was used to match lines of one-by-four trim used elsewhere in room. When working with molding, dull point of nail by tapping with hammer to avoid splitting wood.

BUILT-IN SMALL APPLIANCES

That took care of the big troublemakers, but there was still lots of countertop and cabinet clutter from the collection of small appliances. I took care of most of that—all of the motorized appliances, in fact—by installing Nu-Tone's Food Center. It consists of a power unit that's built into the countertop and houses a ⅓ horsepower motor and solid-state speed control, plus various accessories ranging from a knife sharpener to food processor. The only visible part (when it's not in use) is an attractive panel on the countertop. The accessories include a complete array of compact appliances including mixer, blender, food processor, knife sharpener, etc.—all cordless since they simply lock in place on the power unit output on the countertop panel. Now I have more appliances than before and store them in far less space, using special shelves with a vacuum-formed compartment for each component.

All of the accessories for this unit are super-efficient, although not necessarily of conventional design. The mixer, for instance, has only one large beater and mounts in the middle of a special mixing bowl. The motor drives not only the beater but also a turntable that rotates the bowl. It works great, and it's safer than many conventional mixers. I've found that all of the accessories perform unexpectedly well because the motor is much more powerful than that found on typical portable appliances.

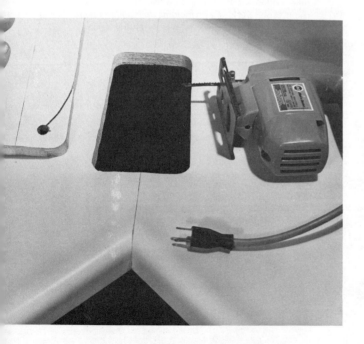

NuTone Food Center was installed in less than an hour. First and hardest step is to make cutout in countertop, using template provided with power unit.

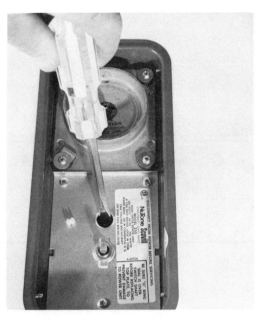

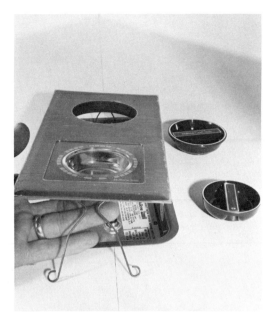

Next step is to drop in power unit and tighten one screw to pull clamp into position and secure. Top-mounting feature lets you place it above inaccessible location such as inside corner.

With power unit mounted, decorative cover snaps in place like recessed lamp lens, then control knob can be pressed into position. Special vacuum-formed shelves for accessories are available for cabinet mounting; power unit and shelves can also be mounted in optional roll-around cart.

UNLIMITED POSSIBILITIES

There's almost no limit to the possibilities of gaining more space by building in appliances. The only precaution, other than those specified in your equipment's installation and owner's manual, is to be sure that adequate ventilation is provided. This is especially important with refrigerators and freezers. Unless you're installing a special model intended for built-in use, be sure to provide the proper clearances on sides and at the rear, and don't use a model with a back-mounted or in-the-

GE's innovative Spacemaker microwave contains range vent system and work light, takes place of conventional range hood. Unit comes complete with instructions and template for installation.

Closeup of another Spacemaker model illustrates "thinline" construction, but cavity of oven is big enough for complete meal preparations. Grille at top vents microwave oven cavity only—cooktop vent exits from top of microwave housing.

MicroMate is combination microwave shelf, range hood, and work light. Twin blowers are located in upper part of housing, provide effective cooktop coverage. "Heat Sentry" control protects microwave by automatically turning blower to high speed if excessive heat is detected.

MicroMate anchors to both wall and soffit for secure mounting, accepts virtually every brand of microwave. Twin activated charcoal filters can be used for ductfree installation as shown; on ducted installations, entire panel can be covered with wood trim or doors.

wall condenser. Models with a fan-forced air system for cooling the condenser usually work very well, but proper side clearance must still be provided.

Don't overlook the laundry equipment when you're thinking built-in. One good project is to design your own home laundry center, surrounding washer and dryer with convenient shelves and supply storage. Locating an ironing board and sorting table in the same area speeds the laundry chore and makes it easier.

You'll find that built-ins do much more than simply free up your kitchen space. The added convenience of a microwave oven at eye level is far better than bending over the counter. And most built-in appliances are quieter, especially the microwave and compactor.

Your imagination can find places for other appliances; as an example, consider this Whirlpool upright freezer. Note grille installed above unit to provide proper ventilation; that's especially important for refrigeration appliances, and many require side clearances also.

Through-the-wall air conditioning installations save valuable window space. Most window units can be converted by using special sleeves; others, like the GE heat pump shown here, are designed for this type of installation and are suitable for room additions and remodeling.

27
Where to Get
Repair Parts

Repair parts for home appliances can be obtained from one of three sources—a servicing dealer (perhaps the one from whom you bought the appliance), the manufacturer of the appliance, or an appliance parts distributor. If your dealer can't supply what you need, he may be able to help you decide whether you should turn next to the manufacturer or a parts distributor, and perhaps tell you the name, address, and telephone number of a distributor who provides parts service in your area.

The servicing dealer makes his living by selling and servicing appliances, or sometimes by merely servicing them. He will likely have the most frequently needed parts on hand, for he is penalizing himself as well as his customers if he doesn't.

A letter to the appliance manufacturer will get you either the name of a nearby supplier for the part or the part itself. Manufacturers are interested in assisting you because they would like for you to have a good image of their company and buy their product again in the future. Address your letter to the "Customer Service Division" of the company, whose address will be on the nameplate of the appliance or on the warranty that you should have.

An appliance parts distributor usually represents one or more manufacturers and keeps on hand a complete line of parts. Some distributors, however, will not sell to individuals since they prefer to operate only a wholesale business. Others not only will sell to you but may give you a discount (if asked). See the accompanying lists for the name and address of distributors with whom you may be able to do business. Distributors may also be listed in the telephone book Yellow Pages, in major cities, under such headings as ''Electrical Appliances—Major'' or ''Electrical Appliances, Small, Repairing.'' If you live in a rural area or small town, check the Yellow Pages in the telephone book for the nearest large city.

Be sure you know exactly what part you need—before writing, telephoning, or approaching a dealer, manufacturer, or parts distributor. Get the full model number of your appliance from the nameplate or your warranty. Using this number, the parts supplier can look up an exploded diagram of your machine that will give him the current part number of what you need. At many parts distributors, these books or microfilm machines are placed on the counter where you can look them up yourself. It is also wise to have the serial number (sometimes necessary when running changes have been made in a model run), and the purchase date of the appliance. For cabinet parts, the color must also be stated.

It is important to *you* that you give the proper information. In many instances, especially when the part must be ordered, you are held responsible and must pay for the part even if it turns out to be the wrong one (provided, of course, the error was yours and not the dealer's or the manufacturer's).

Many parts are furnished as a kit, especially when an improvement has been made in a part. These kits will have an instruction sheet enclosed. Be sure to follow them specifically. They will tell you how to install the part and often give you information about adjustments that should be made.

A major stride was taken with General Electric's introduction of their Quick Fix system for GE and Hotpoint appliances. The system consists of special display modules containing the most frequently used parts for five major appliance lines—ranges, washers, dryers, refrigerator-freezers, and dishwashers. Each package contains illustrated instructions for replacement, and manuals are also made available for each of the product lines. I've worked closely with this effort to make parts and information available to the consumer; it's a new course for an appliance manufacturer to follow, and we hope it sets a goal for others.

If a defect should occur with a replacement part, vendors of high-quality parts and original equipment manufacturers will replace it for you; their parts carry a reasonable warranty. But the warranty varies, depending upon the part and the manufacturer. So be sure that you find out about it when making your purchase. When returning a part to a dealer or distributor for warranty purposes, give him the model and serial number of the machine that it was installed on, the date that it was installed, and a description of the problem.

The best advice of all about appliance parts takes us right back where we started in this book. Be sure of your diagnosis. Be a professional, not a parts changer. Find which part is defective and what is wrong with that part before you purchase a new one. You'll save both time and money—and add to your stock of pride in a job well done.

DISTRIBUTORS OF MAJOR APPLIANCE PARTS IN THE U.S AND CANADA

Supplying parts for appliance repairs has become an important business. Companies engaged in this business are now located in practically every state of the U.S. and in many provinces of Canada. Some of these companies, however, prefer to operate on a wholesale basis and do not seek orders from individual homeowners who repair their own machines. For that reason, it is suggested that you check out any company located in your vicinity to see whether it can or will supply the part you need. The companies listed here deal primarily in parts for the repair of major appliances. For a list of repair shops that also supply parts for small appliances, write the National Appliance Service Assoc., 1308 Pennsylvania, Kansas City, MO 64105.

ALABAMA

Washer and Refrigeration Supply Co., Inc.
716-2nd Avenue, N.
Birmingham 35201
205 322-8693

Appliance Parts & Supply Co., Inc.
805 Church
Mobile 36602
205 432-6634

AAA Appliance Parts, Inc.
810-2nd Avenue, N.
Birmingham 35203
205 328-2142

ARIZONA

Appliance Dealer Supply Co., Inc.
P.O. Box 2017
740 West Grant
Phoenix 85007
602 252-7506

Appliance Parts Co.
2215 East University Drive
Phoenix 85034

Akrit Appliance Supply Co.
1132 N. Richey Boulevard
Tucson 85716

G & N Appliance Parts
1537 S. 4th Avenue
Tucson 85713
602 624-2102

ARKANSAS

Mid-South Appliance Parts Co.
1020 West 14th Street
P.O. Box 2722
Little Rock 72201
501 376-8351

720 North 11th Street
Fort Smith 72901

CALIFORNIA

Appliance Parts Co.,
Division of Washing Machine Parts Co.
15040 Oxnard Street
Van Nuys 91401
213 787-9220

1575 Mable Street
Anaheim 92802

372 North Mt. Vernon
Colton 92324

9870 Baldwin Place
El Monte 91731

Cal Sales Corp.
641 Monterey Pass Road
Monterey Park 91754
213 283-7741

2945 West 5th Street
Oxnard 93030

Cal-Tex Appliance Parts Distributors
7747 Ostrow Street
San Diego 92111

Orange County Appliance Pts.
10466 Stanford
Garden Grove 92640
714 547-7068

P & S Washer Parts Corp.
6909 S. Western
Los Angeles 90047
213 753-1205

Hughes Appliance Parts Supply
12513 Venice Boulevard
Los Angeles 90066
213 397-2117

Appliance Parts Distributors
850 San Antonio Road
Palo Alto 94303
415 967-0595

Coast Appliance Parts Co.
5915 North Kester Avenue
Van Nuys 91401
213 782-5770

269 South Arrowhead Avenue
San Bernardino 92101

764 14th Street
San Diego 92101

8222 Lankershim Boulevard
North Hollywood 91605

9817 Inglewood Avenue
Inglewood 90301

Appliance Parts Distributors
1645 Old County Road
San Carlos 94070
415 591-4467

Appliance Parts Distributors
16200 E. 14th Street
San Leandro 94578
415 357-8200

Appliance Parts & Equipment Dist.
4936 N. Blackstone Avenue
Fresno 93726
209 222-8484

Appliance Parts & Equip. Dist.
1152 N. Union
Stockton 95205
209 466-0573

Appliance Parts House
105 Starlite
S. San Francisco 94080
415 589-2616

Standard Appliance Parts Co.
1820 "S" Street
Sacramento 95801
916 444-6650

Standard Appliance Parts Co.
3430 Fulton Avenue
Sacramento 95801
916 481-6353

Genuine Appliance Parts Dis.
127 E. 18th Street
Bakersfield 93305
805 324-9891

Appliance Parts Center
222 E. 8th Avenue
National City 92050
714 474-6781

Don Erickson Inc.
2606 Lee Avenue
S. El Monte 91733
213 579-1500

Major Appliance Parts
9126 East Valley Road
Rosemead 91770
213 280-6783

Coast Appliance Parts Company
5915 No. Kester Avenue
Van Nuys 91401
213 782-5770

269 So. Arrowhead Avenue
San Bernardino 92408

764 14th Street
San Diego 92101

8222 Lankershim Boulevard
No. Hollywood 91605

9817 Inglewood Avenue
Inglewood 90301

Electrical Appliance Service Co.
1434 Howard Street
San Francisco 94103
415 777-1900

820 East Shields Street
Fresno 93721

1140 Lincoln Avenue
San Jose 95125

4238 Broadway
Oakland 94611

1116 "F" Street
Sacramento 95814

Washing Machine Parts Co., Inc.
1275 Folsom Street
San Francisco 94103
415 413-4686

763 The Alameda
San Jose 95113

CANADA

Mossmanis Appliance Parts Ltd.
746 Ellice Avenue
Winnipeg, Manitoba R3G 0B6

Waugh & MacKewn Limited
1025 Elias Street
P.O. Box 2277 STN A
London, Ontario N6A 4E9
519 432-1115

5325 Crowley Avenue
Montreal, Quebec H4A 2C6

24 Brydon Drive
Toronto, Ontario (Rexdale) M9W 5R6

2285A Gladwin Cres
Ottawa, Ontario K1B 4K9

Trinity Bay
Blaketown, Newfoundland A0B 1C0

3913 Manchester Road
Calgary, Alberta T2G 4A1

Fleet Appliances and Furn. Ltd.
700 Ellice Avenue
Winnipeg, Manitoba R3G 0B1
204 774-2426

Wrights Appliance Parts Ltd.
2225 First Avenue, North
Saskatoon, Saskatchewan
306 652-9522

P.O. Box 7373
Regina, Saskatoon S4P 3A8
306 522-7533

Reliable Parts Ltd.
860 Kingsway
Vancouver 10, British Columbia
604 872-1291

COLORADO

Ray Jones Washing Machine Co.
376 South Broadway
Denver 80209
303 744-6263

1436 North Hancock
Colorado Springs 80903

1813 East Mulberry St.
Ft. Collins 80521

Niles-Noel Inc.
562 South Broadway
Denver 80209

Akrit Appliance Supply Co.
402 Arrawanna Street
Colorado Springs 80909

CONNECTICUT

American Appliance Parts Co., Inc.
2516 Whitney Avenue
Hamden 06518

963 Farmington Avenue
Kensington 06037

10 Boston Avenue
Stratford 06497

Electric Appliance Parts, Inc.
175 Freight Street
Waterbury 06708

Westchester Appliance Parts, Inc.
194 Richmond Hill Avenue
Stamford 06902

Arcand Distributors, Inc.
845 Windsor Street
Hartford 06120
203 522-2214

61 Erna Avenue
Milford 06460

DELAWARE

Appliance Parts Co., Inc.
111-121 S. Lincoln Street
Wilmington 19805
302-652-3701

DISTRICT OF COLUMBIA

Trible's Incorporated
2240 25th Place, N.E.
Washington 20018
202 832-9300

Gaghan & Shaw
35 New York Avenue N.E.
Washington 20002
202 393-4500

FLORIDA

Marcone Appliance Parts Center
777 N.W. 79th Street
Miami 33150

1515 Cypress Street
Tampa 33606

2108 W. Central Boulevard
Orlando 32805

1019 Rosselle Street
Jacksonville 32204

Moore's Appliance Parts
2907-47th Avenue N.
St. Petersburg 33714
813 526-4740

A.P.D. Associates
P.O. Box 1389
Hollywood 33022
305 923-1534

GEORGIA

Harris Appliance Parts Co.
227 West Dougherty Street
Athens 30601

5129 Montgomery Street
Savannah 31405

1801 Atlanta Highway
Gainesville 30501

Fox Appliance Parts
2142 Milledgeville Road
Augusta 30901
404 722-4361

Fox Appliance Parts of Atlanta
P.O. Box 11191
Atlanta 30310
404 524-1979

Fox Appliance Parts
2601 Cusseta Road
Columbus 31903
404 687-5171

Fox Appliance Parts
2724 Houston Avenue
Macon 31206
912 788-6352

Automatic Appliance Parts Co.
243 N. 5th Avenue
Rome 30161
404 232-1073

D & L Appliance Parts Co.
5799 New Peachtree Road
Atlanta 30340

HAWAII

Appliance Parts Company, Inc.
1550 Kalani Street
Honolulu 96817
808 847-3271

731 Kamehameha Highway
Pearl City 96782

3057 Waialae Avenue
Honolulu 96816

118 Hekili Street
Kailua 96734

IDAHO

W. L. May Co. Inc.
202 E. 33rd Street
Boise 83704
208 345-7411

IASCO Distributing Co.
919 Pancheri Drive
Idaho Falls 83401

ILLINOIS

Automatic Appliance Parts Corp.
2730 North Central Avenue
Chicago 60639
312 622-7515

Automatic Appliance Parts Corp.
1506 East Asgonquin Road
Arlington Heights 60005

Midwest Appliance Parts Co.
3645-51 W. Fullerton Avenue
Chicago 60647
312 278-1300

C. E. Sundberg Co.
615 West 79th Street
Chicago 60620
312 723-2700

York Radio & TV—Appliance Parts Division
590 N. Broadway
Decatur 62525
217 423-3484

Triangle Electric
224 E. Cass
Joliet 60432
815 726-4429

INDIANA

Appliance Parts, Inc.
1734 West 15th Street
Indianapolis 46207
317 635-3657

Appliance Parts Supply Co.
1241 Wells Street
Fort Wayne 46808

Bell Appliance Parts
4730 Hohman Avenue
Hammond 46327
219 932-5960

Bells Parts Supply
2819 45th Street
Highland 46322
219 924-1200

4730 Hohman
Hammond 46327

1718 South Michigan
South Bend 46613

Evansville Appliance Parts
920 West Pennsylvania Street
Evansville 47708
812 423-8867

Appliance Parts Supply Co.
1241 Wells Street
Fort Wayne 46808

IOWA

The Ricketts Company, Inc.
809-11 University Avenue
Des Moines 50314
515 244-7236

Iowa Parts Supply
123 Franklin
Des Moines 50314
515 282-1392

Mid-States Supply, Inc.
216-5th Street, S. W.,
Mason City 50401
515 423-1808

KANSAS

Washer Specialties
1640 E. 2nd Street
Wichita 67214
316 267-3343

KENTUCKY

The Collins Co., Inc.
Appliance Parts Division
819 South Floyd Street
Louisville 40203
502 583-1723

Triple A Appliance Parts, Inc.
150 Indiana Avenue, Box 24
Lexington 40508
606 254-7765

The Collins Co., Inc.
3071 Breckenridge Lane
Louisville 40220

150 Indiana Avenue
Box 24
Lexington 40508

LOUISANA

Bruce's Distributing Co.
509 East 70th Street
Shreveport 71106
318 861-7662

Sunseri's Washing Machine Parts
2254-60 St. Claude Avenue
New Orleans 70117
504 944-6762

Appliance Parts Co.
2214 Lee Street
Alexandria 71301

Superior Appliance Parts
3348 Dalton Street
Baton Rouge 70805
504 356-2472

MAINE

Appliance Parts Co.
255 Danforth Street
Portland 04102

Supply Distributors
456 Riverside Industrial Parkway
Portland 04103

MARYLAND

Trible's Incorporated
140 Halpine Road
Rockville 20852

2210 North Howard Street
Baltimore 21218

United Appliance Parts
5003 Harford Road
Baltimore 21214
301 426-0800

Gray's Appliance Parts
316 Bow Street
Cumberland 21502
301 722-7278

Coastline Parts Co.
637 Roland St.
Salisbury 21801
301 742-8634

Trible's Inc.
3533 Fort Meade Road
Laurel 20810

MASSACHUSETTS

Hall Electric Supply Co. (HESCO)
33 Brighton Street
Belmont 02178
617 489-3450

M. G. M. S. Associates, Inc.
22 Water Street
Cambridge 02141
617 868-8360

Appliance Parts Co., Inc.
112 Dartmouth Street
Boston 02116
617-536-0138

Gene's Appliance Parts
124 Lakeview Avenue
Lowell 01850
617 453-2896

Mass Appliance Parts, Inc.
721 Warren Avenue
Brockton 02401
617 587-7100

A.A.A. Appliance Parts Co.
142 Park Street
Dorchester 02122
617 288-2928

Supply Distributors
50 Revere Beach Parkway
Medford 02141
617 395-8100

MICHIGAN

Bussard Appliance Parts Co.
454 Orchard Lake Avenue
Pontiac 48053
313 332-6445

Detroit Appliance Parts Co.
4936 Allen Road
Allen Park 48101
313 928-3211

Sevall Co.
228 East Baltimore Street
Detroit 48202
313 872-3655

26500 Grand River Avenue
Detroit 48240

24312 Gratiot Avenue
East Detroit 48021

6619 Schaefer
Dearborn 48126

630 West Kearsley
Flint 48503

440 Lake Michigan Drive, N.W.
Grand Rapids 49504

1100 South Water Street
Saginaw 48601

Park Appliance Parts
13545 Northline
Southgate 48192
313 282-2666

Park Appliance Parts, Inc.
27726 Plymouth Road
Livonia 48150
313 427-8280

Park Appliance Parts, Inc.
923 E. 11 Mile Road
Royal Oak 48067
313 541-8848

Apco, Inc.
3305 S. Pennsylvania
Lansing 48910
517 882-5745

2841 S. Division
Grand Rapids 49508

412 East Elm Street
Lansing 48912

1900 Ecorse Road
Allen Park 48101

MINNESOTA

Appliance Parts, Inc.
250 3rd Avenue North
Minneapolis 55401
612 335-0931

964 Rice Street
St. Paul 55117

Dey Appliance Parts
150 East 13th Street
St. Paul 55101

MISSISSIPPI

Appliance Parts Co., Inc.
727 S. Gallatin Street
Jackson 39204
601 948-4680

May & Company
P.O. Box 1111
Jackson 29205
601 354-5781

MISSOURI

Marcone Appliance Parts Co.
2320 Pine Street
St. Louis 63103
314 231-7141

Marcone Appliance Parts Co.
3113 Main Street
Kansas City, 64111

St. Louis Appliance Parts, Inc.
2911-13 South Jefferson
St. Louis 63118
314 776-1445

Washer Equipment Co.
1715 Main Street
Kansas City 64108
816 842-9593

NEBRASKA

Lincoln Appliance Pts. Supply, Inc.
728 S. 27th Street
Lincoln 68510
402 432-6908

Appliance Parts Supply, Inc.
14647 Industrial Road
Omaha 68144
402 334-1555

NEVADA

Cal Sales Corp.
3453 Industrial Road
Las Vegas 89109
702 734-1104

Electrical Appliance Service Co.
611 Kuenzli Street
Reno 89502

NEW HAMPSHIRE

Gene's Appliance Parts, Inc.
58-½ Kinsley Street
Nashua 03060
603 889-5331

Supply Distributors
148 Merrimack Street
Manchester 03101

NEW JERSEY

Jacoby Appliance Parts
269 Main Street
Hackensack 07601
201 489-6444

57 Albany Street
New Brunswick 08901

1374 Springfield Avenue
Irvington 07101

923 North Olden Avenue
Trenton 08611

Westchester Appliance Parts, Inc.
470 U. S. Highway #46
Teterboro 07608

Rex Electric Supply
1034 Clinton Avenue
Irvington 07111

All Brand Appliance Parts, Inc.
12 West Kings Highway
Mt. Ephraim 08059
609 933-2300

Maco Electrical & Appliance Parts
800 South Egg Harbor Road
Hammonton 08037
609 561-7270

Pyramid Supply Co.
1707 New York Avenue
Union City 07087
201 866-3900

Valley Appliance Parts
754 Hamburg Turnpike
Pomptom Lakes 07442
201 835-2157

NEW MEXICO

Akrit Appliance Supply Co.
2820 Vassar N.E.
Albuquerque 87107
505 345-8651

NEW YORK

All Appliance Parts of New York, Inc.
1345 New York Avenue
Huntington Station 11746
516 427-4600

2580 Sunrise Highway
Bellmore 11710

113-02 Atlantic Avenue
Richmond Hill
W. Hempstead 11419

600-C Middle Country Road
Selden, NY 11784

Seneca Appliance Parts
1317 Genesee Street
Buffalo 14211
716 896-6757

Westchester Appliance Parts, Inc.
1034 Yonkers Avenue
Yonkers 10714
914 237-0500

Richmond Distributors
1452 Myrtle Avenue
Brooklyn 11237
212 455-3079

Ardco Supply Co.
125 W. Main Street
Endicott 13760
607 754-6706

Alan Appliance Parts Co.
184 Old Country Road
Hicksville 11801
516 681-3535

Buffalo Appliance Parts Co., Inc.
1175 Williams Street
Buffalo 14206
716 856-5005

Nichols Appliance Parts, Inc.
801 South Salina Street
Syracuse 13202

Rochester Appliance Parts Distributors
189 North Water Street
Rochester 14604

Jacoby Appliance Parts
1023 Allerton Avenue
Bronx 10469

214 Route 59
Suffern 10901

1654 Central Avenue
Albany 12205

NORTH CAROLINA

D & L Appliance Parts Co., Inc.
2100 Freedom Drive
P.O. Box 31816
Charlotte 28208
704 375-7306

Moore and Stewart, Inc.
316 East Franklin Avenue
Gastonia 28052
704 864-8334

Appliance Parts Co., Inc.
612 Person Street
Fayetteville 28301
919 483-4700

Cashwell Appliance Parts, Inc.
3924 Bragg Boulevard
Fayetteville 28303
919 867-1135

Morton Distributing Co., Inc.
P.O. Box 6095
Asheville 28806
704 254-0703

2811 Firestone Drive
Greensboro 27406

2324 Atlantic Avenue
Raleigh 27601

1730 10th Avenue S.W.
Hickory 28601

603 Wellons Village
Durham 27703

1925-A Vargrave Street
Winston-Salem 27107

Appliance Parts, Inc.
20 North University Avenue
Fargo 55108

NORTH DAKOTA

Appliance Parts, Inc.
20 North University Avenue
Fargo 55108

OHIO

American Electric Washer Co
988 East Market Street
Akron 44305

2801 Detroit Avenue
Cleveland

405 East Market Street
Akron 44309

Appliance Parts Supply Co.
235 Broadway Street
Toledo 43602
419 244-6741

1408 Cherry Street
Toledo 43608

Dayton Appliance Parts Co.
122 Sears Street
Dayton 45402
513 224-3531

Golden Rule Electric, Inc.
808 Elm Street
Cincinnati 45202
513 241-3701

6944 Plainfield Road
Cincinnati 45202

Mason Supply Co.
985 Joyce Avenue
Columbus 43203
614 253-8607

3929 Apple Street
Cincinnati 45223

Pearsol Appliance Corp.
2319 Gilbert Avenue
Cincinnati 45206

Pearsol Corporation Of Ohio
1847 East 40th Street
Cleveland 44103
216 881-5085

Shore Appliance Co.
17630 South Waterloo Road
Cleveland 44110
216 481-1790

Shore Appliance Co.
6573 Pearl Road
Parma Heights 44130
216 888-4646

Stone's Appliance Co.
7580 Mentor Avenue
Mentor 44060
216 942-4807

Dayco Appliance Parts
338 East Spring Street
Columbus 43215

Brand Service Center, Inc.
808 Elm Street
Cincinnati 56202
513 241-3701

V & V Appliance Parts, Inc.
27 West Myrtle Avenue
Youngstown 44507
216 743-5144

630 High Street, N.E.
Warren 44481

OKLAHOMA

Greer Electric Co.
1018 South Rockford
Tulsa 74104
918 587-3347

Pritchard Electric Co., Inc.
3100 North Santa Fe
Oklahoma City 73101
405 528-0592

OREGON

W. L. May Co., Inc.
1120 S.E. Madison Street
Portland 97214
503 231-9398

3619 Franklin Boulevard
Eugene 97403
503 726-7696

Pacific Appliance Parts, Inc.
835 E. Burnside
Portland 97214
503 235-3161

Appliance Parts Co.
4220 S.E. Hawthorne Boulevard
Portland 97215
503 236-1109

PENNSYLVANIA

Collins Appliance Parts, Inc.
1533 Metropolitan Street
Pittsburgh 15233
412 321-3700

All Appliance Parts Co.
5023 Penn Avenue
Pittsburgh 15224
412 362-1500

Kohler Appliance Pts. Supply, Inc.
201-03 Lexington Avenue
Altoona 16601
814 942-8872

Wagner Appliance Parts, Inc.
1814 Tilghman Street
Allentown 18104
215 439-1564

Parts Distributors Corp.
312 North Easton Road
Willow Grove 19090

McCombs Supply Co.
259 South Ann Street
Lancaster 17602
717 394-6248

McKeesport Appliance Parts Co.
434 Shaw Avenue
McKeesport 15132
412 678-1300

Scranton Appliance Parts
830 Capouse Avenue
Scranton 18500
717 347-3211

D. J. Hurley Co.
18 W. Chester Pike
Havertown 19083
215 446-8894

PUERTO RICO

Appliance Parts Corp.
1207 Roosevelt Avenue
Puerto Nuevo 00920
809 783-4195

J. A. Diaz & Co.
1316 San Alfonso Street
Rio Piedras 00921
809 783-4656

RHODE ISLAND

Appliance Parts Co., Inc.
316 Cranston Street
Providence 02907
401 421-6142

Anderberg's Appliance Parts
855 N. Main Street
Providence 02904
401 351-4361

Twin City Supply Co.
885 Westminster Street
Providence 02904
401 331-5930

SOUTH CAROLINA

G & E Parts Center, Inc.
P.O. Box 2466
852 Pine Street
Spartanburg 29302
803 585-6277

P.O. Box 1074
1212 Bluff Road
Columbia 29202

Harris Appliance Parts, Inc
P.O. Box 611
29 Bypass North
Anderson 29621
803 225-7433

Harris Appliance Parts
Box 5988
Greenville 29606
803 233-3977

Coastline Parts Co.
134 East Montague Avenue
Charleston 29406

D & L Appliance Parts, Inc.
901 South Cashua Drive
Florence 29501

Appliance Parts Co.
1907 Huger Street
Columbia 29201
803 252-9047

SOUTH DAKOTA

Dey Appliance Parts
300 N. Phillips
Sioux Falls 57102

TENNESSEE

Brown Appliance Parts Co., Inc.
857 Central Avenue
Knoxville 37917
615 525-9363

2472 Amnicola Highway
Chattanooga 37406

125 New Kingsport Highway
Bristol 37620

Curtis Co.
562 East Street
Memphis 38104
901 572-1611

Napco, Inc.
501 South Second Street
Nashville 37213

5002 Charlotte Avenue
Nashville 37209

111 Old Hickory Boulevard
Madison 37115

Hamilton Appliance Parts
801 Magnolia Avenue
Knoxville 37917
615 525-0418

Appliance Parts Warehouse, Inc.
2311 E. 23rd Street
Chattanooga 37408
615 622-4158

TEXAS

Pearsol Appliance Co.
3127 Main Street
Dallas 75226
214 741-4638

Central Supply
Division of Washing Machine Parts, Inc.
2612 McKinney
P.O. Box 3385
Houston 77001

5365 College Street
Beaumont 77707

1604 South Shaver
Pasadena 77502

7417 Hillcroft
#2C Houston 77081

Standard Appliance Parts Corp.
1214 West Van Buren
Harlington 78550

P.O. Box 7488
4814 Ayers Street
Corpus Christi 78415
512 853-9823

Texas Parts & Supply Co.
P.O. Box 115
1209 South St. Mary's
San Antonio 78291
512 225-2717

2820 Guadalupe
Austin 78765

Washing Machine Parts Co.
704 North Main Street
Fort Worth76106
817 332-5343

3314 Ross Avenue
Dallas 75221

Alltex Appliance Co.
2710 Fielder Court
Dallas 75235
214 357-0101

Stove Parts Supply Co.
2120 Solana Street
Fort Worth 76107
817 831-0381

Nelson's Specialty Supply Co.
1206 E. 6th Street
Austin 78702
512 478-6468

Akrit Appliance Supply Co.
1805 Montana
El Paso 79902
915 533-5503

Brey Washing Machine Parts
1920 N. Piedras
El Paso 79930
915 565-3982

Akrit Appliance Supply Co.
2306 19th Street
Lubbock 79401
806 763-5282

Akrit Appliance Supply Co.
1805 Montana
El Paso 79902

2306 19th Street
Lubbock 79401

Cal-Tex Appliance Parts Distributors
1806 Polk
Houston 77003

UTAH

IASCO Distributing Co.
925 Southwest Temple Street
Salt Lake City 84101
801 328-0505

Ray Jones Appliance Parts Co.
3336 South 300 East
Salt Lake City 84115

VERMONT

Supply Distributors
18 Chaplin Avenue
Rutland 05701

VIRGINIA

Refrigeration Supply Co., Inc.
1657 West Broad Street
Richmond 23261
804 359-3275

1736 Allied Street
Charlottesville 22901

Booth Supply Co., Inc.
926 Vernon Street, S.E.
Roanoke 24103

8304 Orcutt Avenue
Hampton 23605

Wholesale Parts Distributors, Inc.
113 West 11th Street
Norfolk 23510
703 625-3988

Evans Electric Co.
451 Elm Avenue
Portsmouth 23704
804 399-3044

Appliance Parts Co.
609 Rotary
Hampton 23361
804 826-2310

Trible's Inc.
7273 East Arlington Boulevard
Falls Church 22042

WASHINGTON

Appliance Parts & Service Co.
409 9th Avenue North
Seattle 98109
206 MA2-0152

W. 917 Mallon
Spokane 99201

Pacific Appliance Parts
607 W. "A" Street
Yakima 98902
509 248-2308

Inland Appliance Parts
504 East First
Kennewick 99336
509 586-9915

W. L. May Co., Inc.
6536-6th Avenue So.
Seattle 98108
206 762-3160

WEST VIRGINIA

Mason Supply Company
800 Virginia Street W.
Charleston 25301

3303 Eoff Street
Wheeling 26003

WISCONSIN

A & E Distributors, Inc.
1418 N. Irwin Avenue
P.O. Box 1104
Green Bay 54305
414 437-7022

Power Equipment Company
2373 South Kinnickinnic Avenue
Milwaukee 53207
414 744-3210

R & S Parts, Incorporated
5278 N. Pt. Washington Road
Milwaukee 53217
414 964-4750

Garrons Distributing Inc.
333 S. Hawley Road
Milwaukee 53214
414 475-1070

Kenosha Appliance Parts
2601 Roosevelt Road
Kenosha 53140
414 657-7329

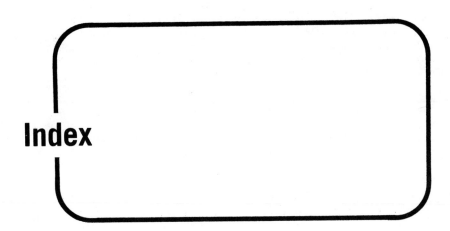

Index

Index